W9-BKD-519

THE *Best American Infographics*

THE BEST AMERICAN *Infographics*

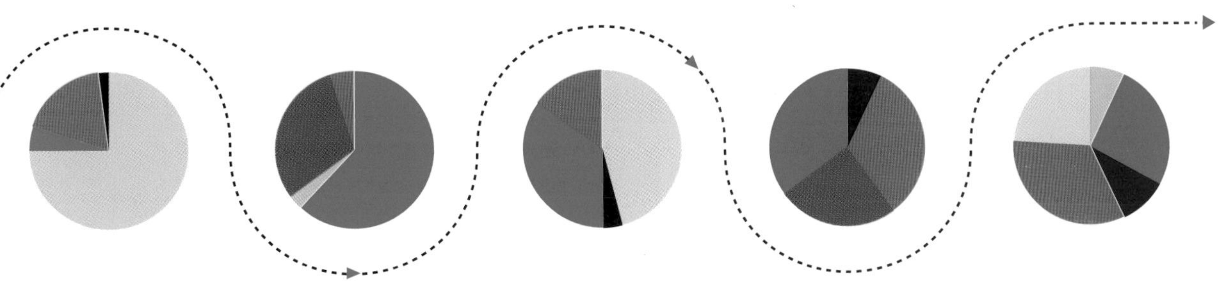

With an Introduction by **DAVID BYRNE**

GARETH COOK, *Series Editor*

MARINER BOOKS
HOUGHTON MIFFLIN HARCOURT
BOSTON | NEW YORK

The Best American Series is a registered trademark of
Houghton Mifflin Harcourt Company.

WWW.HMHBOOKS.COM

Library of Congress Cataloging-in-Publication Data is available.

Book design by Patrick Barry
Cover design by Oliver Munday
Printed in China
SCP 10 9 8 7 6 5 4 3 2
Permissions credits are located on page 164.

CONTENTS

III. THE MATERIAL WORLD

FOREWORD

PRESERVED IN BASALT near the north bank of the Snake River in Idaho is a Native American carving some 10,000 years old that scholars argue is a depiction of the river's course, complete with tributaries. One can easily imagine the work of even earlier cartographers, tracing lines in the dirt to locate a bank of wild berries or a herd of buffalo. Humble as they seem, these sketches represented a dramatic cognitive advance: a recognition, predating the advent of written language, that a whole part of experience, an entire *out there,* could be captured with marks.

With time and technology, cartography grew both more accurate and more ambitious. The German geographer Heinrich Berghaus published dozens of works in the mid-nineteenth century depicting the planet's climate, animal life, and anthropology. Later in the century, Charles Booth published a map that captured the stunning extent of poverty in London, which helped to promote social reforms. In 1869, the French civil engineer Charles Joseph Minard published a depiction of Napoleon's disastrous retreat from Moscow, the dwindling army shown as a narrowing line and the brutal weather neatly annotated below. It was a map, yes, but also an information graphic—still one of the finest ever rendered. For these "thematic maps," as they are sometimes called, the geography served as the backdrop for the real drama. Rich with data, these maps didn't just tell what is where; they told stories.

On this side of the Atlantic, residents of the young United States were eager to deploy cartography to make sense of the New World. In 1769, for example, Benjamin Franklin completed a "Chart of the Gulf Stream," showing it as a dark river off the eastern seaboard, with arrows indicating the direction of flow. Franklin followed what has since become a familiar pattern, starting with specialized data, aggregating it and giving it visual form, leading to a revelation for the public—in this case the idea that a vast, durable current coursed through the chaotic ocean. In the middle of the nineteenth century, with the union falling apart over slavery, came another milestone. The United States Coast Survey issued a map of the southern states, with each county shaded to show how many slaves lived there. South Carolina, the first to secede from the union, features a particularly dark coastline. Another dark band of slave labor surrounded the Mississippi River. Yet other parts of the South (Kentucky, western Virginia) were almost empty of slaves. The map, says the scholar Susan Schulten, carried potent political messages. It made slavery more concrete, and confirmed the impression that secession was about preserving a system of slave labor, not high-minded notions of state's rights. The fact that the terrain of slavery was varied in the extreme also suggested (perhaps too strongly) that swaths of the South might be less ardent in their anti-Union stance. The map captured the public's imagination and was widely reprinted. Abraham Lincoln is said to have enthusiastically studied it. In fact, one can easily make it out in a portrait of him painted by Francis Bicknell Carpenter.

"If traditional topographic maps were akin to description, thematic maps functioned more like an argument," writes Schulten in her history of American cartography, *Mapping the Nation.*

We now find ourselves in a golden age for information graphics. They appear in newspapers and blog posts, on television and in advertisements, in political campaigns and at art openings. Most Americans would be hard-pressed to spend a day without seeing some kind of infographic. The most obvious reason is technological. Data is available for download in vast quantities, covering virtually every imaginable subject. Software has made it easy for amateurs to make infographics and provides the experts with much improved tools. And of course the Internet, combined with mobile computing, has made these twenty-first-century maps sharable.

The other reason is no doubt psychological. The same forces that have made it possible for infographics to proliferate have also made us hungry for them. We are deluged with information, and infographics promise to make sense of it. Sometimes they don't deliver on that promise: plenty of today's infographics are themselves overwhelming, confusing, or distracting. But the best of them bring clarity, answering urgent questions and making us think. Like Franklin's chart of the Gulf Stream, they make us see something we would otherwise miss.

The Best American Infographics seeks to document the rise of this new cartography, to celebrate the finest work being done today by artists, journalists, designers, and data scientists. The winning infographics are divided into three subject areas. The first, You, contains work done at the human scale, from a clever cooking conversion chart to advice on how to dunk a basketball. The second, Us, is the realm of the social, our collective habits and prejudices, our year of political arguments and cultural milestones. The third, The Material World, is, well, everything else—wine labels and oceans, a warhorse and a decommissioned space shuttle. Together, they constitute a journey of scale, from the individual to the far reaches of space (where, the last entry hints, life may have taken hold on some distant world). Finally, we celebrate the top ten interactive infographics of the year, all of which suggest, in their own ways, where the medium is heading.

This volume is also intended to pose questions, to encourage the consumers of this new medium to engage it with a more critical eye. The people who visualize the world for us make choices, and these choices can skew our impressions. Show the fifty states in red or blue and one is left with the impression that each state is a monolith of Democratic or Republican thought. The reality is that the American people are much less polarized, much more purple. Infographics designers make choices, and these choices mean that their works should be seen, as Schulten suggests, as arguments. What is the data, and where did it come from? What was left out? What is emphasized, what is assumed, and what is glossed over?

Each infographic includes a statement from the artists, pulling back the curtain on the creative process. They reveal their diverse inspirations—the impending birth of a child, struggles to express a particular emotion in English, Madonna's appearance at the Super Bowl, questions about the 911 call in the Trayvon Martin killing. You will note a lot of discussion about focus, about how to get to the central point and let the data shine. Tornado tracks are tornado tracks and don't need a lot of commentary, one suggests. Yet many of the contributors also talk about their efforts to make sure they've included enough context, so that the data is fully meaningful. This tension—zoom versus wide angle—lies at the heart of infographic work, and of all storytelling. The captions give us glimpses of the struggle to get it right.

I found picking the "best" of the year to be a daunting task. I decided early on to avoid an overly strict definition of "infographic." I could have articulated a particular set of requirements—excellent data, rigorous labeling, statistical sophistication—which are noble in their way, but which would have left out many examples of excellent work. I have no doubt that purists will have their objections, but I wanted readers to experience the full range of the field's creativity, and that meant going to the borders.

In putting together the collection, I was hunting for four things. The first was intellectual power: Does the work yield insights? Did it challenge me to think? Does it suggest a different view of the world? Do I know something I didn't know before? The second factor was aesthetic sophistication. Some of the infographics are included here because they are simply gorgeous; others were chosen because of their careful use of color or texture or space. The third factor was emotional impact, be it surprise, delight, or awe.

My final consideration was more amorphous, a desire that the collection as a whole tell the story of infographics, and the story of the year. One of the year's winners, for example, leaves much to be desired in terms of polish, but its stark depiction of gun violence is dramatic, it touches on one of the biggest news stories of the year, and the fact that it was done by an amateur on the fly is itself notable. There are many ways to be the best, and in the end perhaps the task I've been given is hopelessly subjective. I can say this: In this book are the pieces that have most stayed with me, the ones I would have been saddest to miss. I hope you come to feel the same way.

As you make your way through the collection, what you see here may seem at best distant cousins to the maps of old. Yet in seeking to understand the new cartography, I'd urge you to bear in mind this long history. The tools have changed, but the motivation has not. Infographics, like the skeletal map scratched in stone near the Snake River, seek to answer two powerful questions that will always be with us: Where are we? Where might we go?

All of the images in *The Best American Infographics 2013* were originally published for an American audience, online or in print, during 2012. The top ten interactive works were selected this year by Eric Rodenbeck, founder of San Francisco's Stamen Design and a leader in the field of data visualization. Selecting the rest of the works fell to me. To nominate infographics for the next volume, see the rules at garethcook.net, or e-mail me at contactgareth@gmail.com.

I'd like to thank David Byrne. He is a tremendous artist and also a keen critic of the ways that new means of expression, be they musical or visual, shape art. I cannot imagine a better person to introduce this project.

I want to thank my wife, Amanda Cook, who helps and inspires me in every possible way. I also want to thank the members of my Brain Trust, who sent me infographics to consider and offered help and advice throughout the year. (They are listed, with their impressive bios, at the end of the book.) Thank you to Oliver Munday, who made the perfect cover. A huge thank you, also, to an all-star team at Houghton Mifflin Harcourt, particularly Patrick Barry (for design wizardry), Michaela Sullivan (creative genius), Mary Dalton-Hoffman (permissions Jedi mastery), Michelle Bonanno (promotional brilliance), and Ashley Gilliam (logistical virtuosity). Lastly, and most importantly, I want to thank my editor at HMH, Deanne Urmy. This new series was entirely her idea, and it's been an honor and a pleasure to work with someone who is so talented, so kind, and so wise about books — and life in general.

GARETH COOK

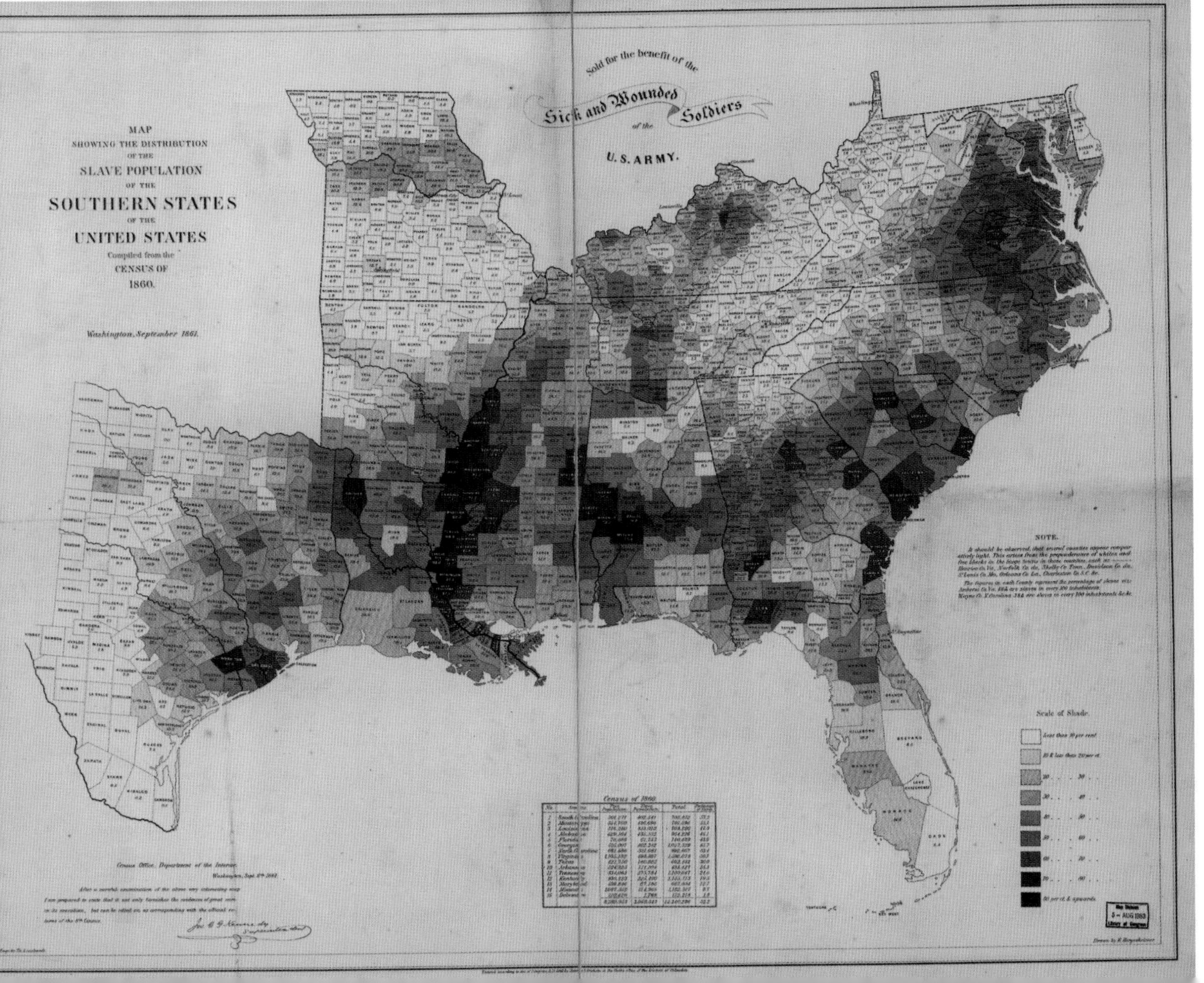
Sold for the benefit of the
Sick and Wounded Soldiers
of the
U.S. ARMY.
MAP
SHOWING THE DISTRIBUTION
OF THE
SLAVE POPULATION
OF THE
SOUTHERN STATES
OF THE
UNITED STATES
Compiled from the
CENSUS OF
1860.
Washington, September 1861.
Census of 1860
NOTE.
Scale of Shade.

Lincoln studied this map of slavery in the South.

Library of Congress, Geography and Map Division

INTRODUCTION

WHAT A THRILL and pleasure it was to be asked to write this introduction. I love these infographic things, and welcomed the excuse to think about them some more.

I was not a judge in this selection, but I spent a good few days examining many infographics that did and didn't make it into the final selected group—some of the best of which are interactive and some of the others designed for broadsheet newspapers with their giant pages or four-page foldouts in glossy magazines. Despite the change in context, you'll be able to make sense of most of the wonderful work going on in this odd corner of the workplace, where assignments to include a lot of information battle it out with a publication's available space, printing specs, web technology, and deadlines.

The very best of these, in my opinion, engender and facilitate an insight by visual means—allow us to grasp some relationship quickly and easily that otherwise would take many pages and illustrations and tables to convey. Insight seems to happen most often when data sets are crossed in the design of the piece—when we can quickly see the effects on something over time, for example, or view how factors like income, race, geography, or diet might affect other data. When that happens, there's an instant "Aha!"—we can see how income affects or at least correlates with, for example, folks' levels of education. Or, less expectedly, we might, for example, see how rainfall seems to have a profound effect on consumption of hard liquor (I made that part up). What we can get in this medium is the instant revelation of a pattern that wasn't noticeable before. We can see that (this part is true) the highest rate of tweeting in New York City runs up and down Broadway. Is that because of tweet-happy tourists who gravitate to that avenue, or is it representative of general heavy NYC foot traffic? I wouldn't know. In "Paths Through New York City," the graphic representation of NYC tweets appears like a weird, beautiful organism—a root system, drainage pattern, or inkblot. A living thing unto itself. In this, it's beautiful—but do people from all walks of life tweet? What inferences can we draw from this city as root system, drainage pattern, or inkblot? That part isn't clear.

Many infographics here spark insights, and they do so super quickly. The interactive "Road to Victory," for example, allows one to see Obama's odds against Romney—how Romney had many more options to lose, given the decision tree of possible wins and losses in various states. Surprising us with before-unseen clarity is the kind of thing this medium can sometimes do far better than any other.

Many of us have delved into Edward Tufte's books, such as *Envisioning Information,* in which he beautifully lays out examples of the good, elegant, efficient, and accurate presentation of information in graphic form and contrasts it with evil, bad, and confusing examples of the same. I remember a graphic showing Napoleon's tragic Russian campaign used as an example of a good graphic. This piece of artwork manages to interweave many kinds of data—location, date, and numbers of soldiers—to show instantly just how ridiculous and tragic that campaign was. It makes you gasp.

A good infographic, like the Tufte example, is—again—elegant, efficient, and accurate. But do they matter? Are infographics just things to liven up a dull page of type or the front page of *USA Today*? Well, yes, they do matter. We know that charts and figures can be used to support almost any argument—anyone remember the Niger yellowcake from Colin Powell's UN speech? Tufte refers to a visual demonstration by the scientist Richard Feynman showing how chilled O-rings on the Challenger booster were in danger of losing their flexibility, and how they could, and in fact did, shatter. This had all been brought to NASA's attention in an infographic in the form of a PowerPoint presentation, but, according to Tufte, the limited information-carrying capacity of PowerPoint, its tendency to reduce complex ideas to simple bullet points, resulted in the "warning" being ignored, and a tragic loss of life. Bad infographics are deadly!

One would hope that we could educate ourselves to be able to spot the evil infographics that are being used to manipulate us, or that are being used to hide important patterns and information. Ideally, an educated consumer of infographics might develop some sort of infographic bullshit detector that would beep when told how the trickle-down economic effect justifies fracking, for example. It's not easy, as one can be seduced relatively easily by colors, diagrams, and funny writing. Like many somewhat nerdy guys, I have a soft spot for charts, decision trees, and graphs—but I've also learned they often don't mean diddly. I've been burned more than once by a slickly rendered diagram.

Before writing this, I spent my days looking at these infographics. Maybe one way to understand what effects infographics are having on us is to analyze them, and as I began that process I noticed they tend to fall into a number of categories. Those are:

LISTS

An awful lot of infographics are essentially illustrated lists. Sports fans and boys love lists—some musicians do too. Top 10 lists, most home runs, most home runs in one month, songs that mention Hennessy cognac and BMWs in the same verse, how many times I visited my mom last year . . . or last month even. OMG, the "Feltron Biennial Report"! He's telling us (and himself) mundane stuff about his life under the assumption that some pattern or larger truth will emerge—but mostly what we get is that he loves telling us about himself! It's so meta. To be fair, I can imagine that he could parse some of his own data to help with his decisions. He might ask, for example, How much time do I spend in Brooklyn? Maybe then I should move there? His data should help him figure out how to manage his life rationally. But the graphic is also a hilarious parody of rationality as the answer to all of life's problems.

As I write this, we've just been through awards season—every magazine and website did their top 10 lists for the year, and then after that we had Grammys, Golden Globes, and Academy Awards—two more months of making lists! And some came with charts illustrating those lists. Some of these are beautiful, amusing, even sad (the one about writers and journalists who make stuff up comes to mind), but sometimes no patterns emerge. It's a list, that's the point; just like I'm making my own list right here.

FLOWCHARTS AND DECISION TREES

Importing the worldview inherent in programming and coding into the real world, these algorithmic diagrams help break down what might seem like a complicated decision process. And, by taking things step by step, the way to move forward is revealed to be self-evident. This is hugely amusing when applied inappropriately—to social situations and personal relationships, for instance. This is not to say that we shouldn't make use of our brains and that our hearts don't ever partake of branching logic structures, but I suspect the amygdala, with its lizard brain origins, has a bit more influence in much of our decision-making. So by making happiness into a flowchart, as happens in "How to Be Happy," for example, one can celebrate the joy and elegance of programming and make fun of its inappropriate use simultaneously.

Rationality and inappropriateness aside, these pieces reveal flowcharts as a form of poetry. And poetry is its own reward.

ILLUSTRATED NARRATIVE/COMICS

By comics, I don't mean paneled drawings of superheroes; I mean a series of drawings, pictures, or graphics that tell a chronological story. The minute-by-minute tale of how the *Titanic* sank after hitting the iceberg, shown from an underwater perspective, is essentially a beautiful graphic novel panel, rendered in realistic detail, as are the sequences that make up the landing and deployment of the Mars rover. Trayvon Martin's last forty-five seconds of life rendered as a graphic is more or less a single comic panel, too (OK, it doesn't look like a comic), with text blocks and bloodstains leading us step by step through this short and tragic narrative. When an infographic like this works, it puts us in the picture—we imagine ourselves as tiny people inside that graphic world. Sims on the *Titanic*.

FAKE NEWS AND TRENDS

The gayest halftime shows, the composition of

cocktails, Oscar winners by locale, an illustration with the surprising news that we don't use Rolodexes anymore. To me, these are essentially space fillers, attractive trinkets that visually seduce us but have been concocted (I imagine) by clever editors or their cohorts to imply a "story" where in fact there is none. Sometimes the seduction works—and sometimes there is actual information imparted (e.g., that Super Bowl halftime shows aren't as manly as some dudes might hope), but mostly these are empty calories.

SEEING THE INVISIBLE

These pieces do something that only this medium can do—they show us things from a perspective that we can never have in real life. I've loved these since I was a child. I drooled over breakaway drawings of fighter jets and hovercraft, and the renderings of Aztec cities filled with people. Things we would never ever be able to see, like the Chinese Emperor's entire army restored and the internal structure of a cheetah as it runs. This category allows us the possibility to grasp how something invisible and un-seeable makes itself manifest in our world. We can see through things, we can see the (imagined) distant past and sometimes our own implied future, as in the interactive graphic video representation of New York City carbon emissions. We see great time and distances compressed into manageable size. In this use of infographics, we experience a kind of geeky rapture as our senses are amplified and expanded through charts and illustrations.

CROSS-REFERENCING OF DATA SETS

These infographics are the ones most likely to lead to new insights. When, for example, time is plotted against the U.S. population's spending in various areas—health, food, entertainment, and so on—you instantly see that a huge shift in consumption has taken place. The same team did "American Education Gets a Grade," which similarly integrates a number of disparate data sets, presents them disarmingly simply, and in the process reveals a somewhat hidden pattern. Wonderful and surprising. There are many other infographics out in the world, however, that show only one data set, and neglect to cross it with something else—time, income, race, voting records—which would actually give us some new insight.

INTERACTIVE

Interactive infographics stake out new territory. Well, relatively new—though one suspects these may have been around for a while, but, being expensive to produce and way inappropriate for print platforms, they've struggled to establish themselves. That said, some of these are for me the most engaging examples of this medium. I mentioned previously the "Road to Victory" graphic, but even a relatively simple piece, like "Wind Map," is also engaging. It's mesmerizing. One wonders, however, what use it actually is to most of us—wind farm investors excluded. The same is true of the interactive census map—a thing of beauty, utterly unique to this medium, but how does one use it? What does it reveal?

The "Bear 71" piece was a total revelation for me. That and the "Network of Violence" seemed to be new ways of storytelling that use this technology in ways that trigger insights and surprises. Many levels of information and data are being brought into play in "Bear 71": actress Mia Kirshner as the bear, and the ability to use surveillance tech to check out crows and deer in Banff National Park—both totally out of left field, but perfect—and all of it threaded together with a narrative. Amazing.

1,000 WORDS

Sometimes a picture or graphic is indeed worth those 1,000 words. Sometimes a graphic is merely a replacement for those words, and sometimes it's an oversized dingbat, merely visually breaking up the blocks of text on the printed or web page. When infographics work, and many of these in *Best American Infographics 2013* do, they take you somewhere no other medium can go; they allow and facilitate intuitive insights; and they reveal the hidden patterns buried in mountains of data.

The graphic nature of these pieces helps them function as metaphors. Democrats become blue shapes and Republicans red ones. Pop songs are an aqua wedge-shaped snake. I get that. We have an inbuilt ability to manipulate visual metaphors in ways we cannot do with the things and concepts they stand for—to use them as malleable, conceptual Tetris blocks or modeling clay that we can more easily squeeze, stack, and reorder. And then—whammo!—a pattern emerges, and we've arrived someplace we would never have gotten to by any other means.

DAVID BYRNE
New York City
2013

THE *Best American Infographics* 2013

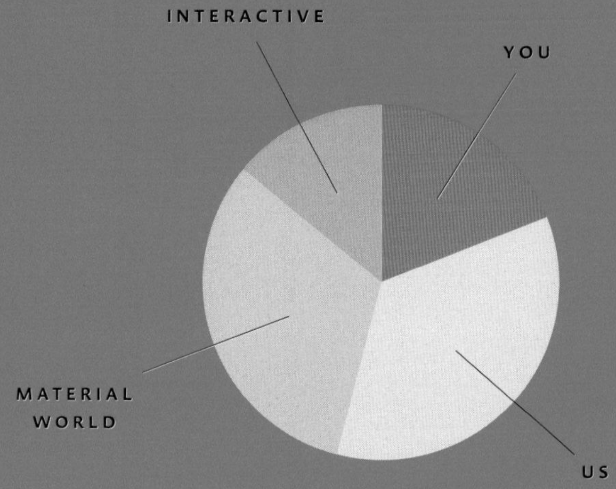
INTERACTIVE
YOU
MATERIAL WORLD
US

I. YOU

America's Most Popular Birthdays

The days of the year, ranked by the number of babies born on each day in the United States.

ARTIST Matt Stiles, a data journalist at National Public Radio in Washington, D.C.

STATEMENT A friend posted a link to the data on my Facebook wall, and that prompted the graphic. I was inspired by the fact that my wife and I were expecting our first baby in 2012, and I wanted to know how common her due date was. Baby Eva came a little early, but still in September—the most common month for births in the United States. Apparently, people like to make babies around the winter holiday season.

PUBLICATION thedailyviz.com (May 12, 2012)

Which Birth Dates Are Most Common?

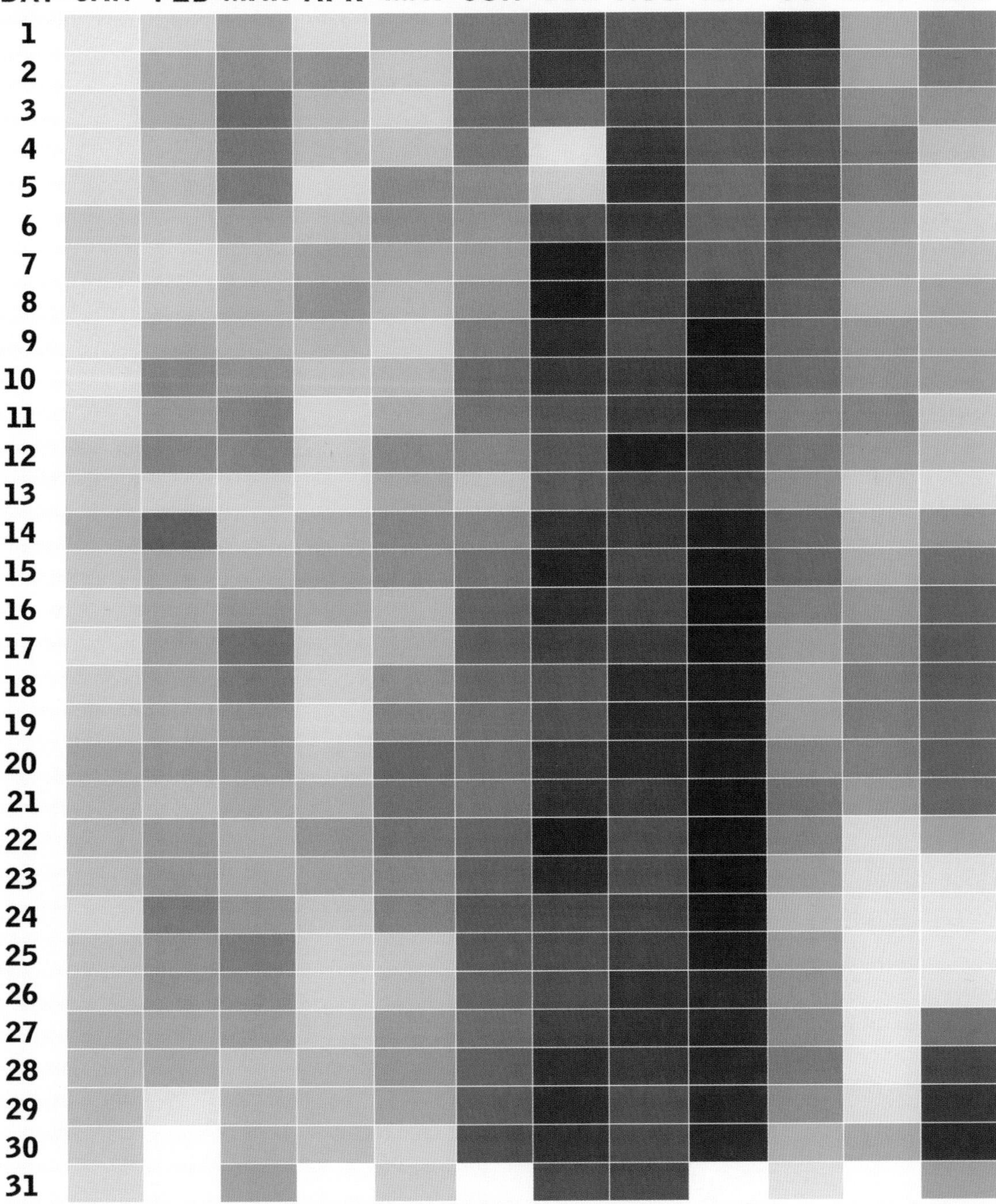
DAY JAN FEB MAR APR MAY JUN JUL AUG SEP OCT NOV DEC
1
2
3
4
5
6
7
8
9
10
11
12
13
14
15
16
17
18
19
20
21
22
23
24
25
26
27
28
29
30
31

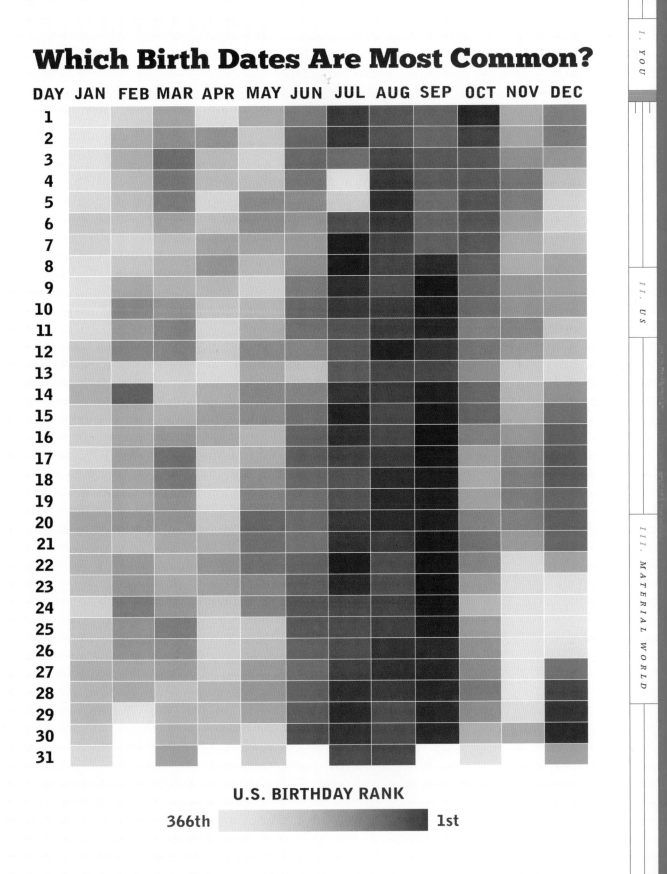

U.S. BIRTHDAY RANK

366th 1st

CAN I MAKE STUFF UP?

NO

STEPHEN GLASS

Journalist
If you make stuff up as a journalist, you will be considered such a liar that the state of California won't let you become a lawyer.

JAMES FREY

Memoirist
If you make stuff up as a memoirist, Oprah will excoriate you on the air, and your publisher will refund duped readers the cost of your book, but you may have a lucrative second career employing young writers to pump out popular fiction.

MITCH ALBOM

Columnist
If you make stuff up as a columnist, you will get suspended. Then you can write your column again.

MIKE DAISEY

Monologist
If you make stuff up as a monologist, Ira Glass will be very disappointed in you, but lots of people will defend the "greater truth" of your story.

TRUMAN CAPOTE

Nonfiction Novelist
If you make stuff up as a "nonfiction novelist," people will call you out on it eventually, but you'll still go down as a great writer (especially if you die prematurely).

DAVID FOSTER WALLACE

Humorous Journalist
If you make stuff up as a humorous journalist, the editor-in-chief of *The New Yorker* will be heartbroken.

TOM HOOPER

Biopic Director
If you make a movie "based on a true story" that includes made-up stuff, journalists will write articles pointing out where you were wrong, but you might win an Oscar anyway.

The Rules of Invention

To make life easier for would-be liars everywhere, a handy visual guide.

DAN BROWN

Historical Novelist
If you make stuff up as a historical novelist, people will point out on Wikipedia that you were wrong and evaluate your claims on TV, but you can still make the best-seller list.

MATTHEW WEINER

Period-Piece Showrunner
If you make stuff up for your mostly historically accurate TV show, linguists will scrutinize your every misstep and magazine journalists will compare your show to their memories, but you'll still be a critical darling.

DAVID SEDARIS

Humorist
If you make stuff up as a humorist, the *New Republic* will fact-check the dickens out of you, but most people will say your lies are OK, especially if they're just about your personal life.

LOUIS C.K.

Stand-Up Comedian
If you make stuff up as a stand-up comedian, no one will care (unless you lie about where your jokes came from).

ICE CUBE

Songwriter
If you say you had a "good day," bloggers will fact-check you twenty years after the fact. But they will still love the song, even if it wasn't exactly true.

ISAAC ASIMOV

Science Fiction Writer
If you make stuff up as a science fiction writer, you will be honored as a visionary. (Unless you convince millions that your stories are true and found a church, in which case you will be derided as a nut.)

J.K. ROWLING

Fantasy Writer
If you make stuff up as a fantasy writer, you will earn a place in the hearts of children everywhere. But some fundamentalist Christians might burn your books.

YES

ARTISTS L. V. Anderson, David Haglund, Natalie Matthews-Ramo, and Jim Pagels, *Slate*.

STATEMENT When Mike Daisey was caught fabricating details during a *This American Life* segment about Apple factories in China (material adapted from his one-man show), we couldn't stop talking about it. We had the usual questions about why he did it and how he got away with it—the questions that come up every time a writer presents fiction as fact. But we had other, knottier questions too, like, Did presenting this material in a one-man show give him any poetic license? When another frequent guest on *This American Life,* David Sedaris, was berated by the *New Republic* for making stuff up, many people seemed to find that berating a little bit ridiculous. How come?

The expectations for truth in storytelling vary from context to context, and those expectations typically come into focus only after someone fails to meet them. Perhaps, we decided, seeing them laid out in a chart would make things a little clearer.

PUBLICATION *Slate* (March 21, 2012)

切ない
(Japanese)
Emotion between bitter-sweet, painful and wistful. A kind of heartrending emotion.

Sorrow

Regret
SHAME
Gu
Displeasure
Shame

Misery
Glumness
Woe
Gloom
Grief
SADNESS
Sadı
Unhappiness
Despair
Sadness
Hopelessness
Melancholy
Depression

SYMPATHY
Pity
Ago
Sympathy

Rage
Vengefulness
Bitterness
Anger
Outrage
Fury
Spite
RAGE
Scorn
Wrath
Loathing
Hate
Resentment
Hostility
Dislike
Ferocity

Annoyance
Grouchiness
Agitation
IRRITATION
Grumpiness
Aggravation
Irritation

Anger

Envy
ENVY
Jealousy

EXASPER-ATION
Exasperation
Frustration

TORMENT
Torment

Contempt
DISGUST
Disgust
Revulsion

Surprise
SURPRISE
Amazement
Astonishment
Surprise

Hiraeth
(Welsh)
Homesickness tinged with grief or sadness over the lost or departed and the the earnest desire fc. the Wales of the past.

懐かしい
(Japanese)
Missing something. The sense of longing, being nostalgic for something, someone, or somewhere.

Тоска
(Russian)
Great spiritual anguish, often without any specific cause. Ache of soul, a longing with nothing to long for.

Saudade
(Portuguese)
A somewhat melancholic feeling of incompleteness. Longing for something that might never return. Yearning.

心疼
(Chinese)
The feeling somev between sympath empathy, to feel the ing of loved on

כואב לי הלב
(Hebrew)
Identifying other's suffering so much that the heart hurts.

Yearning
Longing
LONGING

Liking
Love
Desire
Arousal
Sentimentality
Adoration
Lov
LUST
Infatuation
Lust
Passion
Compassion
AFFECTION
Fondness
Tenderness
Caring
Attraction
Affection

忐忑
(Chinese)
A mixture of feeling uneasy and worried, as if you can feel your own heart beat.

糾結
(Chinese)
Worried, feeling uneasy, don't know what to do.

Anxiety
Tenseness
Uneasiness
Dread
NERVOUS-NESS
Nervousness
Distress
Worry
Apprehension

Fear

Mortification
Alarm
Hysteria
Shock
HORROR
Fear
Panic
Fright
Terror
Horror

Unt… Emotio… other … v.s. Par… Cla…

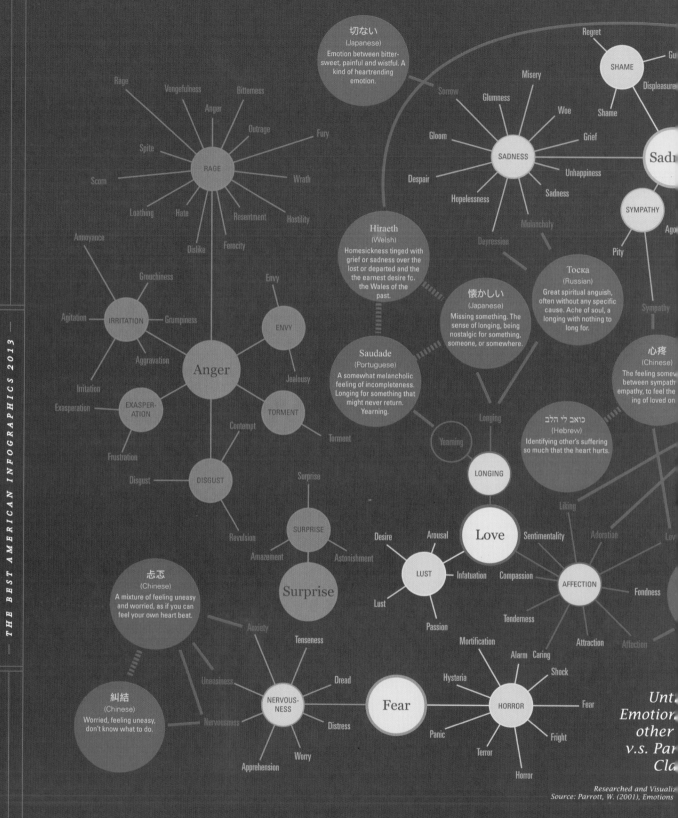

Researched and Visualiz…
Source: Parrott, W. (2001), Emotions …

Feelings That Cannot Be Expressed in English

Untranslatable emotions expose the deficiencies of language.

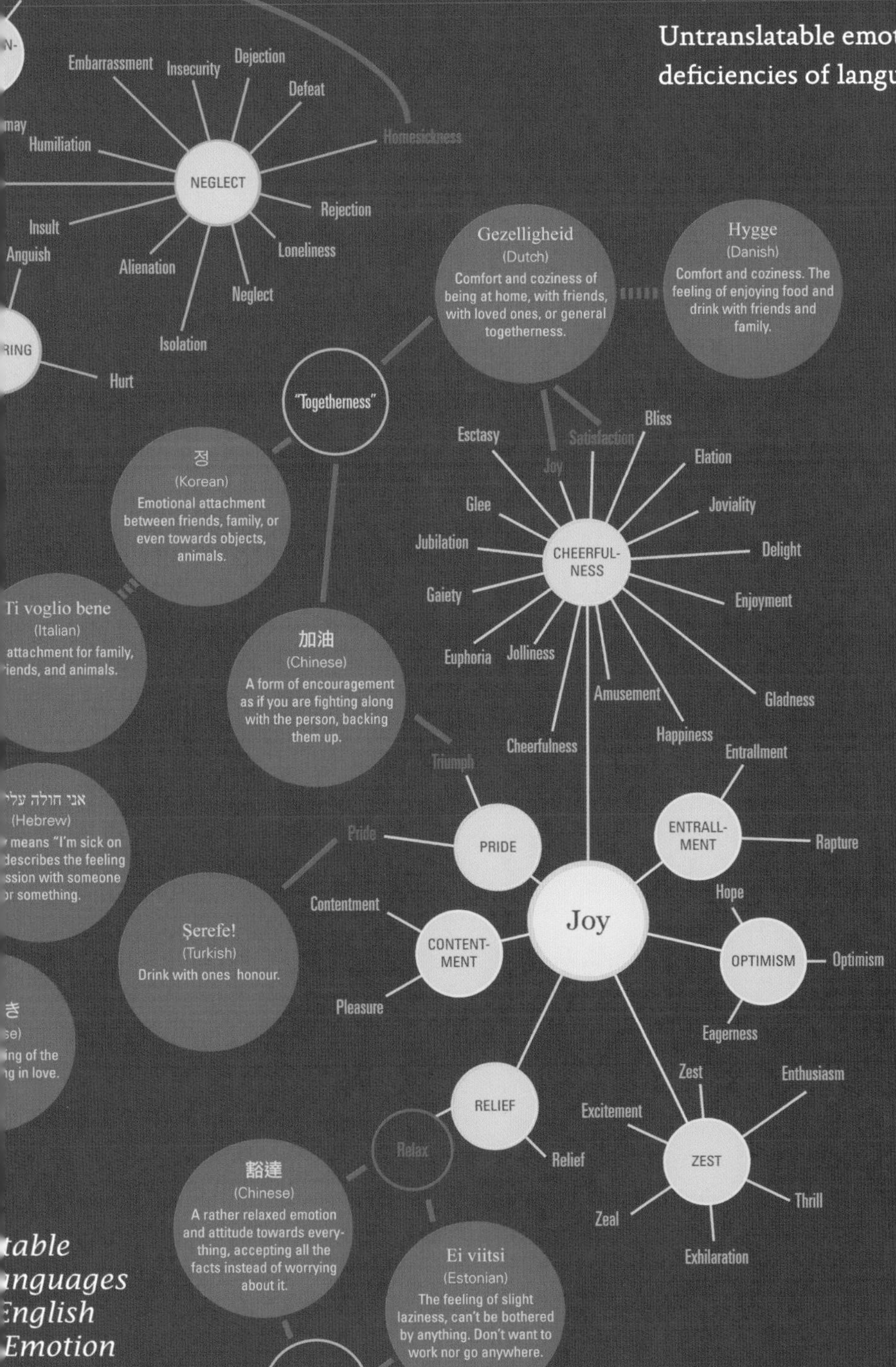
Embarrassment
Insecurity
Dejection
Defeat
Humiliation
NEGLECT
Homesickness
Rejection
Insult
Anguish
Alienation
Loneliness
Neglect
Isolation
Hurt
"Togetherness"
Gezelligheid
(Dutch)
Comfort and coziness of being at home, with friends, with loved ones, or general togetherness.
Hygge
(Danish)
Comfort and coziness. The feeling of enjoying food and drink with friends and family.
정
(Korean)
Emotional attachment between friends, family, or even towards objects, animals.
Ti voglio bene
(Italian)
加油
(Chinese)
A form of encouragement as if you are fighting along with the person, backing them up.
(Hebrew)
Şerefe!
(Turkish)
Drink with ones honour.
豁達
(Chinese)
A rather relaxed emotion and attitude towards everything, accepting all the facts instead of worrying about it.
Ei viitsi
(Estonian)
The feeling of slight laziness, can't be bothered by anything. Don't want to work nor go anywhere.
"Nothingness"
Relax
Esctasy
Satisfaction
Joy
Bliss
Elation
Glee
Joviality
Jubilation
CHEERFUL-NESS
Delight
Gaiety
Enjoyment
Euphoria
Jolliness
Amusement
Gladness
Cheerfulness
Happiness
Entrallment
Triumph
Pride
PRIDE
ENTRALL-MENT
Rapture
Contentment
Joy
Hope
CONTENT-MENT
OPTIMISM
Optimism
Pleasure
Eagerness
Zest
Enthusiasm
RELIEF
Excitement
Relief
ZEST
Thrill
Zeal
Exhilaration

ARTIST Pei-Ying Lin, a freelance designer and artist based in Taiwan.

STATEMENT The basic categorization of emotions in this visualization comes from the book *Emotions in Social Psychology* by W. Gerrod Parrott, an American psychologist. Parrott asked his students to sort out emotions by their similarities, and using their ratings, he drew out the "hierarchical structure of the emotion domain." It is like organizing species of plants or animals using taxonomy, only with emotions.

The project was motivated by my experience as an international student. I often find it hard to find the right word in English to explain how I feel. And when I am finally able to talk about the emotion with another Chinese speaker, there is this "aha!" moment when we understand each other immediately. I sent out a message asking for examples of this throughout the Royal College of Art, where I was studying, and I got back so many sincere and generous replies. This led to the making of this graph, along with a video database in which people explain the emotions in their languages.

PUBLICATION
peiyinglin.net
(February 7, 2012)

Short guys can dunk

Jam. Slam. Flush. *Posterize.* There is no more forceful display of basketball authority than a fabulously executed dunk, and most of the ultra-tall players you'll see in this month's NCAA Tournament can throw one down at will. But what about those who stand far below the 10-foot rims? We posed this question to a kinesiology professor and a trainer who works with college and pro basketball players: Why can some shorter guys jump high enough to dunk?

One step at a time

Practicing over and over again trains the brain to activate muscles in a precise sequence so momentum travels in waves from shoulders to toes in a perfect kinetic chain.

1 **Hands and arms** swing forward and upward. (They don't need to be able to palm the basketball; many players dunk two-handed or cradle the ball against a forearm.)

2 **Head** raises and **trunk** extends.

3 **Core** engages. Legs, core muscles, even feet need to be strong. If one muscle group is under- or overdeveloped, the body won't accumulate as much force as it should.

4 **Gluteus maximus** contracts. The best dunkers have a high percentage of fast-twitch muscle fibers, which fire quickly, providing great power in short bursts.

5 **Quadriceps** contract. If you have shorter-than-average thighs for your height, you have the ideal mechanical setup for leaping, according to kinesiology professor Tim Anderson. It's a lever issue:

How can I learn to dunk?

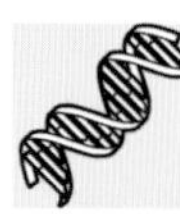

Trade out your genes to grow a few inches taller and acquire a higher percentage of fast-twitch muscle fibers. If that ship has sailed, you have two options left, according to kinesiology professor Tim Anderson and trainer Jacob Ross.

Get stronger Ross suggests leg-strengthening exercises such as single-leg squats, regular squats, leg presses and calf extensions. Anderson recommends specifically strengthening your feet with toe raises and other barefoot exercises.

Practice jumping Plyometric exercises — they often have "jump" or "hop" in the title — require explosive movements that teach muscles in the chain to work together. (Caution: They can also be hard on untrained joints and tendons.)

Shorter femur, better jumper

When you jump, your thigh acts as a lever that propels your body weight upward. A shorter thigh resists movement less than a longer one. (To feel this, try a regular squat. Now imagine how much easier it would be to push yourself upward if your thighs were shorter.)

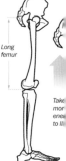

Long femur

Sources: Jacob Ross of EFT Sports Performance, who jumps off two feet to dunk; Tim Anderson of Fresno State, who blames deficient genes for his inability to dunk

7 Small muscles in the **feet** give the final push. People who are very good at transferring forward momentum (running) to vertical momentum will dunk off one foot. Others need raw leg power to lift them, so they jump off two feet.

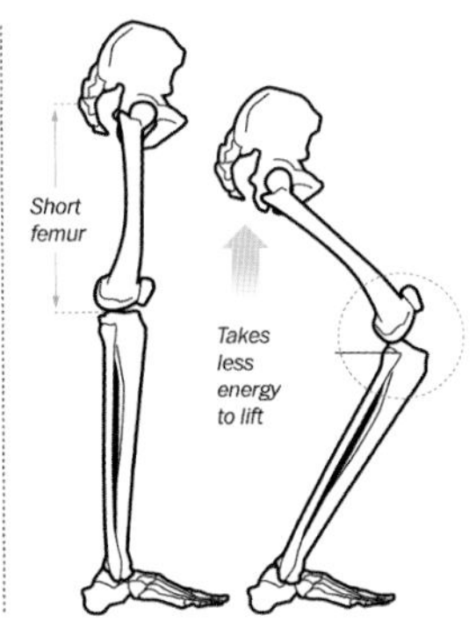

Short femur
Takes less energy to lift

E BERKOWITZ AND ALBERTO CUADRA /THE WASHINGTON POST

Two Points, with Drama

Why can some five foot ten people dunk a basketball and some six foot five people can't?

ARTISTS Alberto Cuadra, a graphic artist, and Bonnie Berkowitz, a graphics reporter, at the *Washington Post*.

STATEMENT Early in the research, the focus of this graphic changed from the generic "how to dunk" to "how a short guy can dunk" because the physiological process has to be so much more precise. (We were not being sexist by using "guys" in the headline, by the way. Experts said that natural physiological differences make it much harder for a woman of any height to dunk, so a short woman has virtually no chance.) Neither of us was entirely happy with this graphic before publication. Some really interesting information wouldn't fit, the perspective had to be altered so the graphic would fit the width of a newspaper page, and the visual reference we had was not ideal. We bickered so much during the process that coworkers started calling us Fred and Ethel.

But after publication we realized none of those things detracted much from the final product, and we had stumbled onto something people liked. The source line at the bottom was one of our favorite parts. Important and relevant note: Although Bonnie is nearly six feet tall and Alberto is six foot one, neither of us can dunk.

PUBLICATION *Washington Post* (March 6, 2012)

Understanding Social Media—with Bacon

The reality is that all social media channels offer the same service: an opportunity for people to get together. The only important difference is the way they allow people to connect.

ARTIST Corey Smith, president of Tribute Media, a web consulting firm based in Meridian, Idaho.

STATEMENT I saw a picture of a whiteboard showing the same concept with donuts. I figured bacon was a bit more inspiring, and so I redesigned it with my own artwork and some variations on how a few of the social media elements were represented. I didn't intend for this infographic to become so popular. I thought I was designing it for me.

PUBLICATION coreysmith.ws/blog (February 13, 2012)

Social Media Explained

- I'm eating bacon
- I like bacon
- I have skills including eating bacon
- This is where I eat bacon
- Watch me eat my bacon
- Here's a vintage photo of my bacon
- Here's a recipe with bacon
- I work for Google and eat bacon
- I'm listening to music about bacon

 coreysmith.ws

The Four Kinds of Dog

The breeds, grouped by their DNA.

FAMILY TIES Analyzing the DNA of 85 dog breeds, scientists found that genetic similarities clustered them into four broad categories. The groupings reveal how breeders have recombined ancestral stock to create new breeds; a few still carry many wolflike genes. Researchers named the groups for a distinguishing trait in the breeds dominating the clusters, though not every dog necessarily shows that trait.

ARTIST John Tomanio, a senior graphics editor, *National Geographic,* Washington, D.C.

STATEMENT While researching graphics for a story about the wide range of physical differentiation in dogs, I came across a scientific paper that analyzed the DNA of a broad selection of breeds. Surprisingly, the DNA clustered into four general categories, with some very different breeds sharing the same category. I found this fascinating. Who would guess that the Basenji belongs to the group genetically closest to wolves? Or that, based on their DNA, pharaoh hounds are most likely modern re-creations made to resemble ancient breeds? Great data can make a simple graphic compelling.

PUBLICATION *National Geographic* (February 2012)

The length of the colored bars in a breed's genetic profile shows how much of the dog's DNA falls into each category.

WOLFLIKE
With roots in Asia, Africa, and the Middle East, these breeds are genetically closest to wolves, suggesting they are the oldest domesticated breeds.

HERDERS
Familiar herding breeds such as the Shetland sheepdog are joined by breeds never known for herding: the greyhound, pug, and borzoi. This suggests those breeds either were used in the creation of classic herding dogs or descended from them.

HUNTERS
Most in this group were developed in recent centuries as hunting dogs. While the pharaoh hound and Ibizan hound are said to descend from dogs seen on ancient Egyptian tombs, their placement here suggests they are re-creations bred to resemble ancient breeds.

MASTIFFLIKE
The German shepherd's appearance in this cluster, anchored by the mastiff, bulldog, and boxer, likely reflects its breeding as a military and police dog.

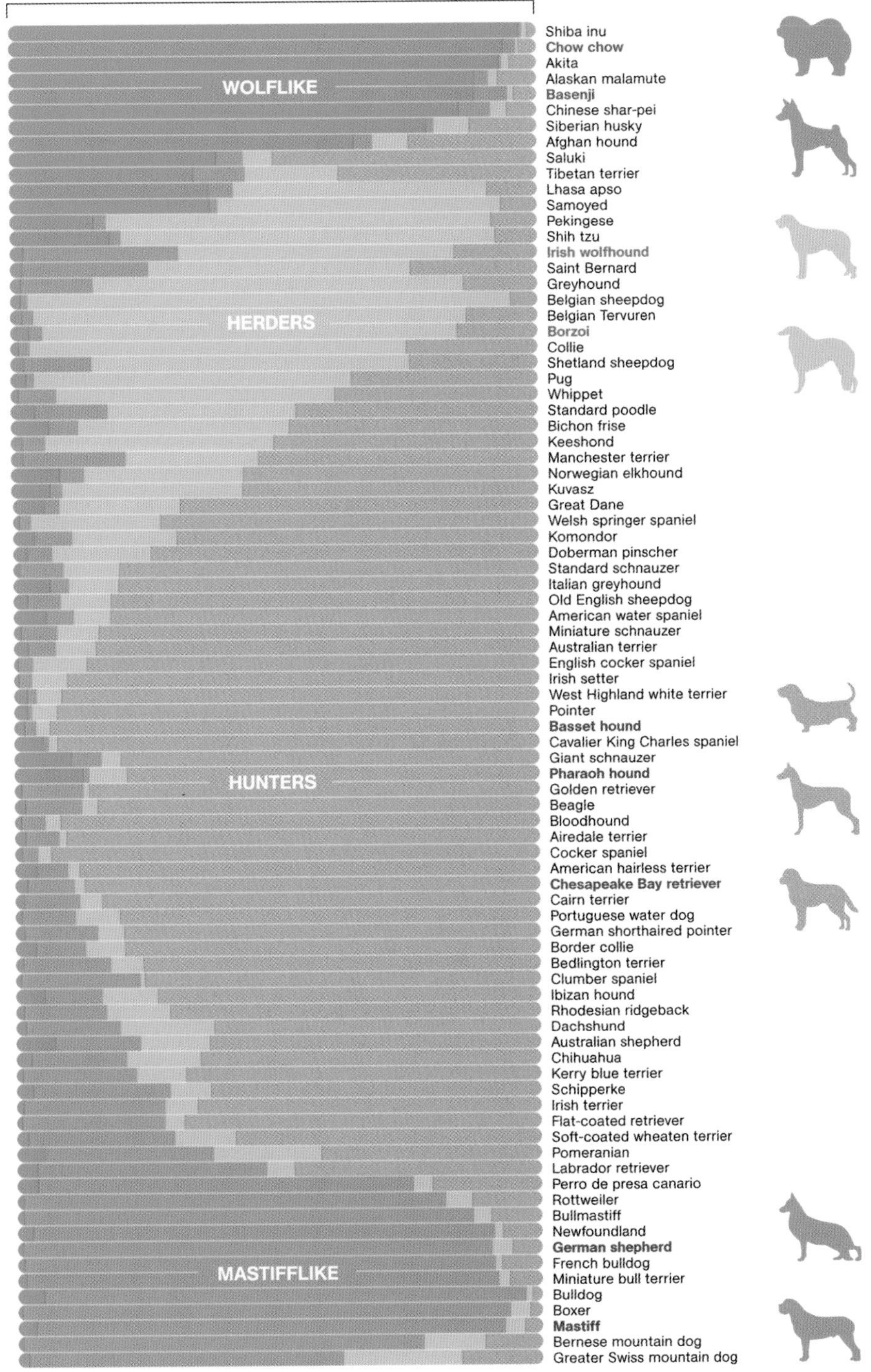

WOLFLIKE
HERDERS
HUNTERS
MASTIFFLIKE
Shiba inu
Chow chow
Akita
Alaskan malamute
Basenji
Chinese shar-pei
Siberian husky
Afghan hound
Saluki
Tibetan terrier
Lhasa apso
Samoyed
Pekingese
Shih tzu
Irish wolfhound
Saint Bernard
Greyhound
Belgian sheepdog
Belgian Tervuren
Borzoi
Collie
Shetland sheepdog
Pug
Whippet
Standard poodle
Bichon frise
Keeshond
Manchester terrier
Norwegian elkhound
Kuvasz
Great Dane
Welsh springer spaniel
Komondor
Doberman pinscher
Standard schnauzer
Italian greyhound
Old English sheepdog
American water spaniel
Miniature schnauzer
Australian terrier
English cocker spaniel
Irish setter
West Highland white terrier
Pointer
Basset hound
Cavalier King Charles spaniel
Giant schnauzer
Pharaoh hound
Golden retriever
Beagle
Bloodhound
Airedale terrier
Cocker spaniel
American hairless terrier
Chesapeake Bay retriever
Cairn terrier
Portuguese water dog
German shorthaired pointer
Border collie
Bedlington terrier
Clumber spaniel
Ibizan hound
Rhodesian ridgeback
Dachshund
Australian shepherd
Chihuahua
Kerry blue terrier
Schipperke
Irish terrier
Flat-coated retriever
Soft-coated wheaten terrier
Pomeranian
Labrador retriever
Perro de presa canario
Rottweiler
Bullmastiff
Newfoundland
German shepherd
French bulldog
Miniature bull terrier
Bulldog
Boxer
Mastiff
Bernese mountain dog
Greater Swiss mountain dog

JOHN TOMANIO, LAWSON PARKER, NGM STAFF
SOURCE: HEIDI G. PARKER, NATIONAL HUMAN GENOME RESEARCH INSTITUTE, NATIONAL INSTITUTES OF HEALTH

From Teaspoon to Gallon and Back Again

The perplexing and hard-to-remember U.S. Standard measuring system, mapped out for easy reference.

ARTIST Shannon Lattin, a freelance graphic designer in Portland, Oregon, on a mission to make useful things beautiful—and vice versa.

STATEMENT This graphic was born partly from a passion for baking and partly from a ghastly inability to remember how to convert gallons to pints, cups to quarts, and tablespoons to anything at all. Knowing that—unlike the sleek symmetry of the metric system—the U.S. Standard system would not lend itself well to a linear conversion chart, I started instead with a constellation-like format. This has the added benefit of allowing for comparisons between multiple measurements at once. Don't have a quarter cup handy? You can quickly find out how to fake it with either tablespoons or teaspoons. A third of a cup can be reached using a combination of the two.

PUBLICATION
sblattindesign.wordpress.com
(September 15, 2012)

THE COMMON COOK'S

HOW-MANY GUIDE

TO KITCHEN CONVERSIONS

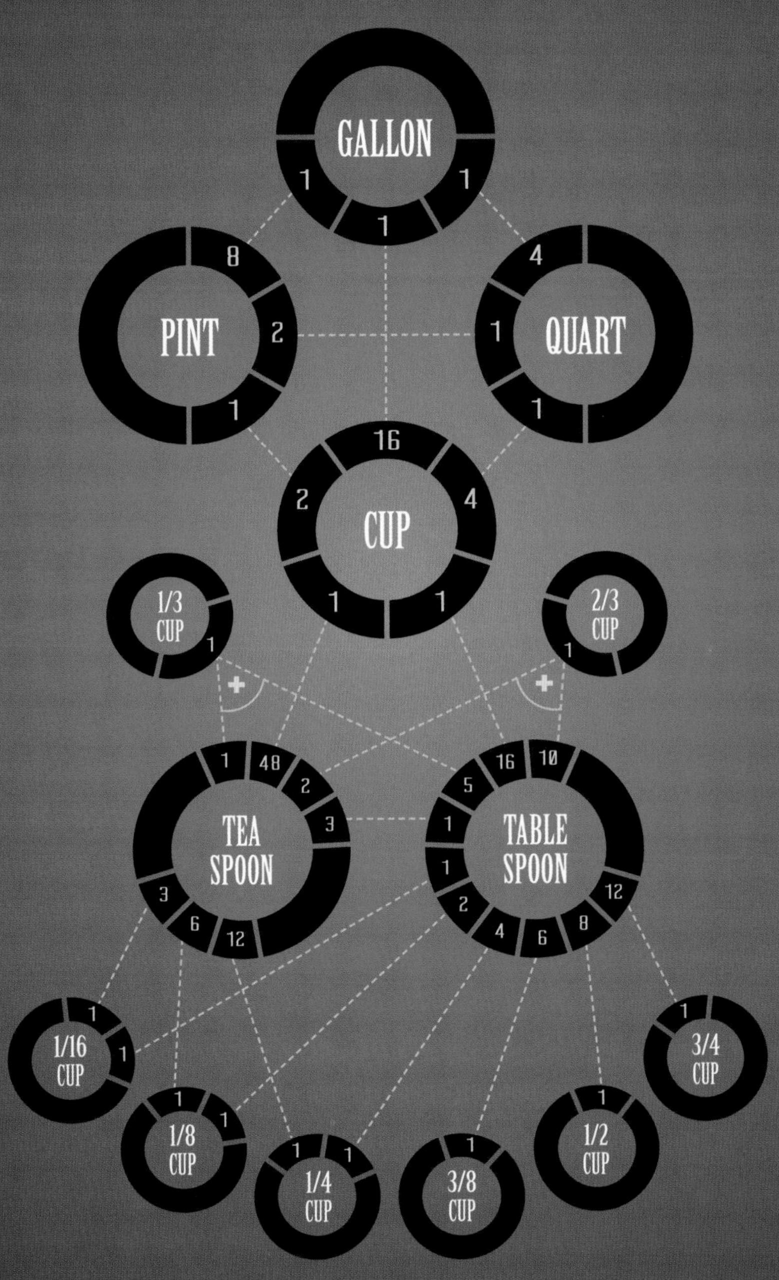
GALLON
1
1
1
PINT
8
2
1
QUART
4
1
1
CUP
16
2
4
1
1
1/3 CUP
1
2/3 CUP
1
+
+
TEA SPOON
1
48
2
3
3
6
12
TABLE SPOON
16
10
5
1
1
2
4
6
8
12
1/16 CUP
1
1
1/8 CUP
1
1
1/4 CUP
1
1
3/8 CUP
1
1/2 CUP
1
3/4 CUP
1

S.B.LATTINDESIGN

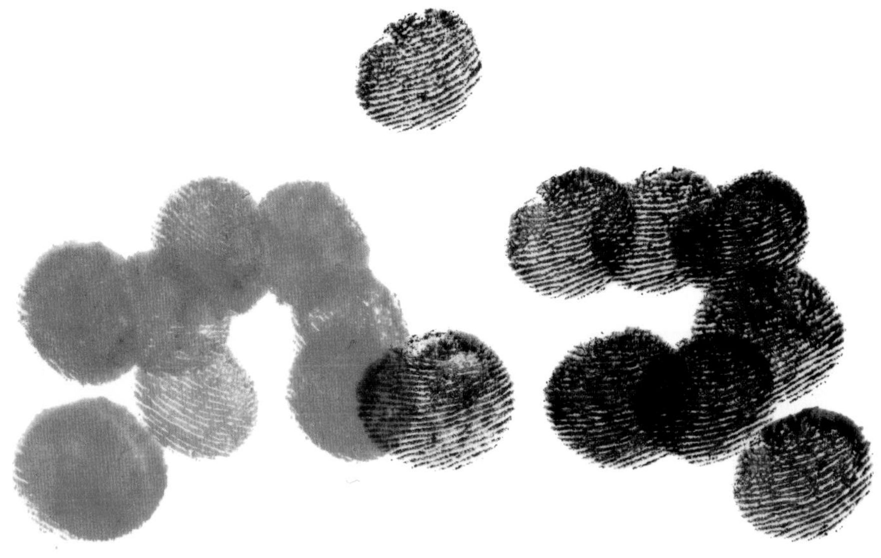

Multi-Touch Paintings

Images created by performing routine tasks on handheld computing devices, ranging from unlocking the device to checking Twitter, with inked fingers.

ARTIST Evan Roth, an American artist currently based in Paris.

STATEMENT The work was not intended as a glorification of this new kind of computing. In addition to visualizing and archiving our first encounters with touching pixels, the pieces also aim to critically question these computers that never leave our pockets and how they command us in certain ways. Many of these gestures that have been dictated to us by companies like Apple or Rovio are now a part of our daily routines and, even though they were prescribed to us only a few years ago, are already ingrained in our physical memories.

The Multi-Touch Painting series also aims to connect something intimate and personal (like a fingerprint) to something that is generic and designed not for the individual but for the masses (e.g., interface design). Part of the motivation for making the piece was to create something through a very analog process (ink on paper) that speaks about our relationship with something digital. There is something very poetic about this imagery that speaks to the more complicated relationship we now have with technology.

PUBLICATION Exhibition at N2 Galeria in Barcelona, Spain (April 19 to June 1, 2012)

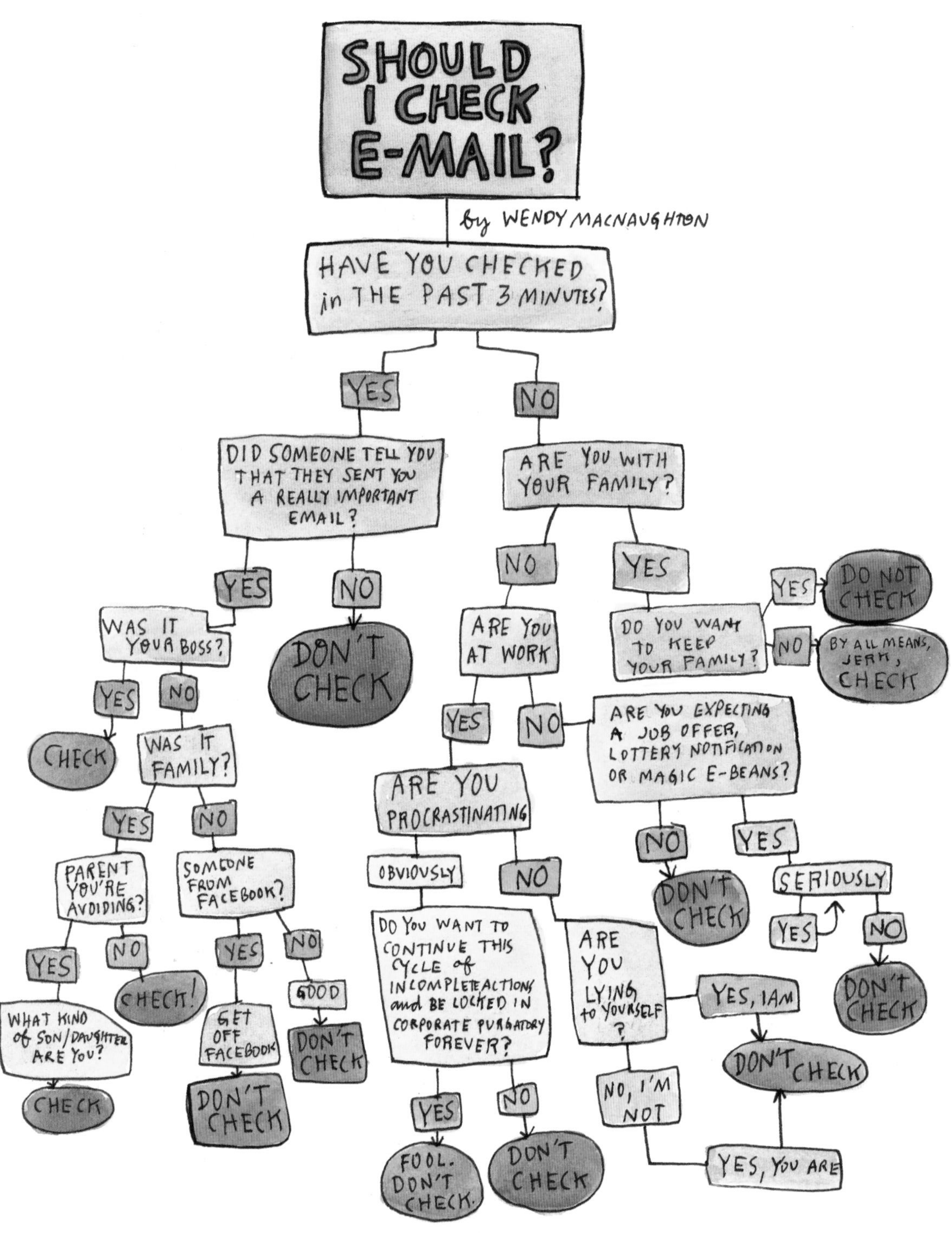
SHOULD I CHECK E-MAIL?
by WENDY MACNAUGHTON
HAVE YOU CHECKED in THE PAST 3 MINUTES?
YES
NO
DID SOMEONE TELL YOU THAT THEY SENT YOU A REALLY IMPORTANT EMAIL?
ARE YOU WITH YOUR FAMILY?
YES
NO
DON'T CHECK
WAS IT YOUR BOSS?
YES
CHECK
NO
WAS IT FAMILY?
YES
PARENT YOU'RE AVOIDING?
YES
WHAT KIND of SON/DAUGHTER ARE YOU?
CHECK
NO
CHECK!
NO
SOMEONE FROM FACEBOOK?
YES
GET OFF FACEBOOK
DON'T CHECK
NO
GOOD
DON'T CHECK
NO
ARE YOU AT WORK
YES
ARE YOU PROCRASTINATING
OBVIOUSLY
DO YOU WANT TO CONTINUE THIS CYCLE of INCOMPLETE ACTIONS and BE LOCKED IN CORPORATE PURGATORY FOREVER?
YES
FOOL. DON'T CHECK.
NO
DON'T CHECK
NO
ARE YOU LYING to YOURSELF?
YES, I AM
DON'T CHECK
NO, I'M NOT
YES, YOU ARE
NO
ARE YOU EXPECTING A JOB OFFER, LOTTERY NOTIFICATION OR MAGIC E-BEANS?
NO
DON'T CHECK
YES
SERIOUSLY
YES
NO
DON'T CHECK
YES
DO YOU WANT TO KEEP YOUR FAMILY?
YES
DO NOT CHECK
NO
BY ALL MEANS, JERK, CHECK

E-mail: Help for Addicts

A handy flowchart to help you decide if you should check your e-mail.

ARTIST Wendy MacNaughton, a freelance illustrator in San Francisco.

STATEMENT I usually make diagrams to make sense of things that are abstract or complex. This flowchart, however, is more about self-help. Like everyone these days, I'm drowning in e-mail. But it's my own fault. I have three e-mail accounts. I check them at least ten times a day (more like an hour). I respond to e-mails with "How are you?," ensuring another e-mail comes my way. I am the reason that I'm drowning. Creating this chart helped me see that I had a problem, accept it, and start on the road to recovery.

Remember: Unless it's a family emergency, Don't Check.

PS: Families don't e-mail emergencies.

PUBLICATION Dell Inc. on Forbes.com (April 19, 2012)

The Quantified Self

Nicholas Felton gathers massive amounts of data about how he spends his time then publishes his own corporate report.

ARTIST Nicholas Felton, cofounder of Daytum.com and a member of the product design team at Facebook.

STATEMENT Philip K. Dick claimed that "a person's authentic nature is a series of shifting, variegated planes that establish themselves as he relates to different people; it is created by and appears within the framework of his interpersonal relationships." The 2010/2011 Feltron Biennial Report explores this notion by overlapping facets of my behavior to visualize how my personality varies based on location and company.

I decided in October 2010 to move to Brooklyn for the first time, and then in April 2011 I began working at Facebook as a member of the product design team. So I now have a life focused on Manhattan and a life focused on the West Coast. In the report, I'm trying to graphically represent the dichotomies.

PUBLICATION Feltron.com (February 27, 2012); print edition (April 27, 2012)

In New York City

2010—2011

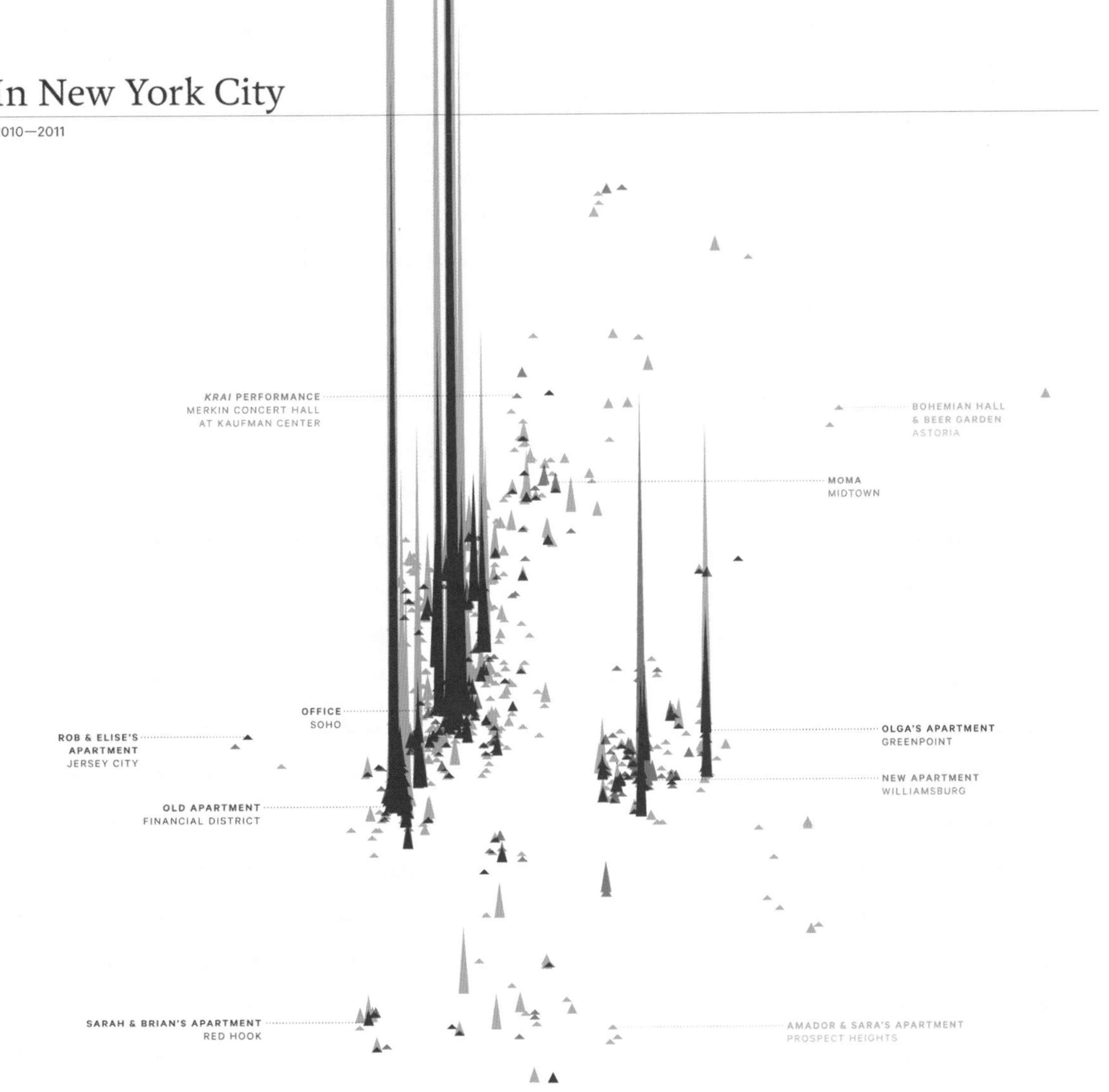

KRAI PERFORMANCE
MERKIN CONCERT HALL
AT KAUFMAN CENTER
BOHEMIAN HALL
& BEER GARDEN
ASTORIA
MOMA
MIDTOWN
OFFICE
SOHO
ROB & ELISE'S
APARTMENT
JERSEY CITY
OLGA'S APARTMENT
GREENPOINT
NEW APARTMENT
WILLIAMSBURG
OLD APARTMENT
FINANCIAL DISTRICT
SARAH & BRIAN'S APARTMENT
RED HOOK
AMADOR & SARA'S APARTMENT
PROSPECT HEIGHTS

DAYS SPENT IN NEW YORK CITY

442¾

61% of each year

TIME IN NYC BOROUGHS

MANHATTAN — 377¾ DAYS

BROOKLYN — 61½ DAYS

QUEENS — 3½ DAYS

BRONX

STATEN ISLAND

NYC PLACES VISITED

648

173 restaurants, 121 shops, 55 bars, 41 outdoor places, 39 offices, 35 delis, 34 coffee shops, 22 homes, 20 venues, 16 grocery stores, 13 galleries, 11 banks, 9 museums, 8 airport terminals, 7 hotels, 7 liquor stores, 7 schools, 6 drug stores, 4 train stations, 4 open houses, 4 post offices, 3 laundromats, 3 movie theaters, 2 parks, 2 rental car locations, a dance studio, a gas station, a gym, mini-storage and work

MOST VISITED NYC SHOPS

FEDEX, SPRING STREET — 9 VISITS

J. CREW LIQUOR STORE — 8 VISITS

PETLAND DISCOUNTS — 7 VISITS

VITSOE — 7 VISITS

APPLE STORE SOHO — 6 VISITS

MOST VISITED DELI

Broadway Gourmet Food Market

584–588 Broadway — 30 visits

RATIO OF NYC SUBWAY TO TAXI TRIPS

5¾:1

1,147 subway vs. 202 taxi trips

FAVORITE NYC BEVERAGE

Filter Coffee

296 servings

TIME IN NYC SPENT IN RESTAURANTS

5%

CONTINUED

With Olga

EVERYWHERE

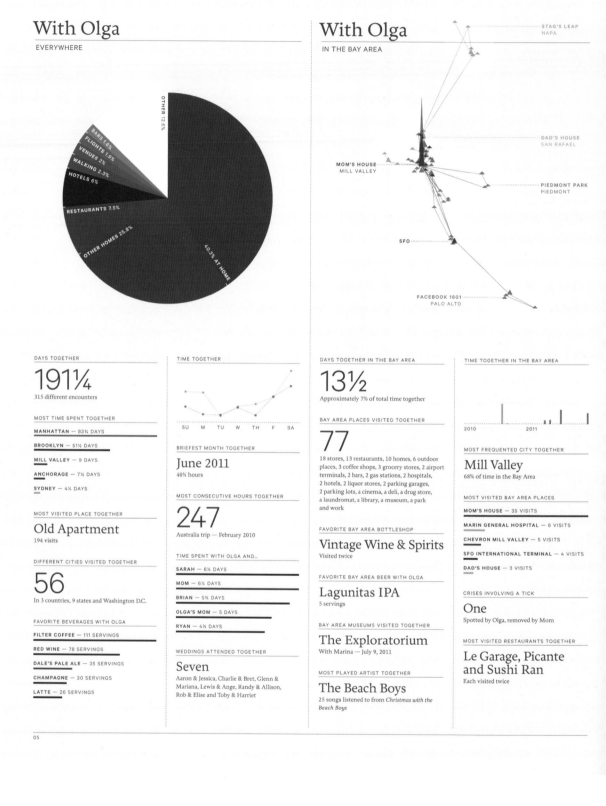

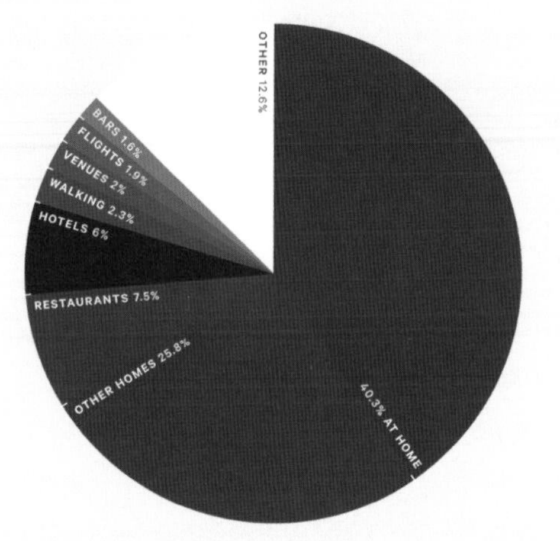
OTHER 12.6%
BARS 1.6%
FLIGHTS 1.9%
VENUES 2%
WALKING 2.3%
HOTELS 6%
RESTAURANTS 7.5%
OTHER HOMES 25.8%
40.3% AT HOME

With Olga

IN THE BAY AREA

STAG'S LEAP
NAPA

DAD'S HOUSE
SAN RAFAEL

MOM'S HOUSE
MILL VALLEY

PIEDMONT PARK
PIEDMONT

SFO

FACEBOOK 1601
PALO ALTO

DAYS TOGETHER

191¼

315 different encounters

MOST TIME SPENT TOGETHER

MANHATTAN — 83¾ DAYS

BROOKLYN — 51½ DAYS

MILL VALLEY — 9 DAYS

ANCHORAGE — 7½ DAYS

SYDNEY — 4¼ DAYS

MOST VISITED PLACE TOGETHER

Old Apartment

194 visits

DIFFERENT CITIES VISITED TOGETHER

56

In 3 countries, 9 states and Washington D.C.

FAVORITE BEVERAGES WITH OLGA

FILTER COFFEE — 111 SERVINGS

RED WINE — 78 SERVINGS

DALE'S PALE ALE — 35 SERVINGS

CHAMPAGNE — 30 SERVINGS

LATTE — 26 SERVINGS

TIME TOGETHER

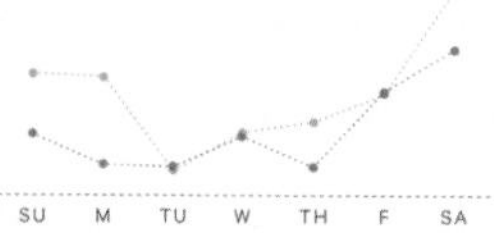
SU
M
TU
W
TH
F
SA

BRIEFEST MONTH TOGETHER

June 2011

40¾ hours

MOST CONSECUTIVE HOURS TOGETHER

247

Australia trip — February 2010

TIME SPENT WITH OLGA AND...

SARAH — 6¼ DAYS

MOM — 6¼ DAYS

BRIAN — 5¾ DAYS

OLGA'S MOM — 5 DAYS

RYAN — 4½ DAYS

WEDDINGS ATTENDED TOGETHER

Seven

Aaron & Jessica, Charlie & Bret, Glenn & Mariana, Lewis & Ange, Randy & Allison, Rob & Elise and Toby & Harriet

DAYS TOGETHER IN THE BAY AREA

13½

Approximately 7% of total time together

BAY AREA PLACES VISITED TOGETHER

77

18 stores, 13 restaurants, 10 homes, 6 outdoor places, 3 coffee shops, 3 grocery stores, 2 airport terminals, 2 bars, 2 gas stations, 2 hospitals, 2 hotels, 2 liquor stores, 2 parking garages, 2 parking lots, a cinema, a deli, a drug store, a laundromat, a library, a museum, a park and work

FAVORITE BAY AREA BOTTLESHOP

Vintage Wine & Spirits

Visited twice

FAVORITE BAY AREA BEER WITH OLGA

Lagunitas IPA

5 servings

BAY AREA MUSEUMS VISITED TOGETHER

The Exploratorium

With Marina — July 9, 2011

MOST PLAYED ARTIST TOGETHER

The Beach Boys

25 songs listened to from *Christmas with the Beach Boys*

TIME TOGETHER IN THE BAY AREA

2010
2011

MOST FREQUENTED CITY TOGETHER

Mill Valley

68% of time in the Bay Area

MOST VISITED BAY AREA PLACES

MOM'S HOUSE — 35 VISITS

MARIN GENERAL HOSPITAL — 6 VISITS

CHEVRON MILL VALLEY — 5 VISITS

SFO INTERNATIONAL TERMINAL — 4 VISITS

DAD'S HOUSE — 3 VISITS

CRISES INVOLVING A TICK

One

Spotted by Olga, removed by Mom

MOST VISITED RESTAURANTS TOGETHER

Le Garage, Picante and Sushi Ran

Each visited twice

05

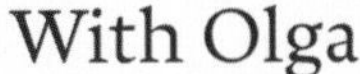

With Olga

IN NEW YORK CITY

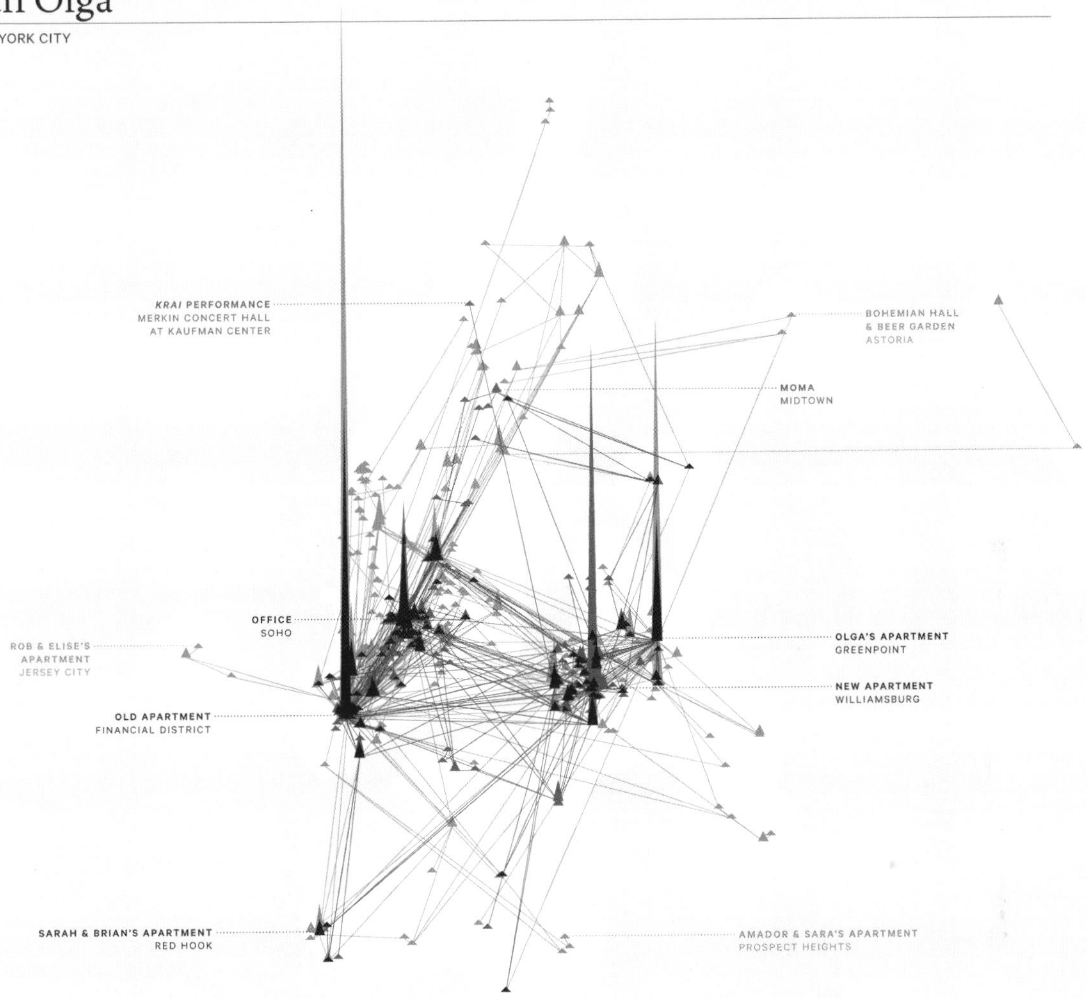

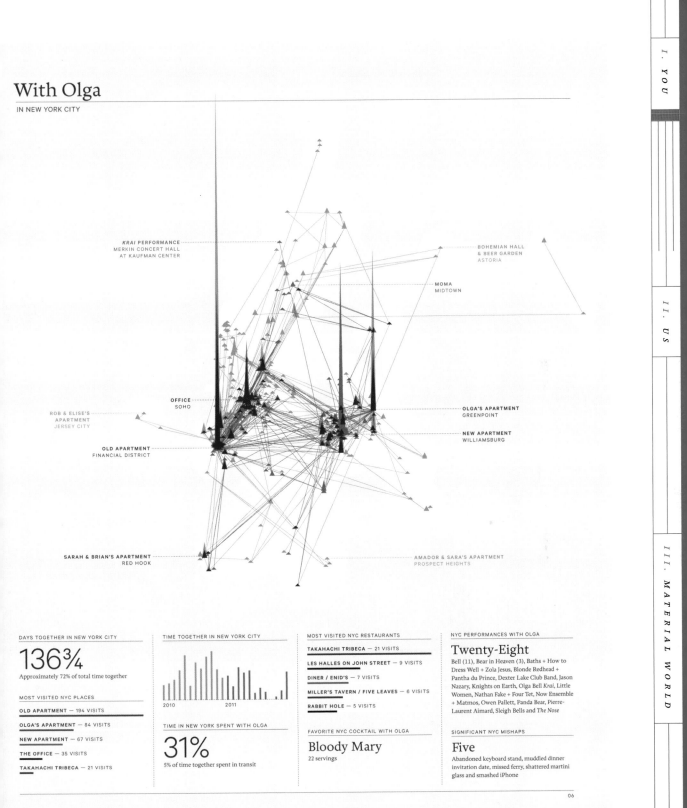

KRAI PERFORMANCE
MERKIN CONCERT HALL
AT KAUFMAN CENTER

BOHEMIAN HALL
& BEER GARDEN
ASTORIA

MOMA
MIDTOWN

OFFICE
SOHO

ROB & ELISE'S
APARTMENT
JERSEY CITY

OLGA'S APARTMENT
GREENPOINT

NEW APARTMENT
WILLIAMSBURG

OLD APARTMENT
FINANCIAL DISTRICT

SARAH & BRIAN'S APARTMENT
RED HOOK

AMADOR & SARA'S APARTMENT
PROSPECT HEIGHTS

DAYS TOGETHER IN NEW YORK CITY

136¾

Approximately 72% of total time together

MOST VISITED NYC PLACES

OLD APARTMENT — 194 VISITS

OLGA'S APARTMENT — 84 VISITS

NEW APARTMENT — 67 VISITS

THE OFFICE — 35 VISITS

TAKAHACHI TRIBECA — 21 VISITS

TIME TOGETHER IN NEW YORK CITY

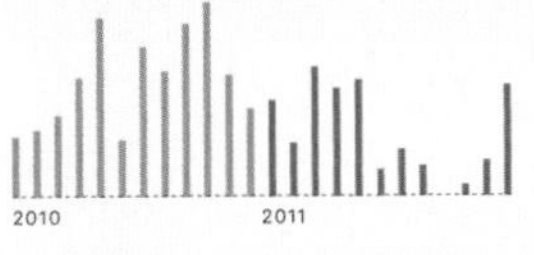
2010
2011

TIME IN NEW YORK SPENT WITH OLGA

31%

5% of time together spent in transit

MOST VISITED NYC RESTAURANTS

TAKAHACHI TRIBECA — 21 VISITS

LES HALLES ON JOHN STREET — 9 VISITS

DINER / ENID'S — 7 VISITS

MILLER'S TAVERN / FIVE LEAVES — 6 VISITS

RABBIT HOLE — 5 VISITS

FAVORITE NYC COCKTAIL WITH OLGA

Bloody Mary

22 servings

NYC PERFORMANCES WITH OLGA

Twenty-Eight

Bell (11), Bear in Heaven (3), Baths + How to Dress Well + Zola Jesus, Blonde Redhead + Pantha du Prince, Dexter Lake Club Band, Jason Nazary, Knights on Earth, Olga Bell *Krai*, Little Women, Nathan Fake + Four Tet, Now Ensemble + Matmos, Owen Pallett, Panda Bear, Pierre-Laurent Aimard, Sleigh Bells and *The Nose*

SIGNIFICANT NYC MISHAPS

Five

Abandoned keyboard stand, muddled dinner invitation date, missed ferry, shattered martini glass and smashed iPhone

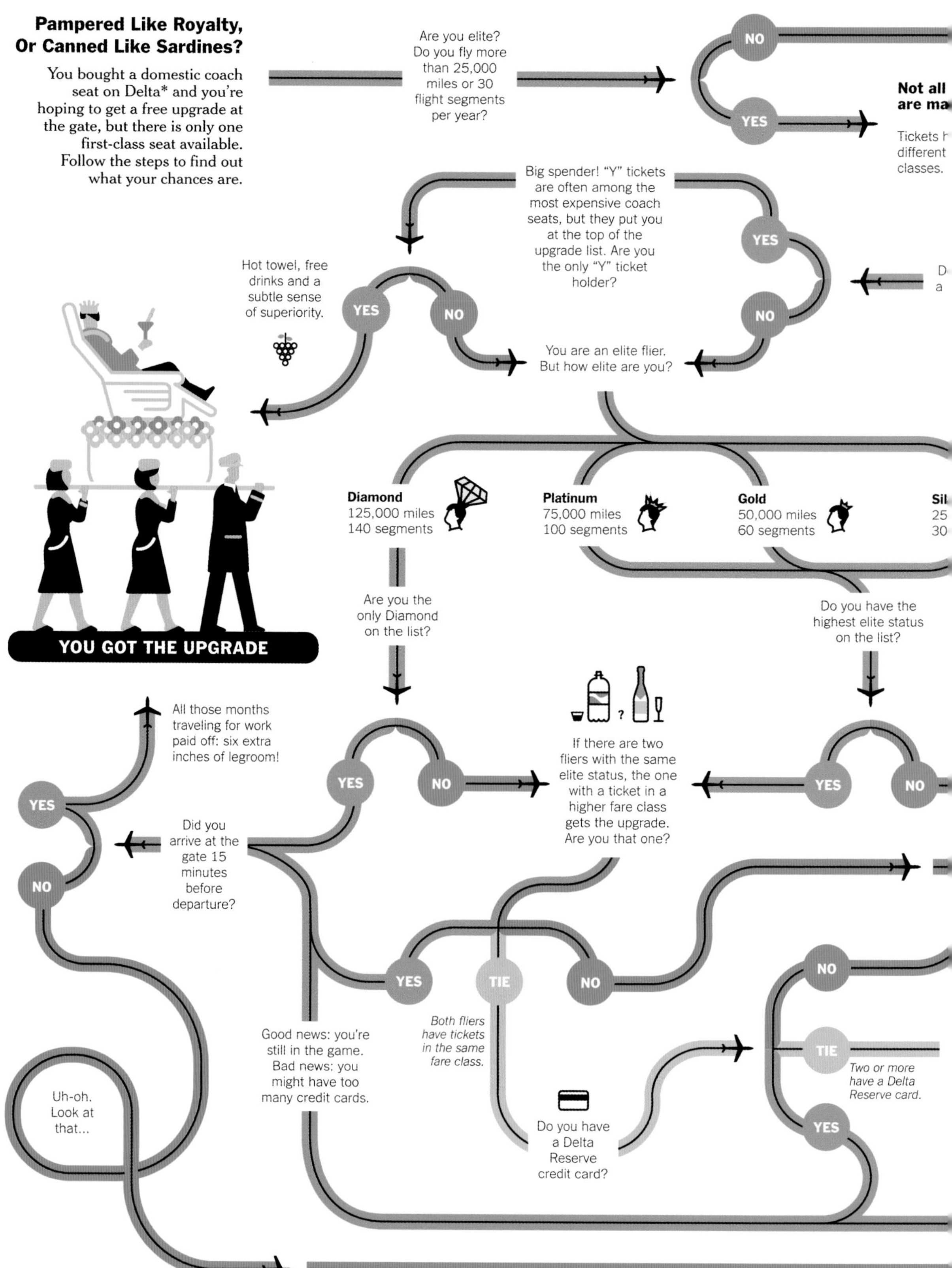

Pampered Like Royalty, Or Canned Like Sardines?
You bought a domestic coach seat on Delta* and you're hoping to get a free upgrade at the gate, but there is only one first-class seat available. Follow the steps to find out what your chances are.
Are you elite? Do you fly more than 25,000 miles or 30 flight segments per year?
NO
YES
Not all
different
classes.
Big spender! "Y" tickets are often among the most expensive coach seats, but they put you at the top of the upgrade list. Are you the only "Y" ticket holder?
YES
NO
Hot towel, free drinks and a subtle sense of superiority.
YES
NO
You are an elite flier. But how elite are you?
YOU GOT THE UPGRADE
Diamond
125,000 miles
140 segments
Platinum
75,000 miles
100 segments
Gold
50,000 miles
60 segments
Are you the only Diamond on the list?
Do you have the highest elite status on the list?
YES
NO
If there are two fliers with the same elite status, the one with a ticket in a higher fare class gets the upgrade. Are you that one?
YES
NO
All those months traveling for work paid off: six extra inches of legroom!
YES
NO
Did you arrive at the gate 15 minutes before departure?
YES
TIE
NO
Both fliers have tickets in the same fare class.
Good news: you're still in the game. Bad news: you might have too many credit cards.
Do you have a Delta Reserve credit card?
NO
TIE
Two or more have a Delta Reserve card.
YES
Uh-oh. Look at that...

* Different airlines have different upgrade criteria. The graphic is based on Delta's.

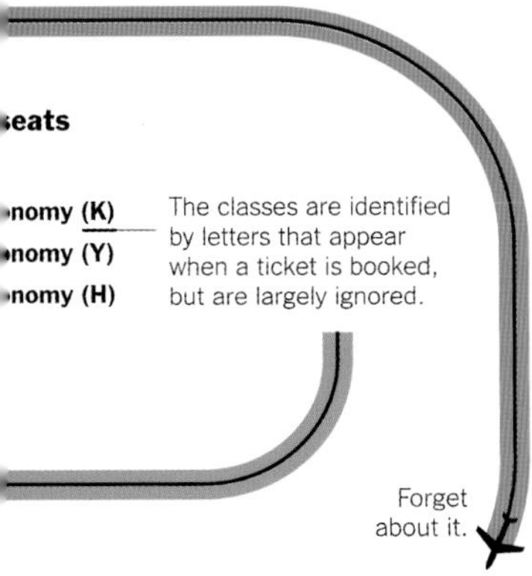
seats
nomy (K)
nomy (Y)
nomy (H)
The classes are identified by letters that appear when a ticket is booked, but are largely ignored.
Forget about it.

PACKED LIKE SARDINES

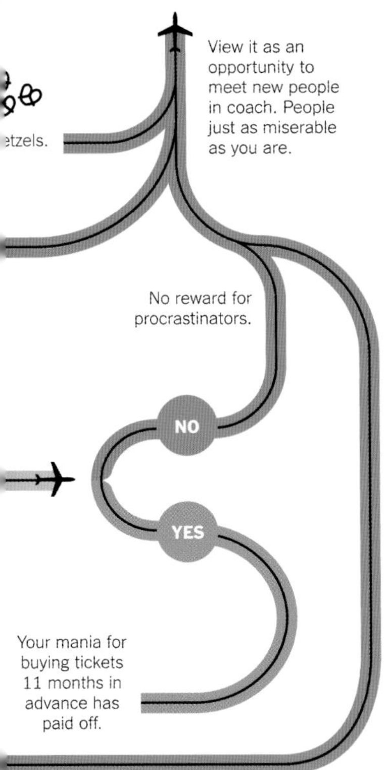
View it as an opportunity to meet new people in coach. People just as miserable as you are.
etzels.
No reward for procrastinators.
NO
YES
Your mania for buying tickets 11 months in advance has paid off.

SERGIO PEÇANHA/THE NEW YORK TIMES

How to Score a Seat in First Class

You bought a domestic coach seat and you're hoping to get a free upgrade at the gate: What are your chances?

ARTIST Sergio Peçanha, the *New York Times.*

STATEMENT Normally, the Travel section is packed full of pictures of wonderful places. But the cover story for this week took a look at what happens behind the scenes when you are at the gate and hoping to score a free airline upgrade. The stark differences between being pampered like royalty in first class and traveling like a sardine in economy seemed like a good opportunity to explain the complex process airlines use to determine whether you make the cut or not—and also a chance to have some fun with the graphic. One piece of trivia: The faces of the people inside the sardine can were based on those of some of my colleagues at the *New York Times.* The pampered king on the left side looks, coincidentally, like me.

PUBLICATION *New York Times* (June 10, 2012)

A Better Food Label

Give consumers a quick numerical and color-coded rating.

ARTISTS Mark Bittman, Bill Marsh, Matthew Dorfman, and Erich Nagler, the *New York Times;* Sharon Werner and Sarah Forss, WDW, a design studio in Minneapolis–St. Paul.

STATEMENT WDW worked with Mark Bittman and the *New York Times* to develop the "dream food label." The overall rating is based on the total of three different scales: nutrition (a summary of the existing nutrition facts), foodness (how close the food is to being real, unadulterated food), and welfare (the impact the food's production has on the welfare of laborers, animals, land, water, air, etc., as well as its carbon footprint and drug and chemical residues). The information is presented in two levels of content—quick color-coding, for at-a-glance readability, and numerically, for a deeper level of meaning. As designers who could potentially have to work with this label on a package design, we were sensitive to giving the label maximum impact with a minimal design footprint.

PUBLICATION *New York Times* (October 14, 2012)

What We Have: Information Overload

THE STATUS QUO This appears in an out-of-the-way spot on every package, and — even if you're inclined to look at it — it's not easy to decipher. Below, the label for Multi Grain Cheerios.

Nutrition Facts
Serving Size: 1 cup (29g)
Servings Per Container: about 8

Amount Per Serving	Cereal	with ½ cup skim milk
Calories	110	150
Calories from Fat	10	10
	% Daily Value**	
Total Fat 1g*	**2%**	**2%**
Saturated Fat 0g	**0%**	**0%**
Trans Fat 0g		
Polyunsaturated Fat 0.5g		
Monounsaturated Fat 0g		
Cholesterol 0mg	**0%**	**1%**
Sodim 120mg	**5%**	**7%**
Potassium 140mg	**4%**	**10%**
Total Carbohydrate 24mg	**8%**	**10%**
Dietary Fiber 3g	**10%**	**10%**
Sugars 6g		
Other Carbohydrate 15g		
Protein 2g		
Vitamin A	10%	15%
Vitamin C	10%	10%
Calcium	10%	25%
Iron	45%	45%
Vitamin D	10%	25%
Thiamin	25%	30%
Riboflavin	25%	35%
Niacin	25%	25%
Vitamin B_6	25%	25%
Folic Acid	50%	50%
Vitamin B_{12}	25%	35%
Phosphorus	8%	20%
Magnesium	4%	8%
Zinc	25%	30%

* Amount in cereal. A serving of cereal plus skim milk provides 1g total fat, less than 5mg cholesterol, 180mg sodium, 340 mg potassium, 29g total carbohydrate (12g sugars), and 7g protein.

** Percent Daily Values are based on a 2,000 calorie diet. Your daily values may be higher or lower depending on your calorie needs:

	Calories	2,000	2,500
Total Fat	Less than	65g	80g
Sat Fat	Less than	20g	25g
Cholesterol	Less than	300mg	300mg
Sodium	Less than	2,400mg	2,400mg
Potassium		3,500mg	3,500mg
Total Carbohydrate		300g	375g
Dietary Fiber		25g	30g

INGREDIENTS: Whole Grain Corn, Whole Grain Oats, Sugar, Whole Grain Barley, Whole Grain Wheat, Whole Grain Rice, Corn Starch, Brown Sugar Syrup, Corn Bran, Salt, Canola and/or Rice Bran Oil, Tripotassium Phosphate, color added. Vitamin E (mixed tocopherols) added to preserve freshness.

Vitamins and Minerals: Calcium Carbonate, Zinc and Iron (mineral nutrients), Vitamin C (sodium ascorbate), A B Vitamin (niacinamide), Vitamin B_6 (pyridoxine hydrochoride), Vitamin B_2 (riboflavin), Vitamin B_1 thiamin mononitrate, Vitamin A (palmitate), A B Vitamin (folic acid), Vitamin B_{12}, Vitamin D.

CONTAINS WHEAT INGREDIENTS

LIST OF INGREDIENTS The most useful information currently on packaged foods. A quick but crude way to figure out whether something is actually worth eating: if the list of ingredients spans an entire paragraph, chances are you don't need it.

osed Addition: Read, Out Front

Here's how the new label would work.

NUTRITION This new scale is essentially a summary of the "nutrition facts" box into one easy-to-understand rating, on a scale of 0 to 5.

FOODNESS A measure of how close a product is to being real, unadulterated food. (You might think of it as "naturalness.") A piece of fruit gets 5 points, whereas fruit-flavored candy gets 0.

WELFARE A measure of the impact of the food's production on the overall welfare of everything involved: laborers, animals, land, water, air, etc. This rating also accounts for carbon footprint and chemical (pesticide, for example) and drug (like antibiotic) residues.

RATING BARS Top score per category: 5. Bottom score: 0.

COLOR CODE A visual representation of the total score: eat **green**-coded food freely; **yellow** food with restraint or consideration; and **red** food rarely or never. Of course if you're more concerned about Welfare than Nutrition, or Foodness than either, you can make your own judgments.

11-15 points
6-10
0-5

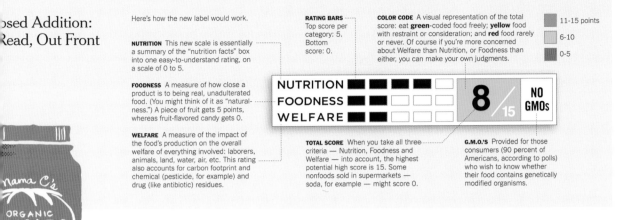

NUTRITION
FOODNESS
WELFARE
8/15
NO GMOs

TOTAL SCORE When you take all three criteria — Nutrition, Foodness and Welfare — into account, the highest potential high score is 15. Some nonfoods sold in supermarkets — soda, for example — might score 0.

G.M.O.'S Provided for those consumers (90 percent of Americans, according to polls) who wish to know whether their food contains genetically modified organisms.

Labels on Four Made-Up Products

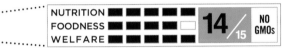

NUTRITION
FOODNESS
WELFARE
14/15
NO GMOs

MAMA C'S ORGANIC TOMATO SAUCE This contains organic tomatoes, extra virgin olive oil, and fresh herbs; it's even refrigerated, so it contains no preservatives.

Since Mama C runs an organic operation with a full-time labor force receiving benefits, the score here is superhigh all around, and the label is **green**.

FROZEN
ueberries
0% ORGANIC

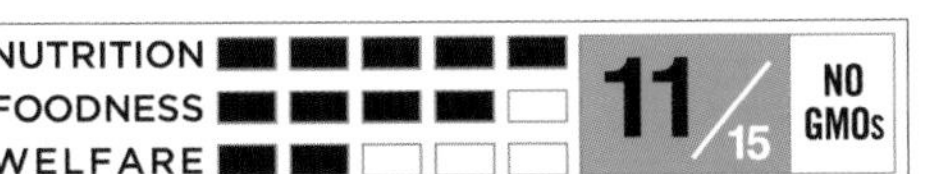
NUTRITION
FOODNESS
WELFARE
11/15
NO GMOs

BERT'S BERRIES FROZEN BLUEBERRIES Barely processed fruit is something we can eat as often as we like, which would give this a Nutrition score of 5. On the other hand, it's not fresh: 4 for Foodness.

Although the blueberries are organic, they're sourced from Chile, where the workers are being paid a dollar a day and little attention is paid to soil quality: 2 for Welfare. Because of those issues, this barely squeaks into the **green**.

Happy
FARMS
Fresh Whole
hicken

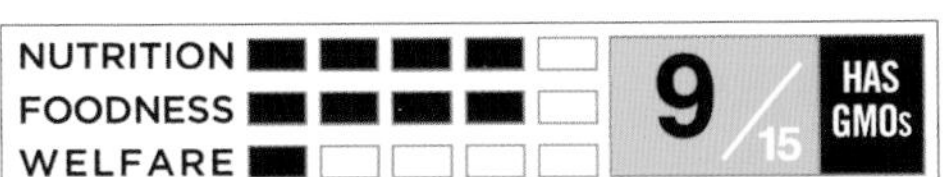
NUTRITION
FOODNESS
WELFARE
9/15
HAS GMOs

HAPPY FARMS FRESH WHOLE CHICKEN Nutrition is good, but saturated fat pulls the score down to 4. Foodness is also high: you can't argue with the fact that it's chicken.

But the birds are raised in cages and fed processed food; there's runoff from the barns; and the working conditions in the processing plant are abysmal. The score of 1 on Welfare pulls the overall score down to the **yellow** range.

CHOCOLATE FROSTED
uper
Krispy
KRUNCHIES

NUTRITION
FOODNESS
WELFARE
4/15
HAS GMOs

CHOCOLATE FROSTED SUPER KRISPY KRUNCHIES Fifty percent sugar; almost all nutrients come from additives. But it does contain 10 percent of the daily allowance of fiber.

It's barely recognizable as food in any near-natural form, and it's made from hyper-processed commodity crops. However, workers in the plant are full time and receive benefits (and no animals are harmed), so a couple of points there (environmentally, however, the welfare is negative, so these points are mitigated): 2. Thus, **red**.

ILLUSTRATIONS AND LABELS BY WERNER DESIGN WERKS FOR THE NEW YORK TIMES

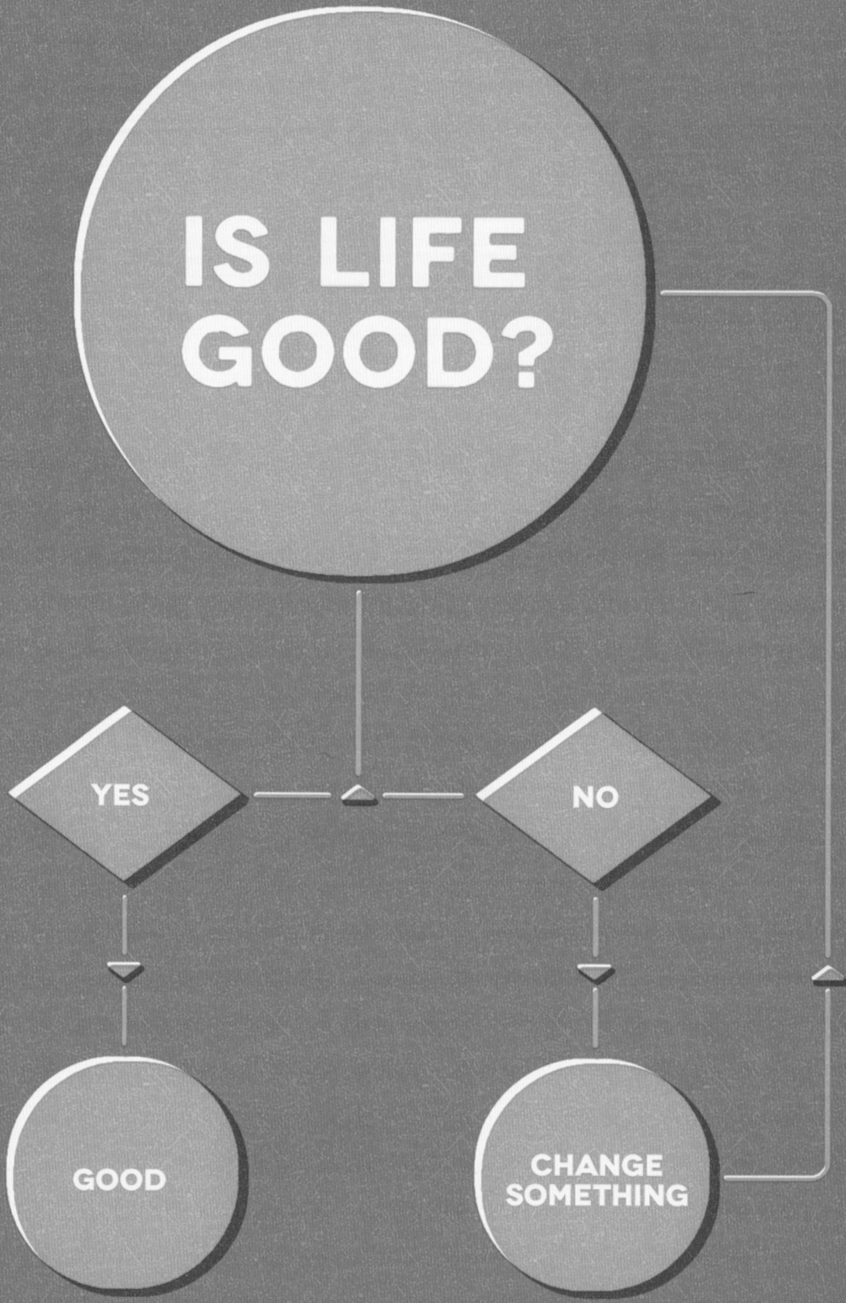

IS LIFE GOOD?

YES

NO

GOOD

CHANGE SOMETHING

How to Be Happy

Just ask yourself one question.

ARTIST Gustavo Vieira Dias, creative director of DDB Tribal Vienna, an advertising agency that belongs to the DDB group and is based in Vienna, Austria.

STATEMENT I'm very happy to be featured in this book, and I'm glad more people will have access to this piece of work. I hope you will be able to answer "yes" to the question "Is life good?"

PUBLICATION Online as a wallpaper for desktop, iPad, and iPhone (January 2012)

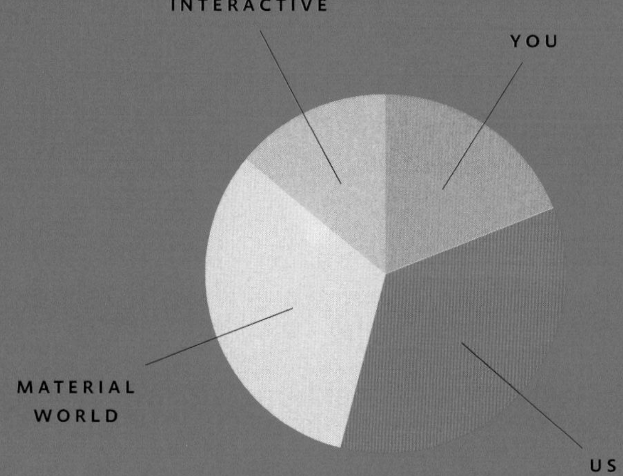
INTERACTIVE
YOU
MATERIAL
WORLD
US

II. US

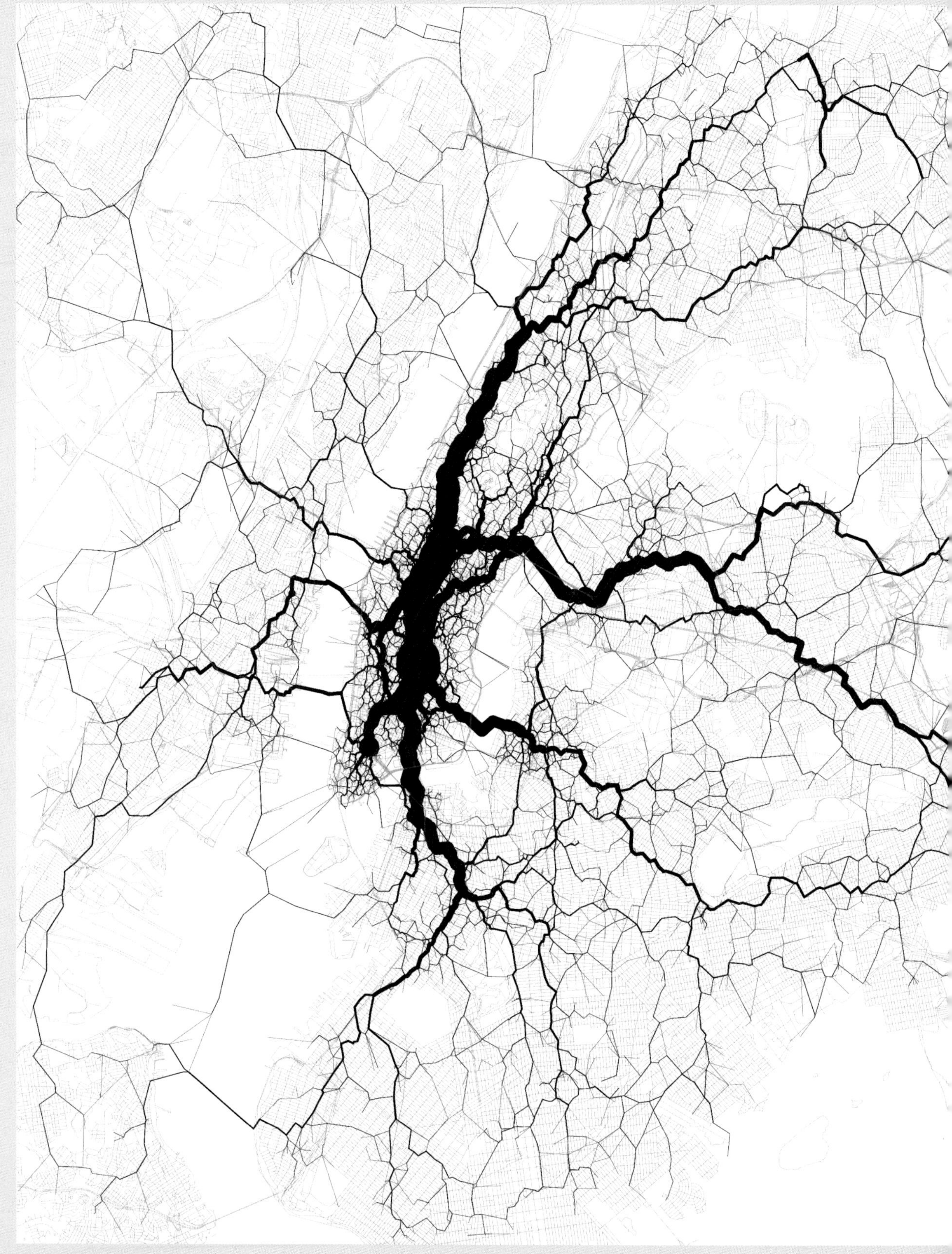

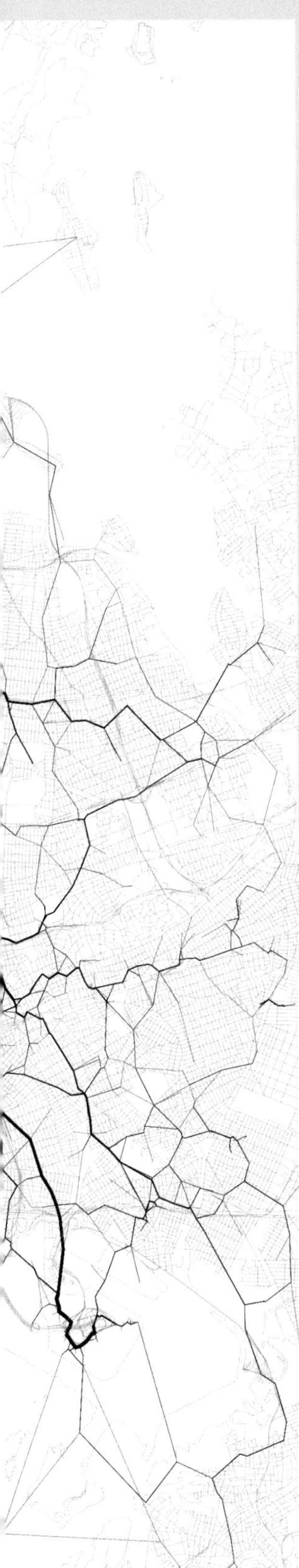

Paths Through New York City

"Flow map" of travel in New York City derived from the locations of tweets tagged with the locations of their senders. The starting and ending points of each trip come from a pair of geotagged tweets by the same person, and the path in between is an estimate, routed along the densest corridor of other people's geotagged tweets.

ARTIST Eric Fischer, artist in residence at the Exploratorium in San Francisco.

STATEMENT One of the major tasks of transportation planning is network analysis: Given a collection of survey data about the origins and destinations of trips that people want to make, what is the system of routes that will enable the most useful mobility with the least infrastructure? This map is one of a series of attempts to do this kind of analysis. It uses the huge mass of information that people provide every day on Twitter about where they go and where they spend their time to produce a "fantasy subway map," highlighting routes and connections that don't necessarily currently exist but that would be heavily used if they did.

PUBLICATION Flickr (flickr.com/photos/walkingsf) (January 22, 2012)

Fifty **States** of Grey

What does *your* state think of the publishing phenomenon?

Fifty
Shades
of Grey
E L James
#1 New York Times Bestseller

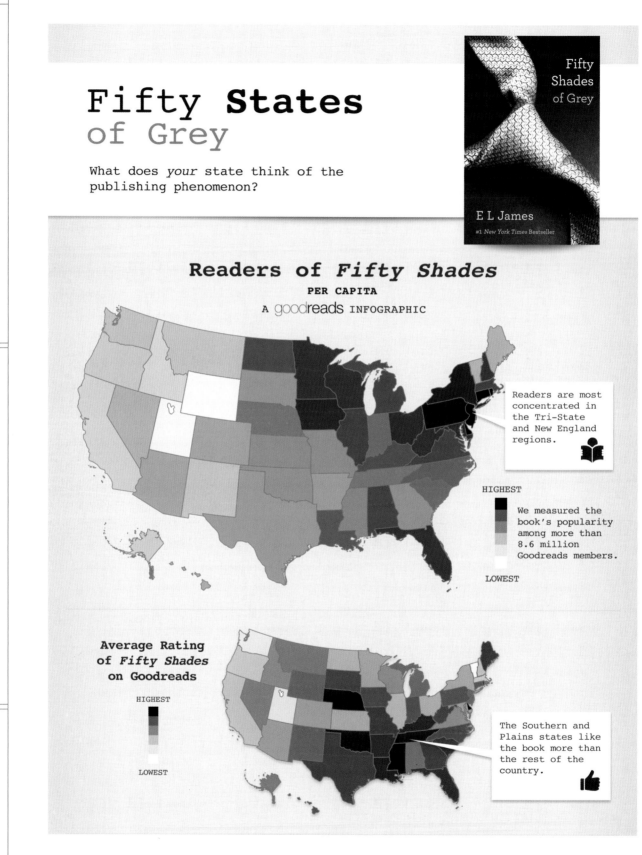

Readers of *Fifty Shades*

PER CAPITA

A goodreads INFOGRAPHIC

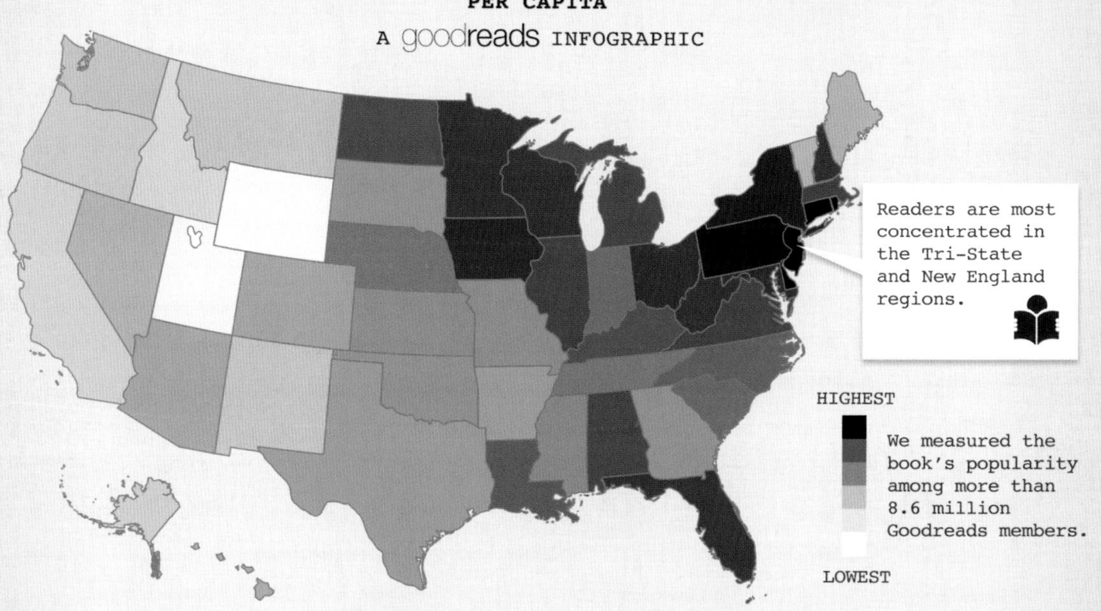
Readers are most concentrated in the Tri-State and New England regions.
HIGHEST
We measured the book's popularity among more than 8.6 million Goodreads members.
LOWEST

Average Rating of *Fifty Shades* on Goodreads

HIGHEST

LOWEST

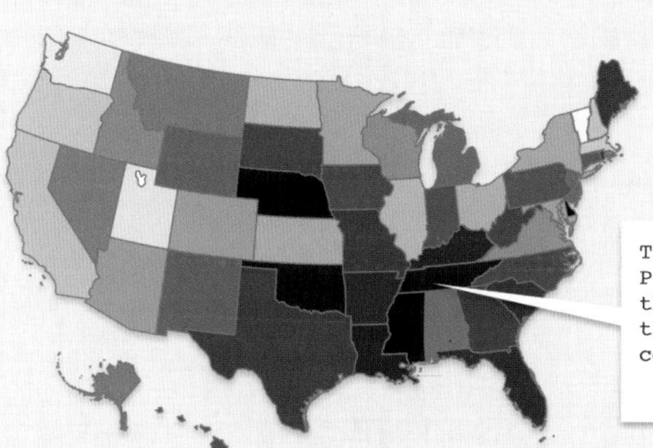

The Southern and Plains states like the book more than the rest of the country.

Who Reads Erotica?

Regional variations in the popularity of *Fifty Shades of Grey.*

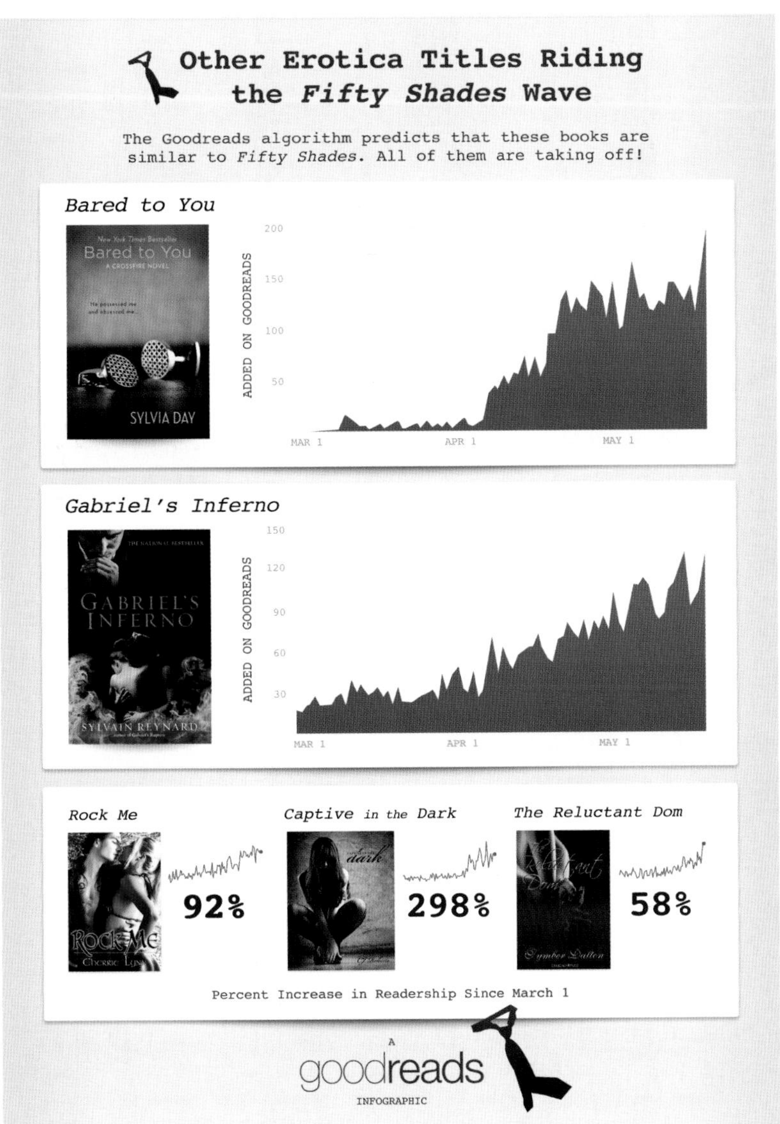
Other Erotica Titles Riding the Fifty Shades Wave
The Goodreads algorithm predicts that these books are similar to Fifty Shades. All of them are taking off!
Bared to You
Bared to You
SYLVIA DAY
ADDED ON GOODREADS
200
150
100
50
MAR 1
APR 1
MAY 1
Gabriel's Inferno
GABRIEL'S INFERNO
SYLVAIN REYNARD
ADDED ON GOODREADS
150
120
90
60
30
MAR 1
APR 1
MAY 1
Rock Me
92%
Captive in the Dark
298%
The Reluctant Dom
58%
Percent Increase in Readership Since March 1
A goodreads INFOGRAPHIC

ARTISTS Patrick Brown, director of community, and Seth Goldstein, director of user experience at Goodreads in San Francisco.

STATEMENT We created the infographic after the publishing phenomenon *Fifty Shades of Grey* had been at the top of the bestseller lists for three months. Our goal was to see if the book was popular across the whole of the United States or if some states were a little more "Grey" than others. Because the book is erotica, we were also interested in seeing whether it had more readers in politically liberal or conservative states. The greatest number of readers lived in the Northeast, but it earned the highest ratings in the southern and plains states.

PUBLICATION *Goodreads* blog (May 24, 2012)

Gay Rights in the U.S., State by State

Gay rights laws in America have evolved to allow—but in some cases ban—rights for gay, lesbian, and transgender people on a range of issues, including marriage, hospital visitation, adoption, housing, employment, and school bullying.

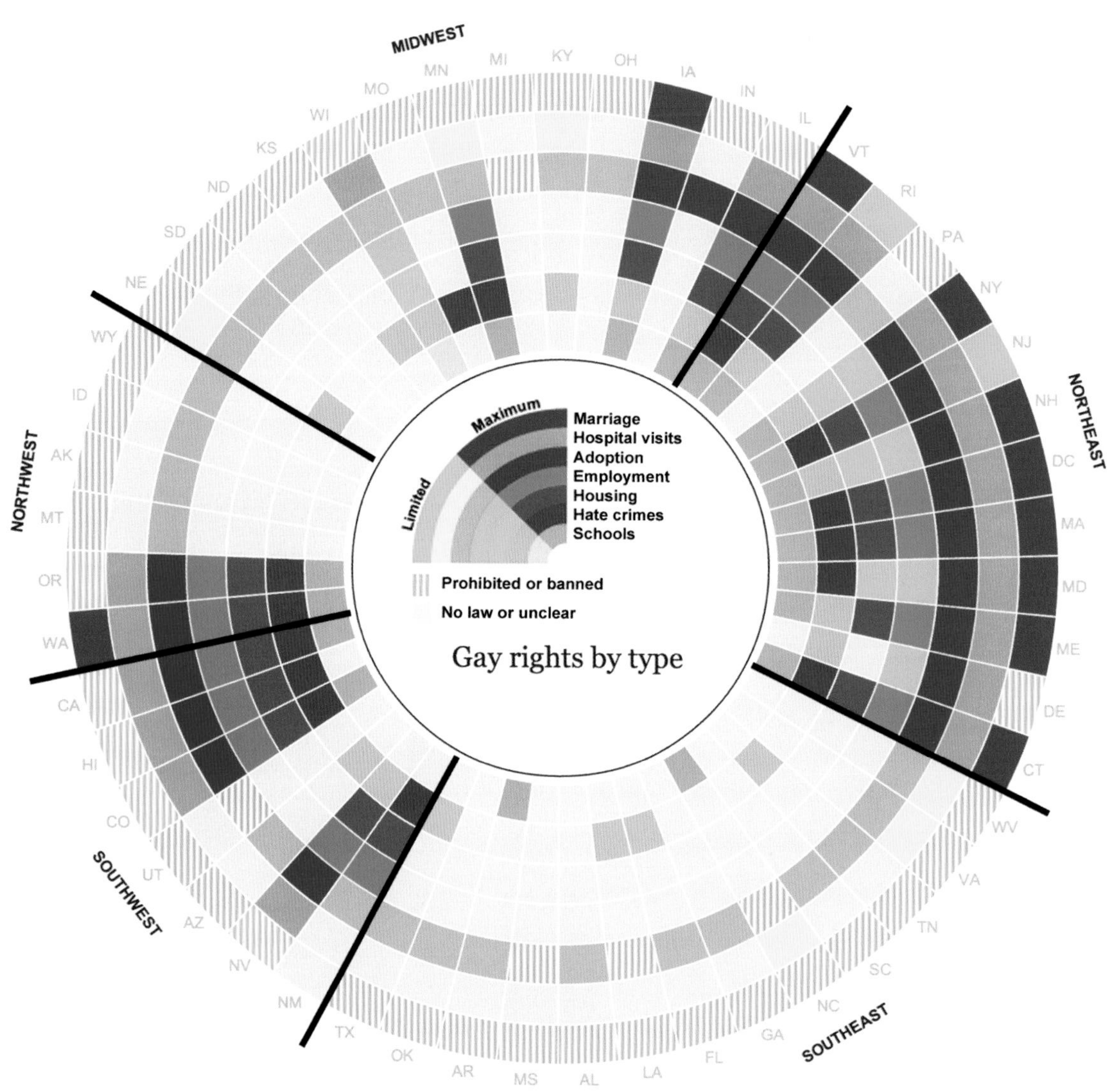
MIDWEST
NORTHEAST
SOUTHEAST
SOUTHWEST
NORTHWEST
MN
MI
KY
OH
IA
IN
IL
VT
RI
PA
NY
NJ
NH
DC
MA
MD
ME
DE
CT
WV
VA
TN
SC
NC
GA
FL
LA
AL
MS
AR
OK
TX
NM
NV
AZ
UT
CO
HI
CA
WA
OR
MT
AK
ID
WY
NE
SD
ND
KS
WI
MO
Maximum
Limited
Marriage
Hospital visits
Adoption
Employment
Housing
Hate crimes
Schools
Prohibited or banned
No law or unclear
Gay rights by type

Marriage

Same-sex marriage or limited alternative is legally recognized in only a few states. The majority of the states have legally defined marriage to be between a man and a woman or amended the state constitution to ban same-sex marriage. Below are the rights legally extended within the given state.

Laws defining same-sex marriage

Marriage
Civil unions
Domestic partnership
Prohibited or banned
None or unclear

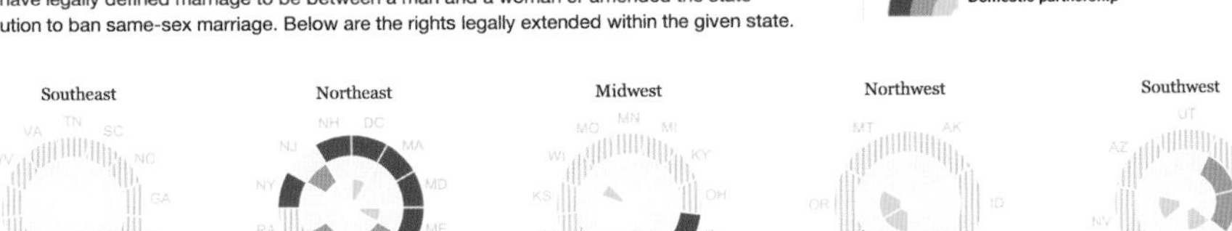
Southeast
Northeast
Midwest
Northwest
Southwest

Notes: In 2012, Maine, Maryland and Washington were the first states to approve same-sex marriage by popular vote. California currently does not offer marriage to same-sex couples due to prop 8 litigation. Colorado affords same-sex couples to register as designated beneficiaries.

Adoption

Laws regarding adoption vary widely by state and are often unclear. All US states allow a single individual the right to petition to adopt a child, though less than half allow a same-sex couple to petition for joint adoption.

Laws allowing adoption

Joint adoption
Single adoption
Ban
None or unclear

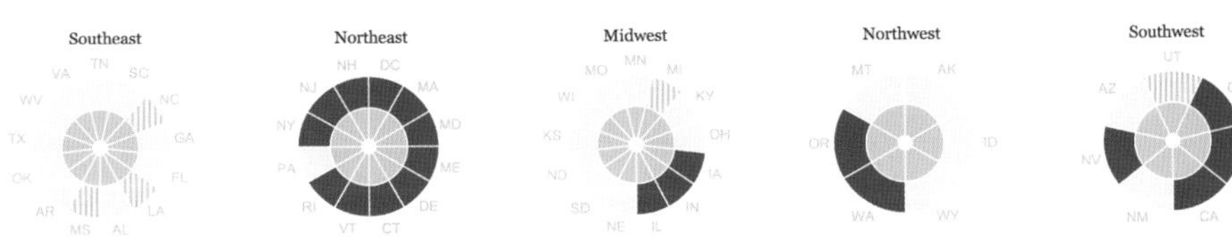
Southeast
Northeast
Midwest
Northwest
Southwest

Note: Only shows statewide joint adoption and not states with some jurisdictions offering joint adoption.

Employment

Anti-discrimination employment laws vary widely by state depending on the inclusion of sexual orientation or gender identity, and whether the law protects those working in the public or private sector. Below are the anti-discrimination laws that protect all workers.

Anti-discrimination employment laws

Gender identity
Sexual orientation
None or unclear

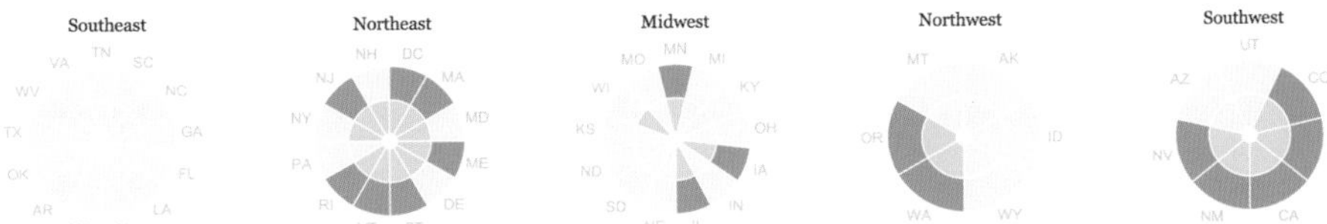
Southeast
Northeast
Midwest
Northwest
Southwest

Hate crimes

Federal hate crime laws extend protection for crimes related to one's sexual orientation or gender identity. At the state level, more than ten states have hate crime laws that lack the inclusion of gender identity or sexual orientation. Of the others, over 30 states include sexual orientation in their hate crime laws with just under half also including gender identity.

Hate crime definition

Gender identity
Sexual orientation
None or unclear

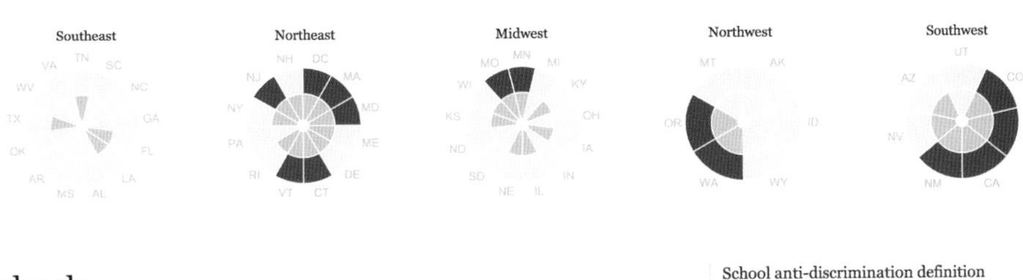
Southeast
Northeast
Midwest
Northwest
Southwest

Schools

Nearly all states address discrimination or bullying as some form of law for elementary and high school students, though almost half do not define categories for protection. Below are the states that have addressed discrimination or bullying based on sexual orientation or gender identity.

School anti-discrimination definition

Gender identity
Sexual orientation
None or unclear

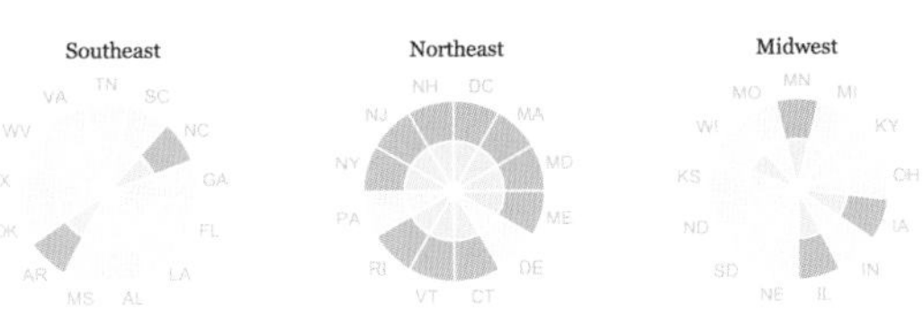
Southeast
Northeast

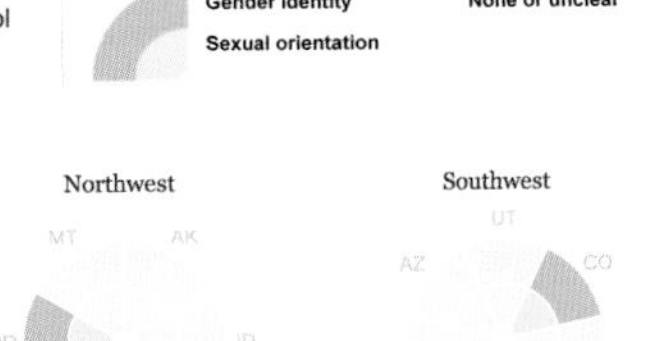
Midwest
Northwest

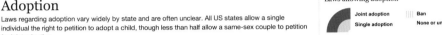

ARTISTS Feilding Cage, interactive designer, and Gabriel Dance, interactive editor, at the *Guardian*'s U.S. office in New York City.

STATEMENT In 2012 gay rights gained a lot of attention, with same-sex marriage appearing on the ballot in five states and President Obama speaking out in favor of the issue. This visualization focuses on the differences between states and regions. Ultimately, the design deviated from the typical map view of the United States and toward a circular view that placed states on a wheel according to geography. This allows the graphic to show multiple dimensions of gay rights side by side, something that would not have been possible with a traditional map. The online graphic also allows users to see how many people are affected by the laws and which of their Facebook friends lived in gay-friendly (or unfriendly) states. This creative use of social networks allowed users to become part of the story, bringing them into the graphic and bucking the normal trend of using social networks solely to distribute content.

PUBLICATION *Guardian* online (www.guardian.co.uk) (May 8, 2012)

The Popification of Top 40

The last twenty years of the Billboard Top 40, showing how the Pop category (shown in aqua) has taken over the charts.

ARTIST Gavin Potenza is a freelance designer and illustrator in Brooklyn, New York.

STATEMENT The data called for a linear-style timeline, and since we were working in such a limited space, we thought utilizing a snakelike formation would work best. There was actually a lot of data to work with, so the real difficulty was trying not to clutter the graphic too much. Sometimes, as infographic designers, we feel obligated to make it more fun by adding illustrations or trying to add too much data, but I really like how this graphic is pure and simple, essentially just blocks of color. Sometimes a simple approach can be the most effective.

PUBLICATION *Billboard* (September 29, 2012)

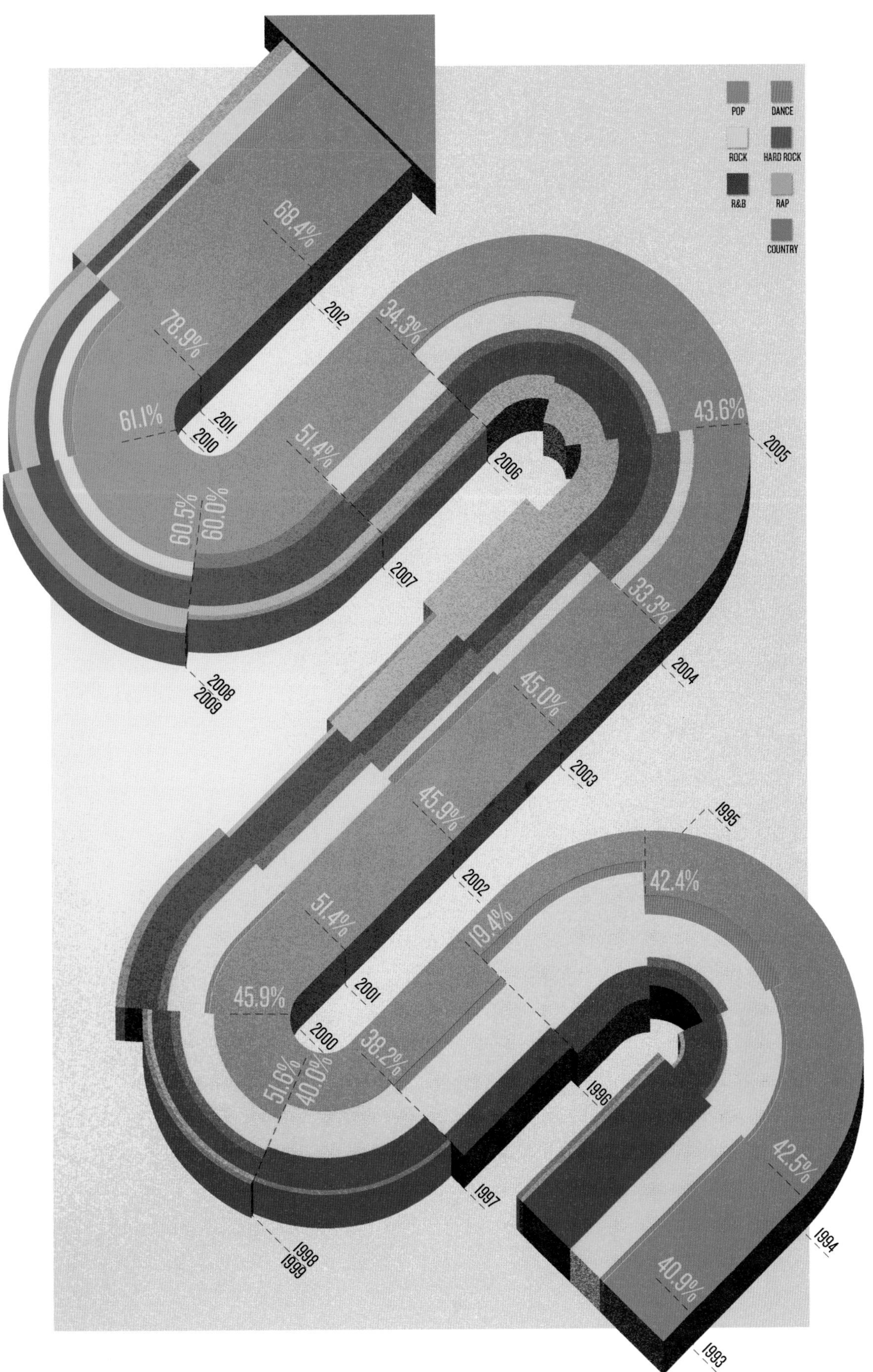
POP
DANCE
ROCK
HARD ROCK
R&B
RAP
COUNTRY
1993
40.9%
1994
42.5%
1995
42.4%
1996
19.4%
1997
38.2%
1998
1999
51.6%
40.0%
2000
45.9%
2001
51.4%
2002
45.9%
2003
45.0%
2004
33.3%
2005
43.6%
2006
34.3%
2007
51.4%
2008
2009
60.5%
60.0%
2010
61.1%
2011
78.9%
2012
68.4%

The Amazing Morphing Campaign Money Map

The familiar electoral map from 2008, with the states warped by the number of electoral votes or the amount of ad spending per voter in each state.

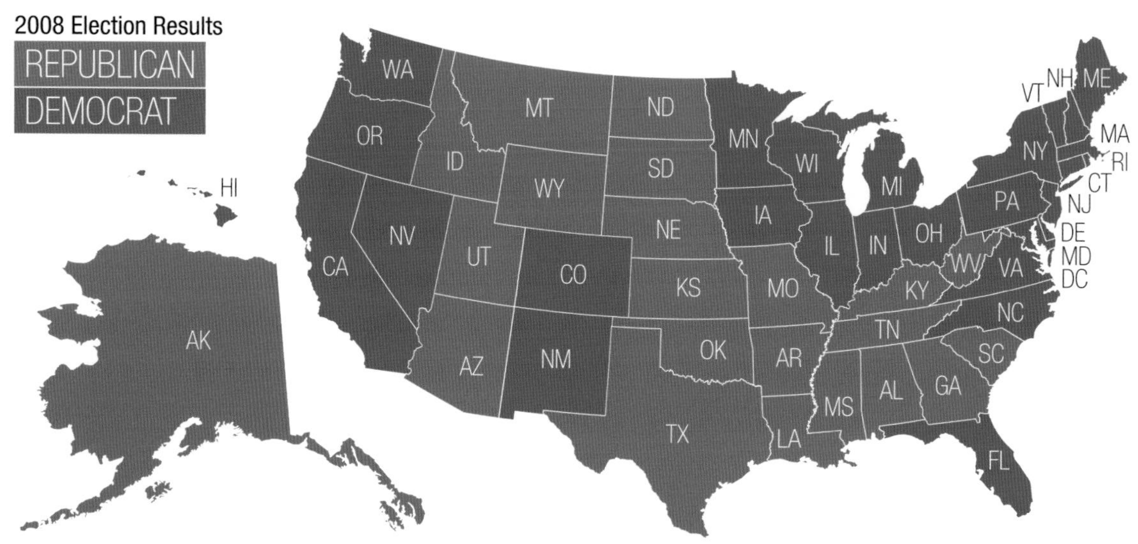

2008 Election Results
REPUBLICAN
DEMOCRAT
WA
OR
CA
NV
ID
MT
WY
UT
AZ
CO
NM
ND
SD
NE
KS
OK
TX
MN
IA
MO
AR
LA
WI
IL
MI
IN
OH
KY
TN
MS
AL
GA
FL
SC
NC
VA
WV
PA
NY
VT
NH
ME
MA
RI
CT
NJ
DE
MD
DC
AK
HI

ARTIST Adam Cole, a multimedia reporter at National Public Radio in Washington, D.C.

STATEMENT In past elections, cartographers have tried to convey the importance of different states by changing their size. The mountain states dominate the center of the country in geographically accurate maps, but in warped "cartograms" (in which size expresses electoral clout), they are dwarfed by the Northeast. The same approach can be applied to a more telling bit of data: the amount of money spent in each state on the presidential race.

In mid-October, I started in on a very involved project—an animation of the electoral map as it morphed and changed color to reflect shifting populations and political allegiances throughout history—but I didn't have time to finish it before the election. I had been playing with these electoral votes and campaign money maps on the side and ended up putting them in a short video, with no inkling that they would be so popular. The maps shown here are static versions of that video. Looking back, I think these maps were interesting—and even comical—because they showed a perversion of the familiar. It's fun to see something as sober as a map bloated and twisted by an interesting data set.

PUBLICATION *It's All Politics* blog on npr.com (November 1, 2012)

Electoral Votes

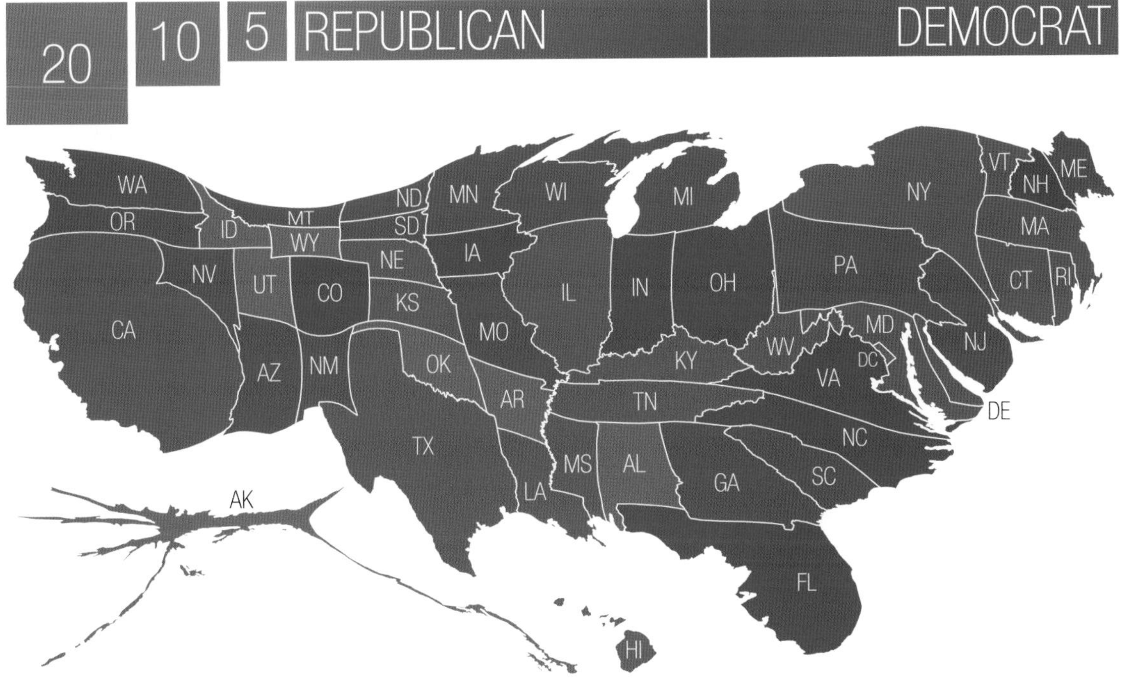
20
10
5
REPUBLICAN
DEMOCRAT
WA
OR
ID
MT
WY
ND
SD
NE
MN
WI
MI
NY
VT
NH
ME
MA
CT
RI
IA
NV
UT
CO
KS
IL
IN
OH
PA
CA
MO
KY
WV
MD
DC
NJ
VA
DE
AZ
NM
OK
AR
TN
NC
TX
MS
AL
GA
SC
LA
AK
FL
HI

Ad Spending Per Voter In Dollars

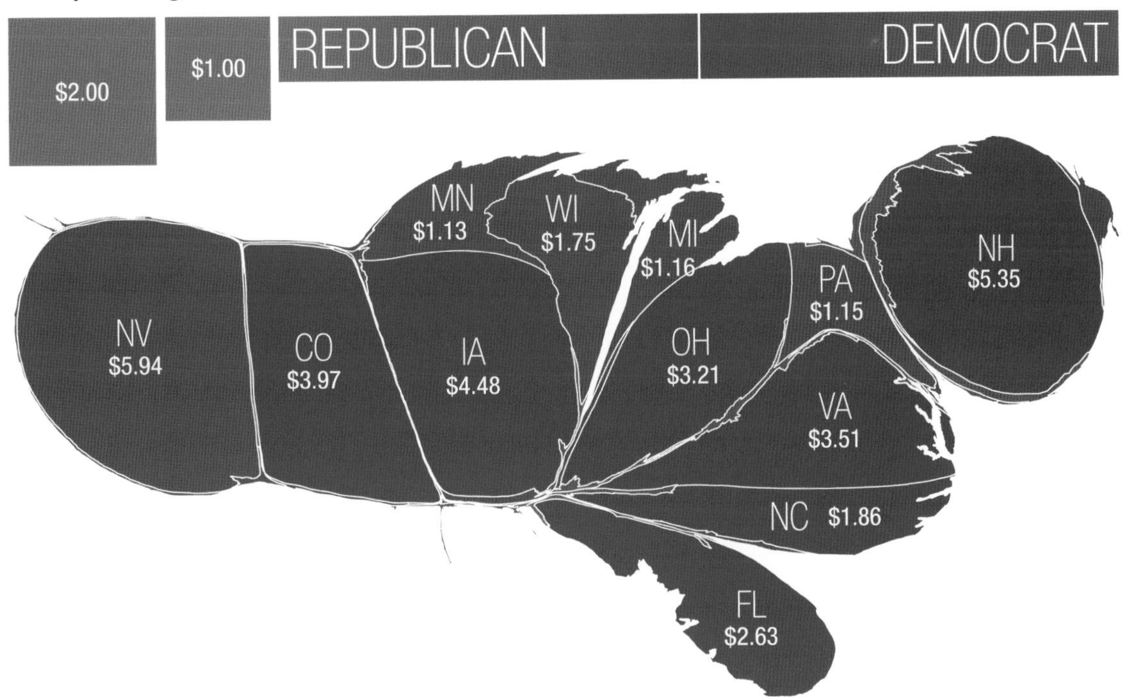
$2.00
$1.00
REPUBLICAN
DEMOCRAT
MN $1.13
WI $1.75
MI $1.16
PA $1.15
NH $5.35
NV $5.94
CO $3.97
IA $4.48
OH $3.21
VA $3.51
NC $1.86
FL $2.63

What Happens After the I.P.O.?

There have been about 2,400 technology, Internet and telecom I.P.O.'s since 1980. On the first day of trading, the average s
offer price. But in the three years after that, most companies had negative returns, according to statistics compiled by Jay Ri
University of Florida. Companies with higher values compared with their revenue before the I.P.O. have fared especially poo

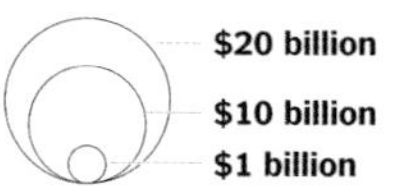

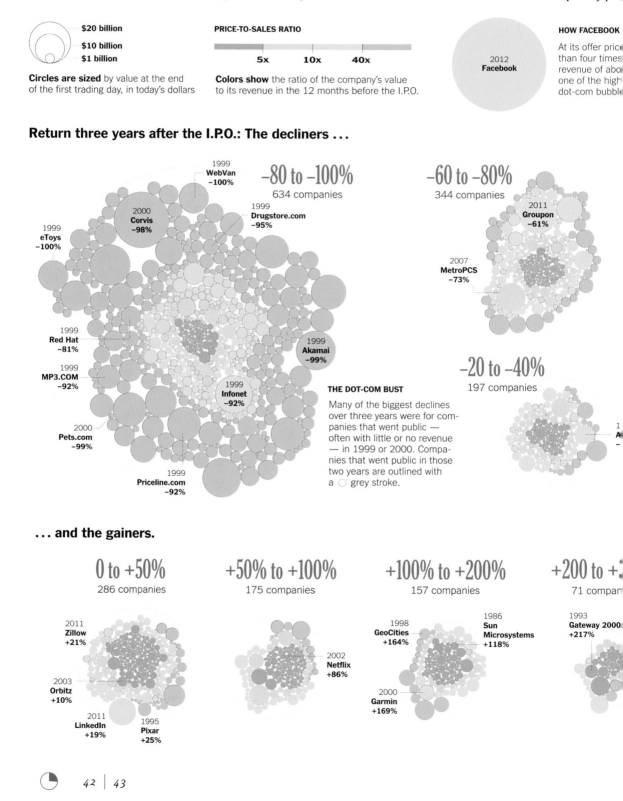

$20 billion
$10 billion
$1 billion

Circles are sized by value at the end of the first trading day, in today's dollars

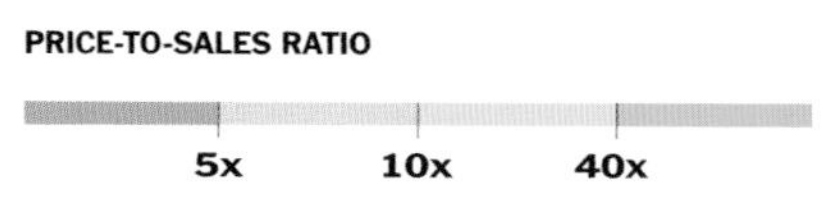

PRICE-TO-SALES RATIO
5x
10x
40x

Colors show the ratio of the company's value to its revenue in the 12 months before the I.P.O.

2012
Facebook

HOW FACEBOOK

At its offer pric
than four times
revenue of abo
one of the high
dot-com bubbl

Return three years after the I.P.O.: The decliners . . .

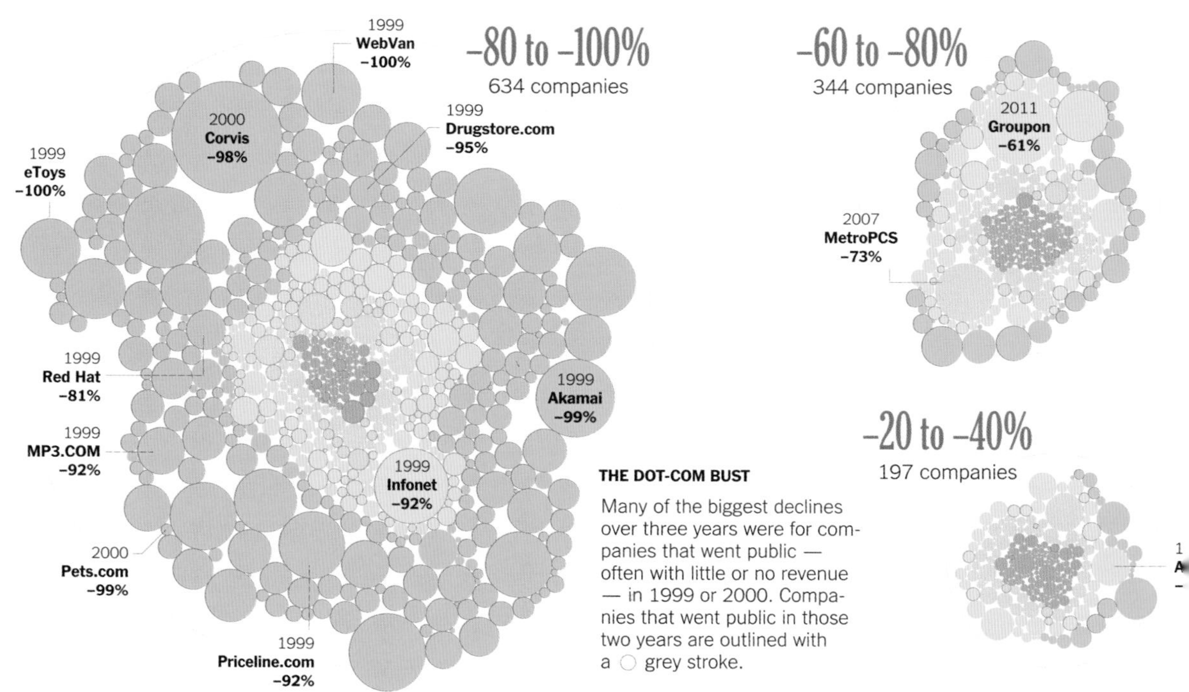

−80 to −100%
634 companies
1999
WebVan
−100%
2000
Corvis
−98%
1999
Drugstore.com
−95%
1999
eToys
−100%
1999
Red Hat
−81%
1999
MP3.COM
−92%
1999
Akamai
−99%
1999
Infonet
−92%
2000
Pets.com
−99%
1999
Priceline.com
−92%
−60 to −80%
344 companies
2011
Groupon
−61%
2007
MetroPCS
−73%
−20 to −40%
197 companies

THE DOT-COM BUST

Many of the biggest declines over three years were for companies that went public — often with little or no revenue — in 1999 or 2000. Companies that went public in those two years are outlined with a ○ grey stroke.

. . . and the gainers.

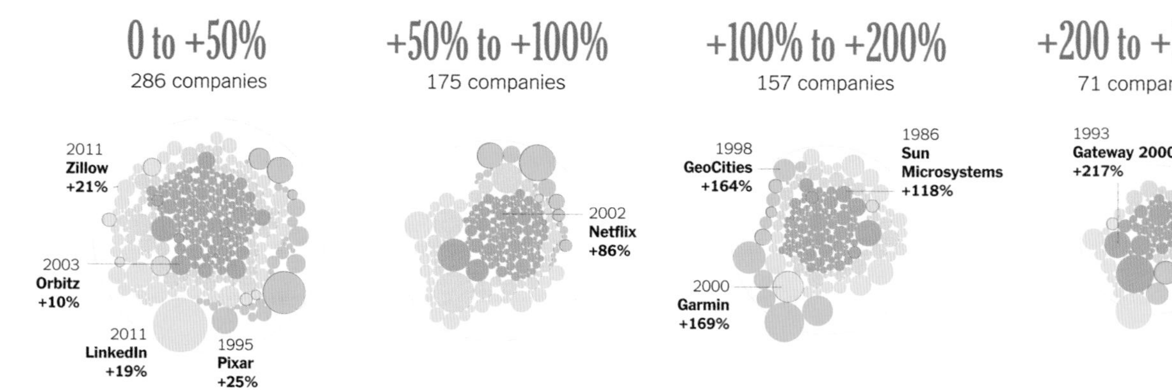

0 to +50%
286 companies
2011
Zillow
+21%
2003
Orbitz
+10%
2011
LinkedIn
+19%
1995
Pixar
+25%
+50% to +100%
175 companies
2002
Netflix
+86%
+100% to +200%
157 companies
1998
GeoCities
+164%
1986
Sun
Microsystems
+118%
2000
Garmin
+169%
1993
Gateway 2000
+217%

percent above its
sor of finance at the

market value is $tk billion, more
e at its I.P.O. in 2004. Facebook had
the last year, meaning it will have
les ratios, especially outside of the

to –60%

5 companies

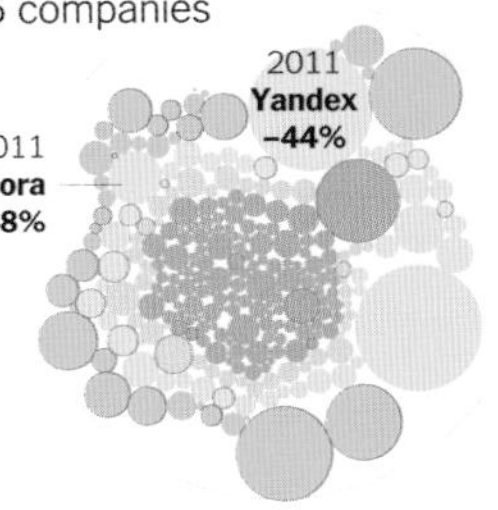
2011
Yandex
–44%
011
ora
48%

to –20%

3 companies

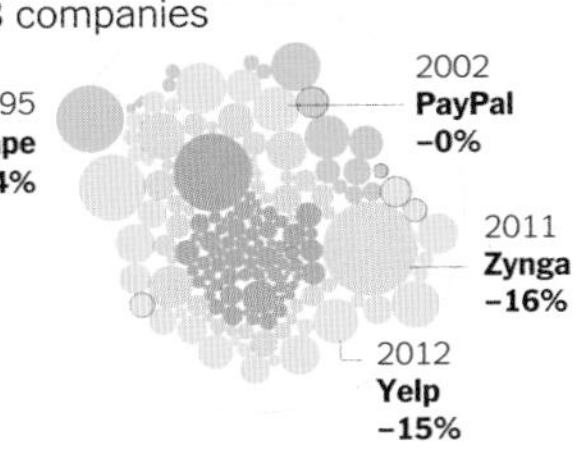
2002
PayPal
–0%
995
ape
4%
2011
Zynga
–16%
2012
Yelp
–15%

+300% or more

115 companies

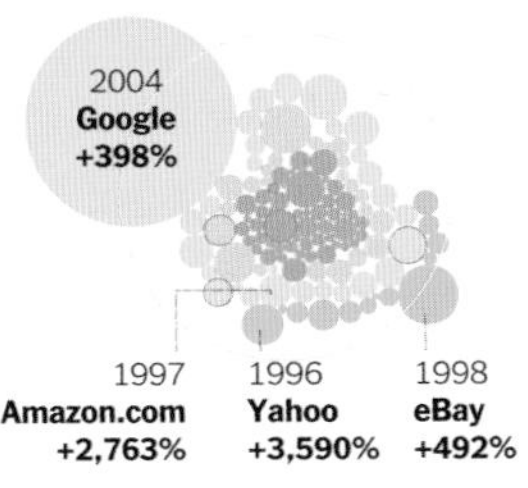
2004
Google
+398%
1997
Amazon.com
+2,763%
1996
Yahoo
+3,590%
1998
eBay
+492%

Facebook: A Risky Investment

How companies fare after they go public.

ARTISTS Amanda Cox and Seth W. Feaster, the *New York Times*.

STATEMENT Too often, words like "billion" and "trillion" feel like synonyms for "a lot." "Congress passed a $2 a lot bill today" may sound ridiculous, but that's how most of us hear it. So, just how big was the $104 billion Facebook I.P.O.? And how often do new technology stocks turn out to be good investments? We tried to answer these questions.

PUBLICATION *New York Times* (May 18, 2012)

Accuracy of Google influenza predictions, 2003–2011.

PREVALENCE OF U.S. INFLUEN

BY THE NUMBERS

Fever Flow

Visualizing data patterns to help get ahead of the flu

STORY BY Katie Peek and Ryan Bradley
ILLUSTRATION BY Pitch Interactive

Strains of seasonal influenza behave slightly differently season to season and strain to strain. The differences are revealing. The rate of transmission of the 1918 pandemic, which killed 40 million people, closely mirrors the data from the 2009 H1N1 pandemic. The two strains are, in fact, closely related. At the Centers for Disease Control and Prevention (CDC), epidemiologists study the patterns of flu data from the current season against historic data. The comparison helps them make informed decisions about how to respond to the virus: what kind of vaccine to make, how to make it, and how and where to distribute it. As data sets improve, scientists will be able to better predict how future strains of seasonal influenza will spread.

DOUBLE DIPS
Seasonal influenza usually arrives in two waves: a small peak in mid-December followed by a doubling in the rate of transmission that spikes in early February. The first wave can be telling—high incident rates early in the season hint at particularly contagious strains. Data from 2007 versus 2008 seasons [in blue] shows an improved response.

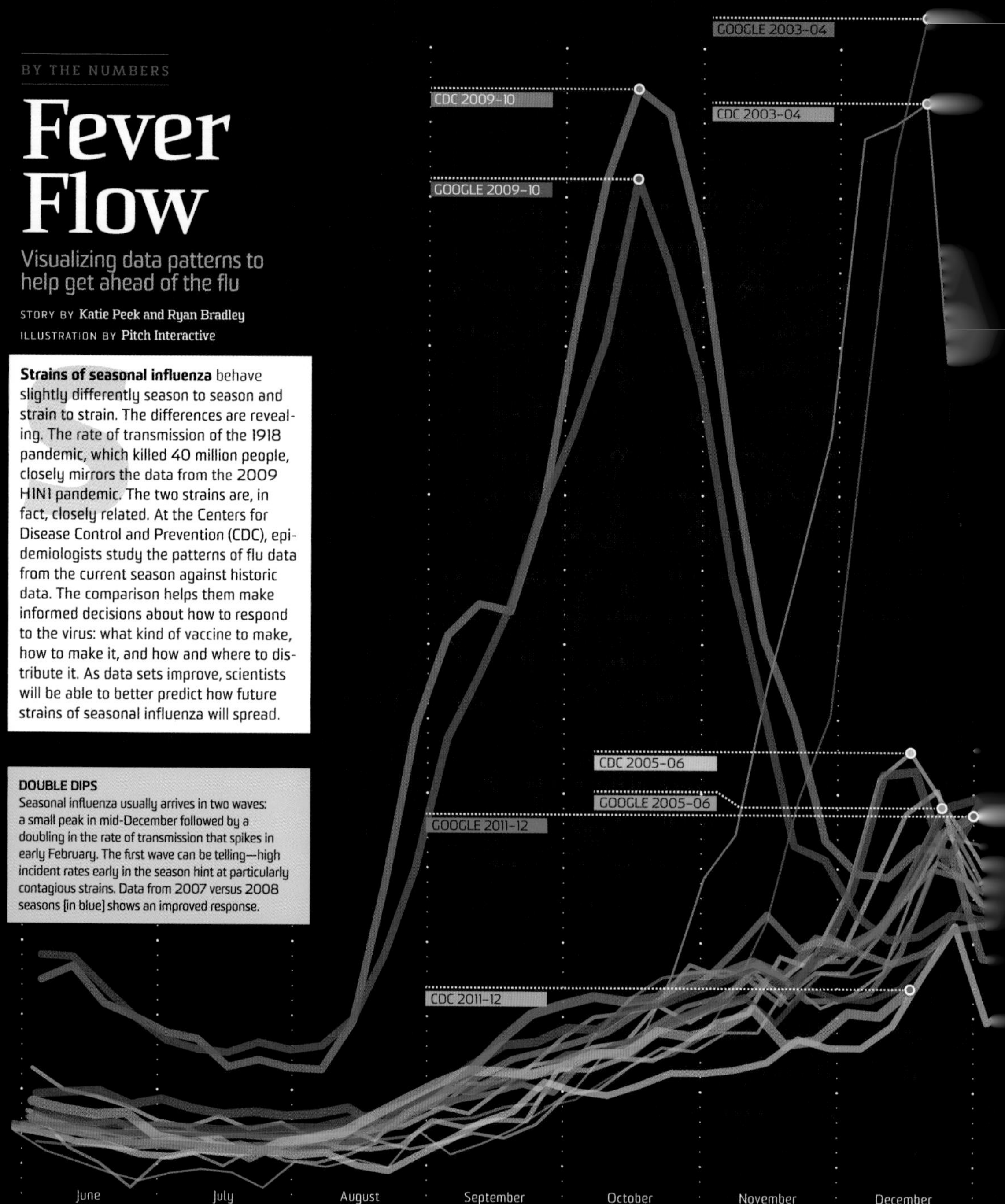
GOOGLE 2003-04
CDC 2009-10
CDC 2003-04
GOOGLE 2009-10
CDC 2005-06
GOOGLE 2005-06
GOOGLE 2011-12
CDC 2011-12
June
July
August
September
October
November
December

CDC numbers are the best estimated fractional percentage of doctor and emergency-room visits each week that are related to influenza-like illness. Google scales its search-term data to CDC numbers

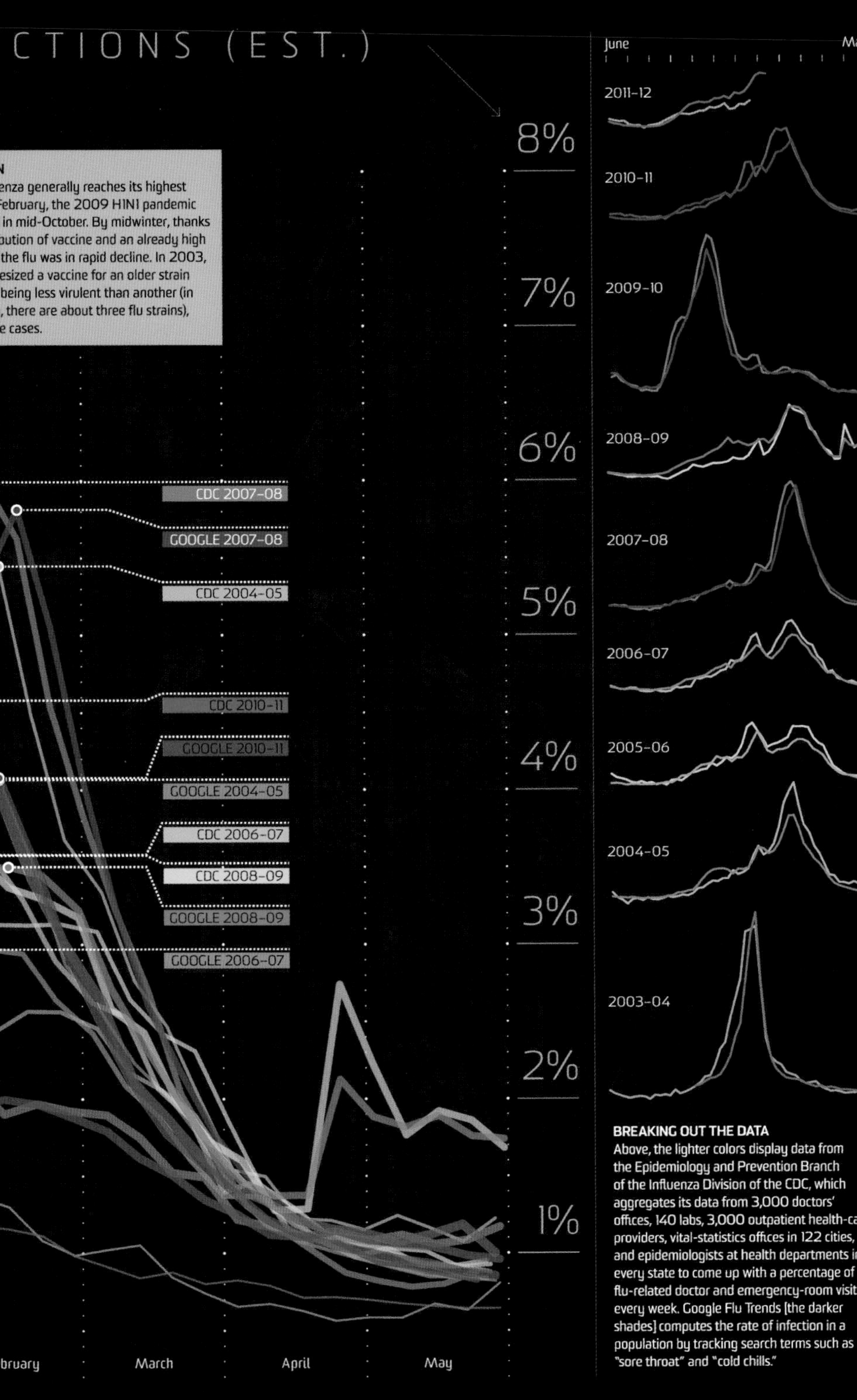
CTIONS (EST.)
enza generally reaches its highest
February, the 2009 H1N1 pandemic
in mid-October. By midwinter, thanks
bution of vaccine and an already high
the flu was in rapid decline. In 2003,
esized a vaccine for an older strain
being less virulent than another (in
, there are about three flu strains),
e cases.
8%
7%
6%
5%
4%
3%
2%
1%
CDC 2007-08
GOOGLE 2007-08
CDC 2004-05
CDC 2010-11
GOOGLE 2010-11
GOOGLE 2004-05
CDC 2006-07
CDC 2008-09
GOOGLE 2008-09
GOOGLE 2006-07
bruary
March
April
May
June
May
2011-12
2010-11
2009-10
2008-09
2007-08
2006-07
2005-06
2004-05
2003-04
VIEW/CENTERS FOR DISEASE CONTROL AND PREVENTION
GOOGLE

BREAKING OUT THE DATA
Above, the lighter colors display data from the Epidemiology and Prevention Branch of the Influenza Division of the CDC, which aggregates its data from 3,000 doctors' offices, 140 labs, 3,000 outpatient health-care providers, vital-statistics offices in 122 cities, and epidemiologists at health departments in every state to come up with a percentage of flu-related doctor and emergency-room visits every week. Google Flu Trends [the darker shades] computes the rate of infection in a population by tracking search terms such as "sore throat" and "cold chills."

ARTISTS Wesley Grubbs, Mladen Balog, Kemper Smith, and Nick Yahnke of Pitch Interactive, Inc., in Berkeley, California; Katie Peek and Ryan Bradley at *Popular Science*.

STATEMENT The goal of the graphic was for readers to understand the basic pattern of the flu season and see that divergent years tend to feature stronger, earlier outbreaks. The H1N1 influenza of 2009–10 stands out immediately as a pattern different from the typical flu season. The second anomaly we wanted people to notice is the 2003–04 flu season. That year, the flu vaccine the CDC distributed proved to be a poor match for the most virulent flu strain. It's interesting how well the Google flu trends data—based on web searches for phrases like "cold chills"—matched the reporting patterns by the CDC—based on doctor and emergency-room visits. Neither is a perfect reporting system, but when considered together, each lends credence to the other.

PUBLICATION *Popular Science* (March 2012)

And the Oscar Goes to . . . New York City

A world map in which the land has been proportionally rescaled to show how many Oscar-nominated films have been set in particular locales.

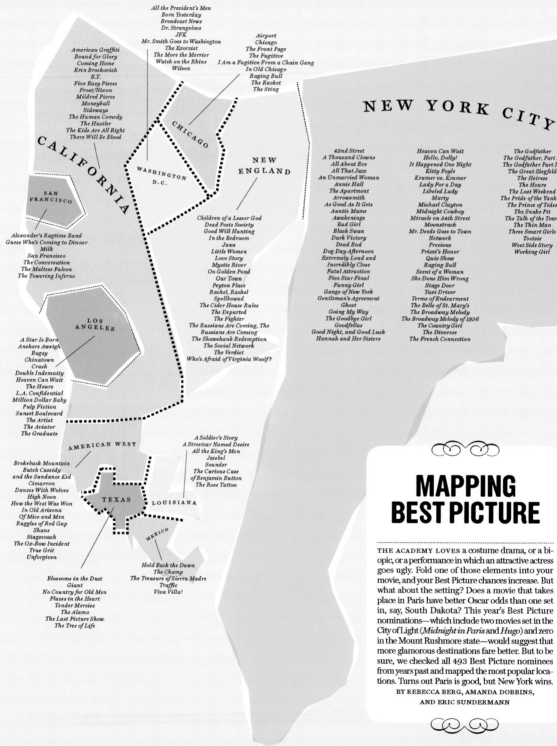

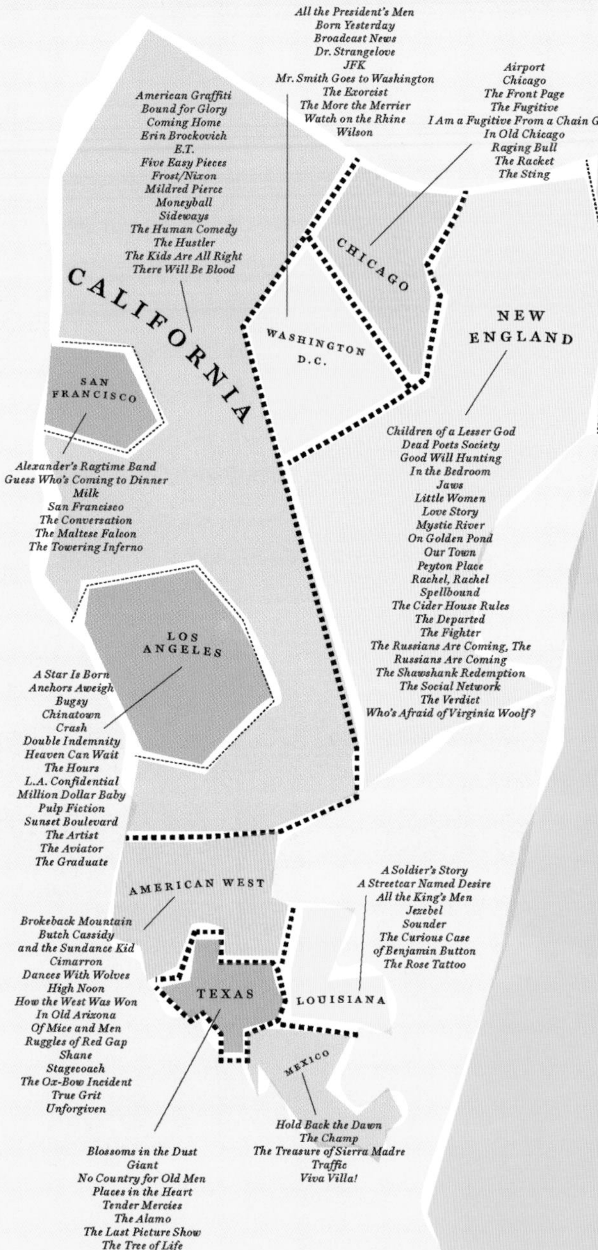

CALIFORNIA
American Graffiti
Bound for Glory
Coming Home
Erin Brockovich
E.T.
Five Easy Pieces
Frost/Nixon
Mildred Pierce
Moneyball
Sideways
The Human Comedy
The Hustler
The Kids Are All Right
There Will Be Blood
WASHINGTON D.C.
All the President's Men
Born Yesterday
Broadcast News
Dr. Strangelove
JFK
Mr. Smith Goes to Washington
The Exorcist
The More the Merrier
Watch on the Rhine
Wilson
CHICAGO
Airport
Chicago
The Front Page
The Fugitive
I Am a Fugitive From a Chain Gang
In Old Chicago
Raging Bull
The Racket
The Sting
SAN FRANCISCO
Alexander's Ragtime Band
Guess Who's Coming to Dinner
Milk
San Francisco
The Conversation
The Maltese Falcon
The Towering Inferno
NEW ENGLAND
Children of a Lesser God
Dead Poets Society
Good Will Hunting
In the Bedroom
Jaws
Little Women
Love Story
Mystic River
On Golden Pond
Our Town
Peyton Place
Rachel, Rachel
Spellbound
The Cider House Rules
The Departed
The Fighter
The Russians Are Coming, The Russians Are Coming
The Shawshank Redemption
The Social Network
The Verdict
Who's Afraid of Virginia Woolf?
LOS ANGELES
A Star Is Born
Anchors Aweigh
Bugsy
Chinatown
Crash
Double Indemnity
Heaven Can Wait
The Hours
L.A. Confidential
Million Dollar Baby
Pulp Fiction
Sunset Boulevard
The Artist
The Aviator
The Graduate
AMERICAN WEST
Brokeback Mountain
Butch Cassidy and the Sundance Kid
Cimarron
Dances With Wolves
High Noon
How the West Was Won
In Old Arizona
Of Mice and Men
Ruggles of Red Gap
Shane
Stagecoach
The Ox-Bow Incident
True Grit
Unforgiven
TEXAS
Blossoms in the Dust
Giant
No Country for Old Men
Places in the Heart
Tender Mercies
The Alamo
The Last Picture Show
The Tree of Life
LOUISIANA
A Soldier's Story
A Streetcar Named Desire
All the King's Men
Jezebel
Sounder
The Curious Case of Benjamin Button
The Rose Tattoo
MEXICO
Hold Back the Dawn
The Champ
The Treasure of Sierra Madre
Traffic
Viva Villa!

NEW YORK CITY
42nd Street
A Thousand Clowns
All About Eve
All That Jazz
An Unmarried Woman
Annie Hall
The Apartment
Arrowsmith
As Good As It Gets
Auntie Mame
Awakenings
Bad Girl
Black Swan
Dark Victory
Dead End
Dog Day Afternoon
Extremely Loud and Incredibly Close
Fatal Attraction
Five Star Final
Funny Girl
Gangs of New York
Gentleman's Agreement
Ghost
Going My Way
The Goodbye Girl
Goodfellas
Good Night, and Good Luck
Hannah and Her Sisters
Heaven Can Wait
Hello, Dolly!
It Happened One Night
Kitty Foyle
Kramer vs. Kramer
Lady For a Day
Libeled Lady
Marty
Michael Clayton
Midnight Cowboy
Miracle on 34th Street
Moonstruck
Mr. Deeds Goes to Town
Network
Precious
Prizzi's Honor
Quiz Show
Raging Bull
Scent of a Woman
She Done Him Wrong
Stage Door
Taxi Driver
Terms of Endearment
The Bells of St. Mary's
The Broadway Melody
The Broadway Melody of 1936
The Country Girl
The Divorcee
The French Connection
The Godfather
The Godfather, Part II
The Godfather Part III
The Great Ziegfeld
The Heiress
The Hours
The Lost Weekend
The Pride of the Yankees
The Prince of Tides
The Snake Pit
The Talk of the Town
The Thin Man
Three Smart Girls
Tootsie
West Side Story
Working Girl

MAPPING BEST PICTURE

THE ACADEMY LOVES a costume drama, or a biopic, or a performance in which an attractive actress goes ugly. Fold one of those elements into your movie, and your Best Picture chances increase. But what about the setting? Does a movie that takes place in Paris have better Oscar odds than one set in, say, South Dakota? This year's Best Picture nominations—which include two movies set in the City of Light (*Midnight in Paris* and *Hugo*) and zero in the Mount Rushmore state—would suggest that more glamorous destinations fare better. But to be sure, we checked all 493 Best Picture nominees from years past and mapped the most popular locations. Turns out Paris is good, but New York wins.

BY REBECCA BERG, AMANDA DOBBINS, AND ERIC SUNDERMANN

A Man for All Seasons
Anne of the Thousand Days
Atonement
Becket
Barry Lyndon
Braveheart
Chariots of Fire
Disraeli
Doctor Doolittle
Finding Neverland
Four Weddings and a Funeral
Goodbye, Mr. Chips
Gosford Park
Great Expectations
Howards End
How Green Was My Valley
Ivanhoe
Julia
Mrs. Miniver
Mutiny on the Bounty
Pygmalion
Random Harvest
Rebecca
The Remains of the Day
Room at the Top
Secrets and Lies
Sense and Sensibility
Separate Tables
Smilin' Through
Sons and Lovers
Tess
The Adventures of Robin Hood
The Barretts of Wimpole Street
The Full Monty
The Gay Divorcee
Tom Jones
War Horse
Witness for the Prosecution
Wuthering Heights
IRELAND
In the Name of the Father
My Left Foot
The Crying Game
The Informer
The Quiet Man
MIDDLE OF THE OCEAN
INCLUDING REMOTE ISLANDS
Captains Courageous
In Which We Serve
Love Affair
Master and Commander
Mister Roberts
Mutiny on the Bounty
Naughty Marietta
Ship of Fools
The Caine Mutiny
The Far Side of the World
The Guns of Navarone
The Long Voyage Home
Titanic
Wake Island
UNITED KINGDOM
Alfie
A Clockwork Orange
A Tale of Two Cities
A Touch of Class
An Education
Cavalcade
Darling; David Copperfield
The Elephant Man
Elizabeth
Foreign Correspondent
Gaslight
Hope and Glory
In the Name of the Father
Mary Poppins
My Fair Lady
Oliver!
The Citadel
The Dresser
The Hours
The King's Speech
The Private Life of Henry VIII
The Queen
Shakespeare in Love
Shine
Top Hat
LONDON
Doctor Zhivago
Fiddler on the Roof
Julia
Nicholas and Alexandra
Reds
The Patriot
RUSSIA/USSR
Crouching Tiger, Hidden Dragon
Shanghai Express
The Good Earth
The Last Emperor
The Sand Pebbles
CHINA
GERMANY
INDIA
A Passage to India
Gandhi
Slumdog Millionaire
The Lives of a Bengal Lancer
The Razor's Edge
FRANCE
ITALY
All Quiet on the Western Front
Cabaret
Decision Before Dawn
Grand Hotel
Grand Illusion
Judgment at Nuremberg
The Reader
Twelve O'Clock High
PARIS
Cleopatra (1934)
Cleopatra (1963)
ders of the Lost Ark
e English Patient
Ten Commandments
GYPT
CA
ROME
Battleground
Beauty and the Beast
Chocolat
Dangerous Liaisons
Fanny
Henry V
Inglourious Basterds
Julia
Saving Private Ryan
The Life of Emile Zola
The Lion in Winter
The Longest Day
The Pied Piper
The Song of Bernadette
The Story of Louis Pasteur
Wings
A Tale of Two Cities
An American in Paris
Chariots of Fire
Gigi
Hugo
Les Miserables
Madame Curie
Midnight in Paris
Moulin Rouge (1952)
Moulin Rouge (2001)
Ninotchka
One Hour With You
Seventh Heaven
The Accidental Tourist
The Razor's Edge
A Farewell to Arms
A Room With a View
Anthony Adverse
Il Postino
Life Is Beautiful
One Night of Love
Romeo and Juliet (1936)
Romeo and Juliet (1968)
The English Patient
Top Hat
Gladiator
Julius Caesar
Quo Vadis?
Roman Holiday
The Robe
Three Coins in the Fountain

ARTISTS Stevie Remsberg, Rebecca Berg, Amanda Dobbins, Eric Sundermann, and Thomas Alberty, *New York* magazine.

STATEMENT We built a world map showing where every nominee for the Best Picture Oscar takes place. (It included 493 films, going back to 1928.) Countries and cities have been proportionally scaled to match the number of films set there, revealing that New York City is, far and away, the location most likely to get a filmmaker an Oscar. Great Britain, and especially London, are also winners. Useful tip if you're trying to win one: Don't make a movie in the Midwest, unless it's in Chicago.

PUBLICATION
New York
(February 6, 2012)

Sexism Visualized

The divide between men and women across American society.

ARTIST Brian McGill, senior graphics editor, *National Journal* in Washington, D.C.

STATEMENT Two things surprised me the most in doing the research. First was that the number of women at the top of Fortune 500 companies was so small. I didn't expect there to be a lot of women running these companies, but I definitely thought there would be more than 3.6 percent. The second surprise was that even in female-dominated sectors of the economy, such as office and administration, men still make more than women. Baffling. It was important to me to keep the design simple so that the focus would be on the information. One color for men, another for women, and a background color.

PUBLICATION
"The Next Economy," a supplement of the *National Journal* (March 2012)

CONTINUED

Women in Power ⬇

Only 18 ***Fortune*** **500 companies** have women in charge. However, that is the most in history.

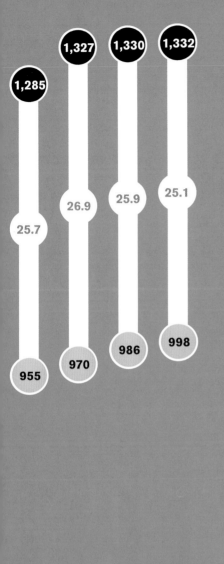

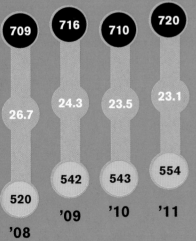

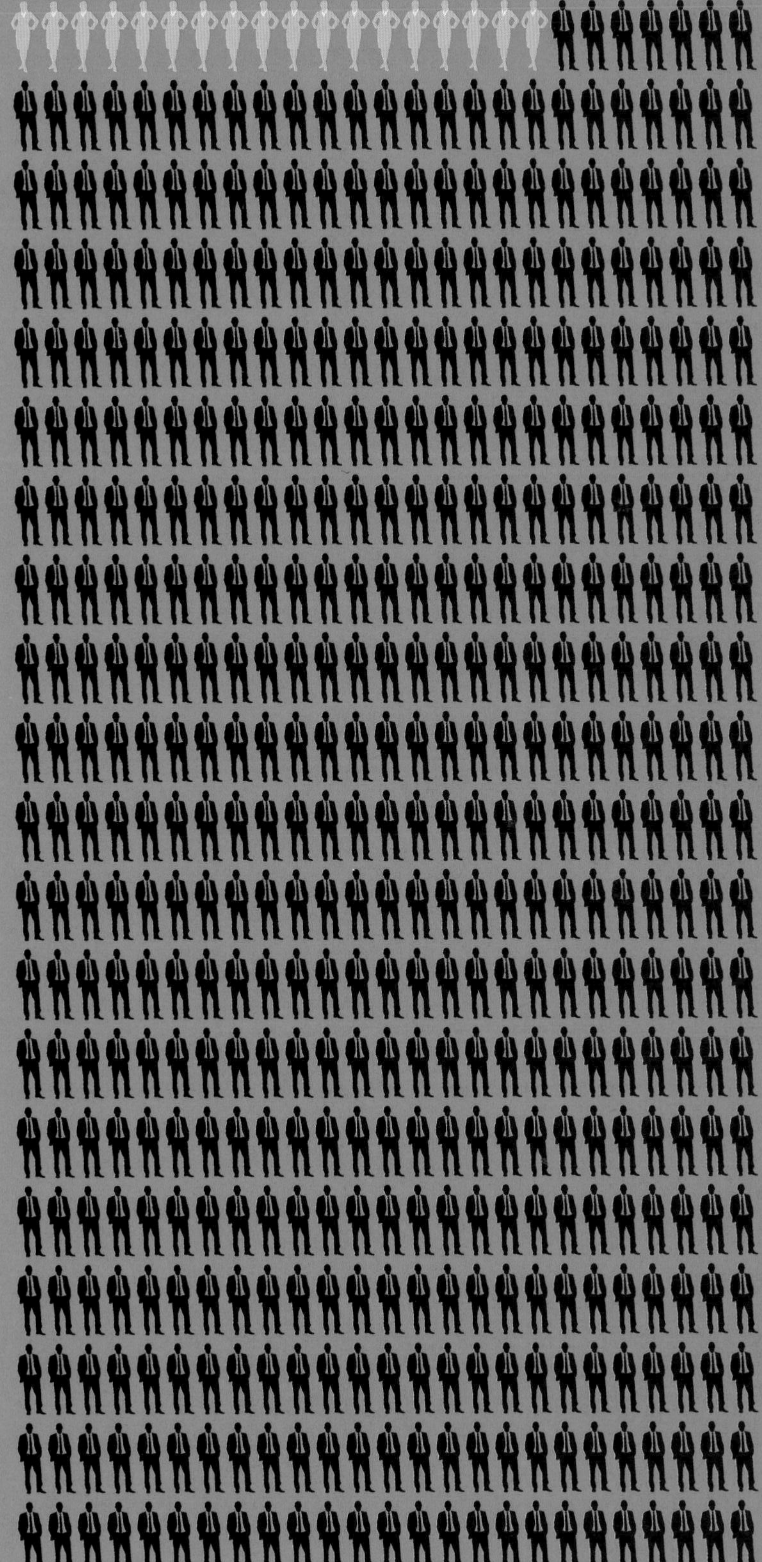

	'08	'09	'10	'11
	1,285	1,327	1,330	1,332
	25.7	26.9	25.9	25.1
	955	970	986	998
	709	716	710	720
	26.7	24.3	23.5	23.1
	520	542	543	554

The Gender Divide

Although women constitute 44 percent of the American workforce, they still fail to get paid as much as men.

Jobs gained/lost as a percentage of total jobs from the second quarter of 2009 through 2011

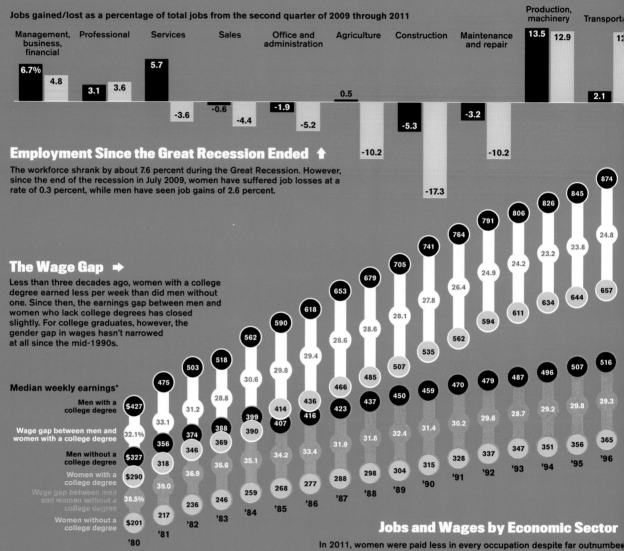

	Men	Women
Management, business, financial	6.7%	4.8
Professional	3.1	3.6
Services	5.7	-3.6
Sales	-0.6	-4.4
Office and administration	-1.9	-5.2
Agriculture	0.5	-10.2
Construction	-5.3	-17.3
Maintenance and repair	-3.2	-10.2
Production, machinery	13.5	12.9
Transport	2.1	1

Employment Since the Great Recession Ended ↑

The workforce shrank by about 7.6 percent during the Great Recession. However, since the end of the recession in July 2009, women have suffered job losses at a rate of 0.3 percent, while men have seen job gains of 2.6 percent.

The Wage Gap ➡

Less than three decades ago, women with a college degree earned less per week than did men without one. Since then, the earnings gap between men and women who lack college degrees has closed slightly. For college graduates, however, the gender gap in wages hasn't narrowed at all since the mid-1990s.

Median weekly earnings*

Year	Men with a college degree	Wage gap between men and women with a college degree	Men without a college degree	Women with a college degree	Wage gap between men and women without a college degree	Women without a college degree
'80	$427	32.1%	$327	$290	38.5%	$201
'81	475	33.1	356	318	39.0	217
'82	503	31.2	374	346	36.9	236
'83	518	28.8	388	369	36.6	246
'84	562	30.6	399	390	35.1	259
'85	590	29.8	407	414	34.2	268
'86	618	29.4	416	436	33.4	277
'87	653	28.6	423	466	31.9	288
'88	679	28.6	437	485	31.8	298
'89	705	28.1	450	507	32.4	304
'90	741	27.8	459	535	31.4	315
'91	764	26.4	470	562	30.2	328
'92	791	24.9	479	594	29.6	337
'93	806	24.2	487	611	28.7	347
'94	826	23.2	496	634	29.2	351
'95	845	23.8	507	644	29.8	356
'96	874	24.8	516	657	29.3	365

Jobs and Wages by Economic Sector

In 2011, women were paid less in every occupation despite far outnumbe[r]ing men among professionals and among office and administration work[ers].

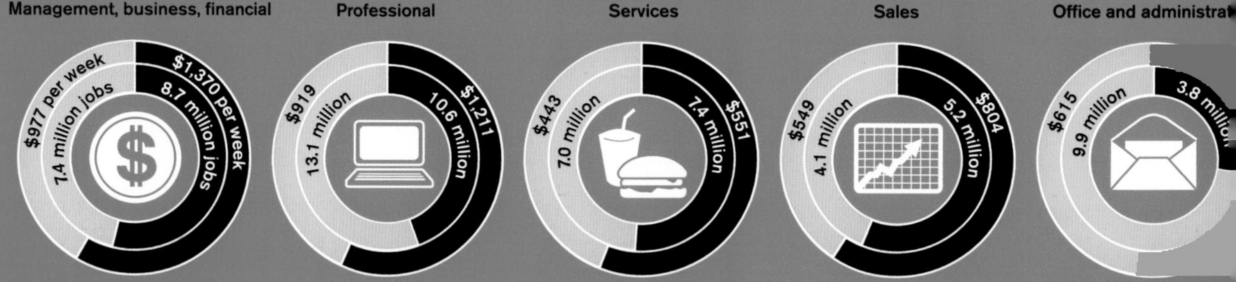

Management, business, financial
$977 per week
7.4 million jobs
$1,370 per week
8.7 million jobs
Professional
$919
13.1 million
$1,211
10.6 million
Services
$443
7.0 million
$551
7.4 million
Sales
$549
4.1 million
$804
5.2 million
Office and administrat
$615
9.9 million
3.8 million

Graphic by BRIAN McGILL

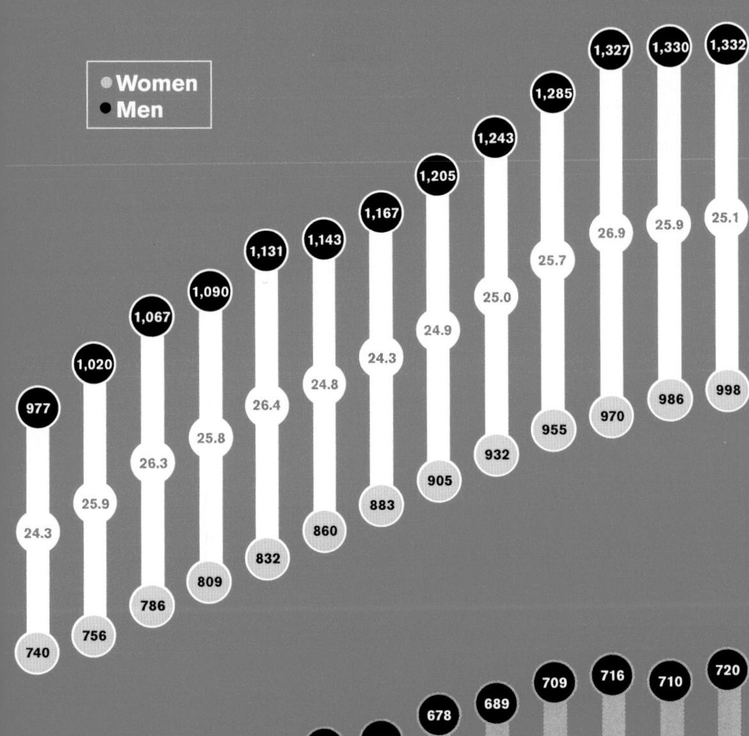
Women
Men
977
24.3
740
1,020
25.9
756
1,067
26.3
786
1,090
25.8
809
1,131
26.4
832
1,143
24.8
860
1,167
24.3
883
1,205
24.9
905
1,243
25.0
932
1,285
25.7
955
1,327
26.9
970
1,330
25.9
986
1,332
25.1
998
580
29.2
405
'99
591
28.9
420
'00
609
27.3
443
'01
617
25.8
458
'02
628
24.5
474
'03
645
24.3
488
'04
652
24.4
493
'05
678
26.3
500
'06
689
25.7
512
'07
709
26.7
520
'08
716
24.3
542
'09
710
23.5
543
'10
720
23.1
554
'11

*For full-time wage and salary workers, in nominal dollars.

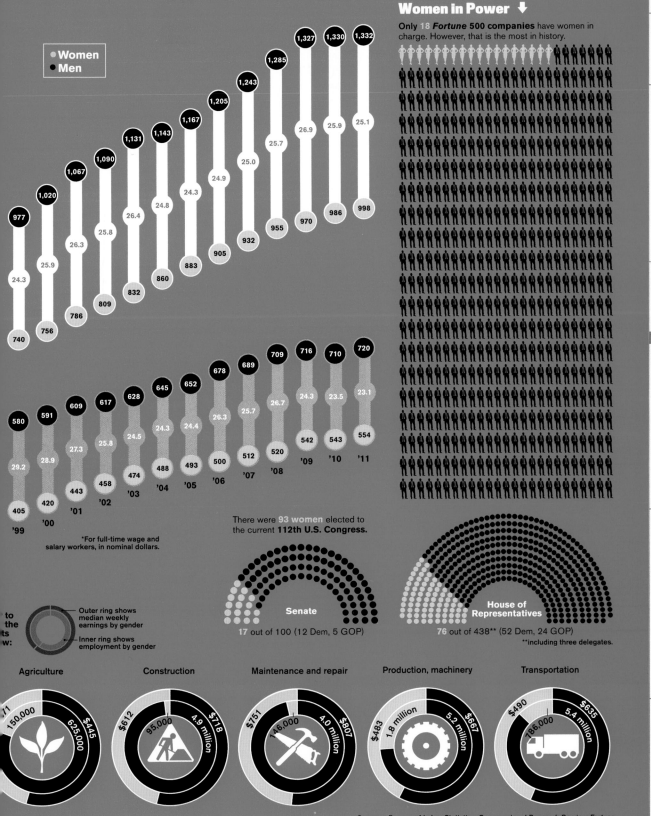

Women in Power

Only 18 ***Fortune* 500 companies** have women in charge. However, that is the most in history.

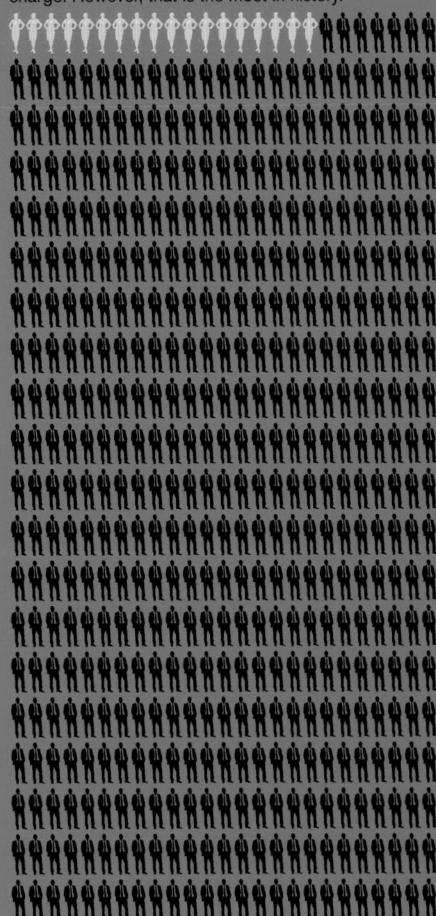

There were **93 women** elected to the current **112th U.S. Congress.**

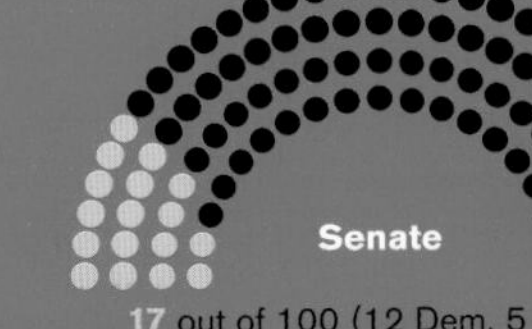
Senate

17 out of 100 (12 Dem, 5 GOP)

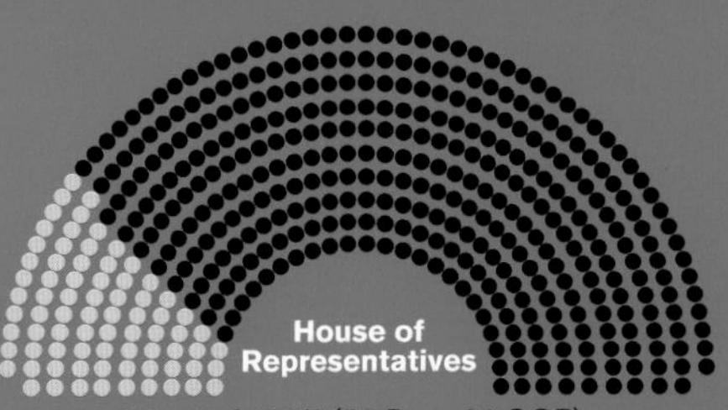
House of Representatives

76 out of 438** (52 Dem, 24 GOP)

**including three delegates.

to the ts w:

Outer ring shows median weekly earnings by gender

Inner ring shows employment by gender

Agriculture

150,000
625,000
$445

Construction

$612
95,000
4.9 million
$718

Maintenance and repair

$751
146,000
4.0 million
$807

Production, machinery

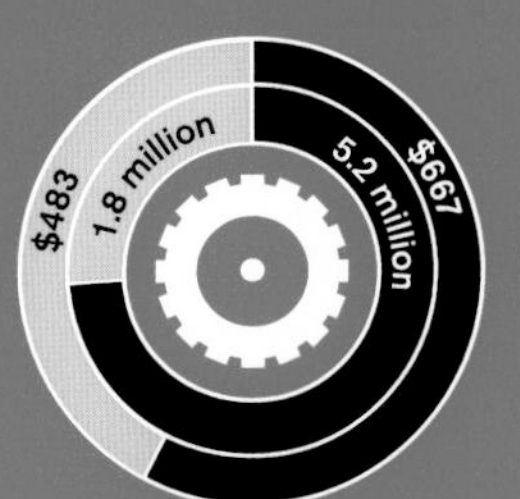
$483
1.8 million
5.2 million
$667

Transportation

$490
786,000
5.4 million
$635

Sources: Bureau of Labor Statistics; Congressional Research Service; *Fortune*

Who ESPN Likes to Talk About

An analysis, based on transcripts, of the NFL players most discussed on *SportsCenter*.

ARTISTS Ritchie S. King, Kevin Quealy, Graham Roberts, and Alicia DeSantis, the *New York Times*.

STATEMENT Drawing on six months of closed-captioning transcripts from the program *SportsCenter*, we showed which NFL players were mentioned the most through 3-D figures on a field. This certainly put the Tim Tebow coverage into perspective.

PUBLICATION *New York Times* online (www.nytimes.com) (February 4, 2012)

Colossi of the N.F.L.

Below, some of the most mentioned players and coaches this season. Each player's height is scaled according to the number of times he was mentioned on "SportsCenter" or "Sunday N.F.L. Countdown."

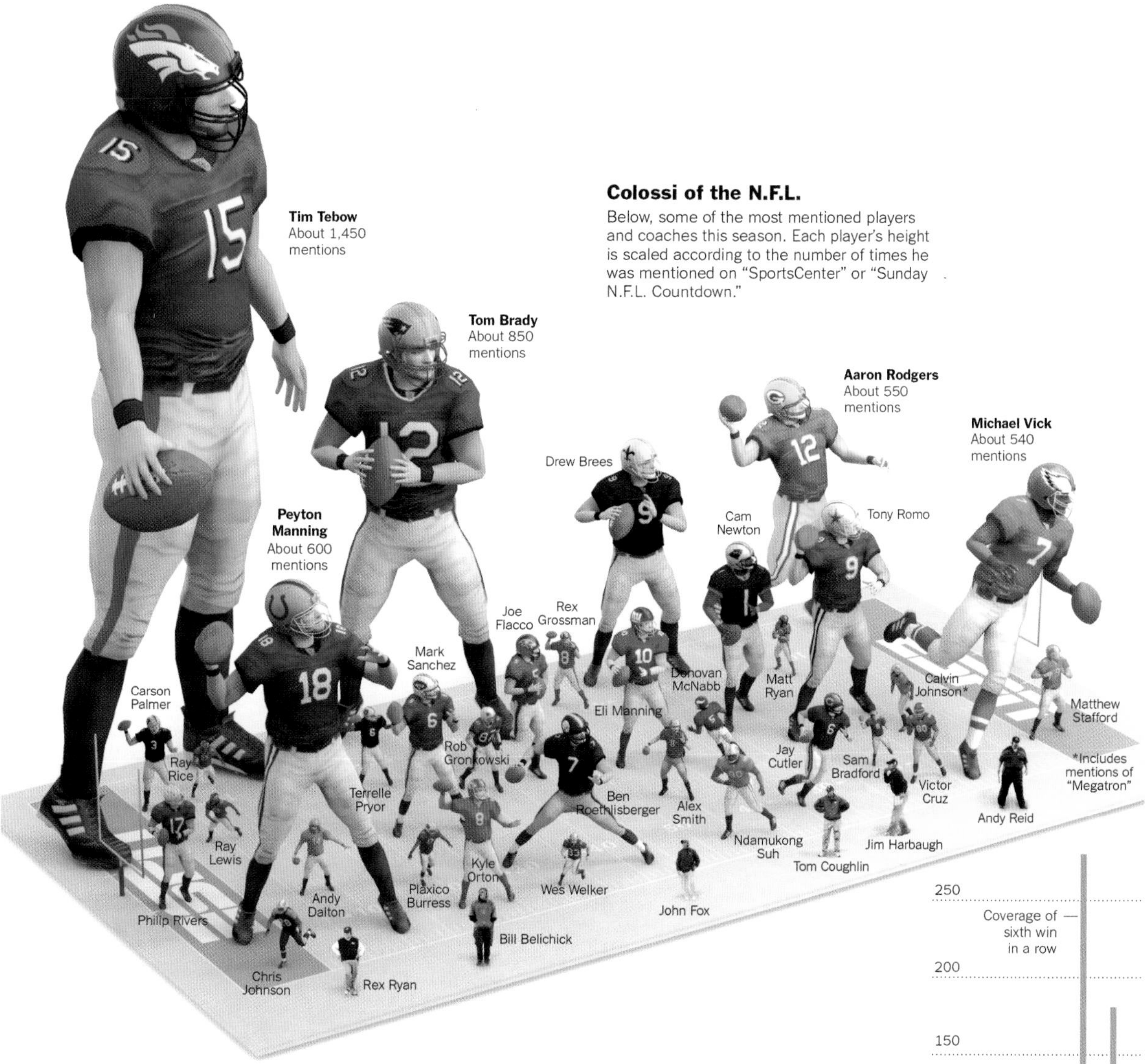

Tim Tebow
About 1,450 mentions

Tom Brady
About 850 mentions

Peyton Manning
About 600 mentions

Aaron Rodgers
About 550 mentions

Michael Vick
About 540 mentions

Drew Brees
Cam Newton
Tony Romo
Joe Flacco
Rex Grossman
Mark Sanchez
Carson Palmer
Eli Manning
Donovan McNabb
Matt Ryan
Calvin Johnson*
Matthew Stafford
Ray Rice
Rob Gronkowski
Jay Cutler
Sam Bradford
Victor Cruz
Terrelle Pryor
Ben Roethlisberger
Alex Smith
Ray Lewis
Ndamukong Suh
Tom Coughlin
Jim Harbaugh
Andy Reid
Kyle Orton
Wes Welker
John Fox
Andy Dalton
Plaxico Burress
Philip Rivers
Bill Belichick
Chris Johnson
Rex Ryan

*Includes mentions of "Megatron"

Transcripts were collected from the 9 a.m. and 11 p.m. editions of "SportsCenter" from Aug. 1, 2011, to Feb. 1, 2012, including the weekly broadcast of "Sunday N.F.L. Countdown" on Sundays. In some cases, a later airing was used to avoid conflicts with "College Gameday" on Saturdays. Closed-captioning transcripts for a small number of dates were not available.

Number of mentions a week

REGULAR SEASON

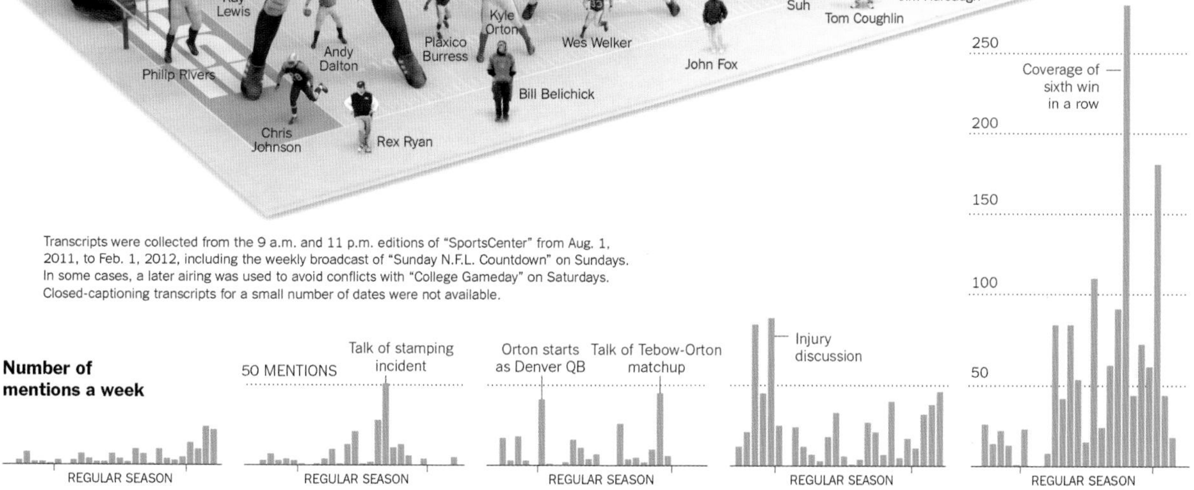

BILL BELICHICK

The anchors were mostly reverent when describing the Patriots' coach, mentioning his secrecy, calling him "tremendous" and a "mastermind."

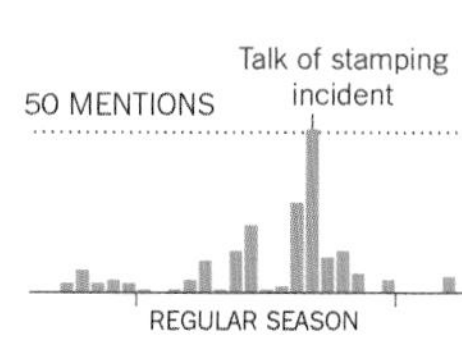
50 MENTIONS
Talk of stamping incident
REGULAR SEASON

NDAMUKONG SUH

The most mentioned defensive player, Suh made the list mostly because of his two-game suspension for stamping on an opponent's arm during Detroit's game against the Green Bay Packers on Nov. 24.

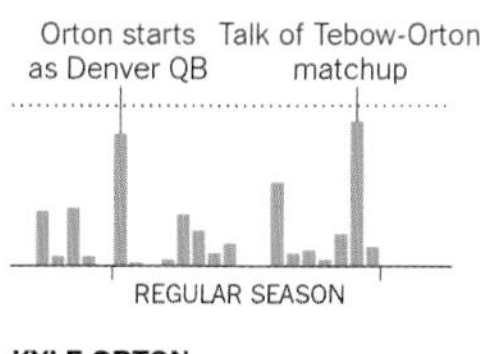
Orton starts as Denver QB
Talk of Tebow-Orton matchup
REGULAR SEASON

KYLE ORTON

In November, Orton went to Kansas City after losing a quarterback battle to Tim Tebow, leading to talk of a potential matchup between the former teammates. He and Tebow did face off in Denver on Jan. 1 — and that time, Orton won.

Injury discussion

REGULAR SEASON

PEYTON MANNING

Despite going the entire season without taking a snap, Manning was discussed more than most of the league's active players — even more than his younger brother, Eli, who led the Giants to Sunday's Super Bowl.

250
Coverage of sixth win in a row
200
150
100
50

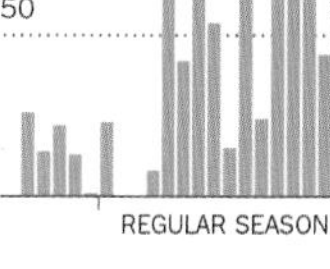
REGULAR SEASON

TIM TEBOW

On "SportsCenter," there was Tebow and then there was everyone else. After the Broncos' sixth consecutive win, he was mentioned more than 40 times in the next morning's edition of the show.

Source: ShadowTV

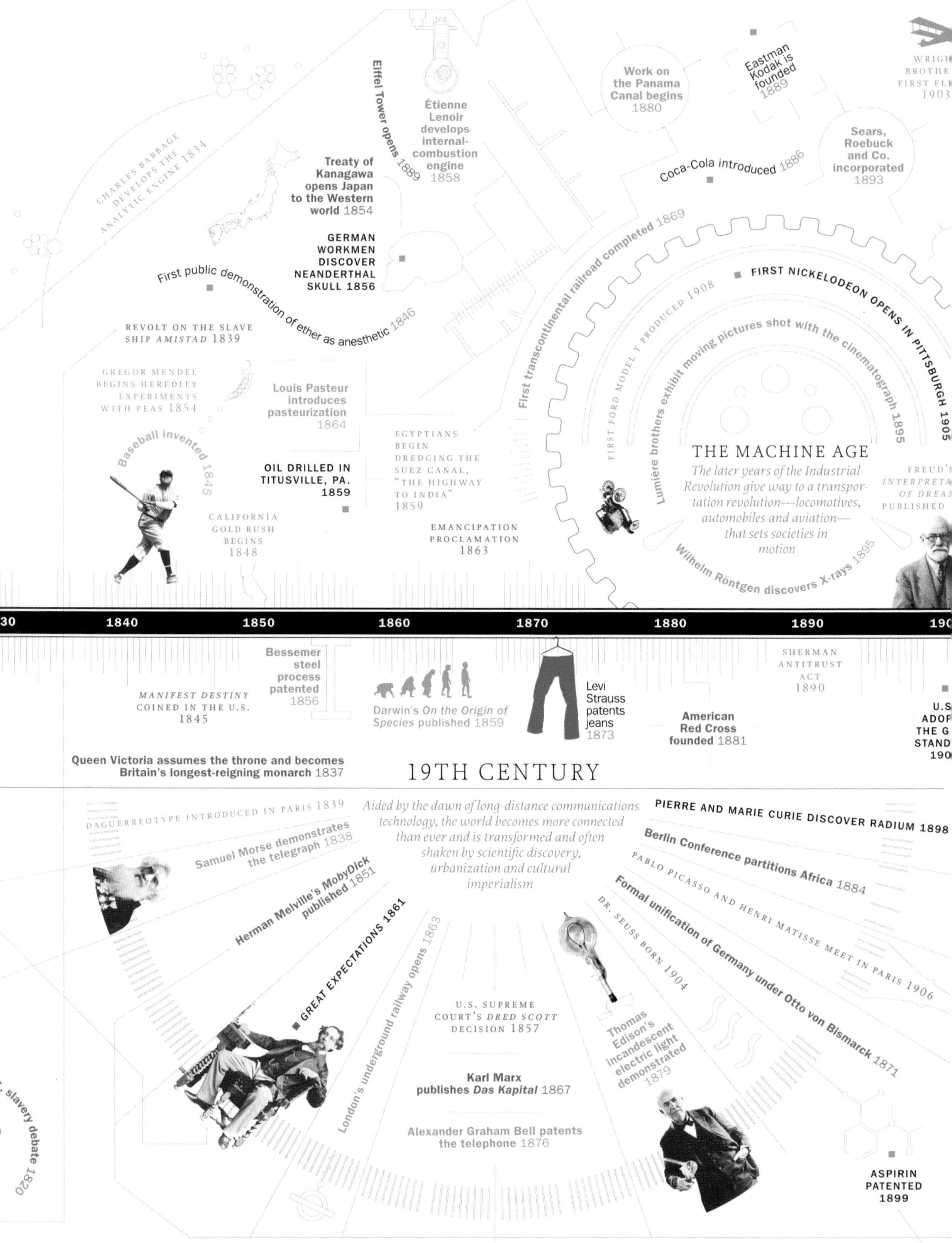

Charles Babbage develops the analytic engine 1834
Eiffel Tower opens 1889
Étienne Lenoir develops internal-combustion engine 1858
Treaty of Kanagawa opens Japan to the Western world 1854
German workmen discover Neanderthal skull 1856
First public demonstration of ether as anesthetic 1846
Revolt on the slave ship *Amistad* 1839
Gregor Mendel begins heredity experiments with peas 1854
Louis Pasteur introduces pasteurization 1864
Baseball invented 1845
Oil drilled in Titusville, Pa. 1859
Egyptians begin dredging the Suez Canal, "The Highway to India" 1859
California Gold Rush begins 1848
Emancipation Proclamation 1863
Work on the Panama Canal begins 1880
Eastman Kodak is founded 1889
Wrigh
Brothe
First Fl
1903
Coca-Cola introduced 1886
Sears, Roebuck and Co. incorporated 1893
First transcontinental railroad completed 1869
First Nickelodeon opens in Pittsburgh 1905
First Ford Model T produced 1908
Lumière brothers exhibit moving pictures shot with the cinematograph 1895
THE MACHINE AGE
The later years of the Industrial Revolution give way to a transportation revolution—locomotives, automobiles and aviation—that sets societies in motion
Freud's
Interpreta
of Drea
published
Wilhelm Röntgen discovers X-rays 1895
1830
1840
1850
1860
1870
1880
1890
190
Manifest Destiny coined in the U.S. 1845
Bessemer steel process patented 1856
Darwin's *On the Origin of Species* published 1859
Levi Strauss patents jeans 1873
American Red Cross founded 1881
Sherman Antitrust Act 1890
U.S.
adop
the G
stand
190
Queen Victoria assumes the throne and becomes Britain's longest-reigning monarch 1837
19TH CENTURY
Aided by the dawn of long-distance communications technology, the world becomes more connected than ever and is transformed and often shaken by scientific discovery, urbanization and cultural imperialism
Daguerreotype introduced in Paris 1839
Samuel Morse demonstrates the telegraph 1838
Herman Melville's MobyDick published 1851
Great Expectations 1861
London's underground railway opens 1863
U.S. Supreme Court's *Dred Scott* decision 1857
Karl Marx publishes *Das Kapital* 1867
Alexander Graham Bell patents the telephone 1876
Pierre and Marie Curie discover radium 1898
Berlin Conference partitions Africa 1884
Pablo Picasso and Henri Matisse meet in Paris 1906
Formal unification of Germany under Otto von Bismarck 1871
Dr. Seuss born 1904
Thomas Edison's incandescent electric light demonstrated 1879
Aspirin patented 1899
.S. slavery debate 1820

Influence: A Brief History

200 years of transformative moments

BY ANDRÉA FORD GRAPHIC BY HEATHER JONES

In 1812, global life expectancy was less than 30 years, it took weeks to cross the Atlantic Ocean by ship, and democracy had just begun to spread around the planet. Today most of the world's people live in cities, more than 30 million commercial flights take off each year, and each day more new smart phones and tablets join the global conversation than babies are born. In two centuries, the world has been dramatically transformed by a series of interconnected moments—the breakthroughs, creations, discoveries, innovations, revolutions and momentous human achievements that have altered the course of history and the way we live our lives.

THE TIME LINE

- Politics and Society
- Economy and Industry
- Science and Technology
- Culture
- Sports

1812 1820

U.S. DECLARES WAR FOR THE FIRST TIME 1812

CHARLES DICKENS BORN 1812

JANE AUSTEN'S *PRIDE AND PREJUDICE* PUBLISHED 1813

17 Luddites executed in England for "machine breaking" 1813

NAPOLEON DEFEATED AT THE BATTLE OF WATERLOO 1815

Baron Karl von Drais introduces the modern bicycle 1817

Mary Shelley publishes Frankenstein 1818

Missouri Compromise magnifies U.

BEETHOVEN'S *SYMPHONY NO. 9* COMPLETED 1824

Erie Canal opens 1825

Slavery abolished the Britis Empire 1834

200 Years of Innovation

The two hundred most influential moments of the past two centuries.

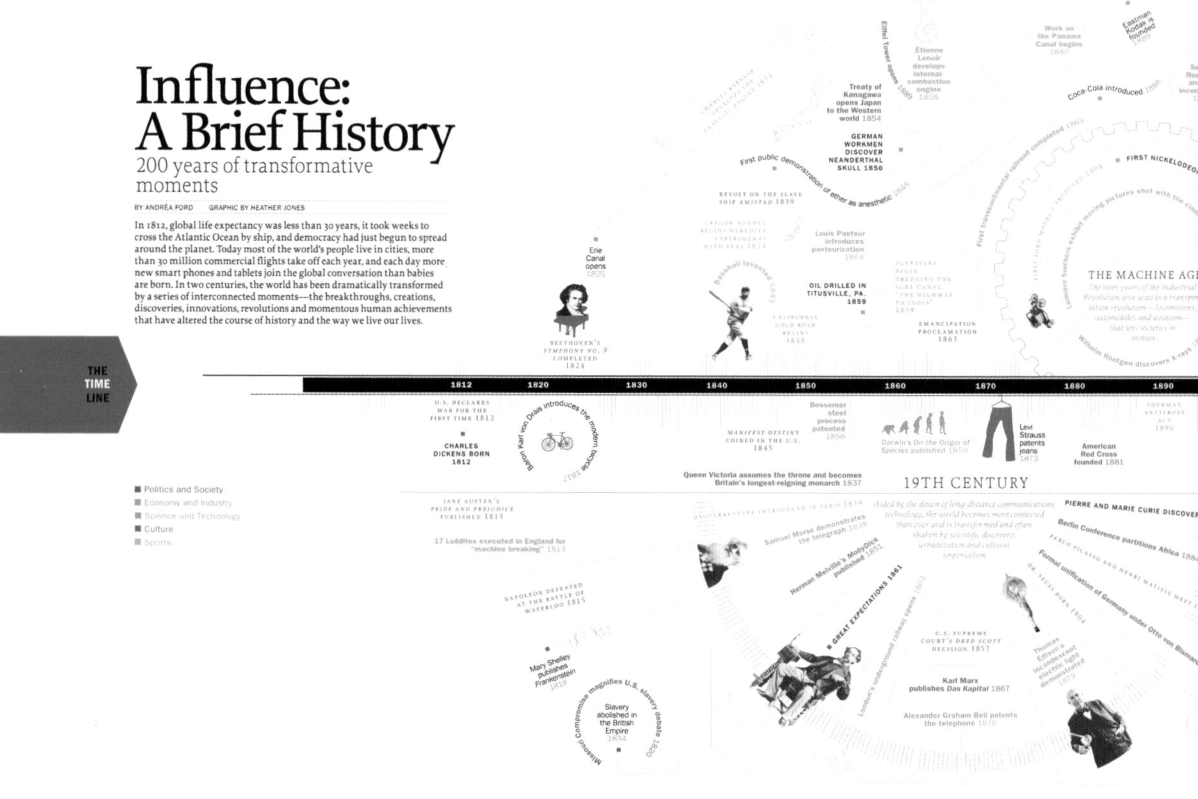

Influence: A Brief History
200 years of transformative moments
BY ANDRÉA FORD GRAPHIC BY HEATHER JONES
In 1812, global life expectancy was less than 30 years, it took weeks to cross the Atlantic Ocean by ship, and democracy had just begun to spread around the planet. Today most of the world's people live in cities, more than 30 million commercial flights take off each year, and each day more new smart phones and tablets join the global conversation than babies are born. In two centuries, the world has been dramatically transformed by a series of interconnected moments—the breakthroughs, creations, discoveries, innovations, revolutions and momentous human achievements that have altered the course of history and the way we live our lives.
THE TIME LINE
Politics and Society
Economy and Industry
Science and Technology
Culture
Sports
1812
1820
1830
1840
1850
1860
1870
1880
1890
Erie Canal opens 1825
BEETHOVEN'S SYMPHONY NO. 9 COMPLETED 1824
REVOLT ON THE SLAVE SHIP AMISTAD 1839
First public demonstration of ether as anesthetic 1846
Treaty of Kanagawa opens Japan to the Western world 1854
GERMAN WORKMEN DISCOVER NEANDERTHAL SKULL 1856
Louis Pasteur introduces pasteurization 1864
OIL DRILLED IN TITUSVILLE, PA. 1859
EMANCIPATION PROCLAMATION 1863
Eiffel Tower opens 1889
Étienne Lenoir develops internal combustion engine 1858
Work on the Panama Canal begins 1880
Eastman Kodak is founded
Coca-Cola introduced 1886
FIRST NICKELODEON
First transcontinental railroad completed 1869
THE MACHINE AGE
Wilhelm Röntgen discovers X-rays
U.S. DECLARES WAR FOR THE FIRST TIME 1812
CHARLES DICKENS BORN 1812
Baron Karl von Drais introduces the modern bicycle 1817
MANIFEST DESTINY COINED IN THE U.S. 1845
Bessemer steel process patented 1856
Darwin's On the Origin of Species published 1859
Levi Strauss patents jeans 1873
American Red Cross founded 1881
Queen Victoria assumes the throne and becomes Britain's longest-reigning monarch 1837
19TH CENTURY
JANE AUSTEN'S PRIDE AND PREJUDICE PUBLISHED 1813
17 Luddites executed in England for "machine breaking" 1813
NAPOLEON DEFEATED AT THE BATTLE OF WATERLOO 1815
Mary Shelley publishes Frankenstein 1818
Missouri Compromise magnifies U.S. slavery debate 1820
Slavery abolished in the British Empire 1834
Samuel Morse demonstrates the telegraph 1838
Herman Melville's Moby-Dick published 1851
GREAT EXPECTATIONS 1861
London's underground railway opens 1863
U.S. SUPREME COURT'S DRED SCOTT DECISION 1857
Karl Marx publishes Das Kapital 1867
Alexander Graham Bell patents the telephone 1876
Thomas Edison's incandescent electric light demonstrated 1879
PIERRE AND MARIE CURIE DISCOVER
Berlin Conference partitions Africa 1884
Formal unification of Germany under Otto von Bismarck

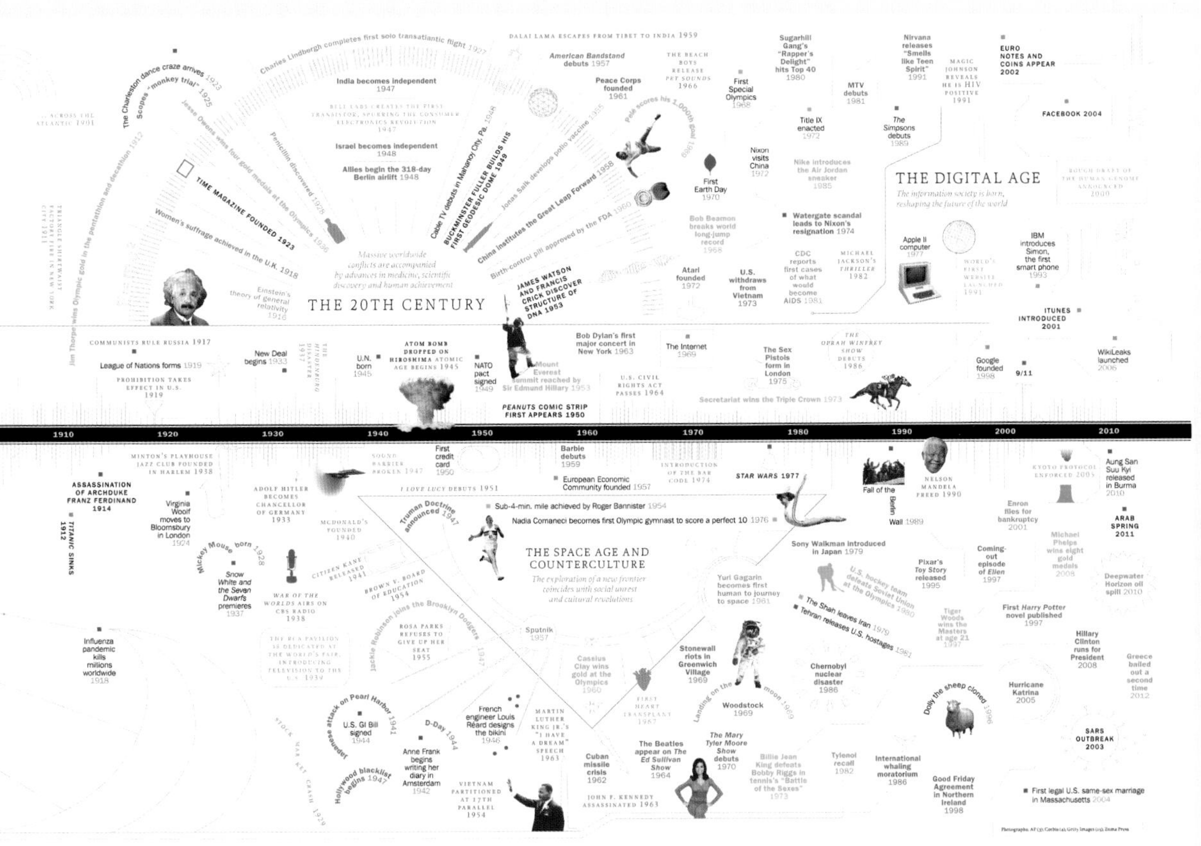
THE 20TH CENTURY
Massive worldwide conflicts are accompanied by advances in medicine, scientific discovery and human achievement
THE SPACE AGE AND COUNTERCULTURE
The exploration of a new frontier coincides with social unrest and cultural revolutions
THE DIGITAL AGE
The information society is born, reshaping the future of the world
1910
1920
1930
1940
1950
1960
1970
1980
1990
2000
2010
The Charleston dance craze arrives 1923
Scopes "monkey trial" 1925
Charles Lindbergh completes first solo transatlantic flight 1927
Jesse Owens wins four gold medals at the Olympics 1936
Penicillin discovered 1928
TIME MAGAZINE FOUNDED 1923
Women's suffrage achieved in the U.K. 1918
Einstein's theory of general relativity 1916
Jim Thorpe wins Olympic gold in the pentathlon and decathlon 1912
India becomes independent 1947
Israel becomes independent 1948
Allies begin the 318-day Berlin airlift 1948
DALAI LAMA ESCAPES FROM TIBET TO INDIA 1959
Cable TV debuts in Mahanoy City, Pa. 1948
BUCKMINSTER FULLER BUILDS HIS FIRST GEODESIC DOME 1949
Jonas Salk develops polio vaccine 1955
China institutes the Great Leap Forward 1958
Birth-control pill approved by the FDA 1960
JAMES WATSON AND FRANCIS CRICK DISCOVER STRUCTURE OF DNA 1953
American Bandstand debuts 1957
Peace Corps founded 1961
Pelé scores his 1,000th goal 1969
First Special Olympics 1968
First Earth Day 1970
Bob Beamon breaks world long-jump record 1968
Atari founded 1972
Nixon visits China 1972
U.S. withdraws from Vietnam 1973
Sugarhill Gang's "Rapper's Delight" hits Top 40 1980
Title IX enacted 1972
Nike introduces the Air Jordan sneaker 1985
Watergate scandal leads to Nixon's resignation 1974
CDC reports first cases of what would become AIDS 1981
MICHAEL JACKSON'S THRILLER 1982
MTV debuts 1981
Nirvana releases "Smells like Teen Spirit" 1991
MAGIC JOHNSON REVEALS HE IS HIV POSITIVE 1991
The Simpsons debuts 1989
Apple II computer 1977
WORLD'S FIRST WEBSITE LAUNCHED 1991
EURO NOTES AND COINS APPEAR 2002
FACEBOOK 2004
ROUGH DRAFT OF THE HUMAN GENOME ANNOUNCED 2000
IBM introduces Simon, the first smart phone 1993
ITUNES INTRODUCED 2001
COMMUNISTS RULE RUSSIA 1917
League of Nations forms 1919
PROHIBITION TAKES EFFECT IN U.S. 1919
New Deal begins 1933
THE HINDENBURG DISASTER 1937
U.N. born 1945
ATOM BOMB DROPPED ON HIROSHIMA ATOMIC AGE BEGINS 1945
NATO pact signed 1949
Mount Everest summit reached by Sir Edmund Hillary 1953
PEANUTS COMIC STRIP FIRST APPEARS 1950
Bob Dylan's first major concert in New York 1963
U.S. CIVIL RIGHTS ACT PASSES 1964
The Internet 1969
The Sex Pistols form in London 1975
THE OPRAH WINFREY SHOW DEBUTS 1986
Secretariat wins the Triple Crown 1973
Google founded 1998
9/11
WikiLeaks launched 2006
ASSASSINATION OF ARCHDUKE FRANZ FERDINAND 1914
TITANIC SINKS 1912
MINTON'S PLAYHOUSE JAZZ CLUB FOUNDED IN HARLEM 1938
Virginia Woolf moves to Bloomsbury in London 1904
ADOLF HITLER BECOMES CHANCELLOR OF GERMANY 1933
McDONALD'S FOUNDED 1940
SOUND BARRIER BROKEN 1947
First credit card 1950
I LOVE LUCY DEBUTS 1951
Barbie debuts 1959
European Economic Community founded 1957
INTRODUCTION OF THE BAR CODE 1974
STAR WARS 1977
Fall of the Berlin Wall 1989
NELSON MANDELA FREED 1990
KYOTO PROTOCOL ENFORCED 2005
Aung San Suu Kyi released in Burma 2010
ARAB SPRING 2011
Mickey Mouse born 1928
Snow White and the Seven Dwarfs premieres 1937
CITIZEN KANE RELEASED 1941
WAR OF THE WORLDS AIRS ON CBS RADIO 1938
BROWN V. BOARD OF EDUCATION 1954
Truman Doctrine announced 1947
Sub-4-min. mile achieved by Roger Bannister 1954
Nadia Comaneci becomes first Olympic gymnast to score a perfect 10 1976
Sony Walkman introduced in Japan 1979
Yuri Gagarin becomes first human to journey to space 1961
U.S. hockey team defeats Soviet Union at the Olympics 1980
The Shah leaves Iran 1979
Tehran releases U.S. hostages 1981
Pixar's Toy Story released 1995
Enron files for bankruptcy 2001
Coming-out episode of Ellen 1997
Michael Phelps wins eight gold medals 2008
Deepwater Horizon oil spill 2010
Tiger Woods wins the Masters at age 21 1997
First Harry Potter novel published 1997
Influenza pandemic kills millions worldwide 1918
THE RCA PAVILION IS DEDICATED AT THE WORLD'S FAIR, INTRODUCING TELEVISION TO THE U.S. 1939
ROSA PARKS REFUSES TO GIVE UP HER SEAT 1955
Jackie Robinson joins the Brooklyn Dodgers 1947
Sputnik 1957
Cassius Clay wins gold at the Olympics 1960
FIRST HEART TRANSPLANT 1967
Stonewall riots in Greenwich Village 1969
Landing on the moon 1969
Woodstock 1969
Chernobyl nuclear disaster 1986
Hillary Clinton runs for President 2008
Greece bailed out a second time 2012
Hurricane Katrina 2005
Dolly the sheep cloned 1996
STOCK MARKET CRASH 1929
Japanese attack on Pearl Harbor 1941
U.S. GI Bill signed 1944
D-Day 1944
Hollywood blacklist begins 1947
Anne Frank begins writing her diary in Amsterdam 1942
French engineer Louis Réard designs the bikini 1946
MARTIN LUTHER KING JR.'S "I HAVE A DREAM" SPEECH 1963
VIETNAM PARTITIONED AT 17TH PARALLEL 1954
Cuban missile crisis 1962
The Beatles appear on The Ed Sullivan Show 1964
JOHN F. KENNEDY ASSASSINATED 1963
The Mary Tyler Moore Show debuts 1970
Billie Jean King defeats Bobby Riggs in tennis's "Battle of the Sexes" 1973
Tylenol recall 1982
International whaling moratorium 1986
Good Friday Agreement in Northern Ireland 1998
SARS OUTBREAK 2003
First legal U.S. same-sex marriage in Massachusetts 2004

ARTISTS Heather Jones and Andréa Ford, *Time.*

STATEMENT There were some obvious moments to include—landing on the moon, women's suffrage, the discovery of the polio vaccine—and then some not necessarily happy, but certainly influential—the dropping of the atomic bomb, the SARS outbreak, and 9/11. I wanted to organize them all into a timeline with subcategories that illustrated the different ages. The machine age had gears and motors connecting its elements, the '50s and '60s were rounded and bubbly, and in the digital age the lines became more angular and pixelated. Our five colored categories (cultural, political, etc.) also emerged, and the whole thing kind of surfaced into an illustrated picture of history: some parts dynamic and lively with other parts serene and isolated (such as the white space around the influenza pandemic). I particularly like how Sir Edmund Hillary climbed up the Mt. Everest type. It was a challenge to keep the eye moving and also put in subtle elements—like the safety pin behind the Sex Pistols and the tiny stitches on Mary Shelley's *Frankenstein* caption.

PUBLICATION
Time (April 30, 2012)

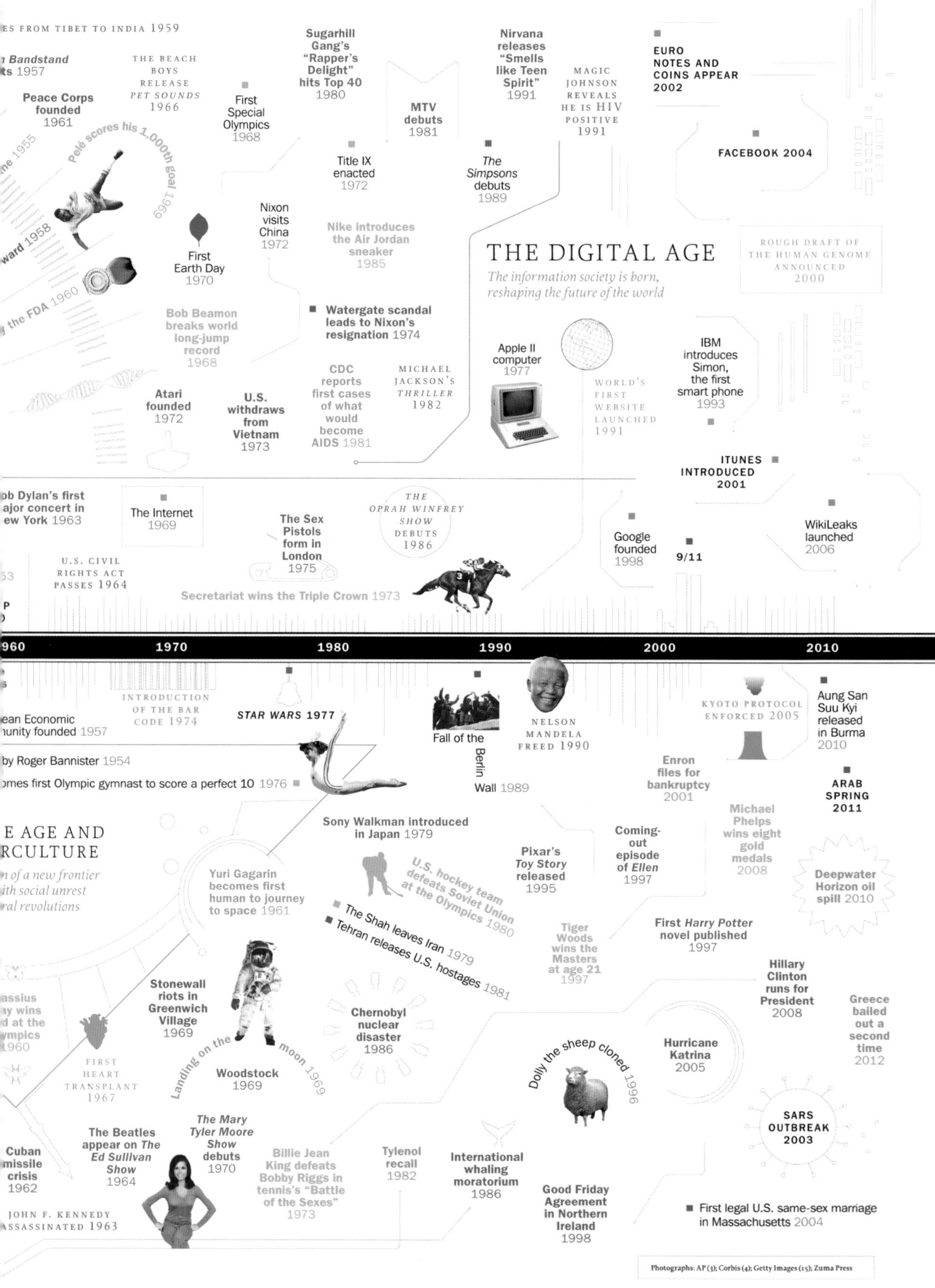
ES FROM TIBET TO INDIA 1959
Bandstand
ts 1957
THE BEACH BOYS RELEASE PET SOUNDS 1966
Peace Corps founded 1961
First Special Olympics 1968
Sugarhill Gang's "Rapper's Delight" hits Top 40 1980
MTV debuts 1981
Nirvana releases "Smells like Teen Spirit" 1991
MAGIC JOHNSON REVEALS HE IS HIV POSITIVE 1991
EURO NOTES AND COINS APPEAR 2002
FACEBOOK 2004
ne 1955
Pelé scores his 1,000th goal 1969
Title IX enacted 1972
The Simpsons debuts 1989
ward 1958
Nixon visits China 1972
First Earth Day 1970
Nike introduces the Air Jordan sneaker 1985
THE DIGITAL AGE
The information society is born, reshaping the future of the world
ROUGH DRAFT OF THE HUMAN GENOME ANNOUNCED 2000
the FDA 1960
Bob Beamon breaks world long-jump record 1968
Watergate scandal leads to Nixon's resignation 1974
Apple II computer 1977
IBM introduces Simon, the first smart phone 1993
WORLD'S FIRST WEBSITE LAUNCHED 1991
Atari founded 1972
U.S. withdraws from Vietnam 1973
CDC reports first cases of what would become AIDS 1981
MICHAEL JACKSON'S THRILLER 1982
ITUNES INTRODUCED 2001
ob Dylan's first ajor concert in ew York 1963
The Internet 1969
The Sex Pistols form in London 1975
THE OPRAH WINFREY SHOW DEBUTS 1986
Google founded 1998
9/11
WikiLeaks launched 2006
U.S. CIVIL RIGHTS ACT PASSES 1964
Secretariat wins the Triple Crown 1973
960
1970
1980
1990
2000
2010
INTRODUCTION OF THE BAR CODE 1974
STAR WARS 1977
Fall of the Berlin Wall 1989
NELSON MANDELA FREED 1990
KYOTO PROTOCOL ENFORCED 2005
Aung San Suu Kyi released in Burma 2010
ean Economic
unity founded 1957
by Roger Bannister 1954
omes first Olympic gymnast to score a perfect 10 1976
Enron files for bankruptcy 2001
ARAB SPRING 2011
Michael Phelps wins eight gold medals 2008
E AGE AND
RCULTURE
n of a new frontier
ith social unrest
ral revolutions
Sony Walkman introduced in Japan 1979
Yuri Gagarin becomes first human to journey to space 1961
U.S. hockey team defeats Soviet Union at the Olympics 1980
Pixar's Toy Story released 1995
Coming-out episode of Ellen 1997
Deepwater Horizon oil spill 2010
The Shah leaves Iran 1979
Tehran releases U.S. hostages 1981
Tiger Woods wins the Masters at age 21 1997
First Harry Potter novel published 1997
Hillary Clinton runs for President 2008
assius
ay wins
d at the
ympics
1960
Stonewall riots in Greenwich Village 1969
Chernobyl nuclear disaster 1986
Greece bailed out a second time 2012
FIRST HEART TRANSPLANT 1967
Landing on the moon 1969
Woodstock 1969
Dolly the sheep cloned 1996
Hurricane Katrina 2005
SARS OUTBREAK 2003
Cuban missile crisis 1962
The Beatles appear on The Ed Sullivan Show 1964
The Mary Tyler Moore Show debuts 1970
Billie Jean King defeats Bobby Riggs in tennis's "Battle of the Sexes" 1973
Tylenol recall 1982
International whaling moratorium 1986
Good Friday Agreement in Northern Ireland 1998
First legal U.S. same-sex marriage in Massachusetts 2004
JOHN F. KENNEDY ASSASSINATED 1963
Photographs: AP (3); Corbis (4); Getty Images (15); Zuma Press

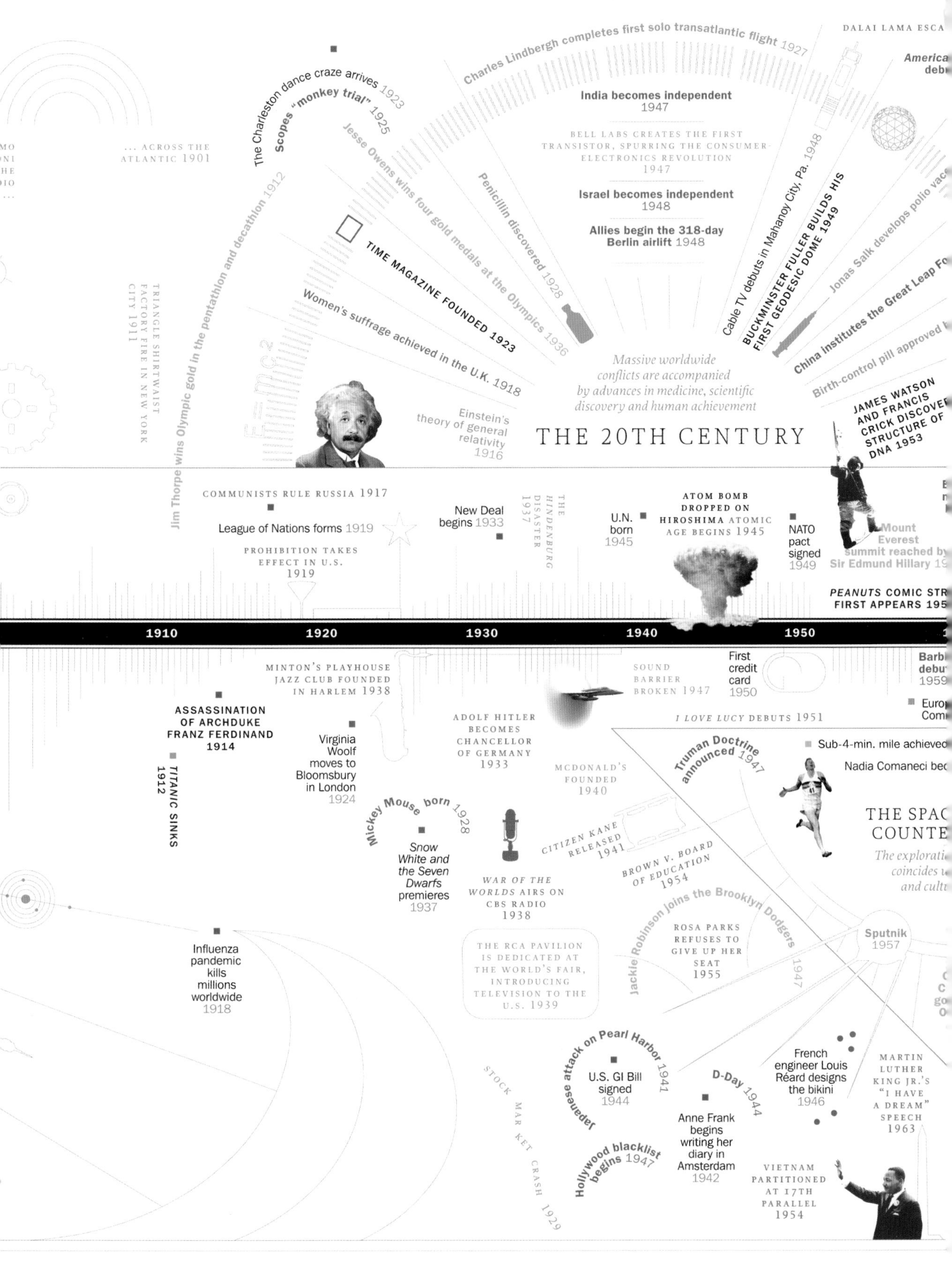
THE 20TH CENTURY
Massive worldwide conflicts are accompanied by advances in medicine, scientific discovery and human achievement
... ACROSS THE ATLANTIC 1901
TRIANGLE SHIRTWAIST FACTORY FIRE IN NEW YORK CITY 1911
Jim Thorpe wins Olympic gold in the pentathlon and decathlon 1912
The Charleston dance craze arrives 1923
Scopes "monkey trial" 1925
Jesse Owens wins four gold medals at the Olympics 1936
TIME MAGAZINE FOUNDED 1923
Women's suffrage achieved in the U.K. 1918
Einstein's theory of general relativity 1916
Penicillin discovered 1928
Charles Lindbergh completes first solo transatlantic flight 1927
India becomes independent 1947
BELL LABS CREATES THE FIRST TRANSISTOR, SPURRING THE CONSUMER-ELECTRONICS REVOLUTION 1947
Israel becomes independent 1948
Allies begin the 318-day Berlin airlift 1948
Cable TV debuts in Mahanoy City, Pa. 1948
BUCKMINSTER FULLER BUILDS HIS FIRST GEODESIC DOME 1949
Jonas Salk develops polio vac
China institutes the Great Leap Fo
Birth-control pill approved
JAMES WATSON AND FRANCIS CRICK DISCOVER STRUCTURE OF DNA 1953
DALAI LAMA ESCA
America deb
COMMUNISTS RULE RUSSIA 1917
League of Nations forms 1919
PROHIBITION TAKES EFFECT IN U.S. 1919
New Deal begins 1933
THE HINDENBURG DISASTER 1937
U.N. born 1945
ATOM BOMB DROPPED ON HIROSHIMA ATOMIC AGE BEGINS 1945
NATO pact signed 1949
Mount Everest summit reached by Sir Edmund Hillary 19
PEANUTS COMIC STR FIRST APPEARS 195
1910
1920
1930
1940
1950
MINTON'S PLAYHOUSE JAZZ CLUB FOUNDED IN HARLEM 1938
ASSASSINATION OF ARCHDUKE FRANZ FERDINAND 1914
TITANIC SINKS 1912
Virginia Woolf moves to Bloomsbury in London 1924
ADOLF HITLER BECOMES CHANCELLOR OF GERMANY 1933
SOUND BARRIER BROKEN 1947
First credit card 1950
Barbi debu 1959
Euro Com
I LOVE LUCY DEBUTS 1951
MCDONALD'S FOUNDED 1940
Truman Doctrine announced 1947
Sub-4-min. mile achieved
Nadia Comaneci bec
THE SPAC COUNTE
The explorati coincides w and cult
Mickey Mouse born 1928
Snow White and the Seven Dwarfs premieres 1937
WAR OF THE WORLDS AIRS ON CBS RADIO 1938
CITIZEN KANE RELEASED 1941
BROWN V. BOARD OF EDUCATION 1954
Jackie Robinson joins the Brooklyn Dodgers 1947
ROSA PARKS REFUSES TO GIVE UP HER SEAT 1955
Sputnik 1957
Influenza pandemic kills millions worldwide 1918
THE RCA PAVILION IS DEDICATED AT THE WORLD'S FAIR, INTRODUCING TELEVISION TO THE U.S. 1939
Japanese attack on Pearl Harbor 1941
U.S. GI Bill signed 1944
Hollywood blacklist begins 1947
D-Day 1944
Anne Frank begins writing her diary in Amsterdam 1942
French engineer Louis Réard designs the bikini 1946
MARTIN LUTHER KING JR.'S "I HAVE A DREAM" SPEECH 1963
VIETNAM PARTITIONED AT 17TH PARALLEL 1954
STOCK MARKET CRASH 1929

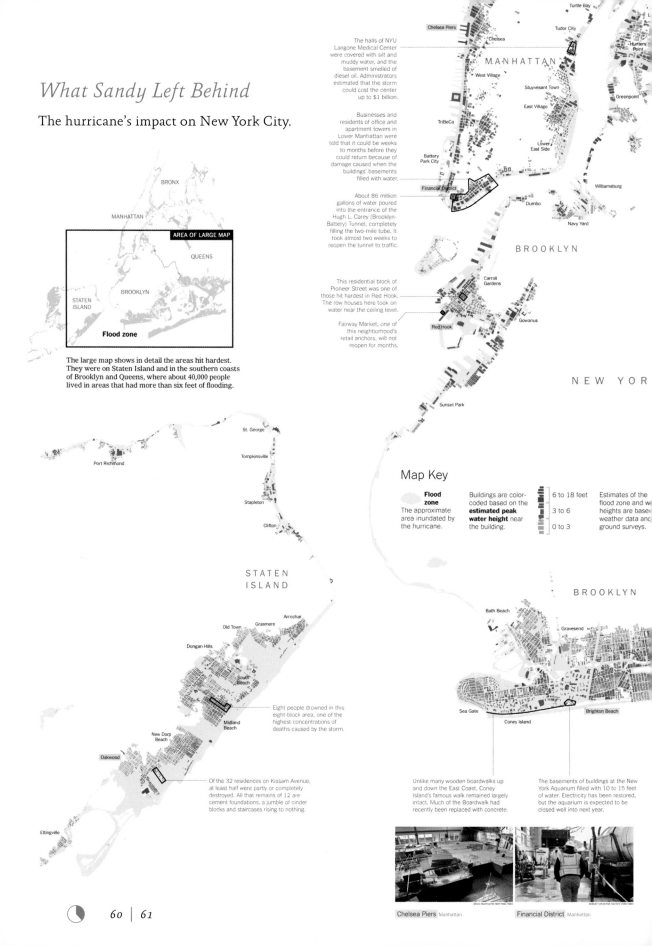

What Sandy Left Behind

The hurricane's impact on New York City.

BRONX
MANHATTAN
AREA OF LARGE MAP
QUEENS
BROOKLYN
STATEN ISLAND
Flood zone

The large map shows in detail the areas hit hardest. They were on Staten Island and in the southern coasts of Brooklyn and Queens, where about 40,000 people lived in areas that had more than six feet of flooding.

Turtle Bay
Chelsea Piers
Chelsea
Tudor City
Hunters Point
MANHATTAN
West Village
Stuyvesant Town
Greenpoint
East Village
TriBeCa
Lower East Side
Battery Park City
Financial District
Williamsburg
Dumbo
Navy Yard
BROOKLYN

The halls of NYU Langone Medical Center were covered with silt and muddy water, and the basement smelled of diesel oil. Administrators estimated that the storm could cost the center up to $1 billion.

Businesses and residents of office and apartment towers in Lower Manhattan were told that it could be weeks to months before they could return because of damage caused when the buildings' basements filled with water.

About 86 million gallons of water poured into the entrance of the Hugh L. Carey (Brooklyn-Battery) Tunnel, completely filling the two-mile tube. It took almost two weeks to reopen the tunnel to traffic.

Carroll Gardens

This residential block of Pioneer Street was one of those hit hardest in Red Hook. The row houses here took on water near the ceiling level.

Fairway Market, one of this neighborhood's retail anchors, will not reopen for months.

Red Hook

Gowanus

NEW YOR

Sunset Park

Map Key

Flood zone The approximate area inundated by the hurricane.

Buildings are color-coded based on the **estimated peak water height** near the building.

6 to 18 feet
3 to 6
0 to 3

Estimates of the flood zone and w heights are base weather data anc ground surveys.

St. George
Port Richmond
Tompkinsville
Stapleton
Clifton
STATEN ISLAND
Arrochar
Old Town
Grasmere
Dongan Hills
South Beach
Midland Beach
New Dorp Beach
Oakwood
Eltingville

Eight people drowned in this eight-block area, one of the highest concentrations of deaths caused by the storm.

Of the 32 residences on Kissam Avenue, at least half were partly or completely destroyed. All that remains of 12 are cement foundations, a jumble of cinder blocks and staircases rising to nothing.

BROOKLYN
Bath Beach
Gravesend
Sea Gate
Coney Island
Brighton Beach

Unlike many wooden boardwalks up and down the East Coast, Coney Island's famous walk remained largely intact. Much of the Boardwalk had recently been replaced with concrete.

The basements of buildings at the New York Aquarium filled with 10 to 15 feet of water. Electricity has been restored, but the aquarium is expected to be closed well into next year.

Chelsea Piers Manhattan

Financial District Manhattan

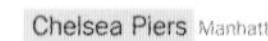

QUEENS

ARTIST Archie Tse, the *New York Times.*

STATEMENT Few anticipated the scale of destruction Hurricane Sandy would bring to New York City. The storm surge topped seventeen feet in some parts, and some neighborhoods in all five boroughs saw floodwaters higher than six feet. We wanted to show readers just how widespread the flooding was and how many people were affected. We gathered flood data from FEMA and combined it with data we had on building footprints and property tax parcels. Once we crunched the data, we found that nearly one in ten New Yorkers saw some flooding, a rate that surprised even those of us who had been covering the storm.

PUBLICATION *New York Times* (November 21, 2012)

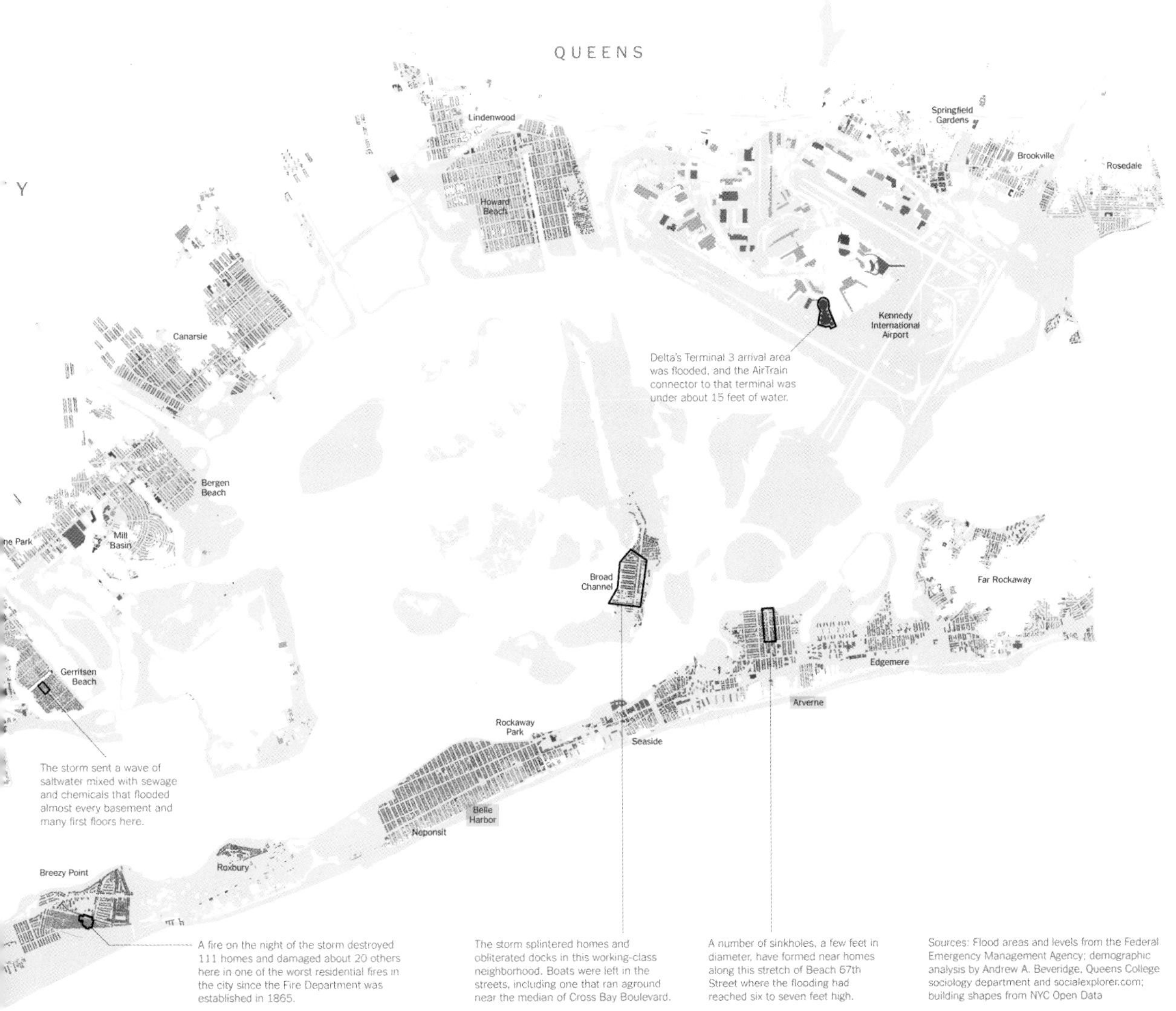

QUEENS

Lindenwood

Howard Beach

Springfield Gardens

Brookville

Rosedale

Canarsie

Kennedy International Airport

Delta's Terminal 3 arrival area was flooded, and the AirTrain connector to that terminal was under about 15 feet of water.

Bergen Beach

Mill Basin

Broad Channel

Far Rockaway

Edgemere

Arverne

Gerritsen Beach

Rockaway Park

Seaside

The storm sent a wave of saltwater mixed with sewage and chemicals that flooded almost every basement and many first floors here.

Belle Harbor

Neponsit

Roxbury

Breezy Point

A fire on the night of the storm destroyed 111 homes and damaged about 20 others here in one of the worst residential fires in the city since the Fire Department was established in 1865.

The storm splintered homes and obliterated docks in this working-class neighborhood. Boats were left in the streets, including one that ran aground near the median of Cross Bay Boulevard.

A number of sinkholes, a few feet in diameter, have formed near homes along this stretch of Beach 67th Street where the flooding had reached six to seven feet high.

Sources: Flood areas and levels from the Federal Emergency Management Agency; demographic analysis by Andrew A. Beveridge, Queens College sociology department and socialexplorer.com; building shapes from NYC Open Data

Red Hook Brooklyn

Oakwood Staten Island

Brighton Beach Brooklyn

Belle Harbor Queens

Arverne Queens

ELECTION 2012 In Brief

gaffe
n.
1: a social or diplomatic blunder
2: a noticeable mistake
3: "when a politician tells the truth" —Michael Kinsley

HAPLESS

The Gaffe

President
really do say t
We ranked t

RYAN
"I had a 2-hour-and-50-some-thing."
Aug. 22, 2012, when asked about his personal best marathon time, which was actually just over four hours

OBAMA
"Voting is the best revenge."
Nov. 2, 2012, trying to motivate Ohio supporters who had booed Romney; the GOP nominee responded by encouraging voters to "vote for love of country"

HUNTSMAN
"When's the delivery food coming?"
Oct. 24, 2011, on *The Colbert Report*, after the show played Chinese-sounding music; the comment, intended to be a joke, was blasted in the blogo-sphere

CAIN
"Ubeki-beki-beki-beki-stan-stan."
Oct. 10, 2011, admitting that he didn't know the President of Uzbekistan because, he explained, it's a "small, insignificant state" that isn't worthy of U.S. attention

ROMNEY
"Rick, I'll tell you what—10,000 bucks. $10,000 bet."
Dec. 10, 2011, in response to Perry's assertion that he was for individual mandates before he was against them

OBAMA
"The private sector is doing fine."
June 8, 2012, explaining that the economy was slowly improving; Republicans used the comment to argue that Obama doesn't understand reality

SANTORUM
"I don't want to make black people's lives better."
Jan. 1, 2012, taking a dig at those who he says abuse the welfare and Medicaid systems; Santorum later said he was misunder-stood

GINGRICH
"I don't think right-wing social engineer-ing is any more desirable than left-wing social engi-neer-ing."
May 15, 2011, criticizing changes to Medicare in Ryan's budget

OBAMA
"After my election, I have more flexibility."
March 26, 2012, asking then Russian President Dmitri Medvedev or "space" on missile-defense negotiations, when Obama thought nobody else was listening

ROMNEY
"I like being able to fire people."
Jan. 9, 2012, arguing that Americans should be allowed to switch insurance companies if they're not happy with their coverage; Democrats used the lin to reinforce their image of Romne as a cold calculatir busines man

The Ultimate Oopses

George Romney said he was "brainwashed" by military brass over the Vietnam War

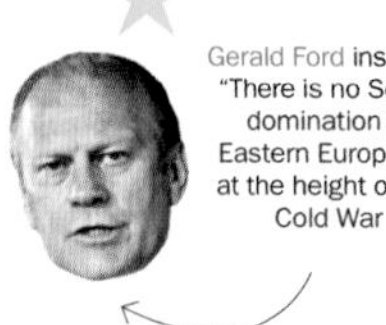
Gerald Ford insisted, "There is no Soviet domination of Eastern Europe"—at the height of the Cold War

Ronald Reagan alleged that most air pollution comes from "plants and trees"

What Not to Say on the Campaign Trail

Gaffes from the presidential election, rated by severity.

ARTISTS Heather Jones, Nick Carbone, Dan Macsai, and Nate Rawlings, *Time*.

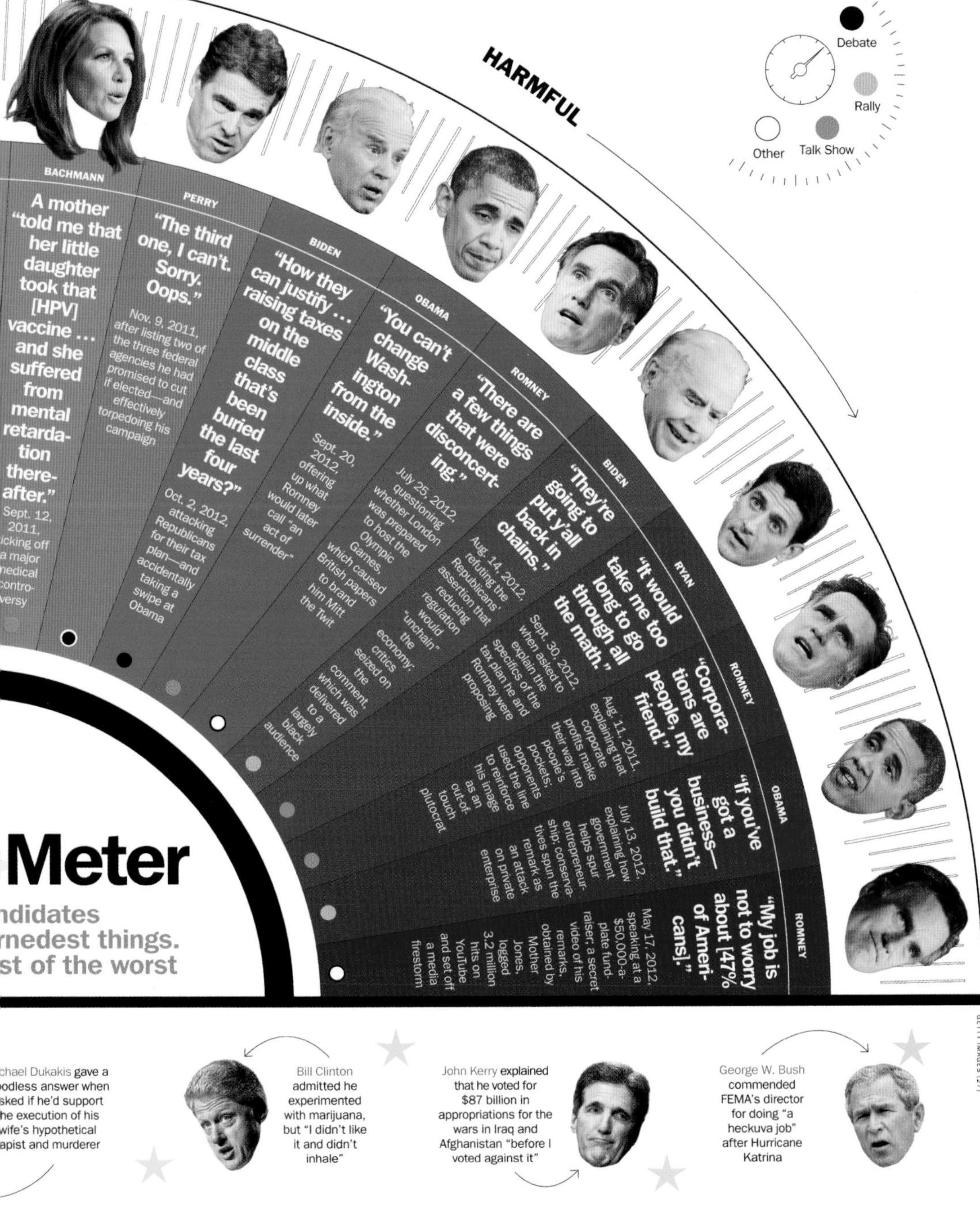

HARMFUL
Debate
Rally
Talk Show
Other
BACHMANN
A mother "told me that her little daughter took that [HPV] vaccine ... and she suffered from mental retarda-tion there-after."
Sept. 12, 2011, kicking off a major medical contro-versy
PERRY
"The third one, I can't. Sorry. Oops."
Nov. 9, 2011, after listing two of the three federal agencies he had promised to cut if elected—and effectively torpedoing his campaign
BIDEN
"How they can justify ... raising taxes on the middle class that's been buried the last four years?"
Oct. 2, 2012, attacking Republicans for their tax plan—and accidentally taking a swipe at Obama
OBAMA
"You can't change Wash-ington from the inside."
Sept. 20, 2012, offering up what Romney would later call "an act of surrender"
ROMNEY
"There are a few things that were disconcert-ing."
July 25, 2012, questioning whether London was prepared to host the Olympic Games, which caused British papers to brand him Mitt the Twit
BIDEN
"They're going to put y'all back in chains."
Aug. 14, 2012, refuting the Republicans' assertion that reducing regulation would "unchain" the economy; critics seized on the comment, which was delivered to a largely black audience
RYAN
"It would take me too long to go through all the math."
Sept. 30, 2012, when asked to explain the specifics of the tax plan he and Romney were proposing
ROMNEY
"Corpora-tions are people, my friend."
Aug. 11, 2011, explaining that corporate profits make their way into people's pockets; opponents used the line to reinforce his image as an out-of-touch plutocrat
OBAMA
"If you've got a business—you didn't build that."
July 13, 2012, explaining how government helps spur entrepreneur-ship; conserva-tives spun the remark as an attack on private enterprise
ROMNEY
"My job is not to worry about [47% of Ameri-cans]."
May 17, 2012, speaking at a $50,000-a-plate fund-raiser; a secret video of his remarks, obtained by Mother Jones, logged 3.2 million hits on YouTube and set off a media firestorm
Meter
ndidates
rnedest things.
st of the worst
chael Dukakis gave a oodless answer when sked if he'd support he execution of his wife's hypothetical apist and murderer
Bill Clinton admitted he experimented with marijuana, but "I didn't like it and didn't inhale"
John Kerry explained that he voted for $87 billion in appropriations for the wars in Iraq and Afghanistan "before I voted against it"
George W. Bush commended FEMA's director for doing "a heckuva job" after Hurricane Katrina
GETTY IMAGES (27)

STATEMENT I was inspired by vintage pinwheels of early Americana that were popular as toys, educational guides, recipe charts, sports trivia meters, etc., and tried to use that look to structure the heads and quotes in a playful way. At first I had a bright, candy-colored key with loads of Joe Biden, Mitt Romney, and Herman Cain quotes and labels such as "Tame" or "Not Enough Caffeine," all the way to "Extremely Uncomfortable to Watch," but we edited these to make them more neutral. Then we simplified the color tints down to "Hapless to Harmful" and added a quick definition, a short historical timeline, and a smaller wheel with the places where the gaffes happened.

PUBLICATION *Time* (November 7, 2012)

SPRINGFIELD IS A MADDENING MESS. COLD, HARD METRICS CLEAN IT UP.

HOW TO BUILD AN NBA HALL OF FAME? FIRST, DEFINE WHAT IT IS—AND ISN'T.
stars and those who played before the 1946 birth of the BAA (all of whom
Rating (see below) and added 36 more (19 active, 17 retired) who did. The

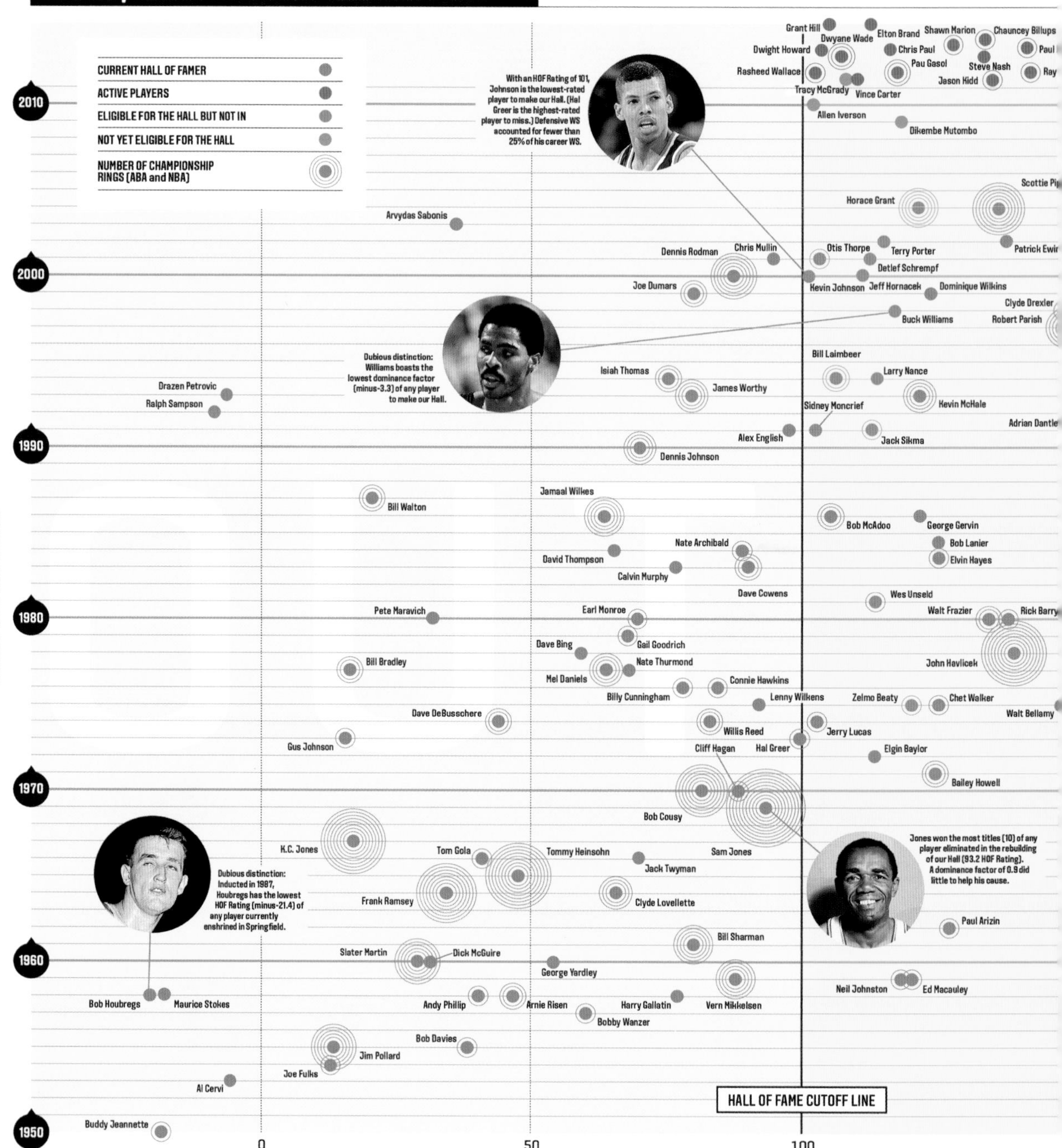

CURRENT HALL OF FAMER
ACTIVE PLAYERS
ELIGIBLE FOR THE HALL BUT NOT IN
NOT YET ELIGIBLE FOR THE HALL
NUMBER OF CHAMPIONSHIP RINGS (ABA and NBA)
With an HOF Rating of 101, Johnson is the lowest-rated player to make our Hall. (Hal Greer is the highest-rated player to miss.) Defensive WS accounted for fewer than 25% of his career WS.
Dubious distinction: Williams boasts the lowest dominance factor (minus-3.3) of any player to make our Hall.
Dubious distinction: Inducted in 1987, Houbregs has the lowest HOF Rating (minus-21.4) of any player currently enshrined in Springfield.
Jones won the most titles (10) of any player eliminated in the rebuilding of our Hall (93.2 HOF Rating). A dominance factor of 0.9 did little to help his cause.
YEAR OF LAST NBA SEASON
2010
2000
1990
1980
1970
1960
1950
0
50
100
HALL OF FAME RATING
HALL OF FAME CUTOFF LINE
Grant Hill
Dwyane Wade
Elton Brand
Shawn Marion
Chauncey Billups
Dwight Howard
Chris Paul
Paul
Rasheed Wallace
Pau Gasol
Steve Nash
Ray
Jason Kidd
Tracy McGrady
Vince Carter
Allen Iverson
Dikembe Mutombo
Scottie Pi
Horace Grant
Arvydas Sabonis
Dennis Rodman
Chris Mullin
Otis Thorpe
Terry Porter
Patrick Ewir
Detlef Schrempf
Joe Dumars
Kevin Johnson
Jeff Hornacek
Dominique Wilkins
Clyde Drexler
Buck Williams
Robert Parish
Bill Laimbeer
Isiah Thomas
Larry Nance
Drazen Petrovic
James Worthy
Kevin McHale
Ralph Sampson
Sidney Moncrief
Adrian Dantle
Alex English
Jack Sikma
Dennis Johnson
Jamaal Wilkes
Bill Walton
Bob McAdoo
George Gervin
Nate Archibald
Bob Lanier
David Thompson
Elvin Hayes
Calvin Murphy
Dave Cowens
Wes Unseld
Pete Maravich
Earl Monroe
Walt Frazier
Rick Barry
Dave Bing
Gail Goodrich
Bill Bradley
Nate Thurmond
John Havlicek
Mel Daniels
Connie Hawkins
Billy Cunningham
Lenny Wilkens
Zelmo Beaty
Chet Walker
Dave DeBusschere
Walt Bellamy
Willis Reed
Jerry Lucas
Gus Johnson
Cliff Hagan
Hal Greer
Elgin Baylor
Bailey Howell
Bob Cousy
K.C. Jones
Tom Gola
Tommy Heinsohn
Sam Jones
Jack Twyman
Frank Ramsey
Clyde Lovellette
Paul Arizin
Bill Sharman
Slater Martin
Dick McGuire
George Yardley
Neil Johnston
Ed Macauley
Bob Houbregs
Maurice Stokes
Andy Phillip
Arnie Risen
Harry Gallatin
Vern Mikkelsen
Bobby Wanzer
Bob Davies
Jim Pollard
Joe Fulks
Al Cervi
Buddy Jeannette

The Basketball Hall of Fame—Fixed

Statistics to the rescue.

e 156 players now enshrined in Springfield, we cut 57 on demographics alone: female players, international-only
e deserving of their own Hall). From there, we cut the 55 who didn't clear our threshold of a 100 Hall of Fame
lly of inductees into *The Mag*'s NBA Hall? A nice round 80—that is, until we enshrine Kevin Durant in two years.

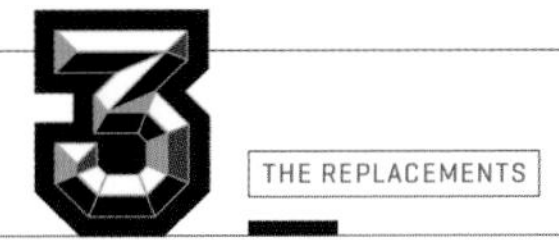

THE REPLACEMENTS

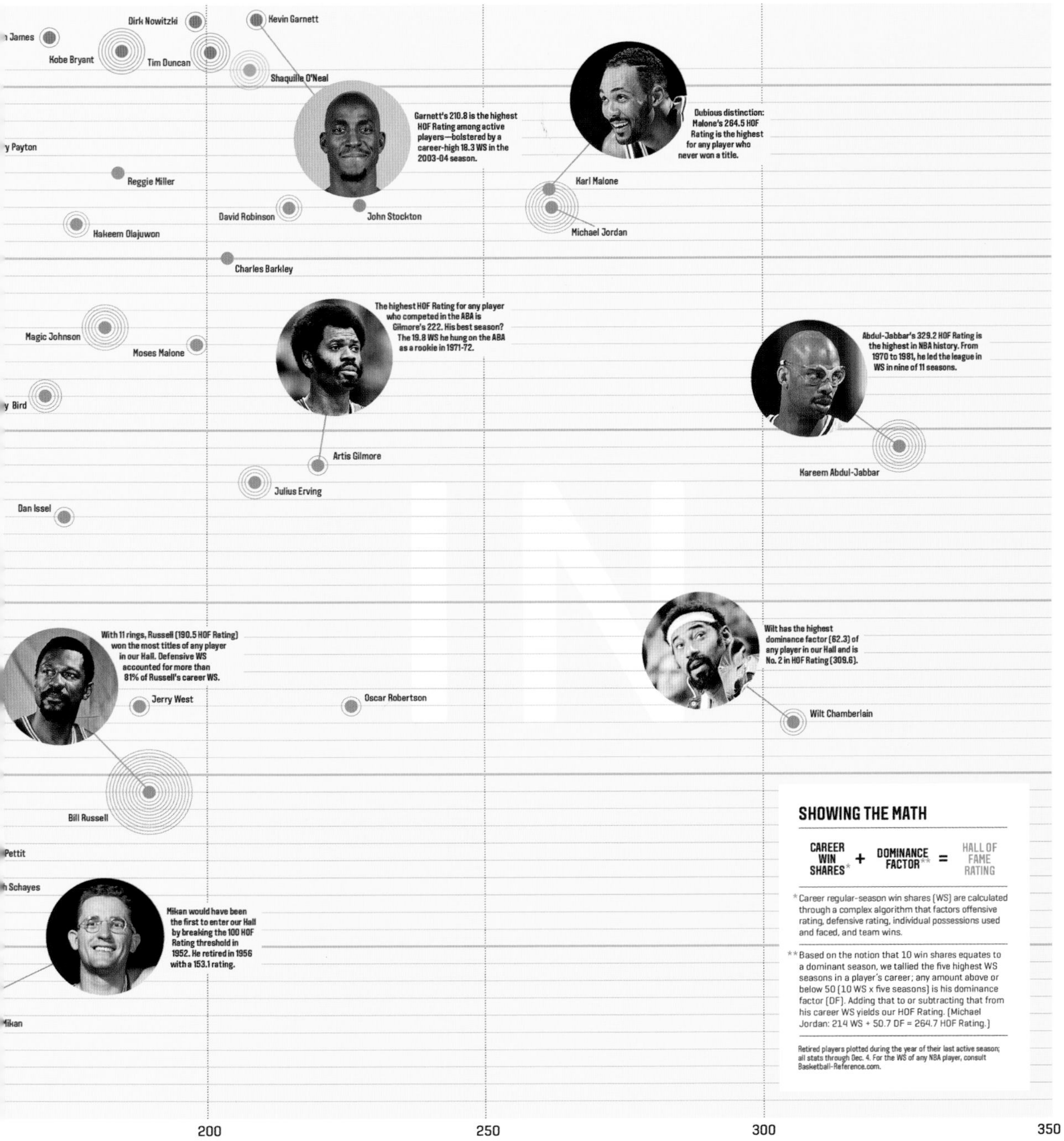

n James
Dirk Nowitzki
Kevin Garnett
Kobe Bryant
Tim Duncan
Shaquille O'Neal
Garnett's 210.8 is the highest HOF Rating among active players—bolstered by a career-high 18.3 WS in the 2003-04 season.
Dubious distinction: Malone's 264.5 HOF Rating is the highest for any player who never won a title.
y Payton
Reggie Miller
Karl Malone
David Robinson
John Stockton
Hakeem Olajuwon
Michael Jordan
Charles Barkley
The highest HOF Rating for any player who competed in the ABA is Gilmore's 222. His best season? The 19.8 WS he hung on the ABA as a rookie in 1971-72.
Magic Johnson
Moses Malone
Abdul-Jabbar's 329.2 HOF Rating is the highest in NBA history. From 1970 to 1981, he led the league in WS in nine of 11 seasons.
y Bird
Artis Gilmore
Kareem Abdul-Jabbar
Julius Erving
Dan Issel
IN
With 11 rings, Russell (190.5 HOF Rating) won the most titles of any player in our Hall. Defensive WS accounted for more than 81% of Russell's career WS.
Wilt has the highest dominance factor (62.3) of any player in our Hall and is No. 2 in HOF Rating (309.6).
Jerry West
Oscar Robertson
Wilt Chamberlain
Bill Russell
Pettit
h Schayes
Mikan would have been the first to enter our Hall by breaking the 100 HOF Rating threshold in 1952. He retired in 1956 with a 153.1 rating.
Mikan
200
250
300
350

SHOWING THE MATH

CAREER WIN SHARES* + DOMINANCE FACTOR** = HALL OF FAME RATING

* Career regular-season win shares (WS) are calculated through a complex algorithm that factors offensive rating, defensive rating, individual possessions used and faced, and team wins.

** Based on the notion that 10 win shares equates to a dominant season, we tallied the five highest WS seasons in a player's career; any amount above or below 50 (10 WS x five seasons) is his dominance factor (DF). Adding that to or subtracting that from his career WS yields our HOF Rating. (Michael Jordan: 214 WS + 50.7 DF = 264.7 HOF Rating.)

Retired players plotted during the year of their last active season; all stats through Dec. 4. For the WS of any NBA player, consult Basketball-Reference.com.

ARTISTS Carl DeTorres, Carl DeTorres Graphic Design in Oakland, California; Munehito Sawada, John Korpics, Jason Lancaster, Bruce Kelley, Ty Wenger, Ross Marrinson, Anthony Olivieri, and Jim Keller, *ESPN The Magazine.*

STATEMENT Working with stats pioneer Dean Oliver, we developed a hall of fame rating. This spread shows which players eclipsed our statistical threshold.

PUBLICATION *ESPN The Magazine* (December 24, 2012)

The Last Forty-Five Seconds

A 3-D drawing of the Florida neighborhood in the moments before Trayvon Martin's death as well as an acoustic forensic analysis of the 911 recording.

A timeline of the moments before Trayvon Martin's death, as outl

Shortcut from street
Clubhouse and mailboxes
Main gat
entran
RETREAT-VIEW CIRCLE
TWIN TREES LANE
TWIN TREES LANE

7:09:34 p.m. *7:10:30* *7:11:41*

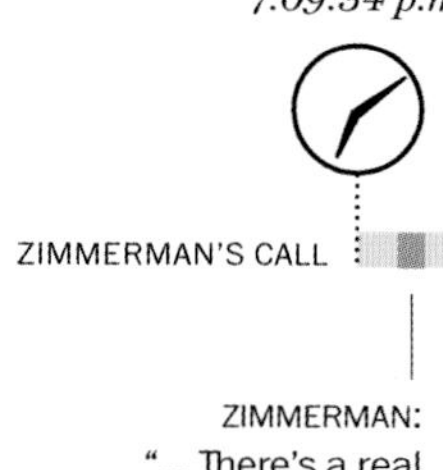

ZIMMERMAN'S CALL

ZIMMERMAN: "... There's a real suspicious guy. It's Retreat View Circle."

ZIMMERMAN: "... He was just staring ..."
DISPATCHER: "... He's just walking around the area?"
ZIMMERMAN: "... looking at all the houses."

DISPATCHER: "He's near the clubhouse right now?"
ZIMMERMAN: "Yeah, now he's coming towards me."

ZIMMERMAN: "... He's running. ... Down towards the other entrance of the neighborhood."
DISPATCHER: "Are you following him
ZIMMERMAN: "Yup."
DISPATCHER: "Okay, we don't need you to do that."

wo calls to the police, by George Zimmerman and an unidentified woman.

proximate area of
nmerman's parked truck.

Approximate location where Trayvon Martin's body was found lying face down.

OREGON AVENUE
Cut-through
RETREAT VIEW CIRCLE
:38
Direction to house where Martin was staying
7:16:11
7:16:56
CALL ENDS
WOMAN'S CALL

Screams and cries

Caller to dispatcher "There's gunshots. ... Just one."

Gap of two minutes, 33 seconds between calls to the police

One expert's view

"There's someone screaming outside. ... I think they're yelling 'help.'"

During the recorded 911 call made by an undentified woman, the sounds of a conflict — a series of seemingly unintelligible cries and shouts from outside her townhouse — can be heard.

Alan R. Reich, a forensic acoustics consultant retained by The Washington Post, analyzed the recording to determine, if possible, what was said and by whom. One of his examinations focused on the final scream just before the gunshot. The one-syllable word being screamed has been interpreted by some as "Help."

Reich concluded the word was "Stop!" based on various forensic acoustics techniques.

CONTINUED

ARTIST Todd Lindeman, a visual journalist at the *Washington Post.*

STATEMENT The science of speech is a fascinating and difficult topic to explain. At first—as more of a curiosity factor—we recorded several of our colleagues saying "Stop" and "Help" and used spectrographic analysis freeware, available online, to generate an image of the spoken words. We shared our findings with an acoustic forensics consultant hired by the *Post,* who then provided his own analysis of the recordings. The results were used to illustrate the science of speech—and to demonstrate how the words "Stop" and "Help" might differ.

PUBLICATION *Washington Post* (May 20, 2012)

Unidentified caller
"Yes"

"Stop"

911 dispatcher
"All right, what is ..."

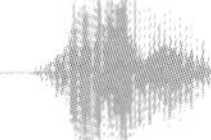

The waveform image (above) represents nearly two seconds of the 911 recording.

REICH'S ANALYSIS

Reich relies heavily on critical listening when examining evidence tapes. Reich amplified this 394-millisecond portion of the audio using computer software. After listening to the segment several hundred times, he perceived the '*a*' phoneme — a linguistic part of a spoken word — pronounced by the 'o' vowel (which sounds like the '*a*' in father).

Reich writes, "When interactively scaled up or amplified by a 10x factor, the word appears to be "stop" not "help" as previously perceived by listeners."

SPECTROGRAPHIC ANALYSIS

Reich also uses acoustic analysis software to create a spectrograph, a visual representation of sound that measures frequencies, time and sound intensity. The intensity is indicated by color — white is the loudest; black represents no intensity. Forensic acoustics experts can use spectrographs to identify phonetic sounds.

REICH'S SPECTROGRAPH OF THE WORD HE CONCLUDED WAS "STOP"

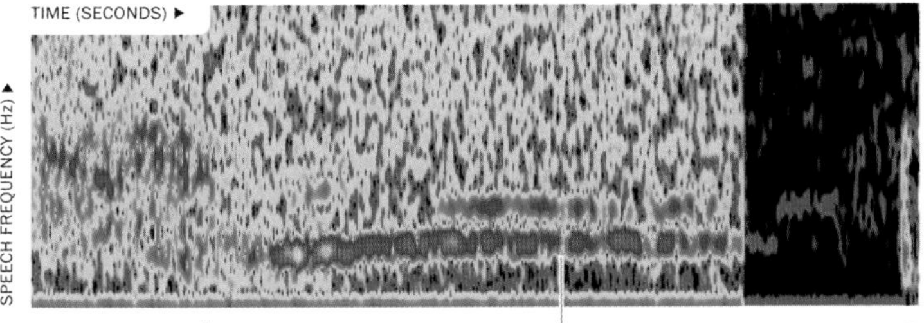
TIME (SECONDS) ▶
SPEECH FREQUENCY (Hz) ▶

Phonetic spelling: *s* *t* *a* Second closure *p*

PHONETICS

Reich used phonetics and speech sounds — how a spoken consonant, vowel or a combination of phonemes are articulated — to try to recognize distinct patterns in the spectrograph:

"Closure"

This gap depicts a micro transition between voiced sounds. A break is caused by a blockage of airflow. As the phoneme "*t*" is pronounced, the tongue touches the upper teeth and blocks air from flowing out of the mouth and nose.

"Formants"

This band of energy depicts the frequency at which the vocal cords vibrate as an '*a*' sound is pronounced. Since vowels require air to pass from the lungs through the vocal cords, the airflow causes the cords to vibrate. Vowels typically have two to four formants that look like oscillating "caterpillars."

"Stop plosive"

This pattern depicts a short, highly explosive noise burst produced by the rapid release of air built up behind the lips as the letter '*p*' is pronounced.

"Stop" vs. "Help"

To illustrate how the words "stop" and "help" might differ in spectrographic analysis, The Washington Post recorded someone saying each word. Using those recordings, Reich generated these two spectrographs:

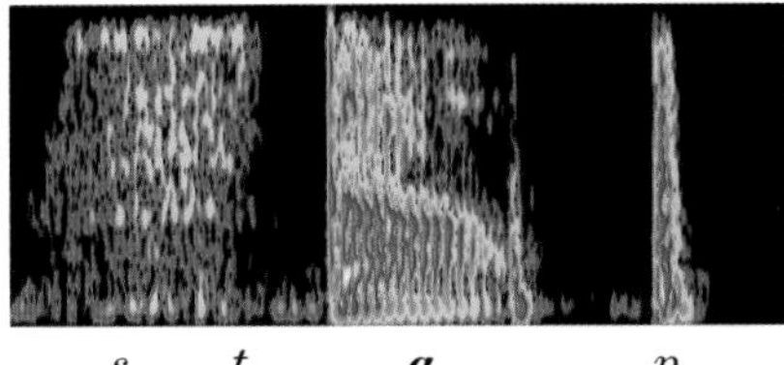

s *t* *a* *p*

As an '*s*' is pronounced, clenched teeth restrict airflow. This blockage creates turbulence, which is displayed on a spectrograph as a louder, higher-intensity sound that has a wider range of frequencies.

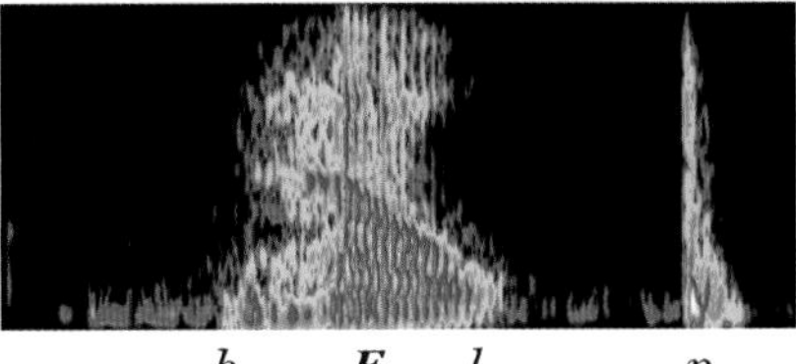

h *E* *l* *p*

Pronouncing an '*h*' is similar to exhaling, as it is spoken with an open mouth. Airflow is low, which means little turbulence and less noise are produced. The phoneme typically has little to no pattern on a spectrograph.

Source: Alan R. Reich, PhD, forensic acoustics expert and former University of Washington professor

TODD LINDEMAN/THE WASHINGTON POST

Obama Was Not as Strong as in 2008, bu

Most demographic groups are less enchanted with President Obama than they once were, but his winning coa

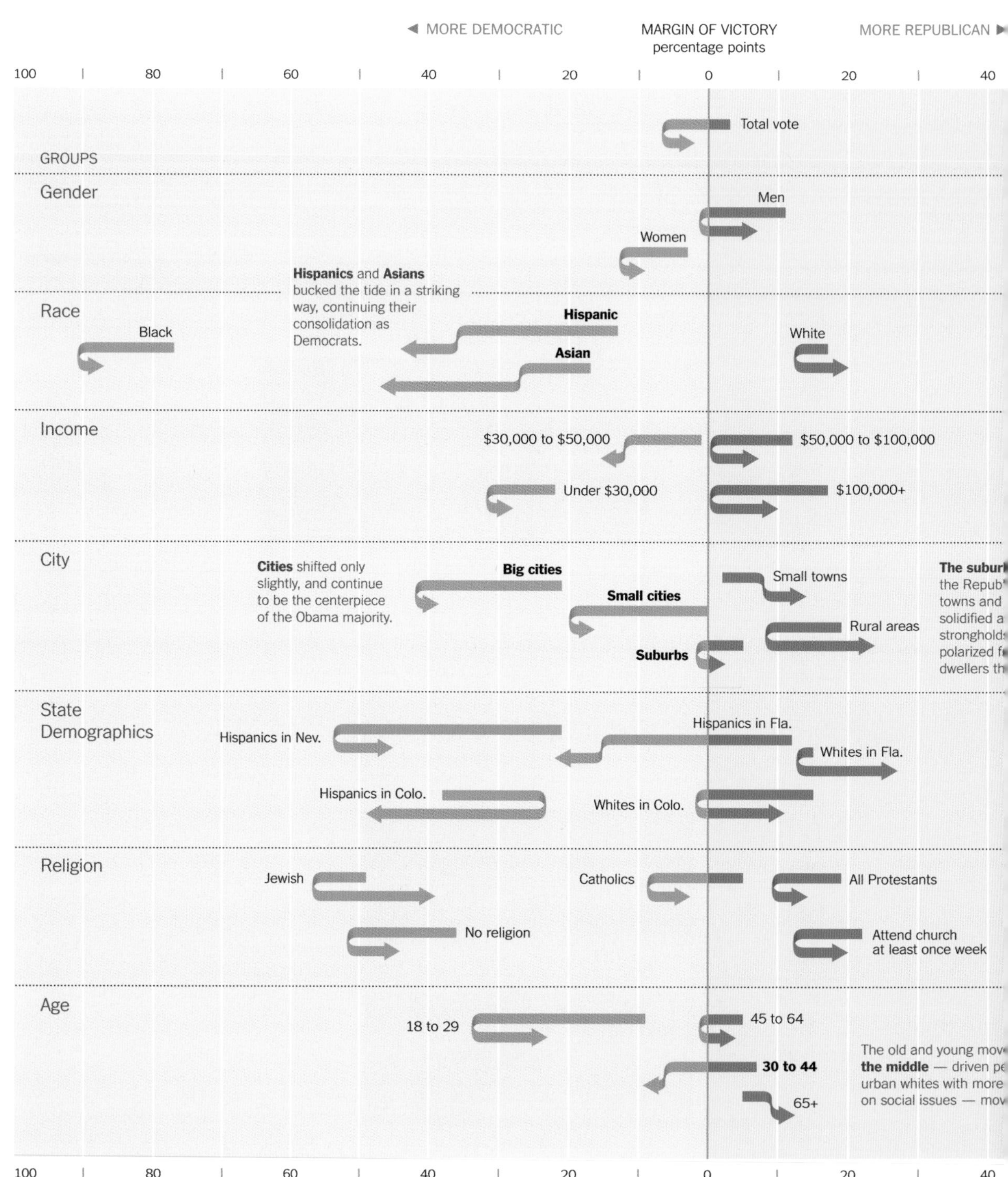
◀ MORE DEMOCRATIC
MARGIN OF VICTORY
percentage points
MORE REPUBLICAN ▶
100
80
60
40
20
0
20
40
Total vote
GROUPS
Gender
Men
Women
Race
Hispanics and Asians bucked the tide in a striking way, continuing their consolidation as Democrats.
Black
Hispanic
Asian
White
Income
$30,000 to $50,000
$50,000 to $100,000
Under $30,000
$100,000+
City
Cities shifted only slightly, and continue to be the centerpiece of the Obama majority.
Big cities
Small cities
Suburbs
Small towns
Rural areas
State Demographics
Hispanics in Nev.
Hispanics in Fla.
Whites in Fla.
Hispanics in Colo.
Whites in Colo.
Religion
Jewish
Catholics
All Protestants
No religion
Attend church at least once week
Age
18 to 29
45 to 64
30 to 44
65+
The old and young mov
the middle — driven pe
urban whites with more
on social issues — mov

Source: Edison Research exit polls

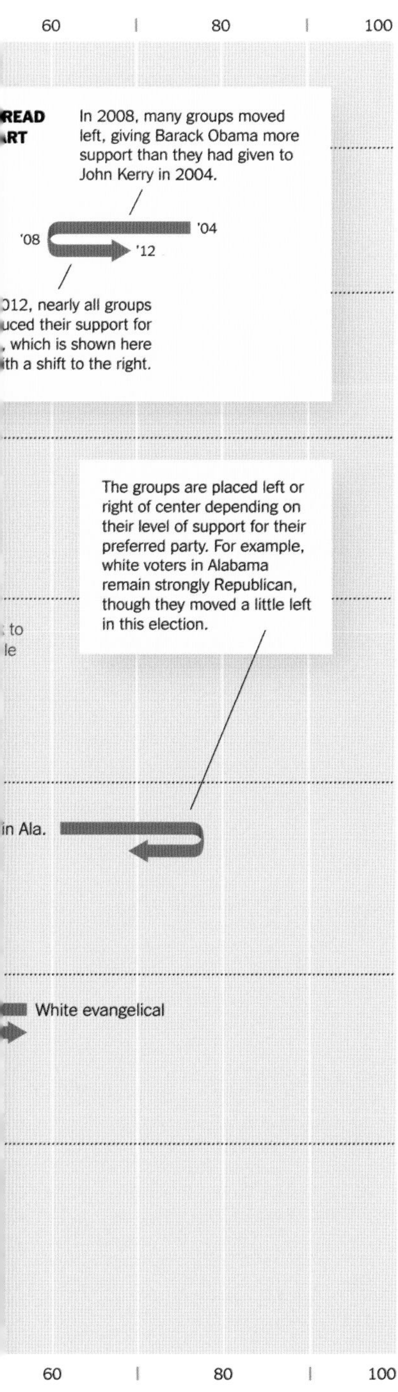

trong Enough
s intact.
60
80
100
In 2008, many groups moved left, giving Barack Obama more support than they had given to John Kerry in 2004.
'08
'04
'12
nearly all groups
which is shown here
The groups are placed left or right of center depending on their level of support for their preferred party. For example, white voters in Alabama remain strongly Republican, though they moved a little left in this election.
in Ala.
White evangelical
60
80
100
AMANDA COX, FORD FESSENDEN AND ALICIA DESANTIS/THE NEW YORK TIMES

Who Gave Obama Victory?

How the president's coalition shifted between the elections of 2008 and 2012.

ARTISTS Amanda Cox, Alicia DeSantis, and Ford Fessenden, the *New York Times*.

STATEMENT We knew that this data told an important story about shifts in voting patterns—the challenge was to come up with a graphic style that made that story accessible. It's a somewhat unfamiliar charting form, and we worked hard to figure out a labeling system and style that would invite readers in and keep them there long enough to absorb the complexity of the message.

PUBLICATION *New York Times* (November 8, 2012)

American Education Gets a Grade

Some states get an A, and some get an F.

AMERICAN SCHOOLS

A National Report Card

By Nicole Allan | Graphics by Kiss Me I'm Polish

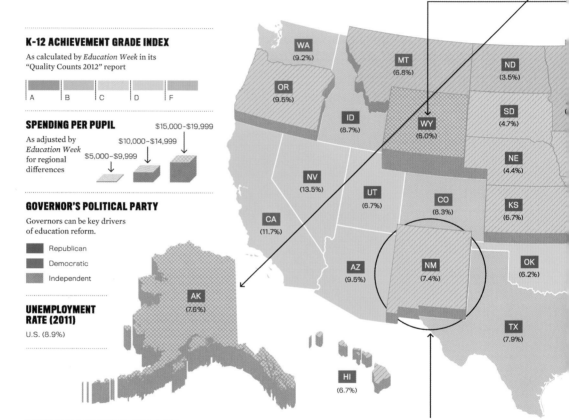

K-12 ACHIEVEMENT GRADE INDEX

As calculated by *Education Week* in its "Quality Counts 2012" report

A | B | C | D | F

SPENDING PER PUPIL

As adjusted by *Education Week* for regional differences

$5,000-$9,999 | $10,000-$14,999 | $15,000-$19,999

GOVERNOR'S POLITICAL PARTY

Governors can be key drivers of education reform.

Republican

Democratic

Independent

UNEMPLOYMENT RATE (2011)

U.S. (8.9%)

WA (9.2%)
OR (9.5%)
MT (6.8%)
ND (3.5%)
ID (8.7%)
WY (6.0%)
SD (4.7%)
NE (4.4%)
NV (13.5%)
UT (6.7%)
CO (8.3%)
KS (6.7%)
CA (11.7%)
AZ (9.5%)
NM (7.4%)
OK (6.2%)
TX (7.9%)
AK (7.6%)
HI (6.7%)

THE CASE OF NEW MEXICO

In 2011, researchers at the Center for American Progress calculated educational return on investment (ROI), district by district. They found wide variation within states, both in terms of money spent and results obtained.

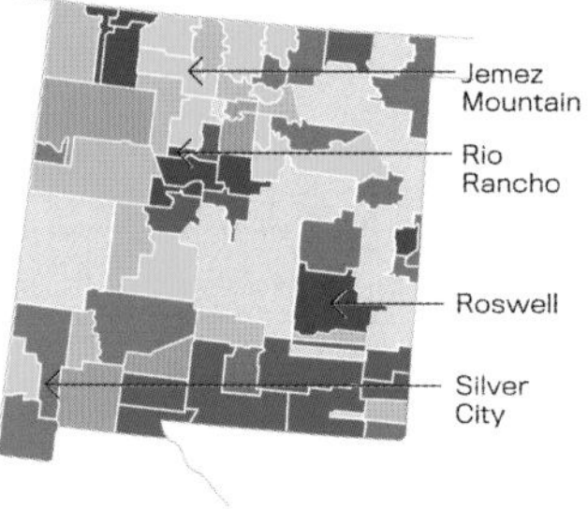

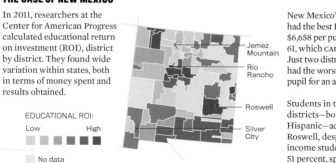

Jemez Mountain
Rio Rancho
Roswell
Silver City

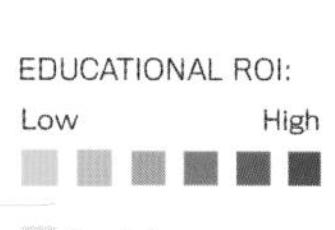

EDUCATIONAL ROI:
Low
High
No data

New Mexico's suburban Rio Rancho district had the best ROI in the state, spending just $6,658 per pupil for an achievement score of 61, which CAP calculated on a scale of 1 to 100. Just two districts away, rural Jemez Mountain had the worst ROI, spending $13,983 per pupil for an achievement score of 25.

Students in the Roswell and Silver City districts—both small, remote, and majority Hispanic—achieved at similar levels. Yet Roswell, despite having 81 percent low-income students compared with Silver City's 51 percent, spent $2,589 less per pupil.

SOURCES: CENTER FOR AMERICAN PROGRESS; COUNCIL OF THE GREAT CITY SCHOOLS; COWEN INSTITUTE; *EDUCATION WEEK*; LOUISIANA DEPARTMENT OF EDUCATION; NATIONAL CENTER FOR EDUCATION STATISTICS; U.S. BUREAU OF LABOR STATISTICS

MORE MONEY, MORE PROBLEMS?

Alaska, Wyoming, and the District of Columbia spend more money per pupil, on a regionally adjusted scale, than almost every other state, yet they get D's or F's in achievement. Seventy percent of the District's students are poor, a factor that drives up its costs, whereas Alaska and Wyoming both struggle to distribute resources to a relatively small number of students spread across vast and isolating geography.

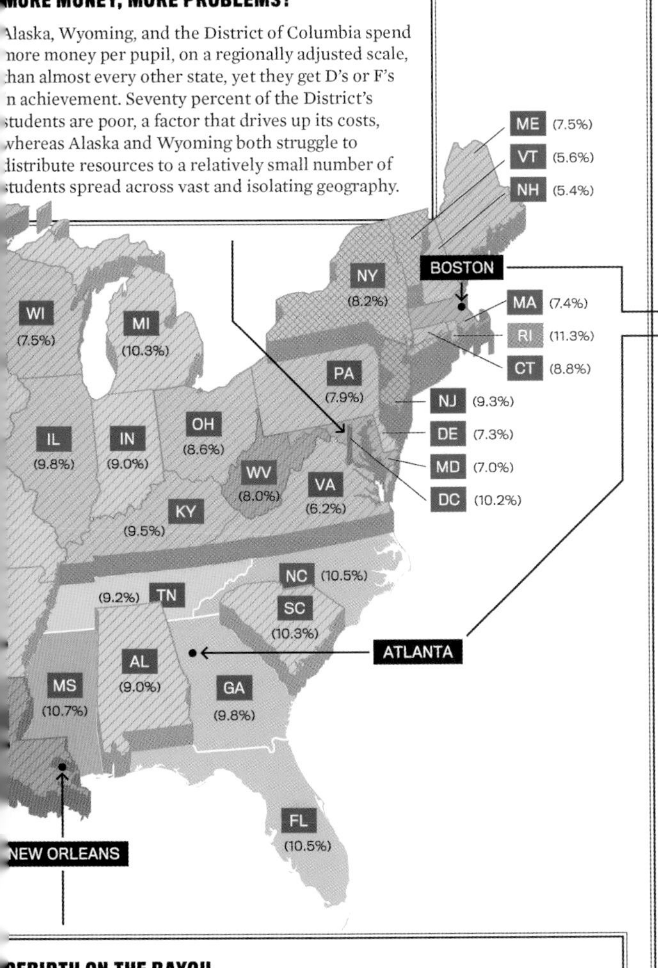
ME (7.5%)
VT (5.6%)
NH (5.4%)
BOSTON
NY (8.2%)
MA (7.4%)
RI (11.3%)
CT (8.8%)
WI (7.5%)
MI (10.3%)
PA (7.9%)
NJ (9.3%)
IL (9.8%)
IN (9.0%)
OH (8.6%)
DE (7.3%)
WV (8.0%)
VA (6.2%)
MD (7.0%)
DC (10.2%)
KY (9.5%)
NC (10.5%)
TN (9.2%)
SC (10.3%)
ATLANTA
AL (9.0%)
MS (10.7%)
GA (9.8%)
FL (10.5%)
NEW ORLEANS

REBIRTH ON THE BAYOU

After Hurricane Katrina, Louisiana transferred most New Orleans schools to the authority of the state-run Recovery School District. With the teachers union effectively obsolete, reform has flourished—about 80 percent of New Orleans students now attend charter schools, the highest proportion in the U.S.—and the city's historically rock-bottom test scores have shot up.

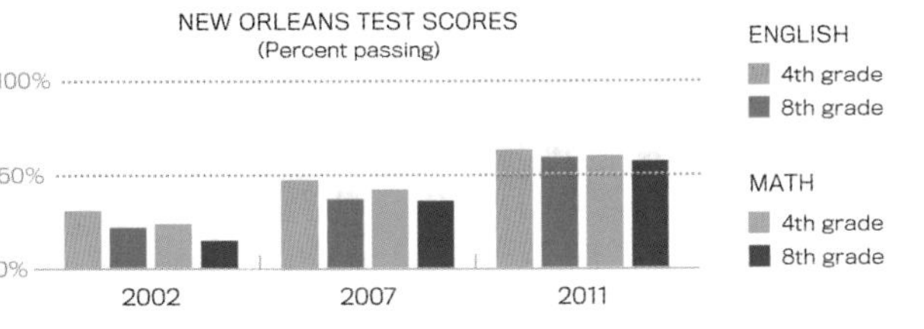
NEW ORLEANS TEST SCORES
(Percent passing)
100%
50%
0%
2002
2007
2011
ENGLISH
4th grade
8th grade
MATH
4th grade
8th grade

CITIES BOUNCE BACK

City schools—dogged by poverty and overcrowding—have traditionally lagged behind their counterparts elsewhere. Achievement in most American cities still trails the national average, but in recent years, urban districts have seen significantly more improvement.

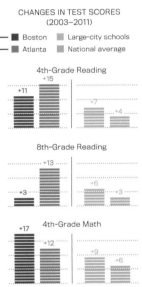

CHANGES IN TEST SCORES (2003–2011)

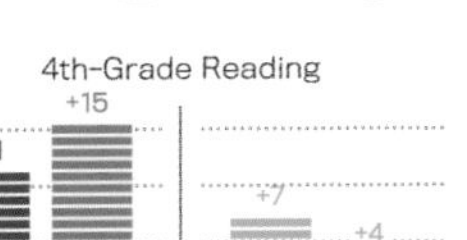
Boston
Atlanta
Large-city schools
National average
4th-Grade Reading
+11
+15
+7
+4

8th-Grade Reading

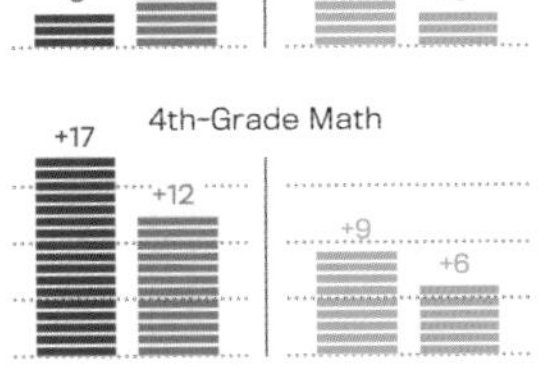
+13
+3
+6
+3
4th-Grade Math
+17
+12
+9
+6

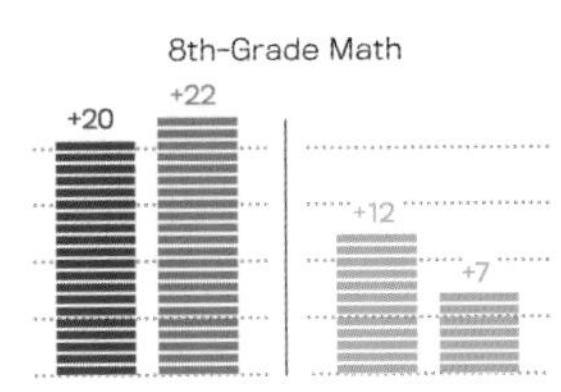
8th-Grade Math
+20
+22
+12
+7

SMART SPENDING PAYS OFF

Atlanta's reading gains and Boston's math gains may be partly attributed to decade-long initiatives in literacy and math, respectively. Boston's program may also have helped narrow its achievement gap: in 2011, the district's black, Hispanic, and poor students all outperformed their national peers in math.

ARTISTS Agnieszka Gasparska of New York design studio Kiss Me I'm Polish; Nicole Allan, senior editor at *The Atlantic*.

STATEMENT Our goal was to convey at a glance how K–12 achievement relates to per pupil spending and party orientation in different states. The core of this design is the map, color-coded and patterned to convey the data. That was the challenge with this design—to find a set of visual cues to allow each state to carry three distinct data points. The solution is what ultimately gives this design all of its color and visual flavor.

PUBLICATION *The Atlantic* (October 2012)

The Breaking Bad *Body Count*

All of the deaths in the first fifty-four episodes of AMC's *Breaking Bad*, with each deceased character represented by a faux chemical formula indicating when he or she died, how they died, and who killed them.

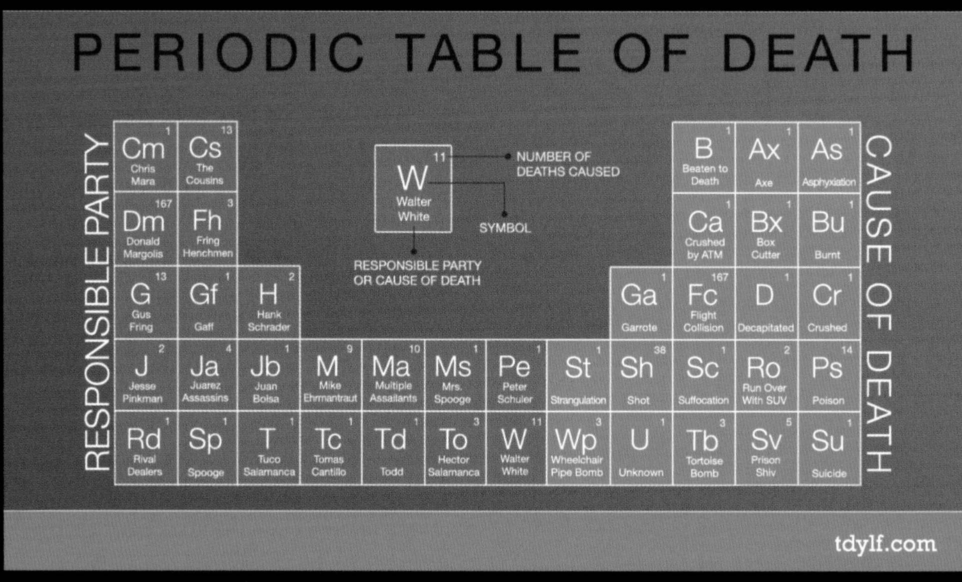
PERIODIC TABLE OF DEATH
RESPONSIBLE PARTY
CAUSE OF DEATH
11 W Walter White
NUMBER OF DEATHS CAUSED
SYMBOL
RESPONSIBLE PARTY OR CAUSE OF DEATH
1 Cm Chris Mara
13 Cs The Cousins
167 Dm Donald Margolis
3 Fh Fring Henchmen
13 G Gus Fring
1 Gf Gaff
2 H Hank Schrader
2 J Jesse Pinkman
4 Ja Juarez Assassins
1 Jb Juan Bolsa
9 M Mike Ehrmantraut
10 Ma Multiple Assailants
1 Ms Mrs. Spooge
1 Pe Peter Schuler
1 Rd Rival Dealers
1 Sp Spooge
1 T Tuco Salamanca
1 Tc Tomas Cantillo
1 Td Todd
3 To Hector Salamanca
11 W Walter White
1 B Beaten to Death
1 Ax Axe
1 As Asphyxiation
1 Ca Crushed by ATM
1 Bx Box Cutter
1 Bu Burnt
1 Ga Garrote
167 Fc Flight Collision
1 D Decapitated
1 Cr Crushed
1 St Strangulation
38 Sh Shot
1 Sc Suffocation
2 Ro Run Over With SUV
14 Ps Poison
3 Wp Wheelchair Pipe Bomb
1 U Unknown
3 Tb Tortoise Bomb
5 Sv Prison Shiv
1 Su Suicide
tdylf.com

ARTIST John D. LaRue, editor, writer, graphic designer, and minister of propaganda for the blog TDYLF, St. Louis, Missouri.

STATEMENT As an avid fan of *Breaking Bad*, I wanted to create something that would allow other fans to remember details they may have forgotten. Given the show's chemistry theme, the chemical death formulas and the "Periodic Table of Death" featured at the bottom meshed well. You will notice in some cases that, instead of a figure of a person, there are icons—the head of a tortoise, a pink teddy bear—which avid fans of the show will appreciate. Everyone else: watch the show.

PUBLICATION *TDYLF* blog (www.tdylf.com) (September 2, 2012, minutes after the *Breaking Bad* season five finale)

THE DEATH TOLL IN Breaking Bad

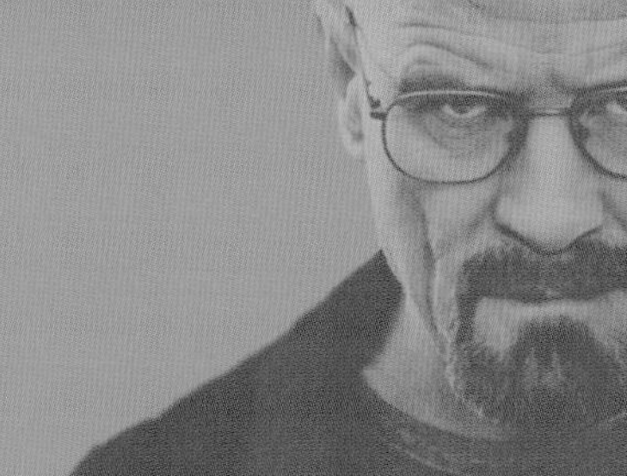

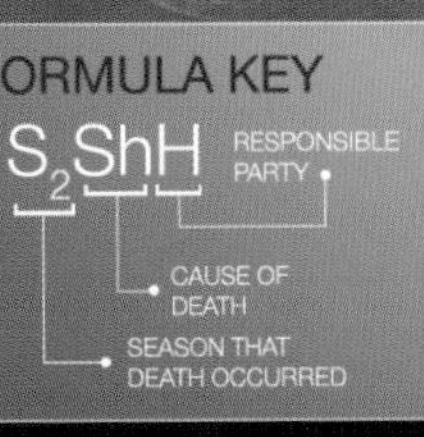
FORMULA KEY
S_2ShH
RESPONSIBLE PARTY
CAUSE OF DEATH
SEASON THAT DEATH OCCURRED

 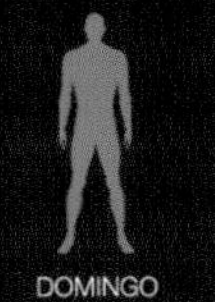 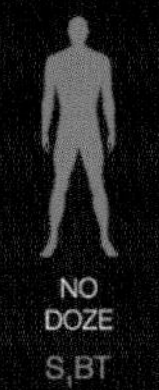 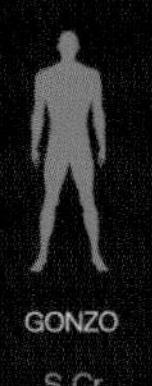  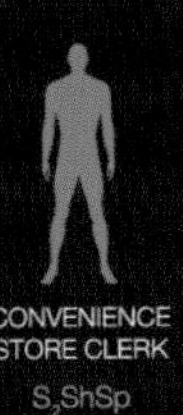 

- EMILIO KOYAMA — S_1PsW
- DOMINGO "KRAZY 8" MOLINA — S_1StW
- NO DOZE — S_1BT
- GONZO — S_2Cr
- TUCO SALAMANCA — S_2ShH
- CONVENIENCE STORE CLERK — S_2ShSp
- SPOOGE — S_2CaMs

 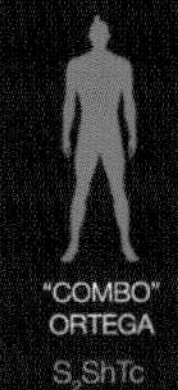 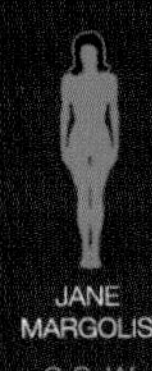      

- TORTUGA — S_2DCs
- UNNAMED DEA AGENT — S_2TbJb
- "COMBO" ORTEGA — S_2ShTc
- JANE MARGOLIS — S_2ScW
- FLIGHT PASSENGERS x167 — S_2FcDm
- TRUCK PASSENGERS x9 — S_3ShCs
- COYOTE DRIVER — S_3ShCs
- MRS. PEYKETEWA — S_3UCs
- DEPUTY BOBBY KEE — S_3AxCs
- UNNAMED MAN — S_3ShCs

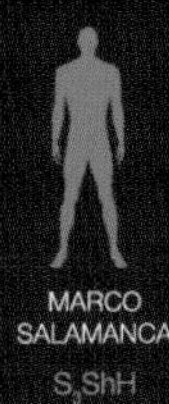     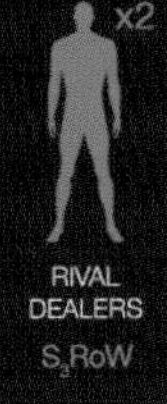    

- MARCO SALAMANCA — S_3ShH
- LEONEL SALAMANCA — S_3PsM
- JUAN BOLSA'S BODYGUARDS x2 — S_3ShFh
- JUAN BOLSA — S_3ShFh
- TOMÁS CANTILLO — S_3ShRd
- RIVAL DEALERS x2 — S_3RoW
- CARTEL ASSASSINS x4 — S_3ShM
- GALE BOETTICHER — S_3ShJ
- VICTOR — S_4BxG
- LOS POLLOS DRIVER — S_4ShJa

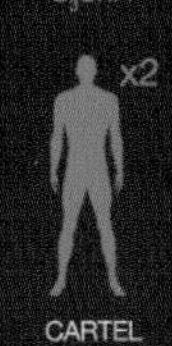     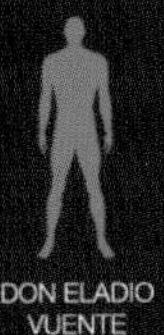   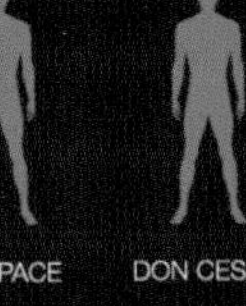 

- CARTEL ASSASSINS #5-6 x2 — S_4ShM
- LOS POLLOS DRIVER #2 — S_4ShJa
- LOS POLLOS GUARDS x2 — S_4ShJa
- MAX ARCINIEGA — S_4ShTo
- FRING HENCHMAN — S_4ShGf
- DON ELADIO VUENTE — S_4PsG
- BENICIO FUENTES — S_4PsG
- MIGUEL — S_4PsG
- DON PACE — S_4PsG
- DON CESAR — S_4PsG

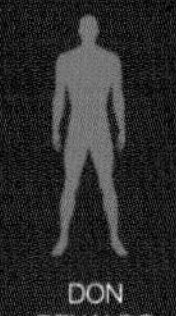    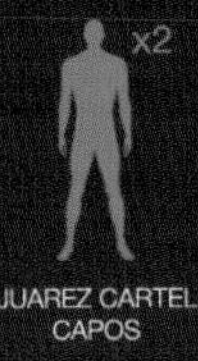  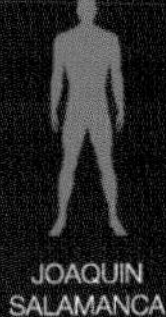  

- DON RENALDO — S_4PsG
- DON FORTUNO — S_4PsG
- DON CISCO — S_4PsG
- DON LUIS — S_4PsG
- DON ESCALARA — S_4PsG
- JUAREZ CARTEL CAPOS x2 — S_4PsG
- GAFF — S_4GaM
- JOAQUIN SALAMANCA — S_4ShJ
- HECTOR SALAMANCA — S_4WpTo
- TYRUS KITT — S_4WpTo

 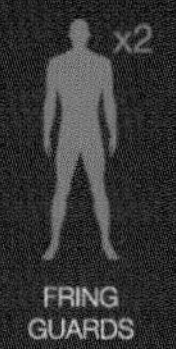 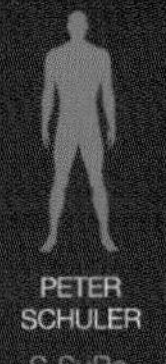   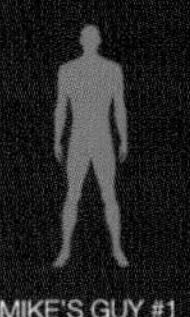 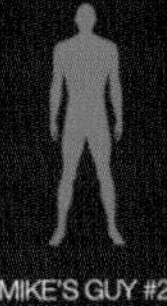

- GUS FRING — S_4WpTo
- FRING GUARDS x2 — S_4ShW
- PETER SCHULER — S_5SuPe
- DUANE CHOW — S_5ShCm
- CHRIS MARA — S_5ShM
- DREW SHARP — S_5ShTd
- MIKE EHRMANTRAUT — S_5ShW
- DAN WACHSBERGER — S_5SvMa
- MIKE'S GUY #1 — S_5BMa
- MIKE'S GUY #2 — S_5BMa

 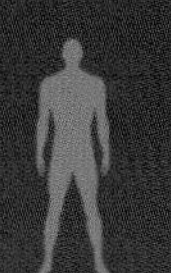 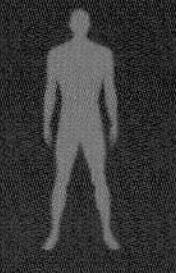  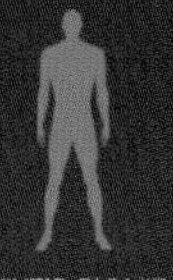  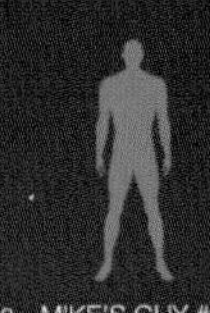   

- MIKE'S GUY #3 — S_5SvMa
- MIKE'S GUY #4 — S_5SvMa
- MIKE'S GUY #5 — S_5SvMa
- MIKE'S GUY #6 — S_5UMa
- MIKE'S GUY #7 — S_5UMa
- MIKE'S GUY #8 — S_5SvMa
- MIKE'S GUY #9 — S_5BuMa

TOTAL NO. OF DEATHS

247

What You Are Buying Now

American consumers reflect the changing economy.

HOW WE SPEND

AND WHAT THAT TELLS US ABOUT THE ECONOMY

By Stephen J. Rose

Graphics by Kiss Me I'm Polish

EVEN AMERICANS WHO think they know where their money goes probably have no idea how their spending compares with that of their parents or grandparents. But such figures yield a surprising picture of how our economy works—and how it's changing. We take for granted, for instance, our much-discussed drift away from manufacturing. Advances in technology and education have created massive productivity gains, which have made things cheaper and easier to obtain. Consider necessities like food and clothing, which gobbled up 42% of our spending in 1947. Six decades later—even in the face of exorbitant spending on frivolities like high-end coffee and designer clothes—food and clothing accounted for only 16% of spending. (In our research, we use 2007 as our end point because some economic relationships have been distorted by our current downturn.) But is spending less on the production of tangible goods such a bad thing? Not necessarily. After all, the shift frees up resources for areas like health care, education, and recreation, where spending has increased.

If we drill down further—to see not just the categories we spend on but where our dollars go within those categories—the picture is even more dramatic. Taking 1967 as our starting point, 30% of the cost of the things we consumed that year went to manufacturing them; by 2007, that figure had fallen to 16%. In contrast, what we spent on business services over the same period jumped from 12% to 26%. That's because baked into the price of everything we buy is the rising cost of advertising, accounting, legal services, insurance, real estate, consulting, and the like—jobs performed by the high-wage workers of our modern economy. These days, 52% of all compensation goes to office workers. That includes the manufacturing sector: nearly a third of workers aren't on the factory floor; they're behind desks.

Stephen J. Rose is a research professor at the Center on Education and the Workforce at Georgetown University. He is a co-author, with Anthony P. Carnevale and Ruy Teixeira, of the forthcoming monograph "Education for What," from which this data was adapted.

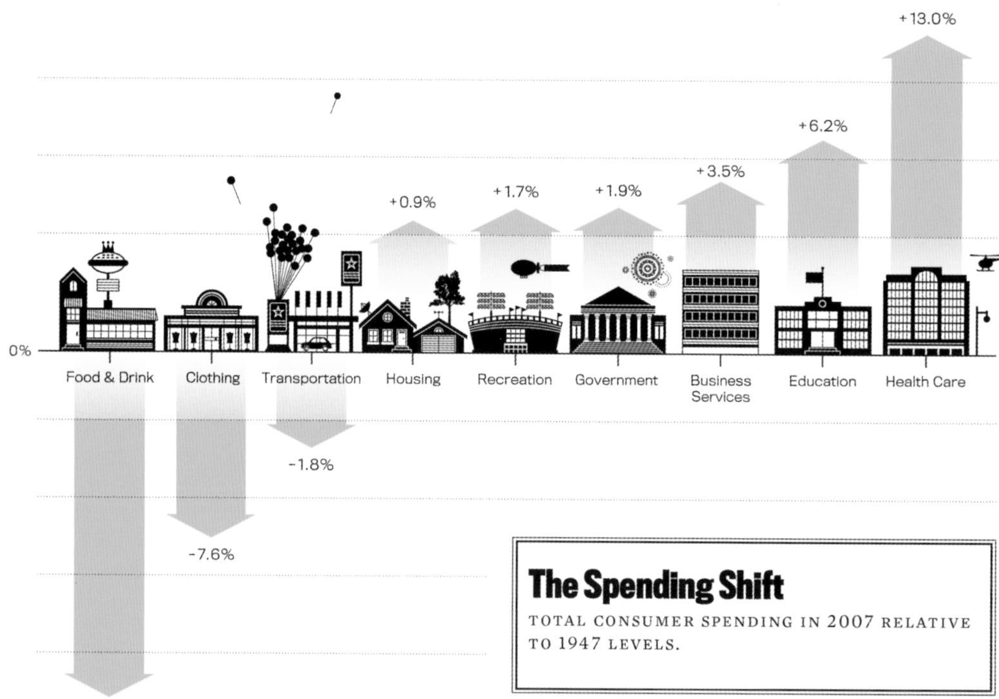
+13.0%
+6.2%
+3.5%
+0.9%
+1.7%
+1.9%
0%
Food & Drink
Clothing
Transportation
Housing
Recreation
Government
Business Services
Education
Health Care
-1.8%
-7.6%
-17.9%

The Spending Shift

TOTAL CONSUMER SPENDING IN 2007 RELATIVE TO 1947 LEVELS.

SOURCES: BUREAU OF ECONOMIC ANALYSIS; U.S. CENSUS BUREAU

1 & Drink
3%
hing
%
sing
9%
sportation
%
reation
%
ernment
%
iness
vices 4.1%
cation
%
th Care
%

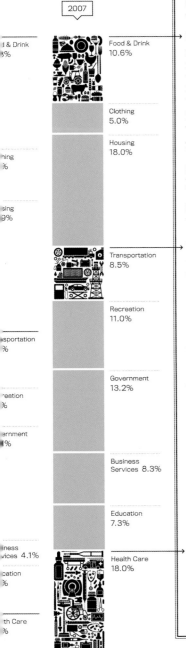

2007
Food & Drink
10.6%
Clothing
5.0%
Housing
18.0%
Transportation
8.5%
Recreation
11.0%
Government
13.2%
Business
Services 8.3%
Education
7.3%
Health Care
18.0%

Breaking It Down

WHERE YOUR DOLLARS ACTUALLY GO

FOOD & DRINK

In 1967, 26% of what we spent on food went to those who made it (farmers and manufacturers), and 6% went to advertisers, lawyers, and other purveyors of business services. In 2007, the business-service people took 15% of spending, while only 14% went to those making the food.

Portion of our food & drink spending going to:

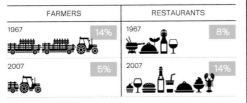

	FARMERS	RESTAURANTS
1967	14%	8%
2007	5%	14%

TRANSPORTATION

Productivity gains give us better automobiles. As a result, we fix them less: repair costs that ate up 7% of our transportation spending in 1967 accounted for less than 2% in 2007. The biggest change has come from the increased complexity of doing business. Costs like legal fees and insurance went from 9% in 1967 to 21% in 2007.

Portion of our transportation spending going to:

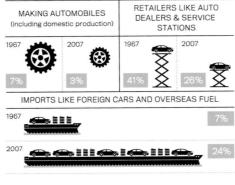

	MAKING AUTOMOBILES (including domestic production)	RETAILERS LIKE AUTO DEALERS & SERVICE STATIONS	IMPORTS LIKE FOREIGN CARS AND OVERSEAS FUEL
1967	7%	41%	7%
2007	3%	26%	24%

HEALTH CARE

Perhaps not surprisingly, health-care spending has grown more than any other category—a fact explained partly by how much education is now required in that field. In 1967, 71% of health-care workers had at most a high-school diploma. Now, almost exactly the same proportion have at least some post-secondary education.

ARTISTS Agnieszka Gasparska of New York design studio Kiss Me I'm Polish; Stephen J. Rose, a research professor at the Center on Education and the Workforce at Georgetown University.

STATEMENT The results remind us—among other things—that the costs of making things or growing them has gone down for Americans. And while this notion that we don't create "things" is frequently remarked upon, the numbers show us something that people sometimes lose sight of: the productivity gains that make things cheaper have led us to create all kinds of jobs thatv in 1947 we wouldn't have ever thought would flourish. More of our money now goes to so-called business services, like advertisers, lawyers, and a variety of other white-collar professionals whose work is now baked into our economy.

What may also not be readily apparent in the final design is how much data was initially gathered and ultimately distilled into this relatively simple layout. Stephen J. Rose provided the team with a vast assortment of data points, numbers, and spreadsheets, and after several attempts at distilling everything into a clear and legible design, we wound up with the final configuration. Interestingly, that hashing-out process took significantly longer than the illustration and visual design that followed. Once everything fell into its right place, the rest was pretty straightforward.

PUBLICATION *The Atlantic* (April 2012)

The Extremely Rich, City by City

What income does it take to join the one percent where you live?

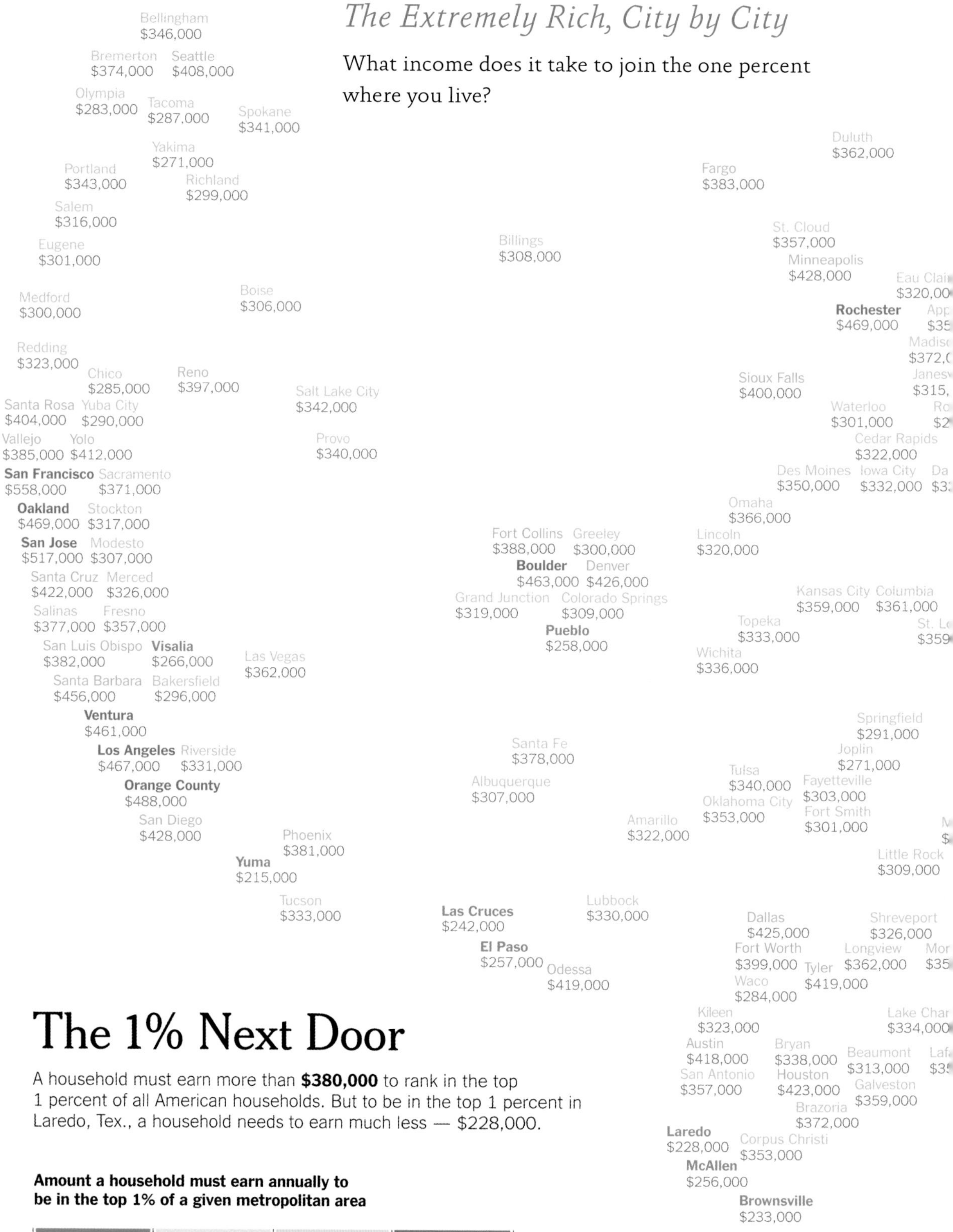

Bellingham $346,000
Bremerton $374,000
Seattle $408,000
Olympia $283,000
Tacoma $287,000
Spokane $341,000
Yakima $271,000
Portland $343,000
Richland $299,000
Salem $316,000
Eugene $301,000
Medford $300,000
Boise $306,000
Redding $323,000
Chico $285,000
Reno $397,000
Salt Lake City $342,000
Santa Rosa $404,000
Yuba City $290,000
Vallejo $385,000
Yolo $412,000
Provo $340,000
San Francisco $558,000
Sacramento $371,000
Oakland $469,000
Stockton $317,000
San Jose $517,000
Modesto $307,000
Santa Cruz $422,000
Merced $326,000
Salinas $377,000
Fresno $357,000
San Luis Obispo $382,000
Visalia $266,000
Las Vegas $362,000
Santa Barbara $456,000
Bakersfield $296,000
Ventura $461,000
Los Angeles $467,000
Riverside $331,000
Orange County $488,000
San Diego $428,000
Phoenix $381,000
Yuma $215,000
Tucson $333,000
Billings $308,000
Fargo $383,000
Duluth $362,000
St. Cloud $357,000
Minneapolis $428,000
Eau Clai $320,00
Rochester $469,000
App $35
Madis $372,
Sioux Falls $400,000
Janes $315,
Waterloo $301,000
Ro $2
Cedar Rapids $322,000
Des Moines $350,000
Iowa City $332,000
Da $3
Omaha $366,000
Fort Collins $388,000
Greeley $300,000
Lincoln $320,000
Boulder $463,000
Denver $426,000
Grand Junction $319,000
Colorado Springs $309,000
Kansas City $359,000
Columbia $361,000
Pueblo $258,000
Topeka $333,000
St. L $359
Wichita $336,000
Springfield $291,000
Santa Fe $378,000
Joplin $271,000
Albuquerque $307,000
Tulsa $340,000
Fayetteville $303,000
Oklahoma City $353,000
Fort Smith $301,000
Amarillo $322,000
Little Rock $309,000
Las Cruces $242,000
Lubbock $330,000
Dallas $425,000
Shreveport $326,000
El Paso $257,000
Fort Worth $399,000
Longview $362,000
Mor $35
Odessa $419,000
Tyler $419,000
Waco $284,000
Kileen $323,000
Lake Char $334,000
Austin $418,000
Bryan $338,000
Beaumont $313,000
Laf $3
San Antonio $357,000
Houston $423,000
Galveston $359,000
Brazoria $372,000
Laredo $228,000
Corpus Christi $353,000
McAllen $256,000
Brownsville $233,000

The 1% Next Door

A household must earn more than **$380,000** to rank in the top 1 percent of all American households. But to be in the top 1 percent in Laredo, Tex., a household needs to earn much less — $228,000.

Amount a household must earn annually to be in the top 1% of a given metropolitan area

$176,000
$266,000
$380,000
$458,000
$908,000

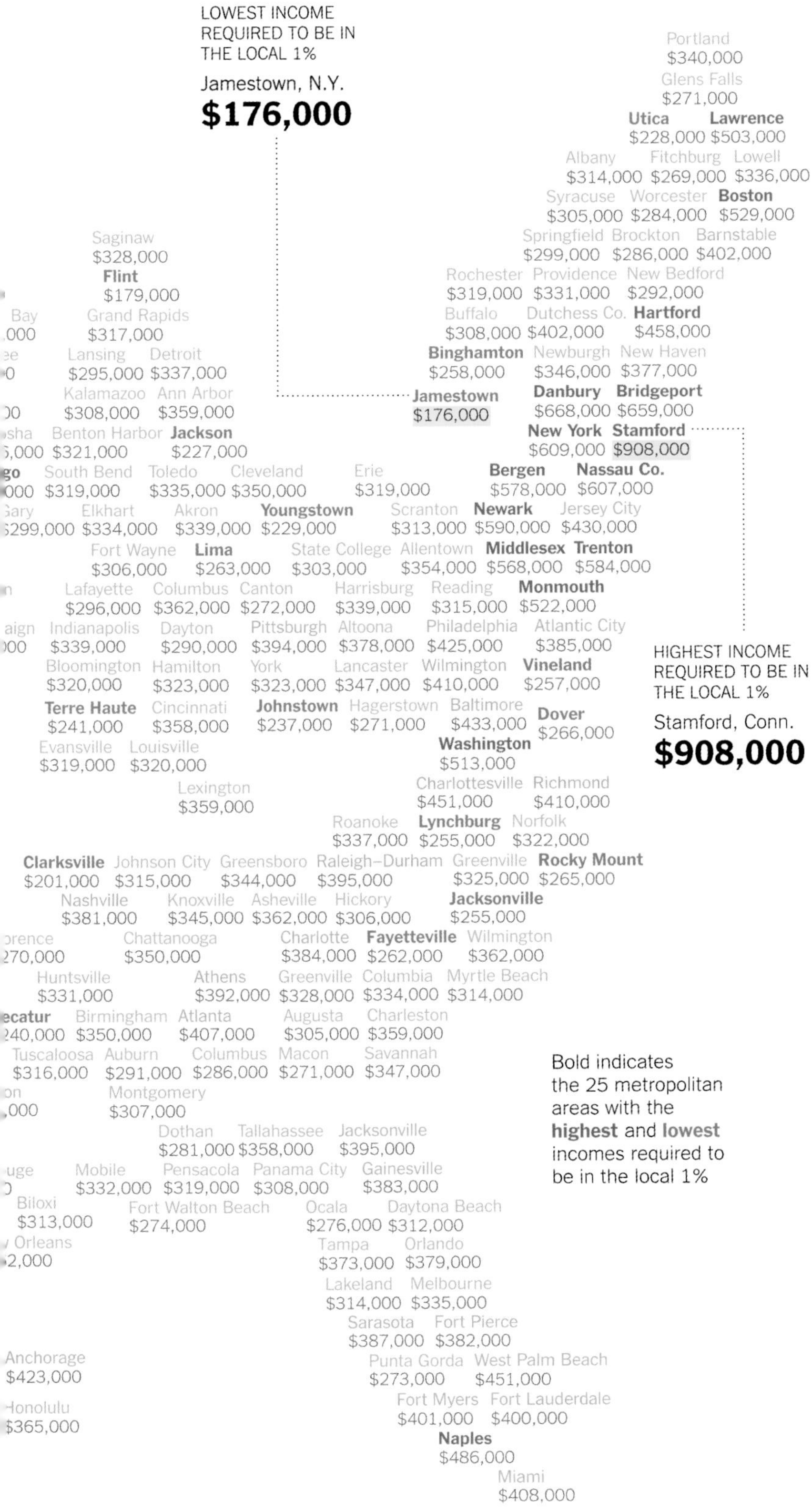

LOWEST INCOME REQUIRED TO BE IN THE LOCAL 1%

Jamestown, N.Y.

$176,000

Portland $340,000
Glens Falls $271,000
Utica $228,000 **Lawrence** $503,000
Albany $314,000 Fitchburg $269,000 Lowell $336,000
Syracuse $305,000 Worcester $284,000 **Boston** $529,000
Saginaw $328,000 Springfield $299,000 Brockton $286,000 Barnstable $402,000
Flint $179,000 Rochester $319,000 Providence $331,000 New Bedford $292,000
Bay ,000 Grand Rapids $317,000 Buffalo $308,000 Dutchess Co. $402,000 **Hartford** $458,000
ee 0 Lansing $295,000 Detroit $337,000 **Binghamton** $258,000 Newburgh $346,000 New Haven $377,000
00 Kalamazoo $308,000 Ann Arbor $359,000 **Jamestown** $176,000 **Danbury** $668,000 **Bridgeport** $659,000
sha ,000 Benton Harbor $321,000 **Jackson** $227,000 **New York** $609,000 **Stamford** $908,000
go 000 South Bend $319,000 Toledo $335,000 Cleveland $350,000 Erie $319,000 **Bergen** $578,000 **Nassau Co.** $607,000
Gary $299,000 Elkhart $334,000 Akron $339,000 **Youngstown** $229,000 Scranton $313,000 **Newark** $590,000 Jersey City $430,000
Fort Wayne $306,000 **Lima** $263,000 State College $303,000 Allentown $354,000 **Middlesex** $568,000 **Trenton** $584,000
n Lafayette $296,000 Columbus $362,000 Canton $272,000 Harrisburg $339,000 Reading $315,000 **Monmouth** $522,000
aign 00 Indianapolis $339,000 Dayton $290,000 Pittsburgh $394,000 Altoona $378,000 Philadelphia $425,000 Atlantic City $385,000
Bloomington $320,000 Hamilton $323,000 York $323,000 Lancaster $347,000 Wilmington $410,000 **Vineland** $257,000
Terre Haute $241,000 Cincinnati $358,000 **Johnstown** $237,000 Hagerstown $271,000 Baltimore $433,000 **Dover** $266,000
Evansville $319,000 Louisville $320,000 **Washington** $513,000
Lexington $359,000 Charlottesville $451,000 Richmond $410,000
Roanoke $337,000 **Lynchburg** $255,000 Norfolk $322,000
Clarksville $201,000 Johnson City $315,000 Greensboro $344,000 Raleigh–Durham $395,000 Greenville $325,000 **Rocky Mount** $265,000
Nashville $381,000 Knoxville $345,000 Asheville $362,000 Hickory $306,000 **Jacksonville** $255,000
orence 270,000 Chattanooga $350,000 Charlotte $384,000 **Fayetteville** $262,000 Wilmington $362,000
Huntsville $331,000 Athens $392,000 Greenville $328,000 Columbia $334,000 Myrtle Beach $314,000
ecatur 240,000 Birmingham $350,000 Atlanta $407,000 Augusta $305,000 Charleston $359,000
Tuscaloosa $316,000 Auburn $291,000 Columbus $286,000 Macon $271,000 Savannah $347,000
on ,000 Montgomery $307,000
Dothan $281,000 Tallahassee $358,000 Jacksonville $395,000
uge 0 Mobile $332,000 Pensacola $319,000 Panama City $308,000 Gainesville $383,000
Biloxi $313,000 Fort Walton Beach $274,000 Ocala $276,000 Daytona Beach $312,000
Orleans 2,000 Tampa $373,000 Orlando $379,000
Lakeland $314,000 Melbourne $335,000
Sarasota $387,000 Fort Pierce $382,000
Anchorage $423,000 Punta Gorda $273,000 West Palm Beach $451,000
Honolulu $365,000 Fort Myers $401,000 Fort Lauderdale $400,000
Naples $486,000
Miami $408,000

HIGHEST INCOME REQUIRED TO BE IN THE LOCAL 1%

Stamford, Conn.

$908,000

Bold indicates the 25 metropolitan areas with the **highest** and **lowest** incomes required to be in the local 1%

Source: New York Times analysis of University of Minnesota Population Center data

ARTISTS Alicia DeSantis, Ford Fessenden, and Rob Gebeloff, the *New York Times.*

STATEMENT The idea for "the local one percent" grew out of our interest in allowing subscribers to *read* the map. We experimented with several different visual approaches—scaled circles, scaled numbers—but the choice to simply assemble a list was our major turning point. Organizing the names geographically required some distortion of the map, but it made great sense as a navigation device. This print piece has some of the qualities of an "interactive" graphic: The reader can find his or her hometown and move on or can investigate at more length.

PUBLICATION *New York Times* (January 15, 2012)

Mixology

A poster-size guide breaks down sixty-nine drinks into their constituent parts. Also included: the proper ratios and serving glasses.

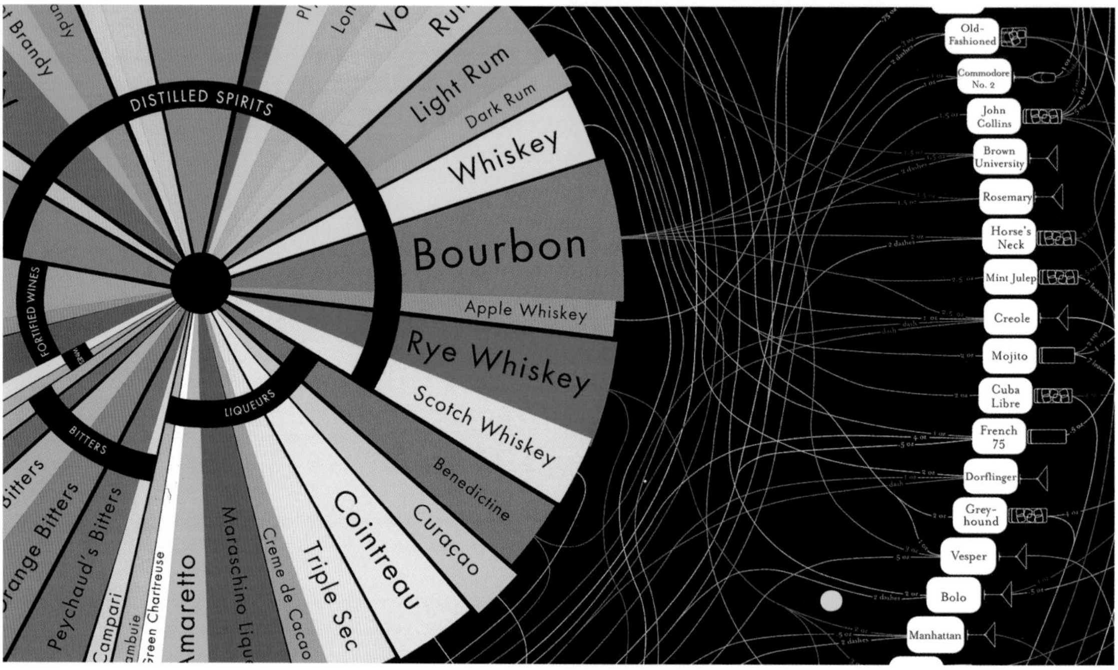

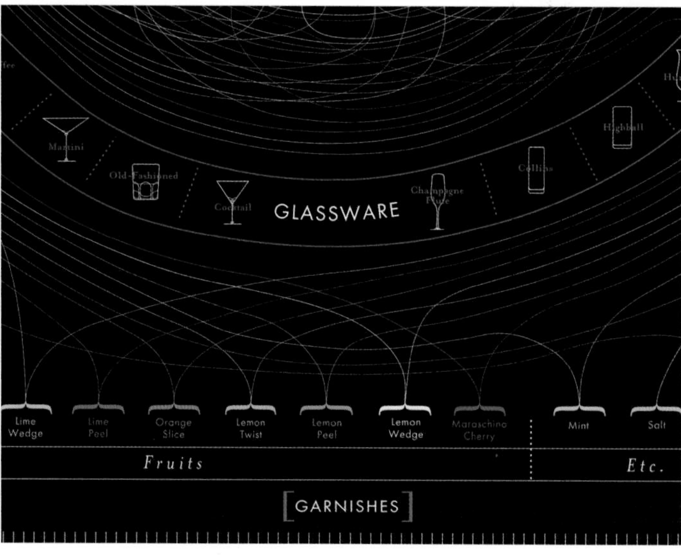

Martini
Old-Fashioned
Cocktail
GLASSWARE
Champagne Flute
Collins
Highball
Lime Wedge
Lime Peel
Orange Slice
Lemon Twist
Lemon Peel
Lemon Wedge
Maraschino Cherry
Mint
Salt
Fruits
Etc.
GARNISHES

ARTISTS Ben Gibson and Patrick Mulligan, cofounders of Pop Chart Lab in Brooklyn, New York.

STATEMENT We actually worked on this for over a year. Coming up with an arrangement that could fit sixty-nine cocktails and all of their ingredients along with the ingredient ratios onto one piece of paper took a lot of doing. Putting the spirits in the middle as a pie chart, the cocktails in a ring around, and the mixers and condiments above and below was our "Aha!" moment.

PUBLICATION popchartlab.com (February 2012)

Constitutions of Classic COCKTAILS

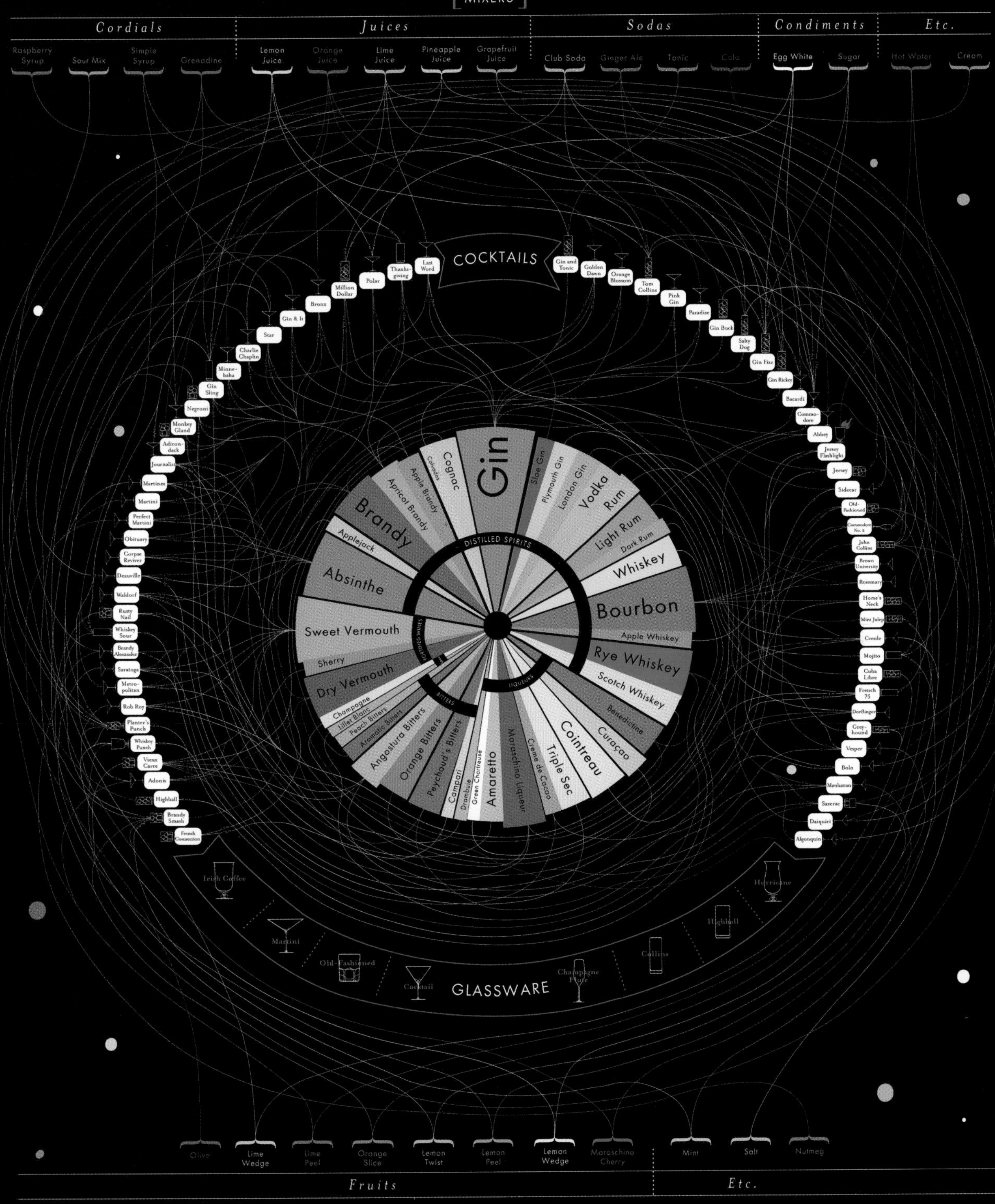
[MIXERS]
Cordials
Raspberry Syrup
Sour Mix
Simple Syrup
Grenadine
Juices
Lemon Juice
Orange Juice
Lime Juice
Pineapple Juice
Grapefruit Juice
Sodas
Club Soda
Ginger Ale
Tonic
Cola
Condiments
Egg White
Sugar
Etc.
Hot Water
Cream
COCKTAILS
Last Word
Thanksgiving
Polar
Million Dollar
Bronx
Gin & It
Star
Charlie Chaplin
Minnehaha
Gin Sling
Negroni
Monkey Gland
Adirondack
Journalist
Martinez
Martini
Perfect Martini
Obituary
Corpse Reviver
Deauville
Waldorf
Rusty Nail
Whiskey Sour
Brandy Alexander
Saratoga
Metropolitan
Rob Roy
Planter's Punch
Whiskey Punch
Vieux Carre
Adonis
Highball
Brandy Smash
French Connection
Gin and Tonic
Golden Dawn
Orange Blossom
Tom Collins
Pink Gin
Paradise
Gin Buck
Salty Dog
Gin Fizz
Gin Rickey
Bacardi
Commodore
Abbey
Jersey Flashlight
Jersey
Sidecar
Old-Fashioned
Commodore No. 2
John Collins
Brown University
Rosemary
Horse's Neck
Mint Julep
Creole
Mojito
Cuba Libre
French 75
Dorflinger
Greyhound
Vesper
Bolo
Manhattan
Sazerac
Daiquiri
Algonquin
DISTILLED SPIRITS
Gin
Sloe Gin
Plymouth Gin
London Gin
Vodka
Rum
Light Rum
Dark Rum
Whiskey
Bourbon
Apple Whiskey
Rye Whiskey
Scotch Whiskey
Cognac
Calvados
Apple Brandy
Apricot Brandy
Brandy
Applejack
Absinthe
FORTIFIED WINES
Sweet Vermouth
Sherry
Dry Vermouth
Champagne
Lillet Blanc
BITTERS
Peach Bitters
Aromatic Bitters
Angostura Bitters
Orange Bitters
Peychaud's Bitters
Campari
LIQUEURS
Drambuie
Green Chartreuse
Amaretto
Maraschino Liqueur
Creme de Cacao
Triple Sec
Cointreau
Curaçao
Benedictine
GLASSWARE
Irish Coffee
Martini
Old-Fashioned
Cocktail
Champagne Flute
Collins
Highball
Hurricane
Olive
Lime Wedge
Lime Peel
Orange Slice
Lemon Twist
Lemon Peel
Lemon Wedge
Maraschino Cherry
Mint
Salt
Nutmeg
Fruits
Etc.
[GARNISHES]

What Were the Gayest (and Straightest) Super Bowl Halftime Shows?

All of the performances, placed on the Kinsey scale of human sexuality.

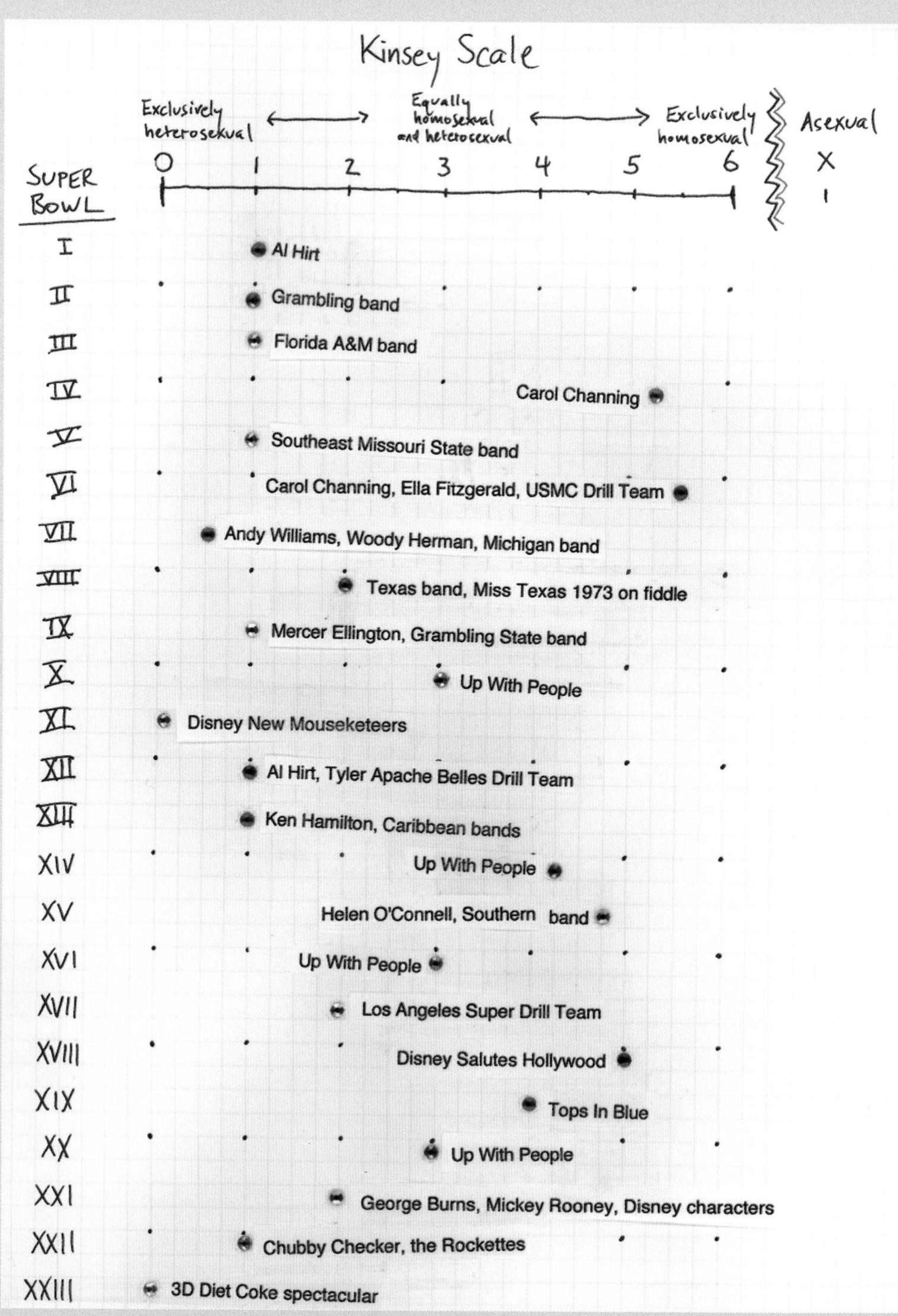
Kinsey Scale
Exclusively heterosexual
Equally homosexual and heterosexual
Exclusively homosexual
Asexual
0
1
2
3
4
5
6
X
SUPER BOWL
I
Al Hirt
II
Grambling band
III
Florida A&M band
IV
Carol Channing
V
Southeast Missouri State band
VI
Carol Channing, Ella Fitzgerald, USMC Drill Team
VII
Andy Williams, Woody Herman, Michigan band
VIII
Texas band, Miss Texas 1973 on fiddle
IX
Mercer Ellington, Grambling State band
X
Up With People
XI
Disney New Mouseketeers
XII
Al Hirt, Tyler Apache Belles Drill Team
XIII
Ken Hamilton, Caribbean bands
XIV
Up With People
XV
Helen O'Connell, Southern band
XVI
Up With People
XVII
Los Angeles Super Drill Team
XVIII
Disney Salutes Hollywood
XIX
Tops In Blue
XX
Up With People
XXI
George Burns, Mickey Rooney, Disney characters
XXII
Chubby Checker, the Rockettes
XXIII
3D Diet Coke spectacular

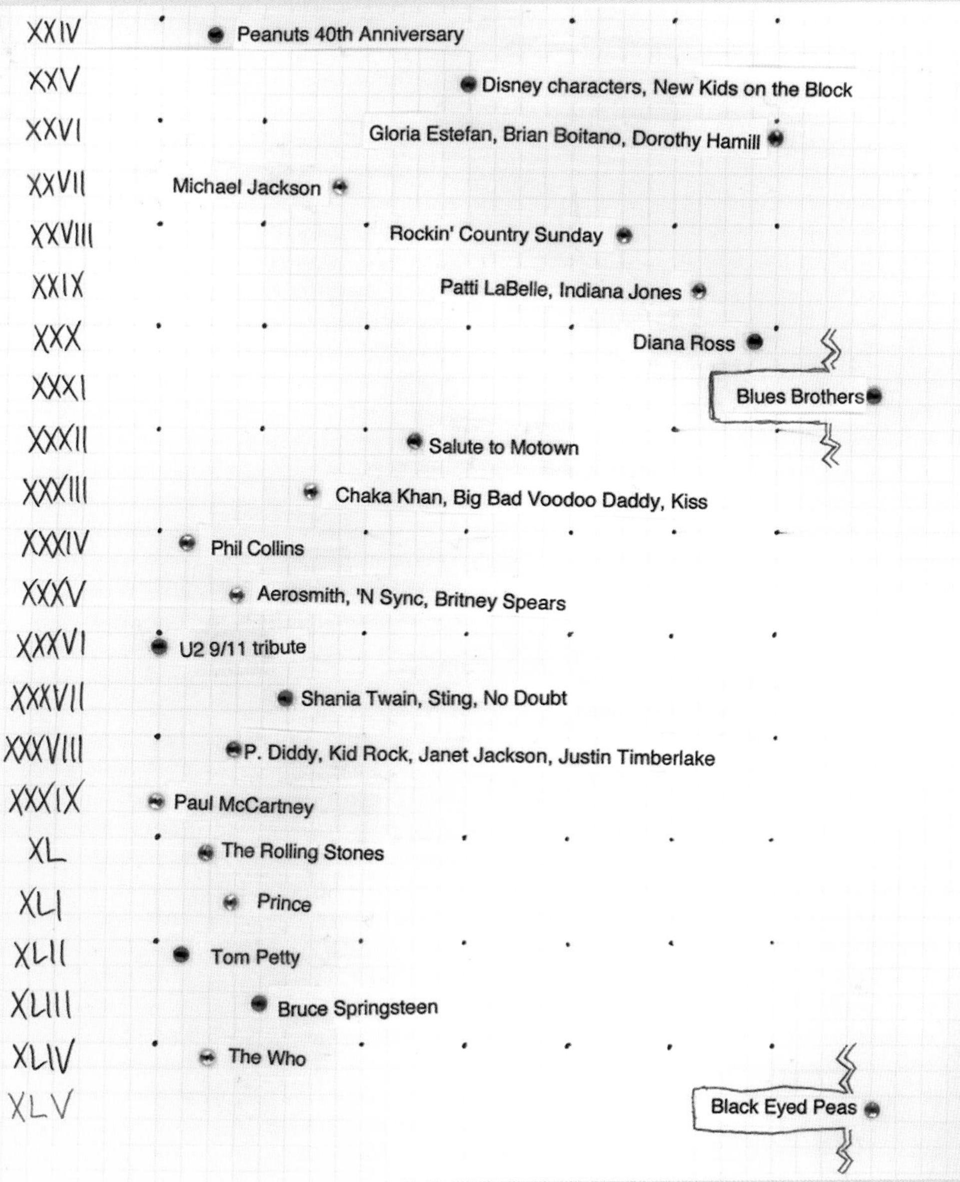

XXIV
Peanuts 40th Anniversary
XXV
Disney characters, New Kids on the Block
XXVI
Gloria Estefan, Brian Boitano, Dorothy Hamill
XXVII
Michael Jackson
XXVIII
Rockin' Country Sunday
XXIX
Patti LaBelle, Indiana Jones
XXX
Diana Ross
XXXI
Blues Brothers
XXXII
Salute to Motown
XXXIII
Chaka Khan, Big Bad Voodoo Daddy, Kiss
XXXIV
Phil Collins
XXXV
Aerosmith, 'N Sync, Britney Spears
XXXVI
U2 9/11 tribute
XXXVII
Shania Twain, Sting, No Doubt
XXXVIII
P. Diddy, Kid Rock, Janet Jackson, Justin Timberlake
XXXIX
Paul McCartney
XL
The Rolling Stones
XLI
Prince
XLII
Tom Petty
XLIII
Bruce Springsteen
XLIV
The Who
XLV
Black Eyed Peas

ARTIST Tom Scocca, deputy editor of *Gawker*.

STATEMENT The chart was born in response to a news story about how Madonna was supposed to be "bringing gay to the Super Bowl" in her upcoming halftime show. This struck me as an inaccurate and self-serving claim—we're talking, after all, about decades' worth of song-and-dance extravaganzas. My first reaction was to try to find a quick, blunt way to refute Madonna's pretensions. Then I started looking at the halftime shows and realized that was too easy—all the way back in 1970, the halftime of Super Bowl IV had starred Carol Channing, who is a definitive gay icon. Moreover, the acts through the years had spanned a broad range of entertainment culture, well beyond Madonna's crude and incorrect binary assumptions about *gay or straight*. The best rebuttal, then, was to try to represent the true diversity and fluidity of the halftime shows. Alfred Kinsey's spectrum of sexuality seemed to suit the task.

So it was a matter of assigning a value to each halftime show—fortunately, nowadays there's a lot of old video online for reference—and figuring out how to make it all into a graph that would fit in our online format. I thought the little jewel stickers would brighten it up a little, given the length of the list; given the length of the list, I ended up in danger of running out of the jewels before I was done. Forty-five Super Bowls is a lot of Super Bowls, it turns out.

PUBLICATION deadspin.com (January 30, 2012)

Just How Fast Is Bolt?

Take every Olympic medalist since 1896 and put them in the same race.

ARTISTS Graham Roberts and Kevin Quealy, the *New York Times*.

STATEMENT When the difference between the gold and silver medals is less than half a second, using a traditional charting form isn't so effective. Instead of explaining the progression of speed in the Olympic men's 100-meter dash by using a scatterplot—though we did do that, too, as a secondary element—we wanted to put the data on a human scale, placing figures on a 3-D track to make it easy to see how far back a split second would put the silver medalist. None of our graphics are simply thought up out of thin air, however; this one in particular was an iteration on a print graphic that we published in 2008, and it was also heavily influenced by a series of "time merge media" mashups posted to the blog kottke.org.

PUBLICATION *New York Times* (August 6, 2012)

INTERNATIONAL OLYMPIC COM

Jesse Owens, 1936 The Dutch bronze medalist i this race later joined the German SS. Owens won three more gold medals in the Berlin Games.

1904
Archie Hahn
U.S., *11.0 sec.*
12.5 meters back

Meters behind Usain Bolt in 2012 → 1

Usain Bolt Against The Olympic Medalist Field Since 1896

Based on the athletes' average speeds, if every Olympic medalist raced one another.

Note: This chart includes medals for the United States and Australia in the Intermediary Games of 1906, which the I.O.C. does not formally recognize.

Sources: "The Complete Book of the Olympics" by David Wallechinsky and Jaime Loucky, International Olympic Committee

Meters behind Usain Bolt in 2012 →

INTERNATIONAL OLYMPIC COMMITTEE

es, 1968 The first to race .0 seconds in the Olympics, d that stood for 20 years.

INTERNATIONAL OLYMPIC COMMITTEE

Carl Lewis, 1984, 1988 In addition to these two victories, he also won the long jump four times in a row.

GETTY IMAGES

Usain Bolt, 2008 Fifteen meters before setting a world record in the 2008 race, Bolt stretched his arms out to celebrate.

JOSH HANER/THE NEW YORK TIMES

Usain Bolt, 2012 He captured his second consecutive gold with a new Olympic record.

d Abrahams
n, *10.6 sec.*
eters back

1936
Jesse Owens
U.S., *10.3 sec.*
6.5 meters back

1984
Carl Lewis
U.S., *9.99 sec.*
3.6 meters back

1968
Jim Hines
U.S. *9.95 sec.*
3.2 meters back

1988
Carl Lewis
U.S., *9.92 sec.*
2.9 meters back

2008
Usain Bolt
Jamaica, *9.69 sec.*
0.6 meters back

2012
Usain Bolt
Jamaica
9.63 sec.

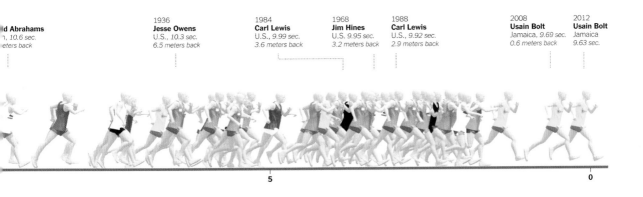

5

0

repeated his win in the 100-meter nday, with a blistering 9.63, an ecord. But how fast is that in the all sprinters ever to land on the he diagram below shows where 116 th of medalists would be relative to finish in London. Among the pack lt: Carl Lewis, the only other win this event back-to-back in the mes, is about 10 feet back. Jesse o won four golds in Berlin in 1936? t back.

VIN QUEALY and GRAHAM ROBERTS

INTERNATIONAL OLYMPIC COMMITTEE

Thomas Burke, 1896 Greek spectators at the Athens Games had never heard the organized chants that the American team used to cheer one another on.

Medal Leaders

United States	**40**
Britain	8
Jamaica	7
Canada	5
Trinidad and Tobago	4
Germany	3
Australia	3

◀ DOMINATED BY AMERICANS

But Jamaica has won three of the last six medals

1896
Thomas Burke
U.S., *12.0 sec.*
19.7 meters back

20

15

Gun Ownership Rates by Country

In a very long chart, the number of privately owned guns per one hundred people in every country in the world.

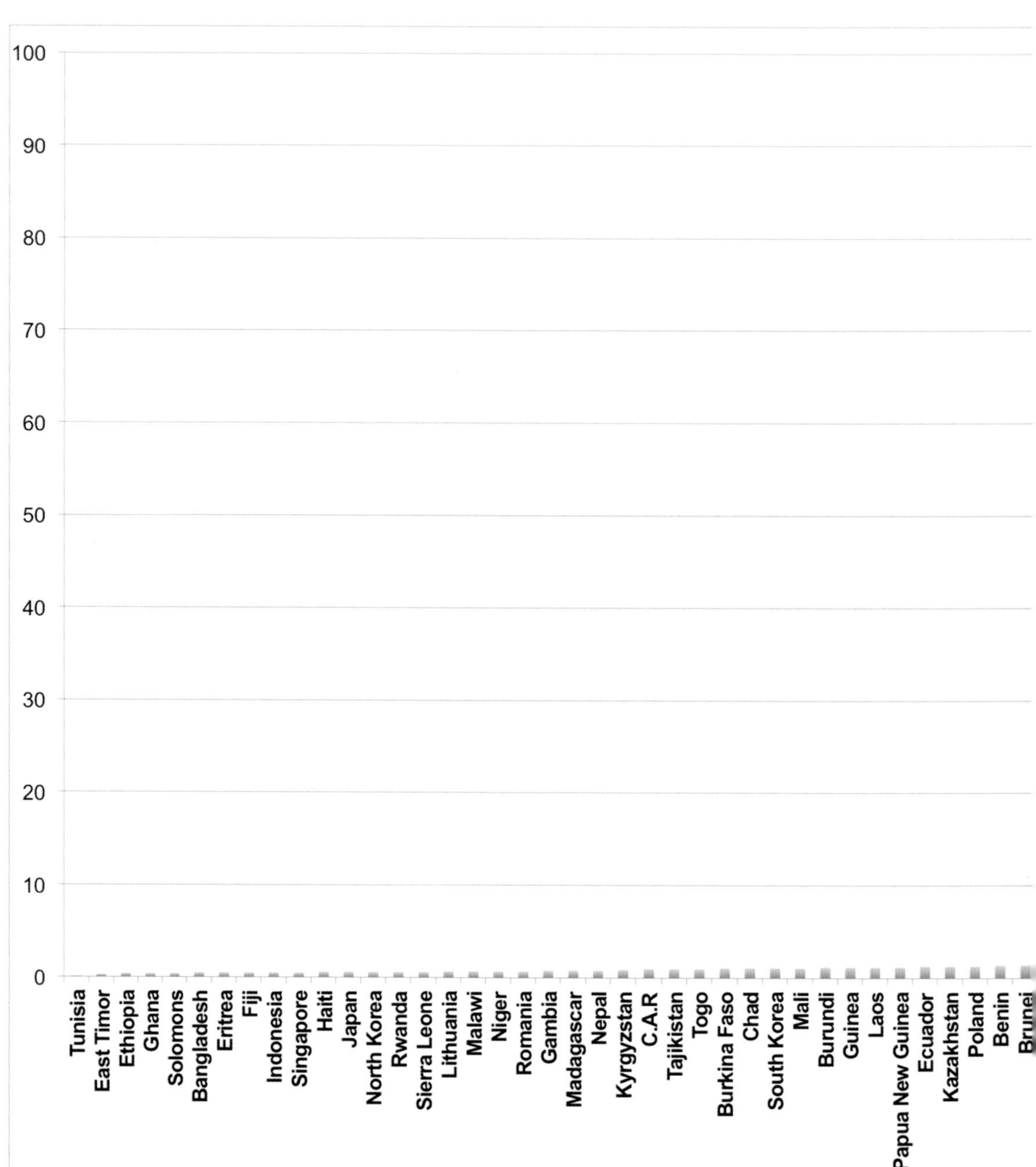
100
90
80
70
60
50
40
30
20
10
0
Tunisia
East Timor
Ethiopia
Ghana
Solomons
Bangladesh
Eritrea
Fiji
Indonesia
Singapore
Haiti
Japan
North Korea
Rwanda
Sierra Leone
Lithuania
Malawi
Niger
Romania
Gambia
Madagascar
Nepal
Kyrgyzstan
C.A.R
Tajikistan
Togo
Burkina Faso
Chad
South Korea
Mali
Burundi
Guinea
Laos
Papua New Guinea
Ecuador
Kazakhstan
Poland
Benin
Brunei

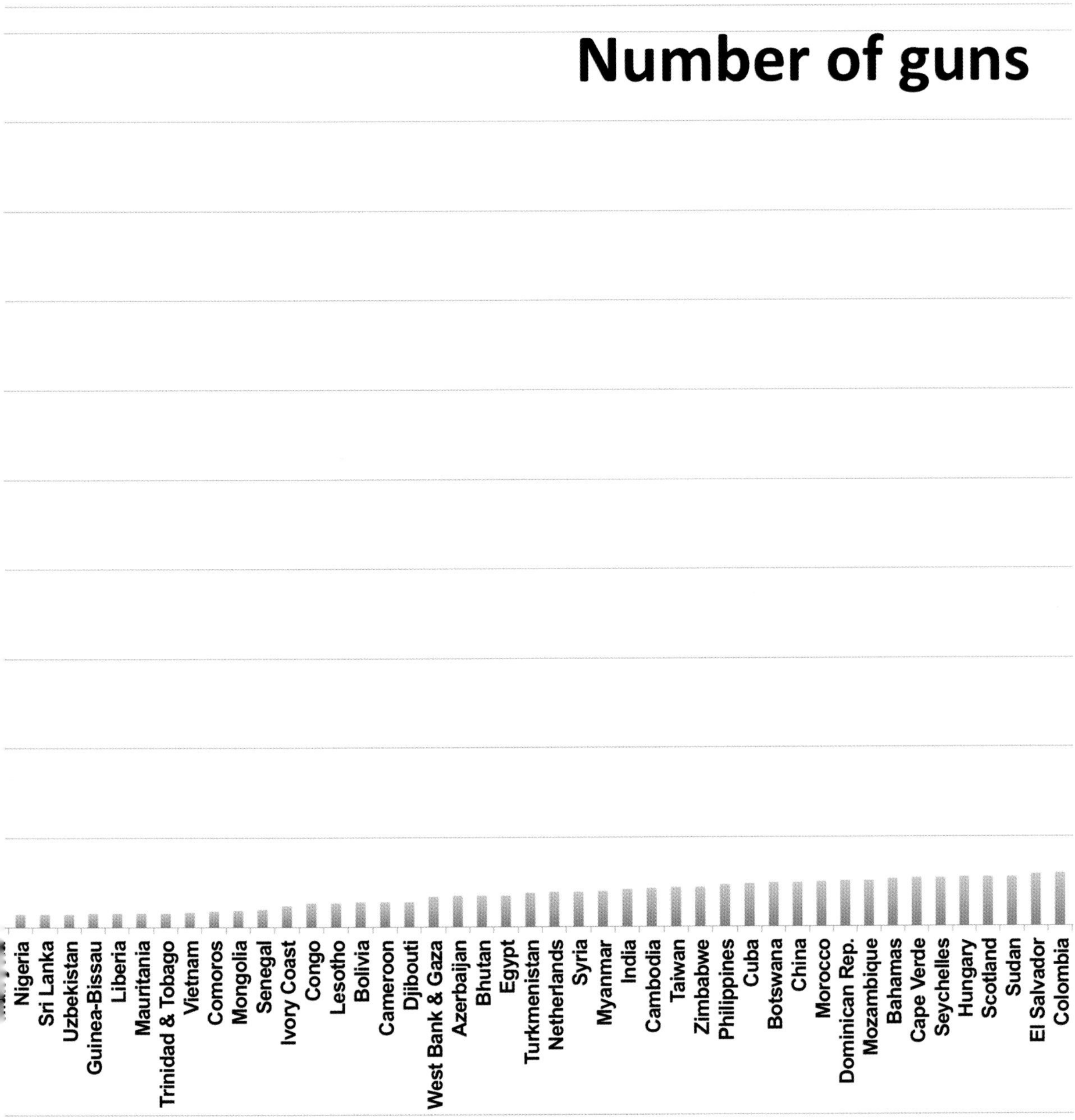

Number of guns

Nigeria
Sri Lanka
Uzbekistan
Guinea-Bissau
Liberia
Mauritania
Trinidad & Tobago
Vietnam
Comoros
Mongolia
Senegal
Ivory Coast
Congo
Lesotho
Bolivia
Cameroon
Djibouti
West Bank & Gaza
Azerbaijan
Bhutan
Egypt
Turkmenistan
Netherlands
Syria
Myanmar
India
Cambodia
Taiwan
Zimbabwe
Philippines
Cuba
Botswana
China
Morocco
Dominican Rep.
Mozambique
Bahamas
Cape Verde
Seychelles
Hungary
Scotland
Sudan
El Salvador
Colombia

CONTINUED

ARTIST Max Fisher, the foreign affairs blogger for the *Washington Post*.

STATEMENT Covering foreign news all day affords me a little bit of perspective on the United States and what makes it unique. One thing that I see again and again is that people in the rest of the world are very aware of—and usually baffled by—American gun culture. In a lot of ways, foreigners tend to be more aware of how unique that culture is than are most Americans. After the shooting at Sandy Hook Elementary, I heard people from Europe to Asia asking the same question they always ask about mass shootings in America: Why do Americans have so many guns?

I'm not a graphic designer, as this chart should make clear, but it doesn't take much to convey the stark contrast in gun owner-

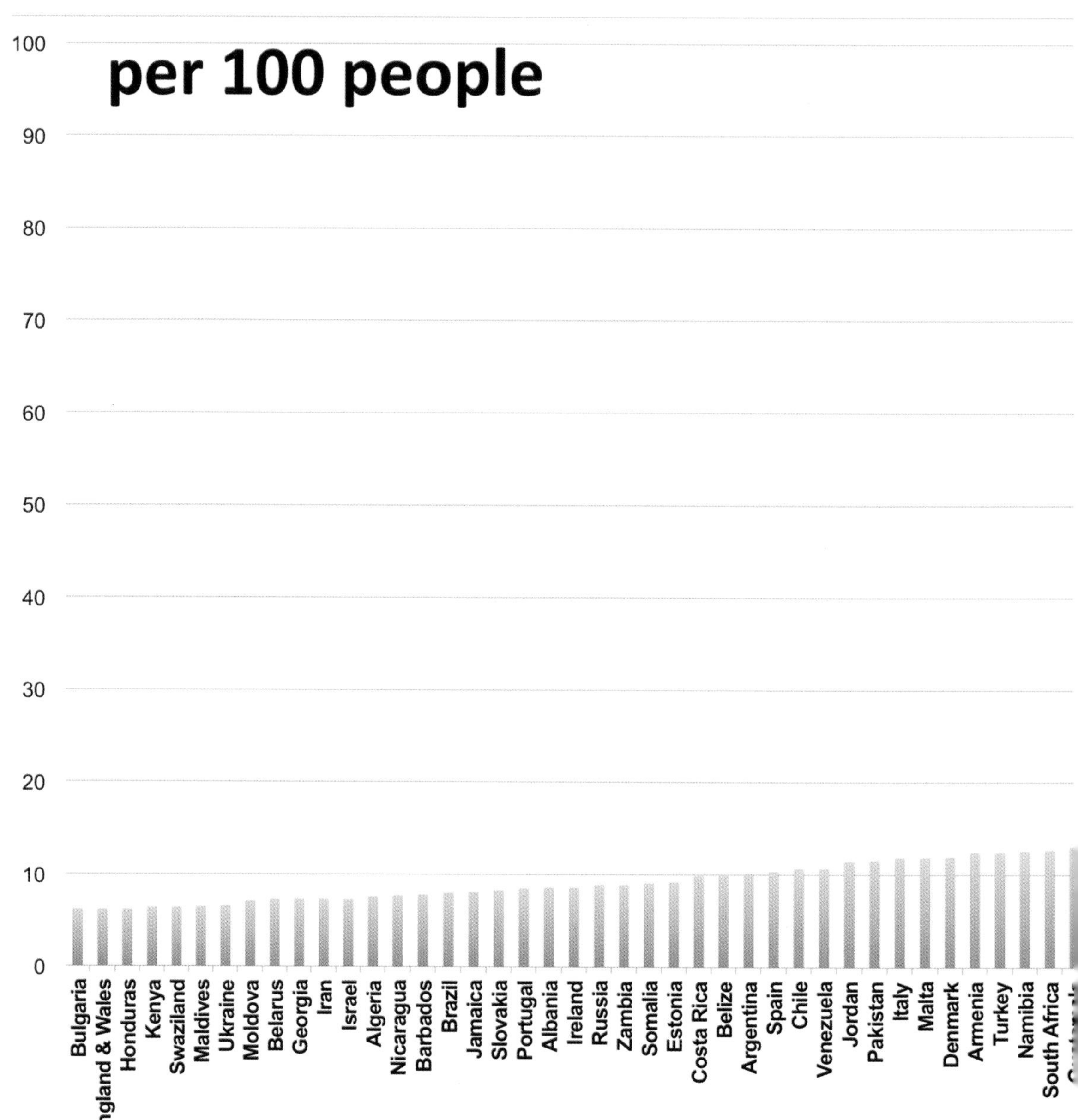

per 100 people
100
90
80
70
60
50
40
30
20
10
0
Bulgaria
England & Wales
Honduras
Kenya
Swaziland
Maldives
Ukraine
Moldova
Belarus
Georgia
Iran
Israel
Algeria
Nicaragua
Barbados
Brazil
Jamaica
Slovakia
Portugal
Albania
Ireland
Russia
Zambia
Somalia
Estonia
Costa Rica
Belize
Argentina
Spain
Chile
Venezuela
Jordan
Pakistan
Italy
Malta
Denmark
Armenia
Turkey
Namibia
South Africa

ship rates between the United States and the rest of the world. There are eighty-nine privately owned guns for every one hundred Americans. In a distant second with fifty-five guns per one hundred people is Yemen, a conflict-torn nation still dealing with political unrest, a separatist Shi'a insurgency, an al-Qaeda branch, and the aftereffects of a 1994 civil war. Most countries have fewer than ten guns per one hundred people.

PUBLICATION
WorldViews blog at WashingtonPost.com (www.washingtonpost.com/blogs/worldviews) (December 15, 2012)

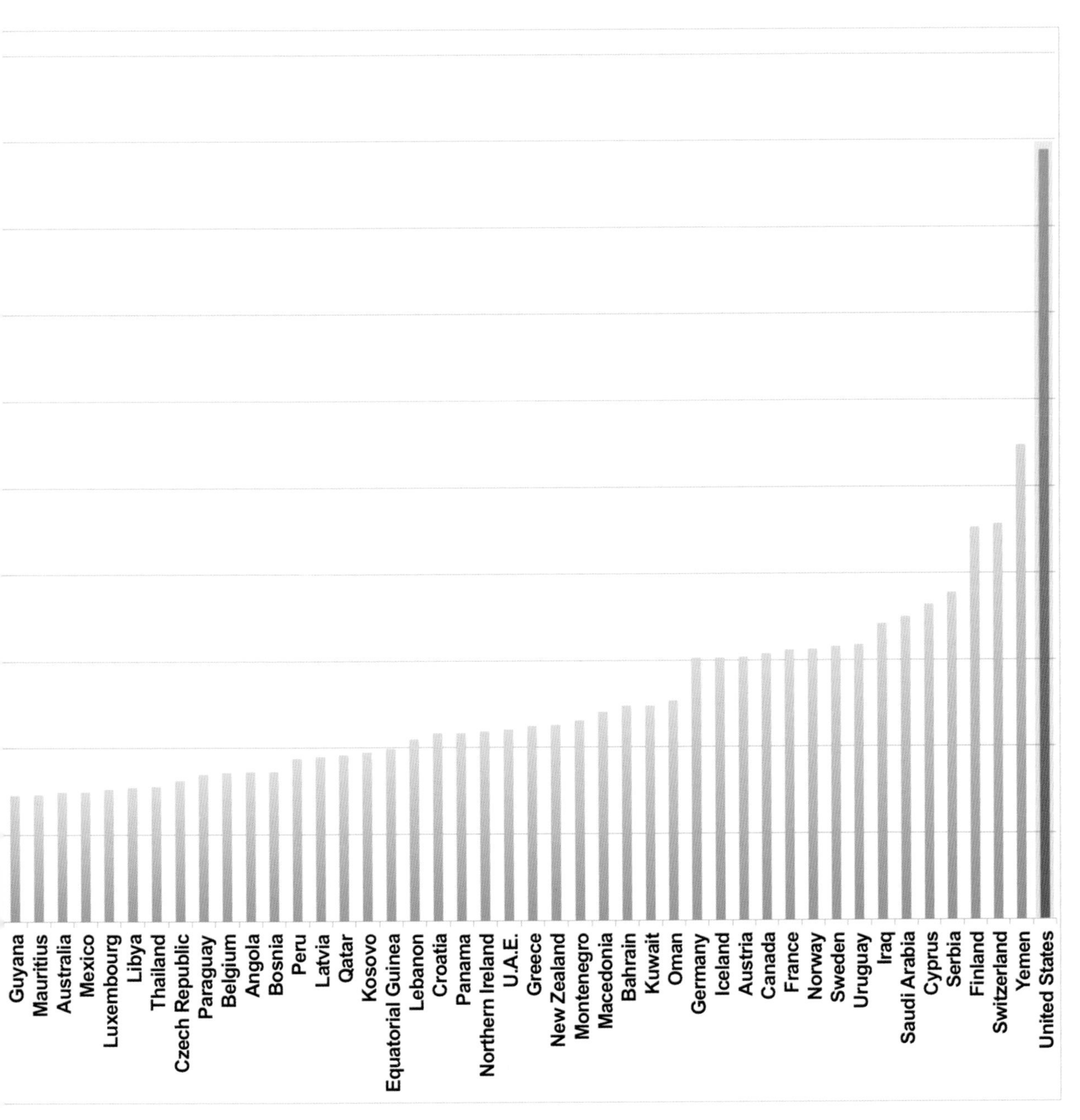
Guyana
Mauritius
Australia
Mexico
Luxembourg
Libya
Thailand
Czech Republic
Paraguay
Belgium
Angola
Bosnia
Peru
Latvia
Qatar
Kosovo
Equatorial Guinea
Lebanon
Croatia
Panama
Northern Ireland
U.A.E.
Greece
New Zealand
Montenegro
Macedonia
Bahrain
Kuwait
Oman
Germany
Iceland
Austria
Canada
France
Norway
Sweden
Uruguay
Iraq
Saudi Arabia
Cyprus
Serbia
Finland
Switzerland
Yemen
United States

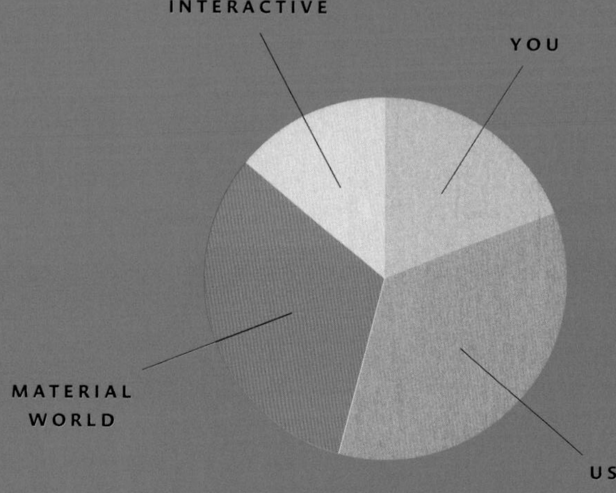
INTERACTIVE
YOU
MATERIAL WORLD
US

III. THE MATERIAL WORLD

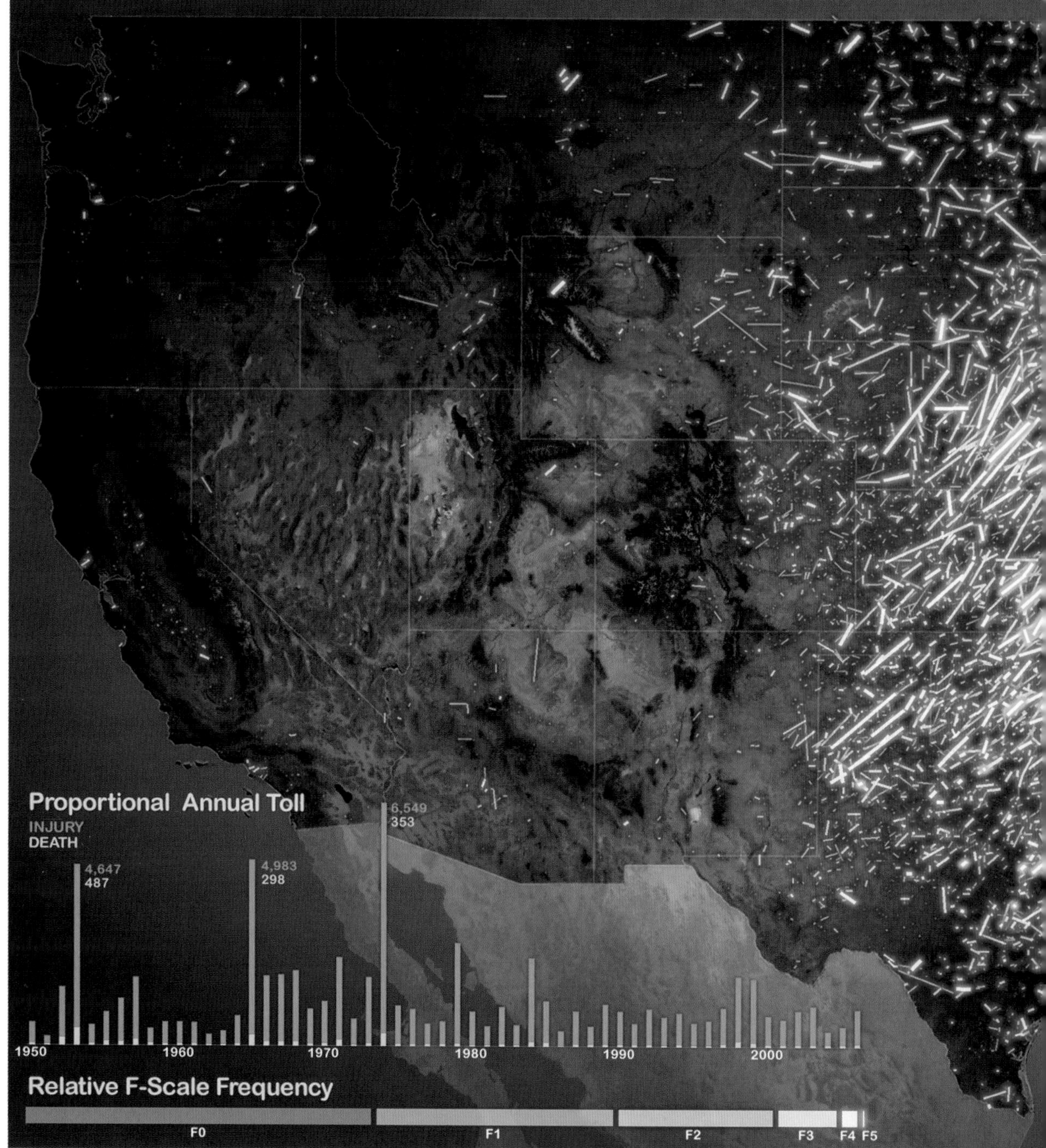
Proportional Annual Toll
INJURY
DEATH
4,647
487
4,983
298
6,549
353
1950
1960
1970
1980
1990
2000
Relative F-Scale Frequency
F0
F1
F2
F3
F4
F5

Where Twisters Touch Down

Fifty-six years of tornado activity within the mainland United States. Start and end points for recorded tornadoes were connected to show approximate paths, which are visually scaled according to severity.

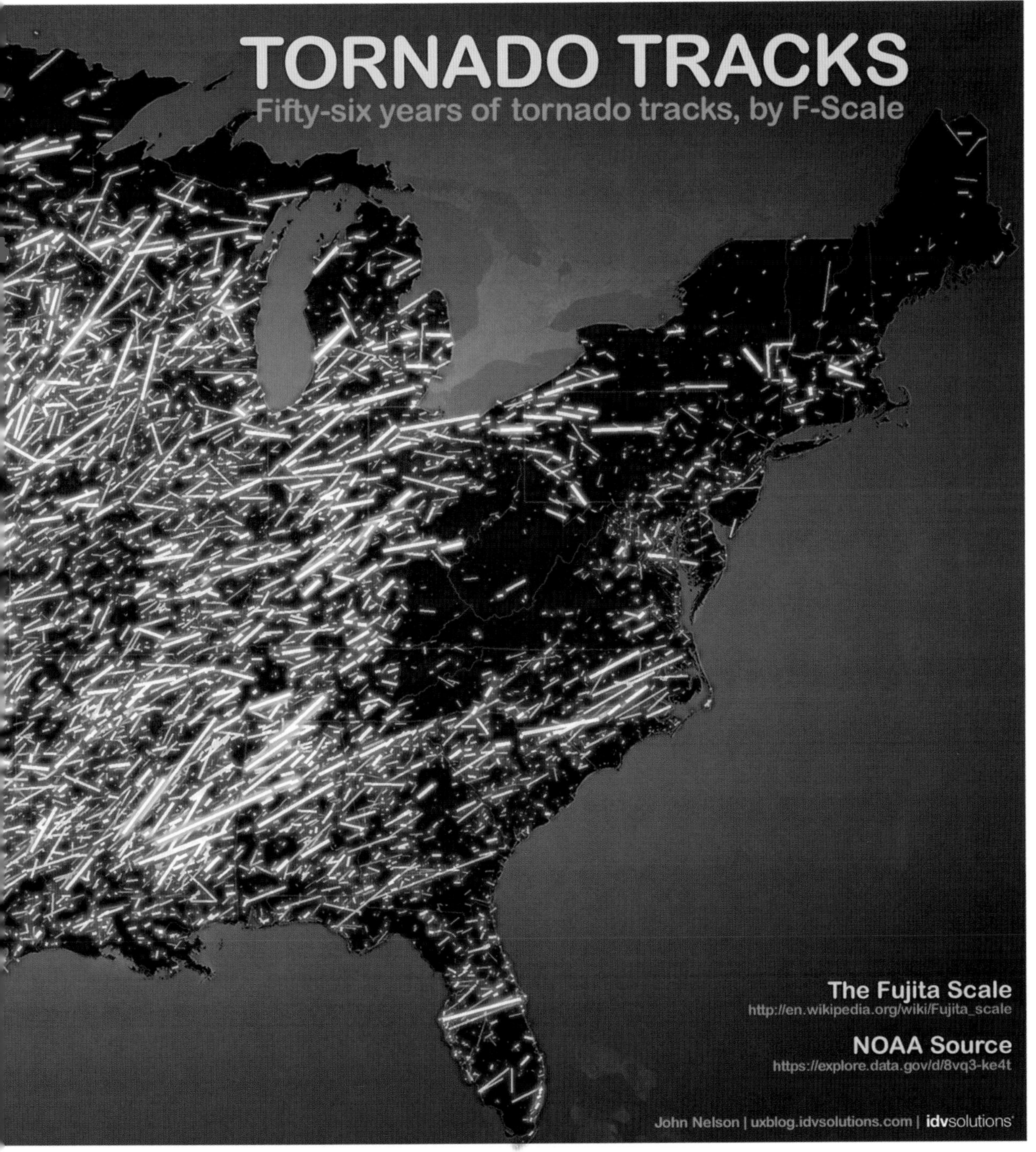
TORNADO TRACKS
Fifty-six years of tornado tracks, by F-Scale
The Fujita Scale
http://en.wikipedia.org/wiki/Fujita_scale
NOAA Source
https://explore.data.gov/d/8vq3-ke4t
John Nelson | uxblog.idvsolutions.com | idvsolutions

ARTIST John Nelson, cartographer at IDV Solutions in Lansing, Michigan.

STATEMENT This map came about because the company I work for focuses on visualizing risk in the hope of reducing it. The production of this map was an exercise in restraint. I applied no aggregation effort and little design process—something that does not come easily to a cartographer, in my experience. By withholding my own editorial analysis of the information, this mostly unfettered presentation invited all sorts of questions, speculations, and insights from readers. What I'm most proud of about this infographic is what I did not do, rather than what I did.

PUBLICATION
UX.Blog
(uxblog.idvsolutions.com)
(May 1, 2012)

Ten Artists, Ten Years

A revolution in color over ten extraordinary years of art history. Each pie chart represents an individual painting, with the five most prominent colors shown proportionally.

ARTIST Arthur Buxton, an artist based in Bristol, UK.

STATEMENT This was made in Illustrator with the help of a color extraction Python script written by Derek Ruths, a Montreal-based computer scientist I met online. I like to keep my designs as simple as possible and let the colors speak for themselves. Every palette has a story to tell. As evidenced by the white space, Gauguin passed away in 1903.

PUBLICATION ArthurBuxton.com (www.arthurbuxton.com) (June 3, 2012)

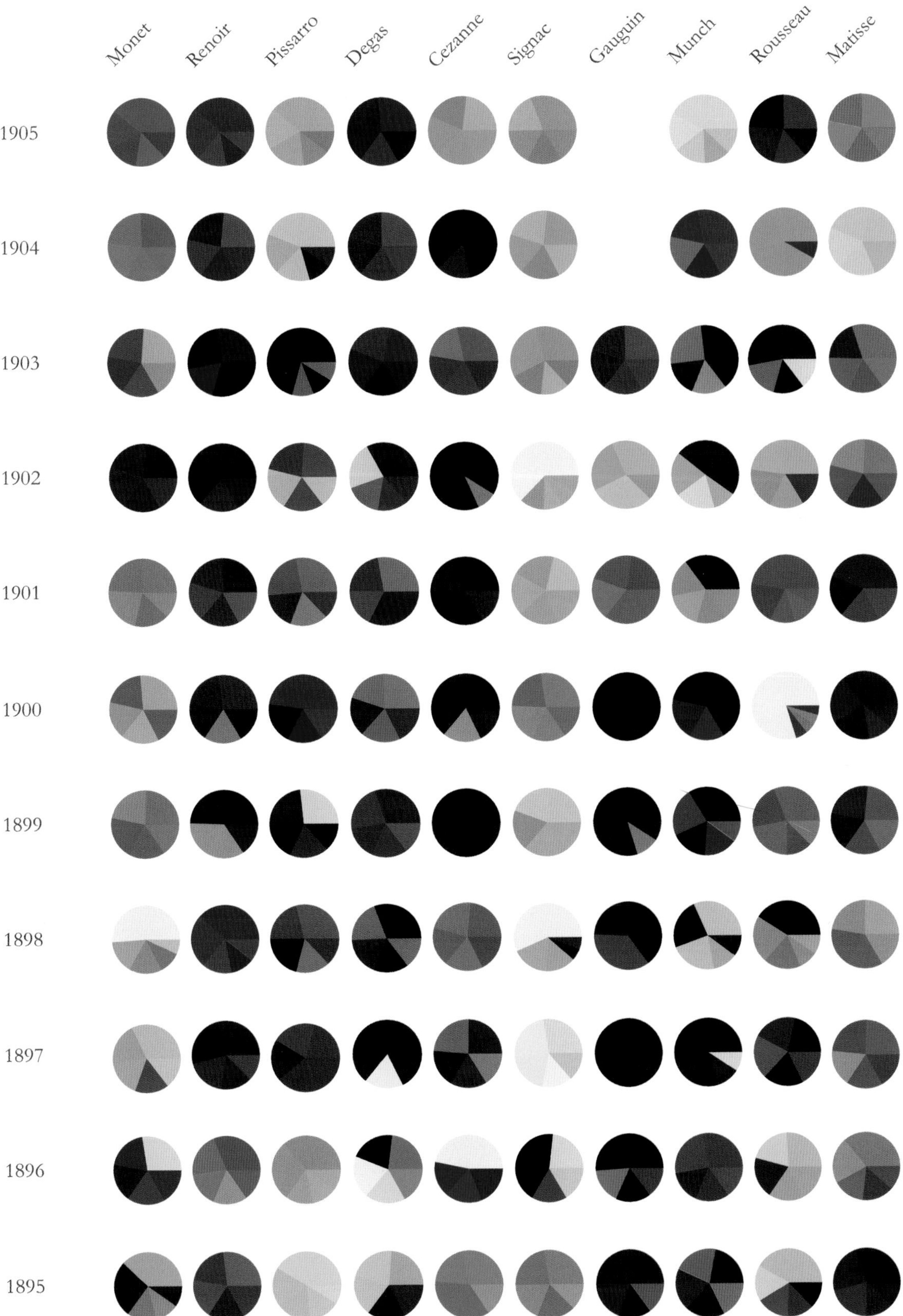
Monet
Renoir
Pissarro
Degas
Cezanne
Signac
Gauguin
Munch
Rousseau
Matisse
1905
1904
1903
1902
1901
1900
1899
1898
1897
1896
1895

Deepest of the Deep

How low can you go?

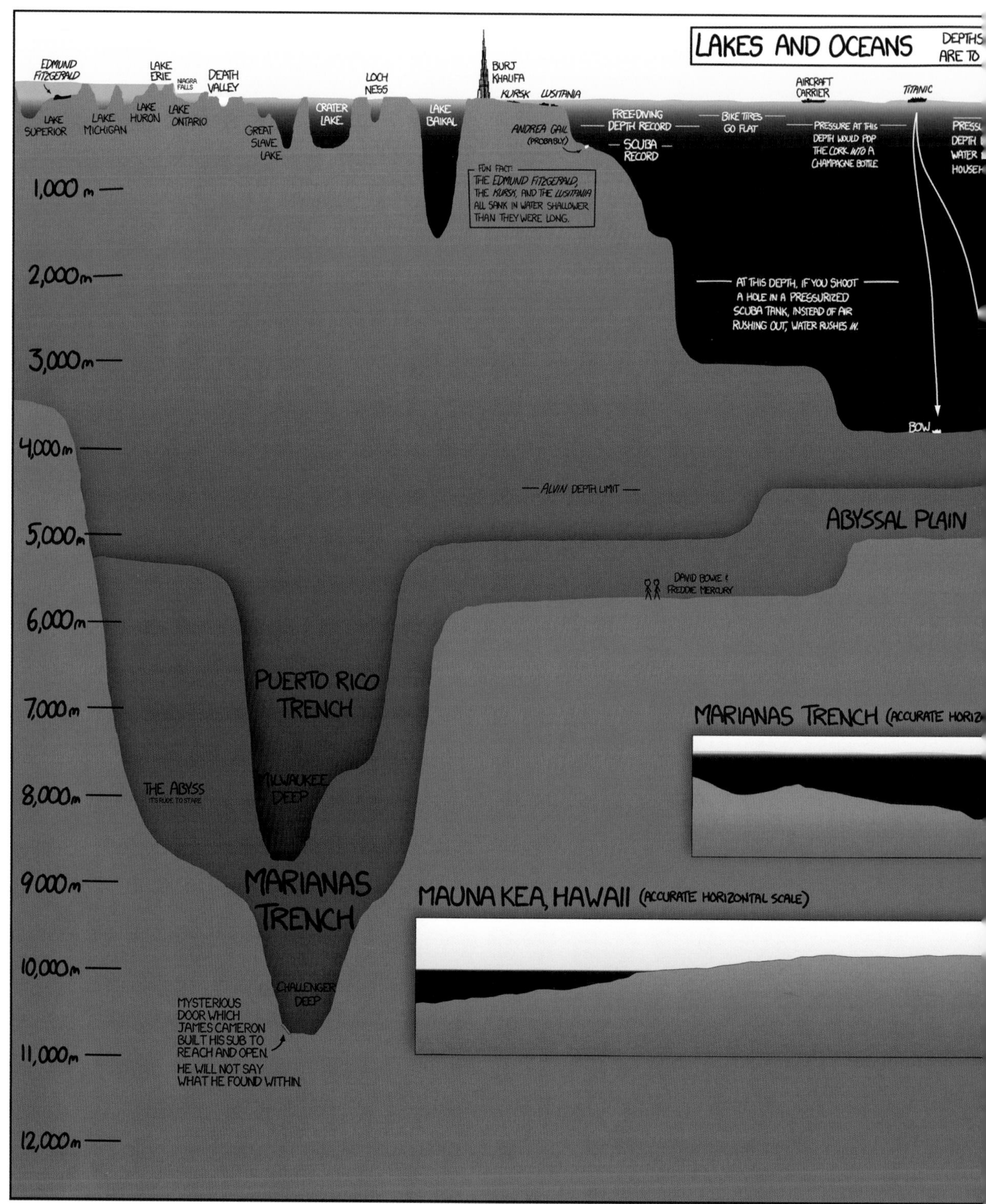
LAKES AND OCEANS
DEPTHS ARE TO
EDMUND FITZGERALD
LAKE ERIE
NIAGRA FALLS
DEATH VALLEY
LOCH NESS
BURJ KHALIFA
KURSK
LUSITANIA
AIRCRAFT CARRIER
TITANIC
LAKE SUPERIOR
LAKE MICHIGAN
LAKE HURON
LAKE ONTARIO
GREAT SLAVE LAKE
CRATER LAKE
LAKE BAIKAL
ANDREA GAIL (PROBABLY)
FREE-DIVING DEPTH RECORD
SCUBA RECORD
BIKE TIRES GO FLAT
PRESSURE AT THIS DEPTH WOULD POP THE CORK INTO A CHAMPAGNE BOTTLE
FUN FACT: THE EDMUND FITZGERALD, THE KURSK, AND THE LUSITANIA ALL SANK IN WATER SHALLOWER THAN THEY WERE LONG.
1,000 m
2,000 m
AT THIS DEPTH, IF YOU SHOOT A HOLE IN A PRESSURIZED SCUBA TANK, INSTEAD OF AIR RUSHING OUT, WATER RUSHES IN.
3,000 m
BOW
4,000 m
ALVIN DEPTH LIMIT
5,000 m
ABYSSAL PLAIN
DAVID BOWIE & FREDDIE MERCURY
6,000 m
PUERTO RICO TRENCH
7,000 m
MARIANAS TRENCH (ACCURATE HORIZ
8,000 m
THE ABYSS
IT'S RUDE TO STARE
MILWAUKEE DEEP
9000 m
MARIANAS TRENCH
MAUNA KEA, HAWAII (ACCURATE HORIZONTAL SCALE)
10,000 m
CHALLENGER DEEP
MYSTERIOUS DOOR WHICH JAMES CAMERON BUILT HIS SUB TO REACH AND OPEN. HE WILL NOT SAY WHAT HE FOUND WITHIN.
11,000 m
12,000 m

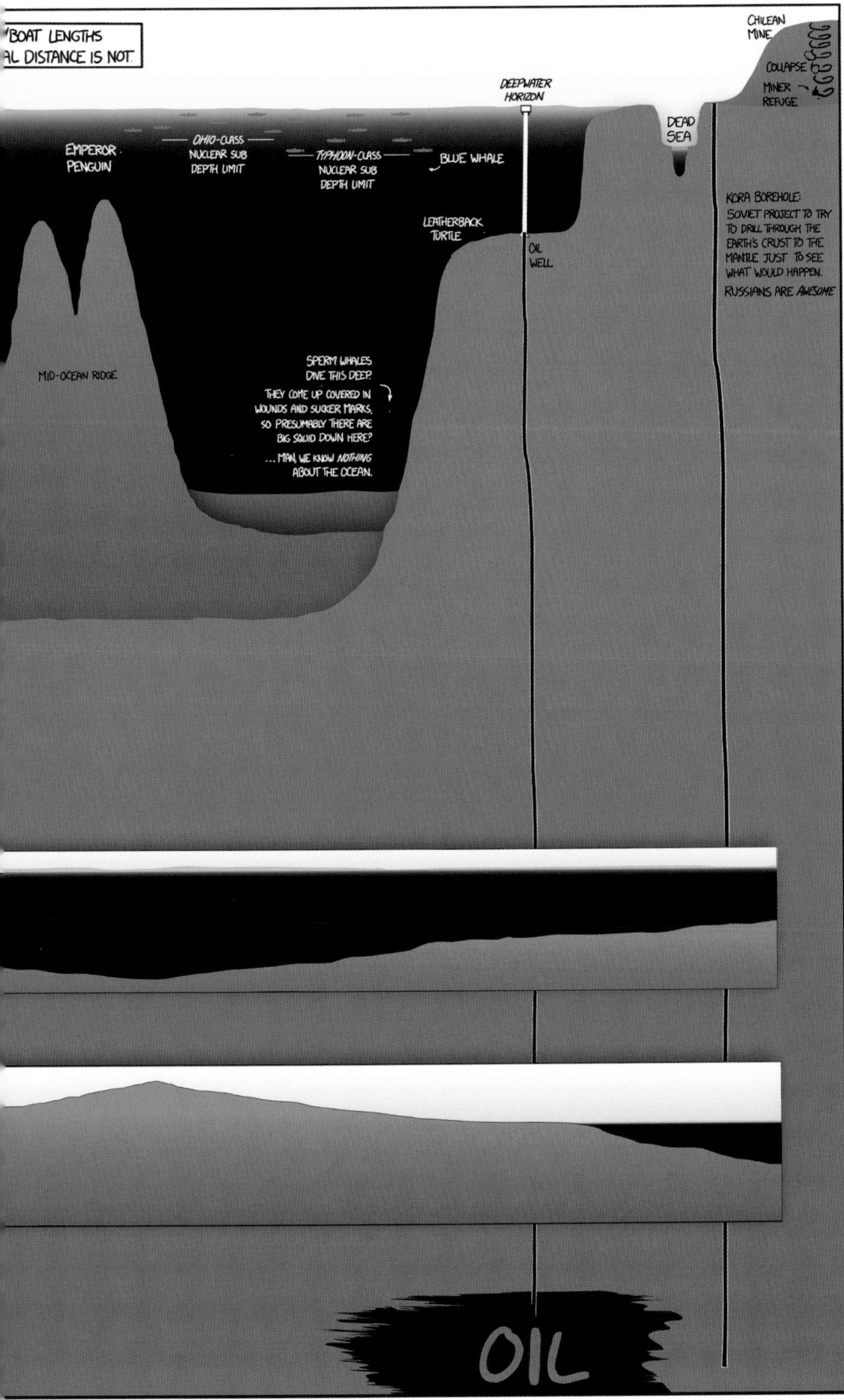

BOAT LENGTHS
AL DISTANCE IS NOT.
DEEPWATER HORIZON
CHILEAN MINE
COLLAPSE
MINER REFUGE
DEAD SEA
EMPEROR PENGUIN
OHIO-CLASS NUCLEAR SUB DEPTH LIMIT
TYPHOON-CLASS NUCLEAR SUB DEPTH LIMIT
BLUE WHALE
LEATHERBACK TURTLE
OIL WELL
KORA BOREHOLE:
SOVIET PROJECT TO TRY TO DRILL THROUGH THE EARTH'S CRUST TO THE MANTLE JUST TO SEE WHAT WOULD HAPPEN.
RUSSIANS ARE AWESOME
MID-OCEAN RIDGE
SPERM WHALES DIVE THIS DEEP.
THEY COME UP COVERED IN WOUNDS AND SUCKER MARKS, SO PRESUMABLY THERE ARE BIG SQUID DOWN HERE?
...MAN, WE KNOW NOTHING ABOUT THE OCEAN.
OIL

ARTIST Randall Munroe, author of the webcomic *xkcd,* based in Boston.

STATEMENT If the *Titanic* were an inch long, the ocean it sank in would be about a foot deep. Yet the crippled 500-foot submarine *Kursk* lay unreachable for days in just 350 feet of water—shallow enough that if the *Kursk* were balanced on end with the stern resting on the seabed, the bow would protrude into the air.

These comparisons were striking to me because I have little sense for how deep the oceans are. I grew up swimming and snorkeling, and occasionally my siblings and I would dive to the lake bottom. Though it was only twenty feet below the surface, the dark, otherworldly landscape seemed terrifyingly remote. Measured against those memories, ocean depth figures—miles rather than feet—seemed utterly incomprehensible. I made this chart to try to get a sense of them. All depths, water levels, ships, and animals are drawn to scale, but horizontal distances are not.

PUBLICATION xkcd.com (www.xkcd.com) (April 9, 2012)

Map of a New America

Fifty states with equal population.

ARTIST Neil Freeman, an artist and urban planner in New York City.

STATEMENT Under the Electoral College, some states receive lavish attention, while others are ignored. In 2000, a few votes in one state (Florida) carried the election, overriding the ballots of thousands of voters elsewhere. I began to consider creative ways to make elections fairer that didn't involve giving up state-by-state voting. I wrote a program that generated groups of counties based on commuting patterns and metropolitan area boundaries. I manually adjusted the borders to create compact shapes and to follow watershed lines where possible. In drafting the states, I developed an idiosyncratic opinion of the character of each state as it took shape. This opinion guided the final step, naming each state. For states centered on a single city, I chose the name of that city. For the others, I picked the names of local mountains, plants, and lakes. A few are taken from history: "Firelands" dates back to the early American settlement of Ohio, and "Yerba Buena" was the village that became San Francisco.

PUBLICATION fakeisthenewreal.org (December 5, 2012)

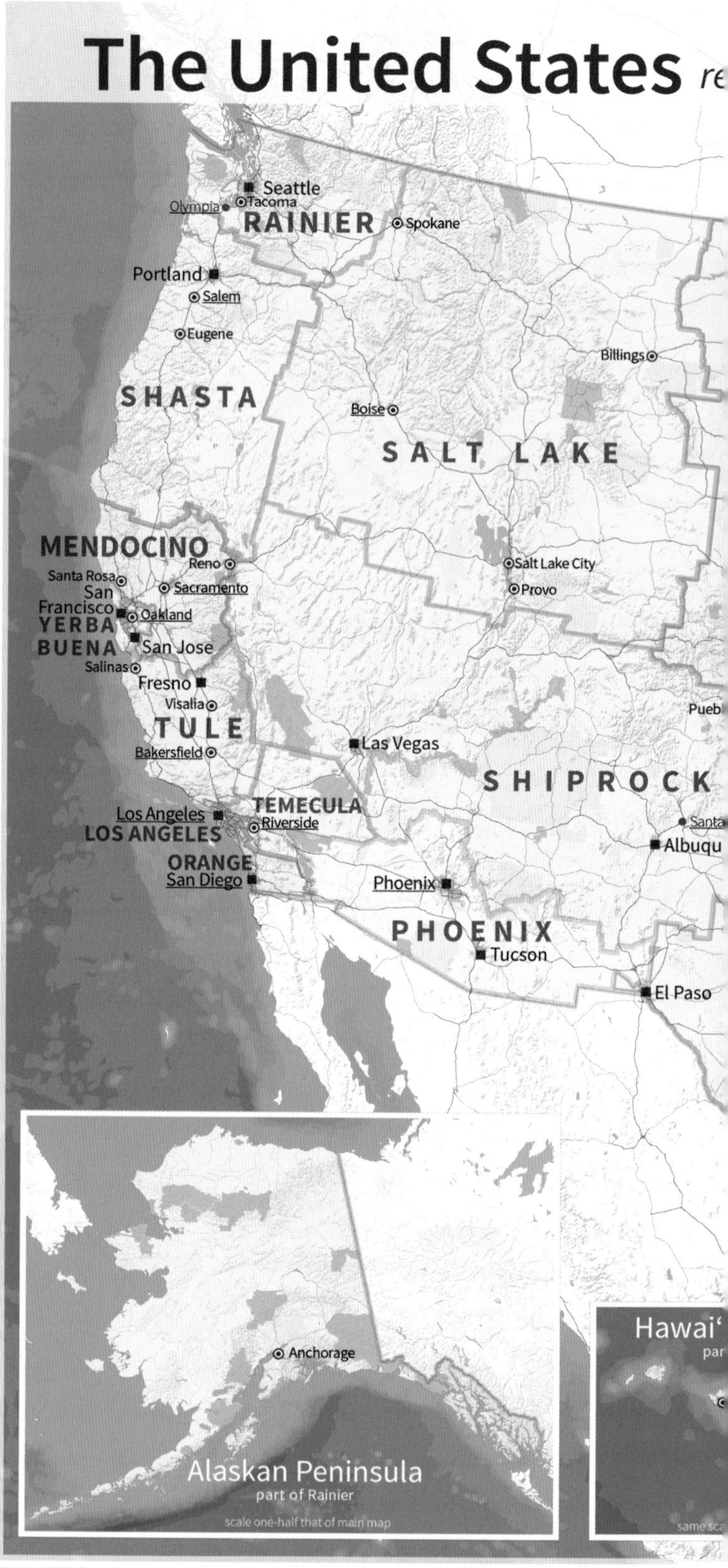

as Fifty States *with* Equal Population

LAKE SUPERIOR
LAKE MICHIGAN
LAKE HURON
LAKE ERIE
LAKE ONTARIO
Fargo
MESABI
MENOMINEE
Minneapolis
St. Paul
Green Bay
Rochester
.LALA
Sioux Falls
Milwaukee
Madison
Rockford
GARY
CHICAGO
Cedar Rapids
Joliet
Des Moines
Lincoln
Peoria
NODAWAY
SANGAMON
Springfield
Topeka
Kansas City
Columbia
St. Louis
Wichita
Springfield
MUSKOGEE
Tulsa
Oklahoma City
Amarillo
OZARK
Memphis
Little Rock
Lubbock
TRINITY
Ft. Worth
Dallas
Abilene
Shreveport
BIG THICKET
Waco
ATI
Austin
San Antonio
Houston
HOUSTON
Laredo
Corpus Christi
McAllen
Brownsville
DETROIT
Grand Rapids
Flint
Detroit
Toledo
Elyria
Cleveland
FIRELANDS
Ft. Wayne
Pittsburgh
Columbus
ALLEGHENY
Indianapolis
Dayton
SCIOTO
MAUMEE
Cincinnati
Louisville
Evansville
Lexington
MAMMOTH
Clarksville
Nashville
BLUE RIDGE
Knoxville
Winston-Salem
Durham
Raleigh
Charlotte
COLUMBIA
Chattanooga
Huntsville
Columbia
Atlanta
Augusta
ATLANTA
Birmingham
Charleston
Savannah
Montgomery
KING
Jackson
ATCHAFALAYA
Mobile
Baton Rouge
Lafayette
New Orleans
CANAVERAL
Tallahassee
Jacksonville
Gainesville
Orlando
Palm Bay
Tampa
St. Petersburg
TAMPA BAY
Port St. Lucie
MIAMI
Cape Coral
Ft. Lauderdale
Miami
ADIRONDACK
CASCO
Manchester
Boston
Rochester
Buffalo
Syracuse
Albany
Providence
Hartford
WILLIMANTIC
POCONO
Erie
Scranton
Yonkers
THROGS NECK
Newark
New York
NEW YORK
NEWARK
SUSQUEHANNA
Harrisburg
Philadelphia
PHILADELPHIA
Baltimore
Arlington
Washington
WASHINGTON
Richmond
SHENANDOAH
Virginia Beach
TIDEWATER
Wilmington
Legend
Cities
Cheyenne 50,000 to 100,000
Shreveport 100,000 to 500,000
Baltimore 500,000 and over
Boise state capital
state borders
international border
American Indian reservation
National Park
urbanized area
river
lake
dry lake
ocean
divided highway
undivided highway
ferry
kilometers 400
miles 400
N
♥ Natural Earth, US Census
Albers Equal Area Conic projection, insets in Alaska & Hawaii State Plane

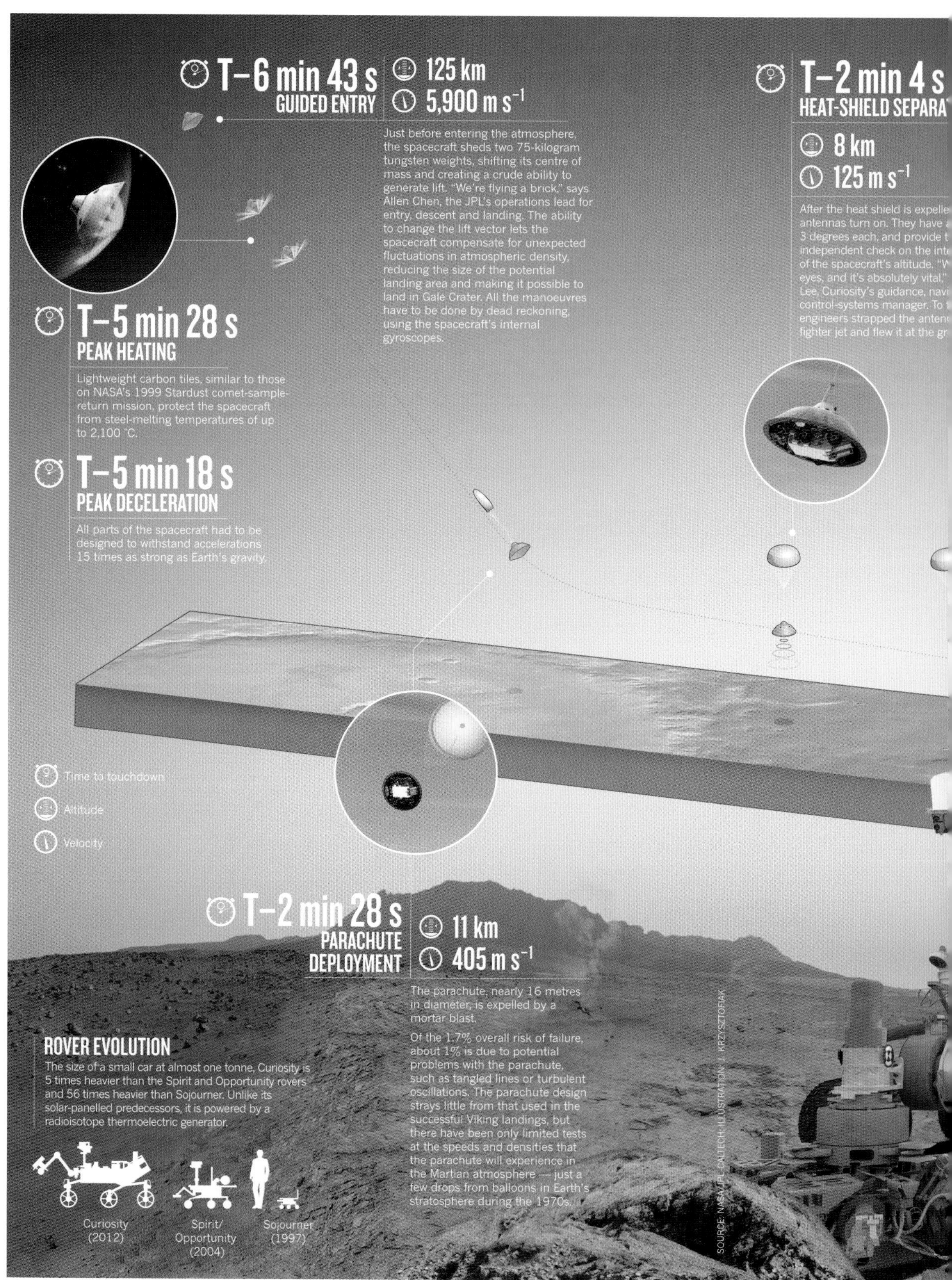

T–6 min 43 s
GUIDED ENTRY
125 km
5,900 m s⁻¹
Just before entering the atmosphere, the spacecraft sheds two 75-kilogram tungsten weights, shifting its centre of mass and creating a crude ability to generate lift. "We're flying a brick," says Allen Chen, the JPL's operations lead for entry, descent and landing. The ability to change the lift vector lets the spacecraft compensate for unexpected fluctuations in atmospheric density, reducing the size of the potential landing area and making it possible to land in Gale Crater. All the manoeuvres have to be done by dead reckoning, using the spacecraft's internal gyroscopes.
T–2 min 4 s
HEAT-SHIELD SEPARA
8 km
125 m s⁻¹
After the heat shield is expelle
antennas turn on. They have
3 degrees each, and provide t
independent check on the inte
of the spacecraft's altitude. "V
eyes, and it's absolutely vital."
Lee, Curiosity's guidance, navi
control-systems manager. To
engineers strapped the anten
fighter jet and flew it at the gr
T–5 min 28 s
PEAK HEATING
Lightweight carbon tiles, similar to those on NASA's 1999 Stardust comet-sample-return mission, protect the spacecraft from steel-melting temperatures of up to 2,100 °C.
T–5 min 18 s
PEAK DECELERATION
All parts of the spacecraft had to be designed to withstand accelerations 15 times as strong as Earth's gravity.
Time to touchdown
Altitude
Velocity
T–2 min 28 s
PARACHUTE DEPLOYMENT
11 km
405 m s⁻¹
The parachute, nearly 16 metres in diameter, is expelled by a mortar blast.
Of the 1.7% overall risk of failure, about 1% is due to potential problems with the parachute, such as tangled lines or turbulent oscillations. The parachute design strays little from that used in the successful Viking landings, but there have been only limited tests at the speeds and densities that the parachute will experience in the Martian atmosphere — just a few drops from balloons in Earth's stratosphere during the 1970s.
ROVER EVOLUTION
The size of a small car at almost one tonne, Curiosity is 5 times heavier than the Spirit and Opportunity rovers and 56 times heavier than Sojourner. Unlike its solar-panelled predecessors, it is powered by a radioisotope thermoelectric generator.
Curiosity (2012)
Spirit/ Opportunity (2004)
Sojourner (1997)
SOURCE: NASA/JPL-CALTECH; ILLUSTRATION: J. KRZYSZTOFIAK

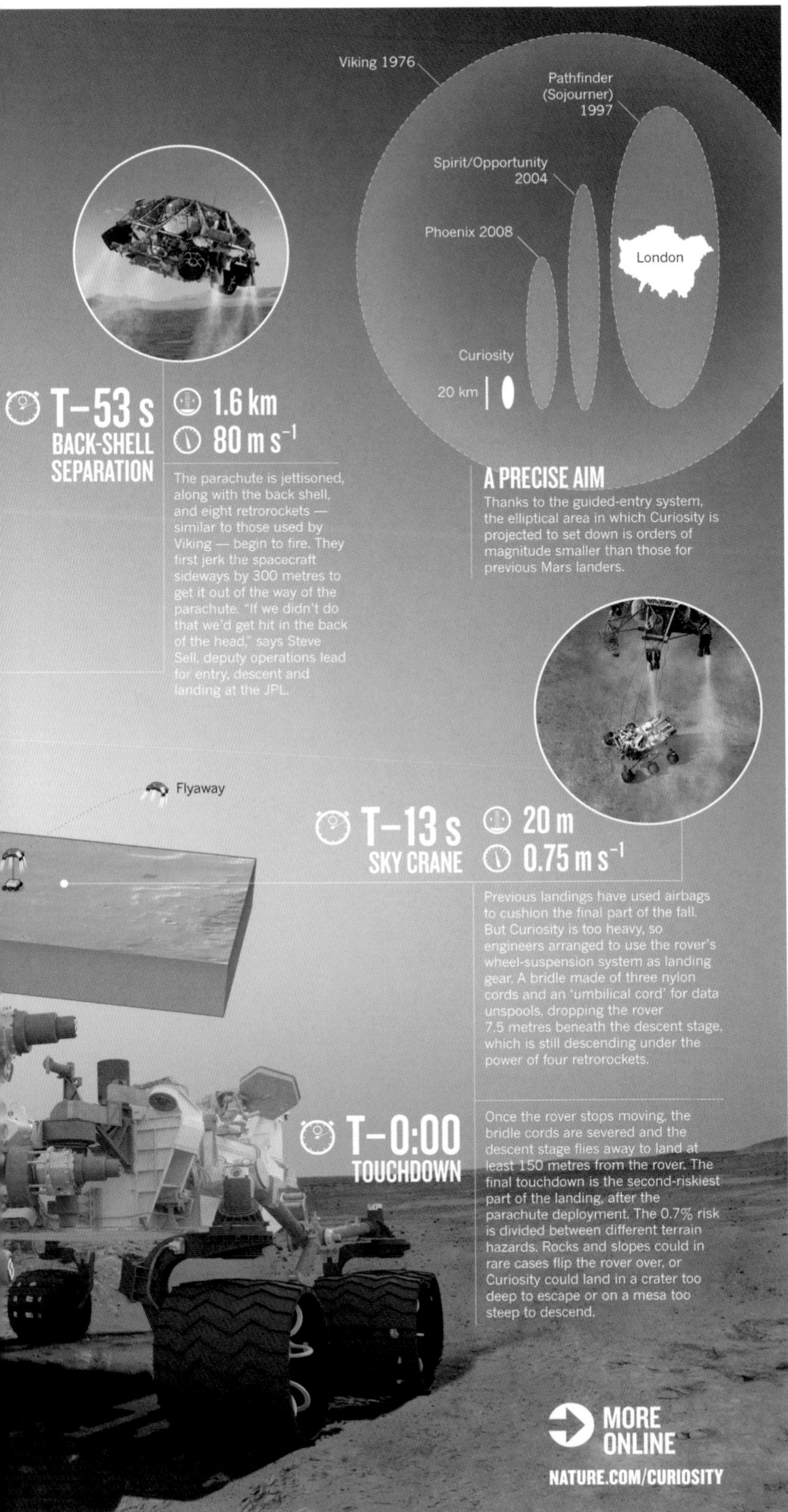
Viking 1976
Pathfinder (Sojourner) 1997
Spirit/Opportunity 2004
Phoenix 2008
London
Curiosity
20 km
T–53 s
BACK-SHELL SEPARATION
1.6 km
80 m s-1
The parachute is jettisoned, along with the back shell, and eight retrorockets — similar to those used by Viking — begin to fire. They first jerk the spacecraft sideways by 300 metres to get it out of the way of the parachute. "If we didn't do that we'd get hit in the back of the head," says Steve Sell, deputy operations lead for entry, descent and landing at the JPL.
A PRECISE AIM
Thanks to the guided-entry system, the elliptical area in which Curiosity is projected to set down is orders of magnitude smaller than those for previous Mars landers.
Flyaway
T–13 s
SKY CRANE
20 m
0.75 m s-1
Previous landings have used airbags to cushion the final part of the fall. But Curiosity is too heavy, so engineers arranged to use the rover's wheel-suspension system as landing gear. A bridle made of three nylon cords and an 'umbilical cord' for data unspools, dropping the rover 7.5 metres beneath the descent stage, which is still descending under the power of four retrorockets.
T–0:00
TOUCHDOWN
Once the rover stops moving, the bridle cords are severed and the descent stage flies away to land at least 150 metres from the rover. The final touchdown is the second-riskiest part of the landing, after the parachute deployment. The 0.7% risk is divided between different terrain hazards. Rocks and slopes could in rare cases flip the rover over, or Curiosity could land in a crater too deep to escape or on a mesa too steep to descend.
MORE ONLINE
NATURE.COM/CURIOSITY

Seven Minutes of Terror

NASA's Curiosity rover landing on Mars in August 2012.

ARTISTS Eric Hand, Jasiek Krzysztofiak, Wesley Fernandes, and Kelly Krause, *Nature*.

STATEMENT We began with gorgeous source illustrations from NASA, and this allowed us to spend more time on information design. There is an amazing amount of information on these two pages, but it all comes together seamlessly, thanks to Jasiek's simple but effective illustration of the landing as a central element, with events and other details arranged around the perimeter. This piece also benefits from a consistent key (time, altitude, velocity) that runs through the events, and a disciplined design (such as each NASA spot image appearing in a circle, consistent typography, and a good text-to-image ratio). *Nature*'s audience is predominantly scientists, so the graphic is heavy on precise measurements.

Our biggest challenge was the legibility of the type, and some might argue that the reverse type is difficult to read. There are compromises to be made in almost every complex graphic. In this case, we felt that mentally transporting the audience to Mars, with the aid of Martian sky and soil background, was an opportunity not to be missed, so we worked hard to place the text in areas without too much background detail.

PUBLICATION *Nature* (August 2, 2012)

Seasonal Produce Calendars

The availability of produce in the northern hemisphere by month and season.

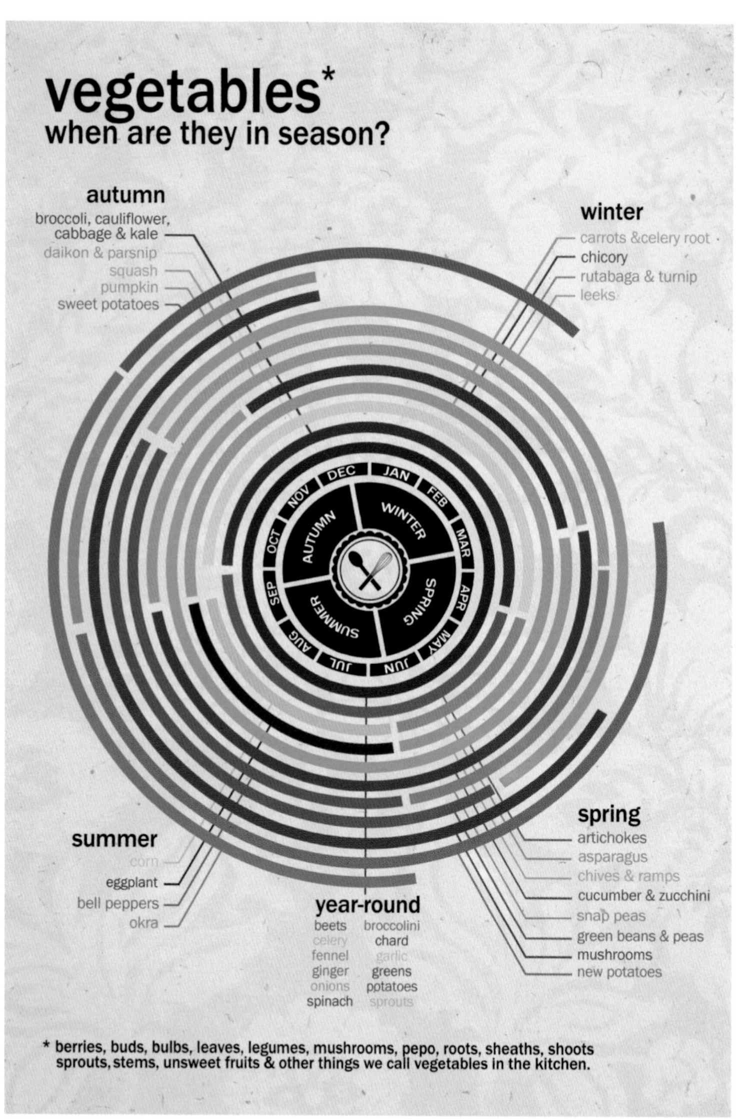
vegetables*
when are they in season?
autumn
broccoli, cauliflower, cabbage & kale
daikon & parsnip
squash
pumpkin
sweet potatoes
winter
carrots &celery root
chicory
rutabaga & turnip
leeks
DEC
JAN
FEB
MAR
APR
MAY
JUN
JUL
AUG
SEP
OCT
NOV
AUTUMN
WINTER
SPRING
SUMMER
summer
corn
eggplant
bell peppers
okra
year-round
beets
broccolini
celery
chard
fennel
garlic
ginger
greens
onions
potatoes
spinach
sprouts
spring
artichokes
asparagus
chives & ramps
cucumber & zucchini
snap peas
green beans & peas
mushrooms
new potatoes
* berries, buds, bulbs, leaves, legumes, mushrooms, pepo, roots, sheaths, shoots sprouts, stems, unsweet fruits & other things we call vegetables in the kitchen.

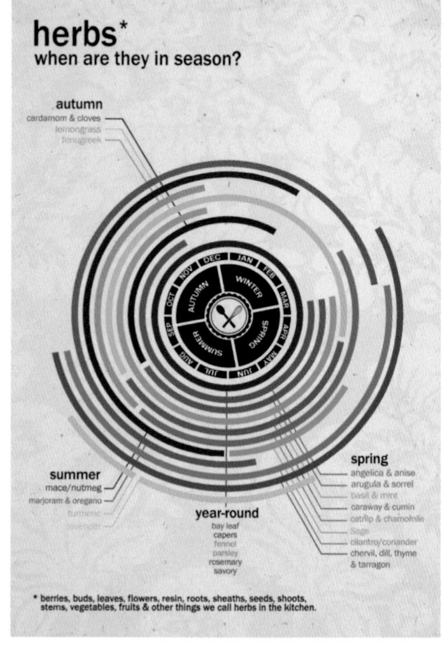
herbs*
when are they in season?
autumn
cardamom & cloves
lemongrass
fenugreek
DEC
JAN
FEB
MAR
APR
MAY
JUN
JUL
AUG
SEP
OCT
NOV
AUTUMN
WINTER
SPRING
SUMMER
summer
mace/nutmeg
marjoram & oregano
turmeric
lavender
year-round
bay leaf
capers
fennel
parsley
rosemary
savory
spring
angelica & anise
arugula & sorrel
basil & mint
caraway & cumin
catnip & chamomile
sage
cilantro/coriander
chervil, dill, thyme & tarragon
* berries, buds, leaves, flowers, resin, roots, sheaths, seeds, shoots, stems, vegetables, fruits & other things we call herbs in the kitchen.

ARTIST Russell van Kraayenburg, founder and managing director of Sweet Tooth Publishing, a small publishing company in Houston, Texas.

STATEMENT I designed the graphics to encourage the adoption of in-season produce shopping. In-season produce is fresher and typically cheaper. Out-of-season produce is often stored in facilities for long periods or shipped long distances, reducing its freshness and increasing its carbon footprint.

PUBLICATION *Chasing Delicious* (chasingdelicious.com) (May 28, 2012)

fruits*
when are they in season?

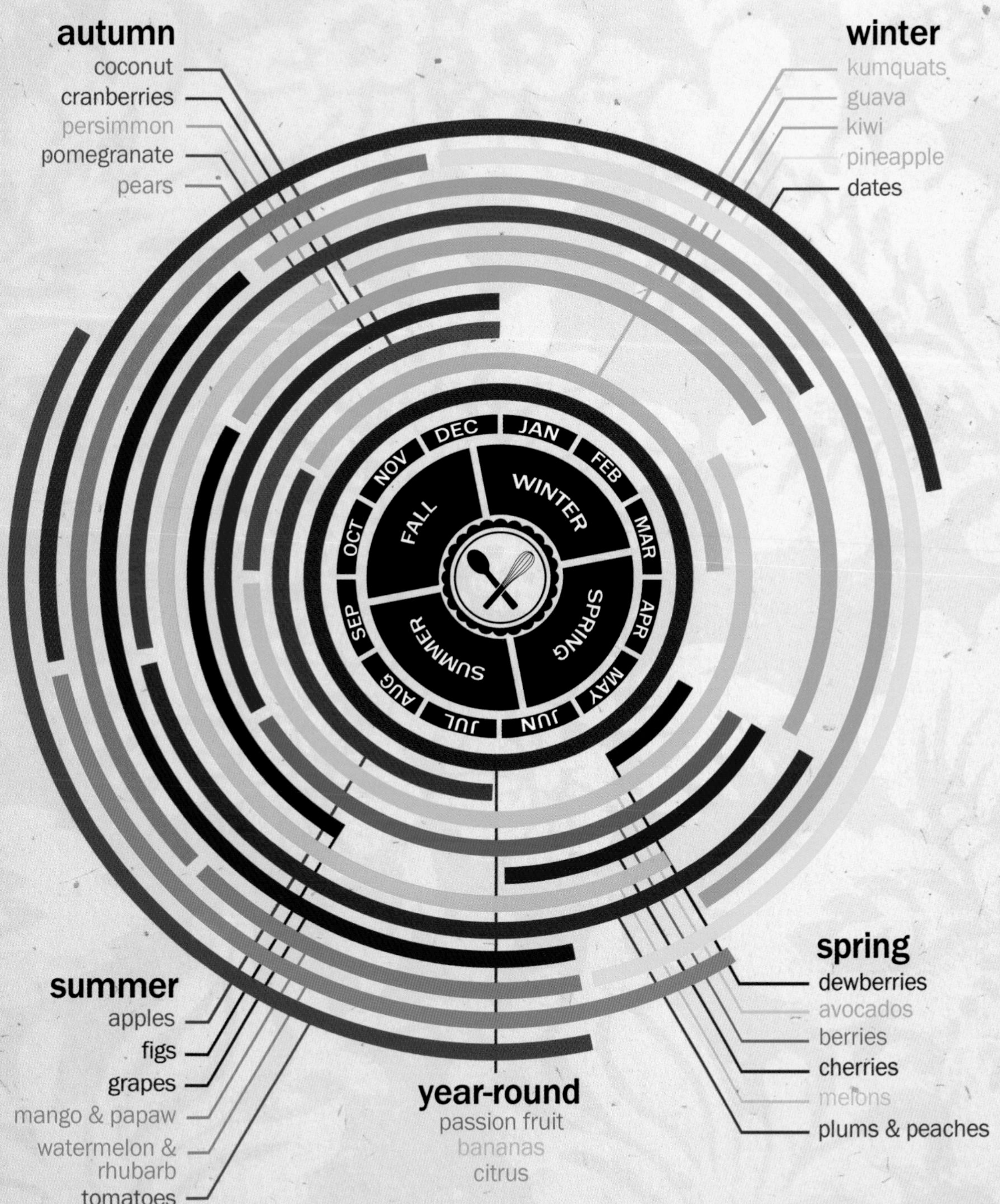
autumn
coconut
cranberries
persimmon
pomegranate
pears
winter
kumquats
guava
kiwi
pineapple
dates
DEC
JAN
NOV
FEB
OCT
MAR
SEP
APR
AUG
MAY
JUL
JUN
FALL
WINTER
SPRING
SUMMER
summer
apples
figs
grapes
mango & papaw
watermelon & rhubarb
tomatoes
year-round
passion fruit
bananas
citrus
spring
dewberries
avocados
berries
cherries
melons
plums & peaches

* achenes, berries, drupes, hesperidia, infructescences, pepo, pomes, sweet vegetables & other things we call fruits in the kitchen.

THE ANATOMY OF SPEED

Virtually every part of a cheetah's body contributes to the cat's undisputed title of fastest land animal. On the hunt, the ultimate sprinter accelerates to 60-plus miles an hour in three seconds, with bones, muscles, and major organs collaborating in a symphony of speed.

Balance and steering
If pursued prey shifts direction, a cheetah turns just as quickly, aided by a tail that acts like a rudder.

Back and front legs
Long, slender bones increase stride yet can take high-speed impact. The way muscle connects to bone at each joint lets the cat quickly kick into high gear.

TOP SPEED OF FIVE LAND ANIMALS

CHEETAH (65 mph)
THOMSON'S GAZELLE (56 mph)
HORSE (38 mph)
GREYHOUND (36 mph)
LION (34 mph)

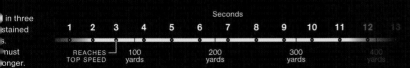

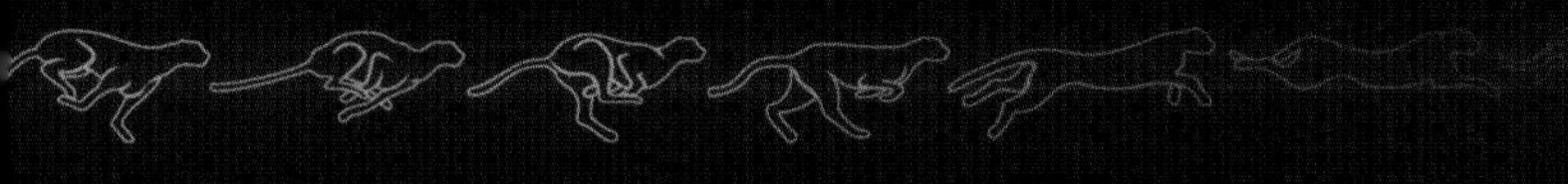

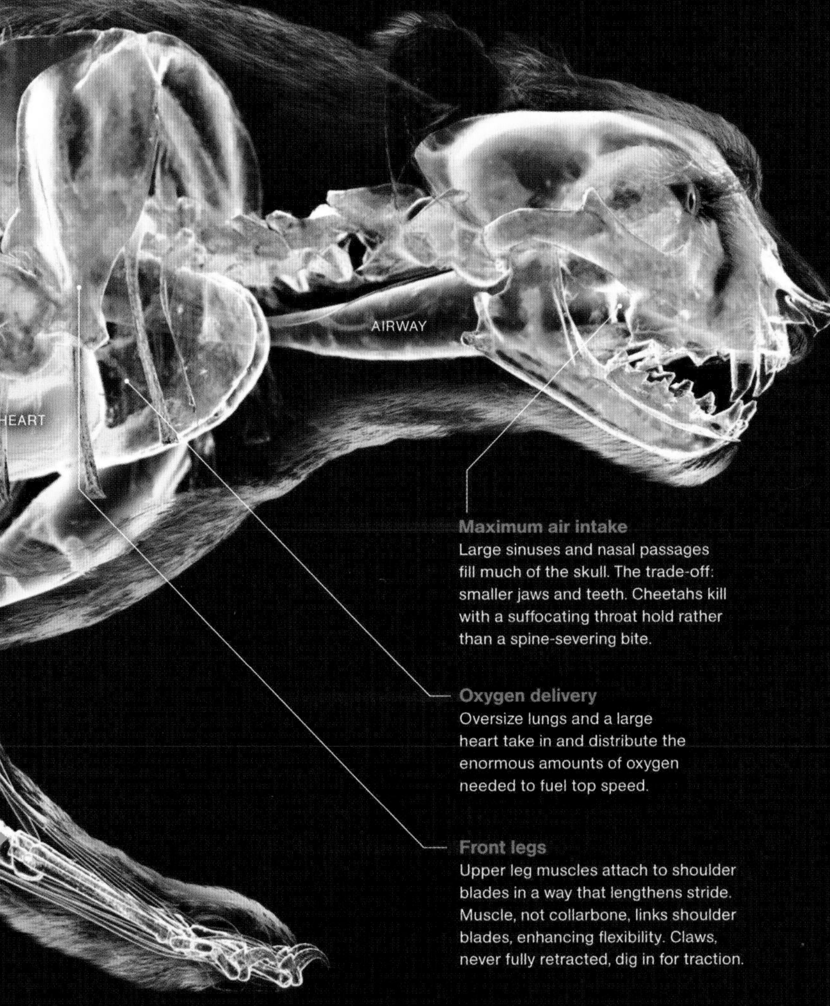
Propulsive spine
A strongly muscled and hyperflexible spine helps a galloping cheetah reach strides that can surpass 25 feet. For half that length, the cat is airborne.
AIRWAY
HEART
Maximum air intake
Large sinuses and nasal passages fill much of the skull. The trade-off: smaller jaws and teeth. Cheetahs kill with a suffocating throat hold rather than a spine-severing bite.
Oxygen delivery
Oversize lungs and a large heart take in and distribute the enormous amounts of oxygen needed to fuel top speed.
Front legs
Upper leg muscles attach to shoulder blades in a way that lengthens stride. Muscle, not collarbone, links shoulder blades, enhancing flexibility. Claws, never fully retracted, dig in for traction.

in three
stained
s.
must
onger.

Seconds

1 2 3 4 5 6 7 8 9 10 11 12 13

REACHES TOP SPEED — 100 yards — 200 yards — 300 yards — 400 yards

JASON TREAT, NGM STAFF. ART: BRYAN CHRISTIE. SOURCES: KRISTOFER M. HELGEN, MATTHEW W. TOCHERI, E. GRACE VEATCH, KATHRYN J. MCGRATH, NATIONAL MUSEUM OF NATURAL HISTORY, SMITHSONIAN INSTITUTION; PENNY HUDSON, ROYAL VETERINARY COLLEGE

ARTISTS Jason Treat, *National Geographic;* Bryan Christie, Bryan Christie Design.

STATEMENT While researching cheetah anatomy for this project, we were struck by the lack of anatomical references. We decided to create our own and enlisted the help of Kris Helgen at the Smithsonian Institution. Kris digitally scanned the bones of a cheetah specimen for us, and Bryan Christie assembled and rendered the beautiful 3-D art. The cheetah is an amazing animal, and I was fascinated to learn how its anatomy is dictated by one thing: speed. From the small size of the skull and the flexibility of the spine to the length of the tail acting as a rudder and the development of oversized lungs and airways to process oxygen—everything in the animal's anatomy is optimized for speed.

PUBLICATION *National Geographic* (November 2012)

Heat Streak

High temperature records set in the United States, January to October 2012.

The Warmup

Dissecting a year of record-breaking heat

A**s of November**, when this issue went to press, 2012 was on track to become the warmest year in the U.S. since 1895, when national record keeping began. From January through October, the 4,451 U.S. weather stations that have been tracking temperatures for at least 30 years measured nearly 28,000 high-temperature records but only 5,200 lows. That's the largest ratio of high to low records ever. "There is a lot of natural variability in these numbers," says Claudia Tebaldi, a senior scientist at the independent research organization Climate Central. "But it's definitely behavior that has the imprint of a warming climate." Scientists say this trend will continue. An Intergovernmental Panel on Climate Change report published last year predicted that the kind of heat records that fall once every 20 years now will be broken every two years by the end of the century.

KEY

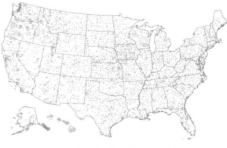

Each circle represents the number of records broken or tied at a weather station from January to October 2012.

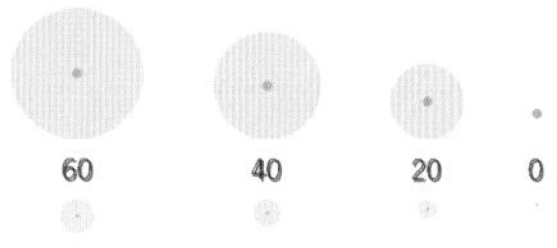
60
40
20
0

STORY AND ILLUSTRATION BY **Katie Peek**

2012 HIGH-TEMPERATURE RECORDS: 27,631

The oldest high-temperature record that fell in 2012 was beaten when the mercury hit 87°F at Elko Regional Airport in Nevada on April 22.

Sidney Municipal Airport in Nebraska logged 54 record highs, the most of any weather station.

The three hottest days were recorded in Death Valley: 128°F on July 12, and 126°F on August 9 and 10.

LOW-TEMPERATURE RECORDS: 5,212

134°F The hottest temperature ever recorded on Earth—Death Valley, California, on July 10, 1913

DES OF HIGHS AND LOWS

h [red] and low [blue] temperature records set from January to October each year.

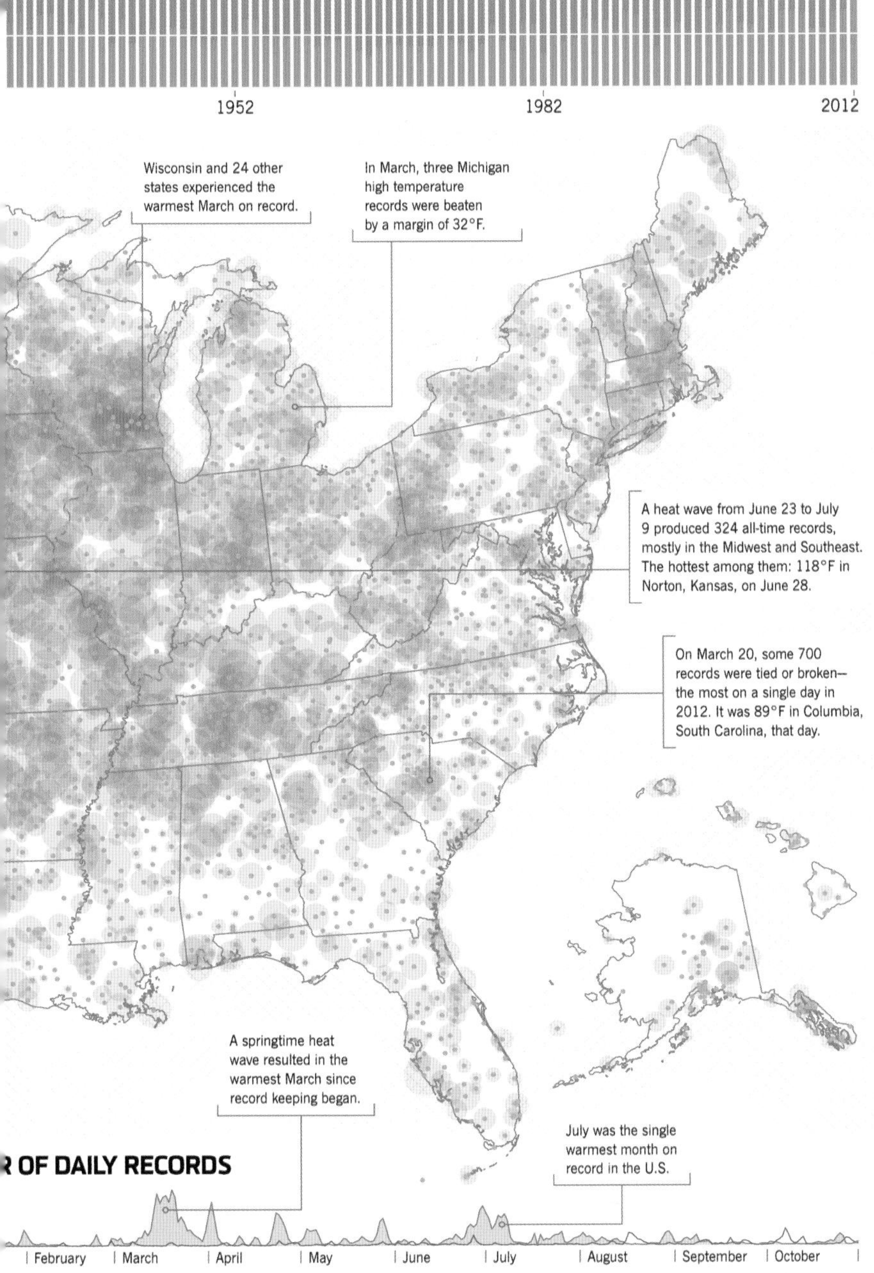

1952
1982
2012
Wisconsin and 24 other states experienced the warmest March on record.
In March, three Michigan high temperature records were beaten by a margin of 32°F.
A heat wave from June 23 to July 9 produced 324 all-time records, mostly in the Midwest and Southeast. The hottest among them: 118°F in Norton, Kansas, on June 28.
On March 20, some 700 records were tied or broken—the most on a single day in 2012. It was 89°F in Columbia, South Carolina, that day.
A springtime heat wave resulted in the warmest March since record keeping began.
July was the single warmest month on record in the U.S.
R OF DAILY RECORDS
February
March
April
May
June
July
August
September
October

ARTIST Katie Peek, data visualization specialist at *Popular Science*.

STATEMENT The National Climatic Data Center keeps a well-maintained database of record temperatures going back to the mid-nineteenth century and including data such as where each record was set, when, and by what margin. A data set that detailed and deep demands visualization. It was the warmest year yet measured in the United States, and I wanted to pull that milestone apart in space and time—just how hot was it, and where, and when?

I settled on a bubble map. The overlapping translucent circles were the right balance of detailed and broad; they allowed readers to investigate their own hometowns while also building up color in a way that exhibited the overall distribution of heat in a glance. The contrasting low temperature map, the two timelines, and the annotations provide important context. It was satisfying to use a single data set to build a detailed graphic with a clear message and plenty of depth. I hope that the numbers, viewed from a fresh, engaging angle, may be an antidote to a climate debate marked by entrenched, repetitious arguments.

PUBLICATION *Popular Science* (January 2013 issue, published December 18, 2012)

The Titanic *Disaster, Step by Step*

How the unsinkable ship broke apart.

ARTISTS Kaitlin Yarnall and Matt Twombly, *National Geographic;* Nick Kaloterakis, 3-D artist, Sydney, Australia.

STATEMENT This graphic was done in collaboration with some of the best minds in the field. Engineer Parks Stephenson was our main source. Parks has worked with James Cameron for years and has the most accurate model depicting how the ship broke apart. During our process, this model was tweaked many times and shared with Nick. James Cameron also consulted on the graphic and provided guidance—few, if any, have spent as much time as James has thinking about this ship. While the art is stunningly beautiful, it is also accurate and represents thousands and thousands of data points.

PUBLICATION
National Geographic (April 2012)

Death of the Titanic

Like her White Star Line sister ships *Olympic* and *Britannic*, *Titanic* was built to withstand practically all kinds of accidents, including a direct ramming by another ship. She would have continued to float with four or perhaps even five of her forward watertight compartments breached. But the iceberg scraping across her starboard hull opened six forward compartments, completely flooding her bow section. A hundred years after the event, explorer and filmmaker James Cameron gathered other *Titanic* experts together to synthesize a new theory of how the great ship sank and broke apart.

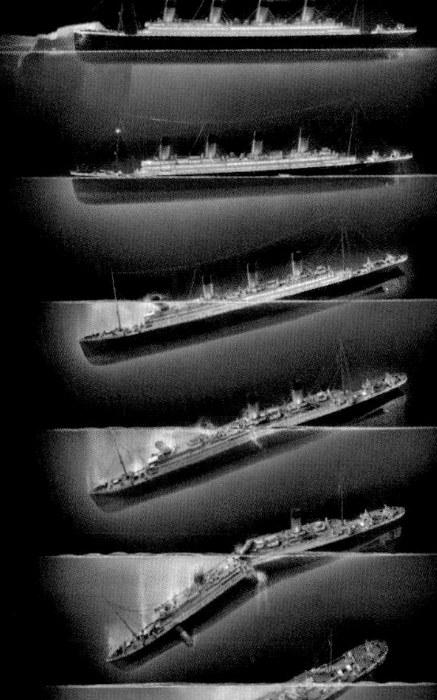

1912

April 14, 11:40 p.m.
An iceberg is sighted dead ahead, but *Titanic* is sailing at almost 21 knots and cannot be turned quickly enough to port to avoid a collision along her starboard side.

April 15, 1:50 a.m.
Two hours of steady flooding settles the bow. The ship gradually lists to port, and by about 1:50 a.m. the water reaches a gangway door open on the port side, increasing the list.

2:15 a.m.
The pressure of rising seawater buckles the boiler uptake supporting the number 1 funnel, and the funnel falls. Water floods in the new opening, accelerating the rate of sinking.

2:18 a.m.
The ship's water-heavy bow and its relatively buoyant stern begin an immense tug-of-war. The stress causes the hull to crack just in front of the third funnel.

2:18 a.m.
Seconds later, maximum bending stress breaks the hull, with bow and stern held together only by the reinforced hull bottom. The stern lurches to port, throwing people against the port rail.

2:19 a.m.
The bow pulls loose from the still buoyant stern, which briefly settles back almost level with the surface before angling down again as water floods its ruptured forward end.

500 ft
1,000 ft
0.5 mile
1 mile
1.5 miles
2 miles
Bow
Stern
2.5 miles
1,970 ft

From Ship to Wreck
The *Titanic* split apart on the surface, its bow and stern taking different paths to the bottom. The sleek bow fell in a fairly straight line, moving forward one length for every five lengths of vertical descent. The less hydrodynamic stern followed minutes later, spiraling down to land almost 2,000 feet to the south of the bow.

2:20 a.m.
As the bow speeds toward the bottom, the stern angles almost to vertical, then disappears from the surface, shedding debris from its open end. Boilers tumble out and head straight down.

2:21 a.m.
Water flowing over the bow snaps the foremast back over the bridge and tears off funnels. About 500 feet down, air pockets in the stern implode, and it flips around to descend aft first.

Because of their flared shapes, both bow and stern descend in an undulating "stall and fall" pattern. The stern corkscrews down clockwise, shedding more debris before smashing into the sea bottom.

Moving at some 30 knots, the bow plows into the bottom at an angle of about 20 degrees, breaking the hull and collapsing decks. The tortured wreck of the stern pays witness to its more violent descent.

Distances not to scale. Final resting pieces of bow and stern are 1,970 feet apart.

NATIONAL GEOGRAPHIC

I. YOU
II. US
III. MATERIAL WORLD

CONTINUED

Death of the Titanic

Like her White Star Line sister ships *Olympic* and *Britannic*, *Titanic* was built to withstand practically all kinds of accidents, including a direct ramming by another ship. She would have continued to float with four or perhaps even five of her forward watertight compartments breached. But the iceberg scraping across her starboard hull opened six forward compartments, completely flooding her bow section. A hundred years after the event, explorer and filmmaker James Cameron gathered other *Titanic* experts together to synthesize a new theory of how the great ship sank and broke apart.

1912

April 14, 11:40 p.m.
An iceberg is sighted dead ahead, but *Titanic* is sailing at almost 21 knots and cannot be turned quickly enough to port to avoid a collision along her starboard side.

April 15, 1:50 a.m.
Two hours of steady flooding settles the bow. The ship gradually lists to port, and by about 1:50 a.m. the water reaches a gangway door open on the port side, increasing the list.

2:15 a.m.
The pressure of rising seawater buckles the boiler uptake supporting the number 1 funnel, and the funnel falls. Water floods in the new opening, accelerating the rate of sinking.

2:18 a.m.
The ship's water-heavy bow and its relatively buoyant stern begin an immense tug-of-war. The stress causes the hull to crack just in front of the third funnel.

2:18 a.m.
Seconds later, maximum bending stress breaks the hull, with bow and stern held together only by the reinforced hull bottom. The stern lurches to port, throwing people against the port rail.

2:19 a.m.
The bow pulls loose from the still buoyant stern, which briefly settles back almost level with the surface before angling down again as water floods its ruptured forward end.

500 ft
1,000 ft
0.5 mile
1 mile
1.5 miles
2 miles
2.5 miles
Bow
Stern
1,970 ft

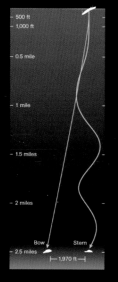

From Ship to Wreck

The *Titanic* split apart on the surface, its bow and stern taking different paths to the bottom. The sleek bow fell in a fairly straight line, moving forward one length for every five lengths of vertical descent. The less hydrodynamic stern followed minutes later, spiraling down to land almost 2,000 feet to the south of the bow.

KAITLIN M. YARNALL AND MATTHEW TWOMBLY, NGM STAFF. ART: NICK KALOTERAKIS

SOURCES: JAMES CAMERON; KEN MARSCHALL; CASEY SCHATZ; LT. CMDR. PARKS STEPHENSON, USN (RET.); CMDR. JEFFREY STETTLER, USN

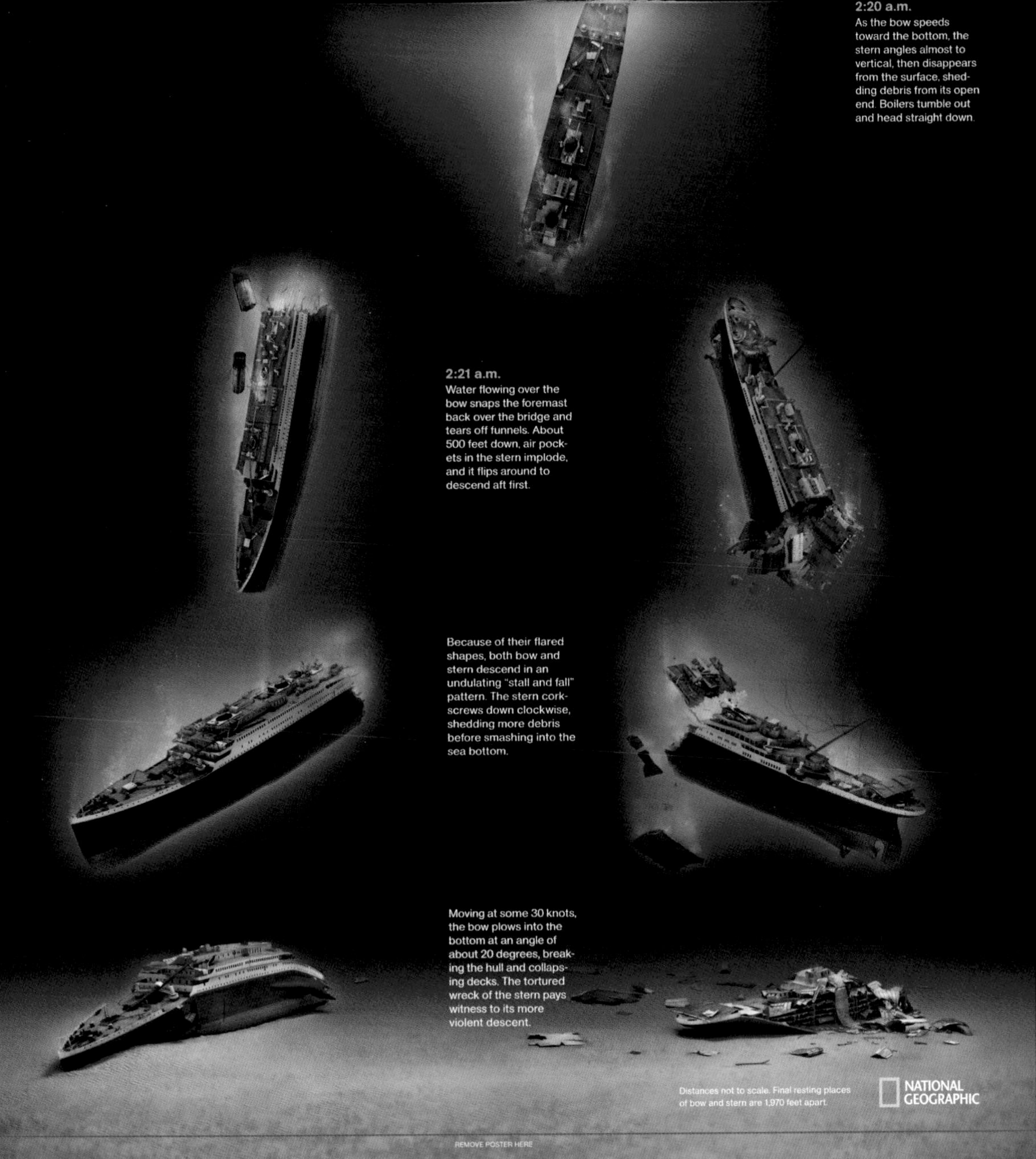
2:20 a.m.
As the bow speeds toward the bottom, the stern angles almost to vertical, then disappears from the surface, shedding debris from its open end. Boilers tumble out and head straight down.
2:21 a.m.
Water flowing over the bow snaps the foremast back over the bridge and tears off funnels. About 500 feet down, air pockets in the stern implode, and it flips around to descend aft first.
Because of their flared shapes, both bow and stern descend in an undulating "stall and fall" pattern. The stern corkscrews down clockwise, shedding more debris before smashing into the sea bottom.
Moving at some 30 knots, the bow plows into the bottom at an angle of about 20 degrees, breaking the hull and collapsing decks. The tortured wreck of the stern pays witness to its more violent descent.
Distances not to scale. Final resting places of bow and stern are 1,970 feet apart.
NATIONAL GEOGRAPHIC
REMOVE POSTER HERE

Mind Control

The steps necessary for a severely paralyzed test patient to operate an experimental robotic arm.

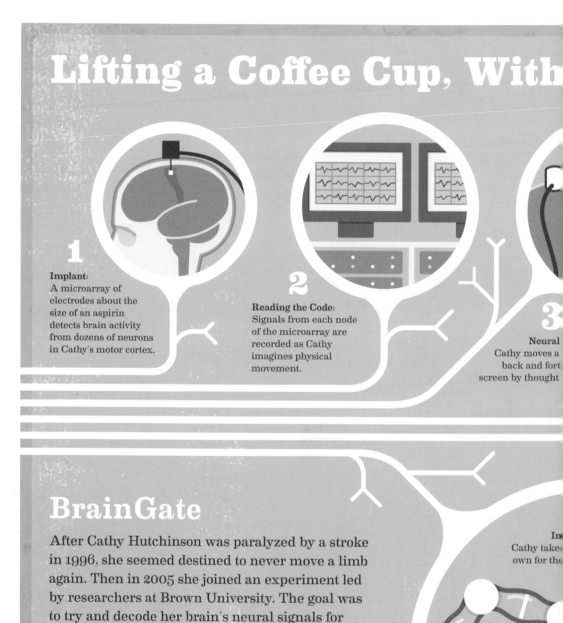

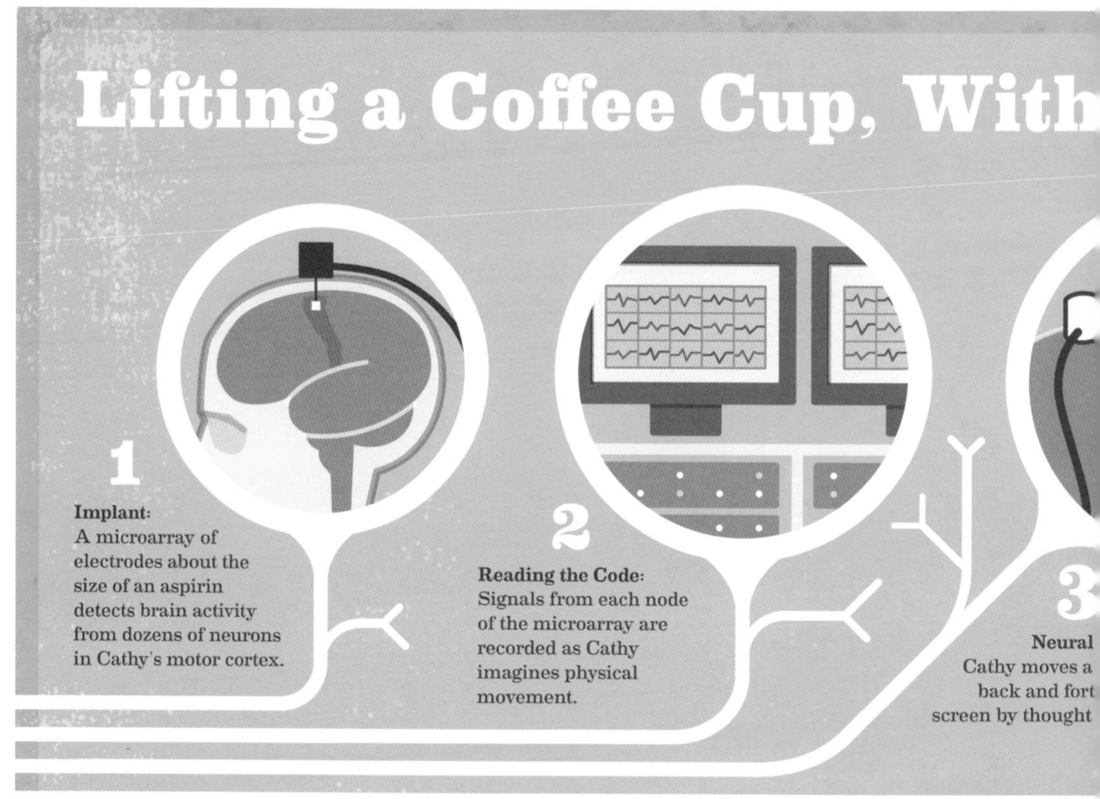
Lifting a Coffee Cup, With
1
Implant:
A microarray of electrodes about the size of an aspirin detects brain activity from dozens of neurons in Cathy's motor cortex.
2
Reading the Code:
Signals from each node of the microarray are recorded as Cathy imagines physical movement.
Neural
Cathy moves a
screen by thought

BrainGate

After Cathy Hutchinson was paralyzed by a stroke in 1996, she seemed destined to never move a limb again. Then in 2005 she joined an experiment led by researchers at Brown University. The goal was to try and decode her brain's neural signals for movement and, then translate them into a robotic arm. In May of 2012, the researchers announced the study's extraordinary success.

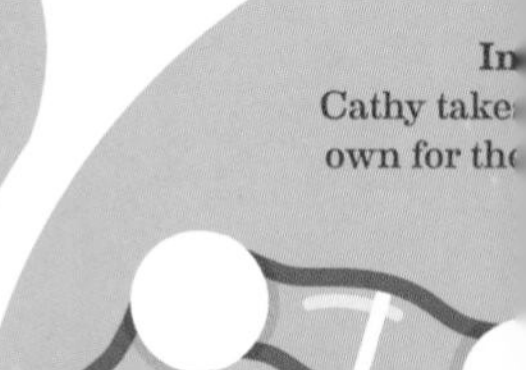

houghts
ATAVIST
4
2D Control:
Cathy learns to move a cursor up, down, left, and right, which allows her to surf the web and type letters.
5
3D Control:
Another dimension of control is added, enabling Cathy to navigate physical space with a robotic arm.
e:
ffee on her
in 15 years
illustration Damien Scogin

ARTIST Damien Scogin, a freelance illustrator in New York City.

STATEMENT This infographic was featured in the story "The Electric Mind" by Jessica Benko. The story concentrated on the unimaginable consequences of a brain-stem stroke and the remarkable determination and attitude of stroke survivor Cathy Hutchinson. Stylistically, I wanted to keep the narrative arc as the primary focus and felt that a flowchart would serve that purpose. The basic shape of neurons gave me a great way to isolate each portion of the research narrative while still keeping the visual flow of the diagram.

I studied neuroscience as an undergrad along with the visual arts. Given my basic background in the subject, this particular story allowed me an incredible opportunity to be a small part of some of the most revolutionary neurobiological research that I have ever heard of.

PUBLICATION *The Atavist* (April 16, 2012)

MLB PREVIEW

GOING, GOING, GONE?

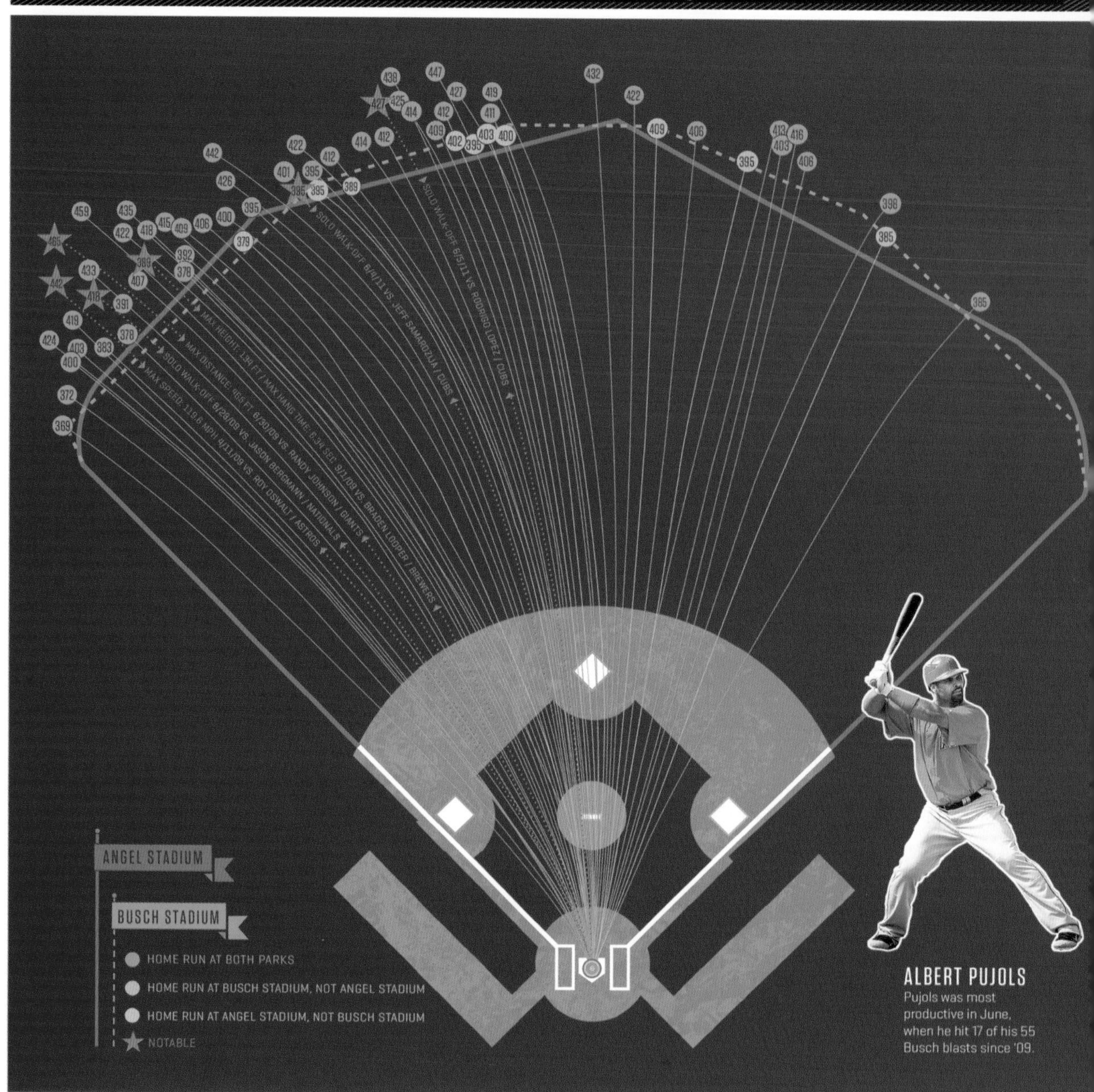

SOLO WALK-OFF 6/5/11 VS. RODRIGO LOPEZ / CUBS
SOLO WALK-OFF 6/4/11 VS. JEFF SAMARDZIJA / CUBS
MAX HEIGHT: 134 FT / MAX HANG TIME: 6.34 SEC 9/1/09 VS. BRADEN LOOPER / BREWERS
MAX DISTANCE: 465 FT 6/30/09 VS. RANDY JOHNSON / GIANTS
SOLO WALK-OFF 8/28/09 VS. JASON BERGMANN / NATIONALS
MAX SPEED: 119.6 MPH 4/11/09 VS. ROY OSWALT / ASTROS
ANGEL STADIUM
BUSCH STADIUM
HOME RUN AT BOTH PARKS
HOME RUN AT BUSCH STADIUM, NOT ANGEL STADIUM
HOME RUN AT ANGEL STADIUM, NOT BUSCH STADIUM
NOTABLE
ALBERT PUJOLS
Pujols was most productive in June, when he hit 17 of his 55 Busch blasts since '09.

Change of Venue

How would two superstar home-run hitters fare in new stadiums?

ARTISTS Ben Gibson, Pop Chart Lab in Brooklyn, New York; John Yun, John Korpics, Jason Lancaster, Amy Brachmann, Bruce Kelley, John B. Morris, Joel Weber, Jim Keller, and the ESPN Stats & Info Group, *ESPN The Magazine*.

IT TOOK MORE THAN $450 MILLION COMBINED TO BRING ALBERT PUJOLS TO ANGEL STADIUM AND PRINCE FIELDER TO COMERICA PARK. MONEY WELL SPENT? ESPN STATS & INFO GROUP CHARTED THEIR HOME-FIELD BOMBS SINCE 2009—AND WHERE THOSE WOULD'VE LANDED IN THEIR NEW PARKS.

infographic by **POP CHART LAB**

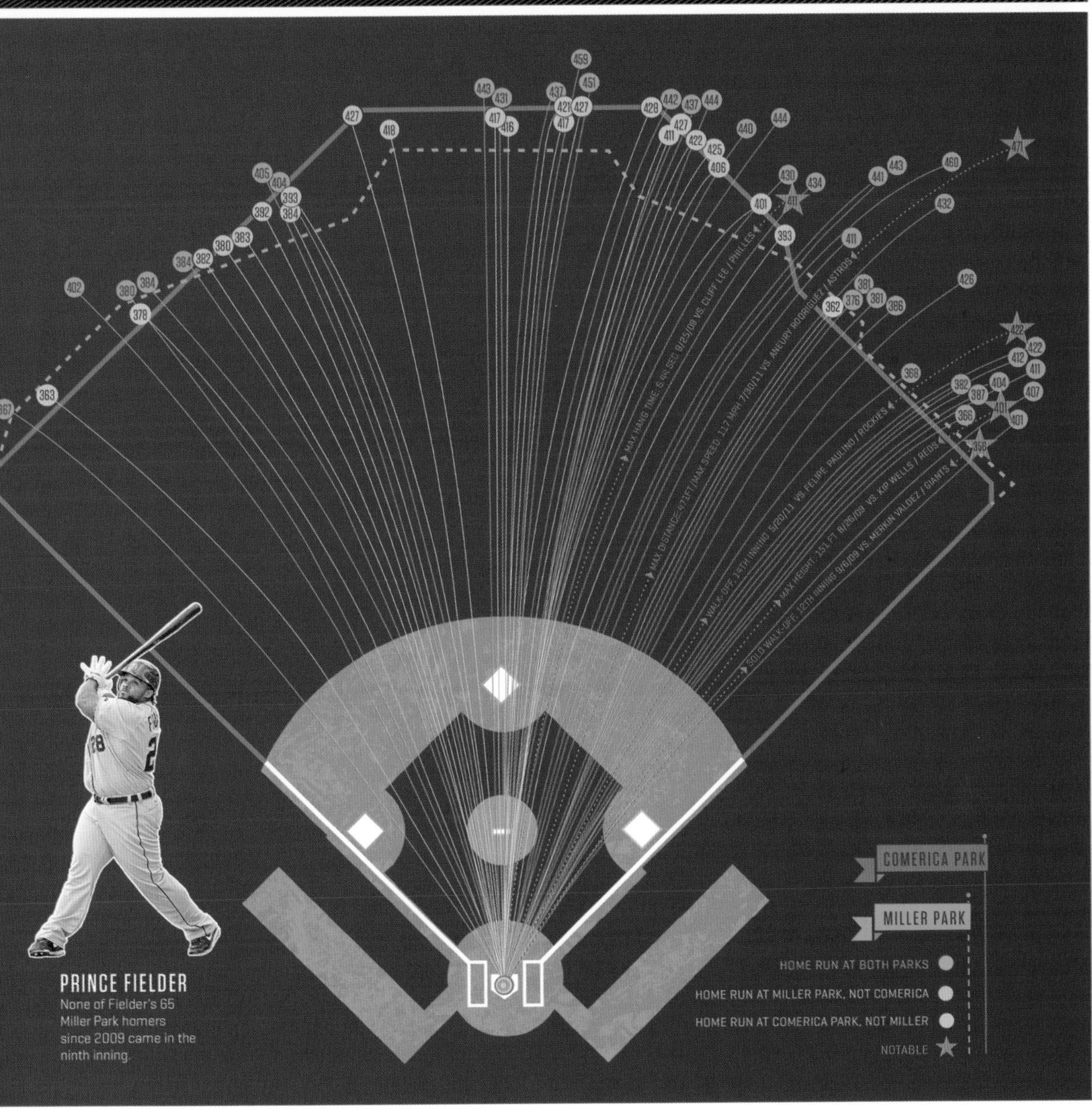
MAX HANG TIME: 6.44 SEC. 9/25/09 VS. CLIFF LEE / PHILLIES
MAX DISTANCE: 471 FT / MAX SPEED: 117 MPH 7/30/11 VS. ANEURY RODRIGUEZ / ASTROS
WALK-OFF, 14TH INNING 5/20/11 VS. FELIPE PAULINO / ROCKIES
MAX HEIGHT: 151 FT 8/26/09 VS. KIP WELLS / REDS
SOLO WALK-OFF, 12TH INNING 9/6/09 VS. MERKIN VALDEZ / GIANTS
COMERICA PARK
MILLER PARK
HOME RUN AT BOTH PARKS
HOME RUN AT MILLER PARK, NOT COMERICA
HOME RUN AT COMERICA PARK, NOT MILLER
NOTABLE
PRINCE FIELDER
None of Fielder's 65 Miller Park homers since 2009 came in the ninth inning.

STATEMENT How would the friendly confines of Angel Stadium handle Albert Pujols's bombs? How exactly would the unfriendly confines of Comerica Park change Prince Fielder's results? To answer those questions for its stat-conscious readers, the ESPN Stats & Info Group calculated the length of every home run Pujols and Fielder hit during the 2011 season and whether those homers would have left their new stadiums. The result was a fascinating picture, lightly drawn but easily understood, showing Pujols potentially gaining homers and Fielder losing many. Included are the outlines of each stadium, where home run balls landed, and where those same balls would land in the new ballparks—with simple color coding revealing the new reality faced by these two ballplayers. Stars highlight homers whose arc, speed, and distance topped the charts.

PUBLICATION *ESPN The Magazine* (April 2, 2012)

The Great Dying

The most detailed available tally of species under threat of extinction.

ARTIST Bill Marsh, the *New York Times.*

STATEMENT Three groups—birds, mammals, and amphibians—have been studied enough for scientists to confidently declare large portions of them at risk of disappearing. Many species in nine other groups, so large that they have not been fully evaluated (or even discovered), are also threatened. But the proportions of those nine groups at risk for extinction are unknown—a race between scientific study and accelerating environmental destruction.

This data was originally graphed as a simple bar chart. Differences in scale between plant and animal groups, and between known and unknown species, reduced some of the relevant numbers to thin, visually indistinct slices. There are certainly less extravagant ways to present these numbers, but the mass of familiar icons makes an arresting image, its circular arrangement evoking the vast web of life that the numbers represent.

PUBLICATION *New York Times* (June 3, 2012)

Are We in the Midst Of a Sixth Mass Extinction?

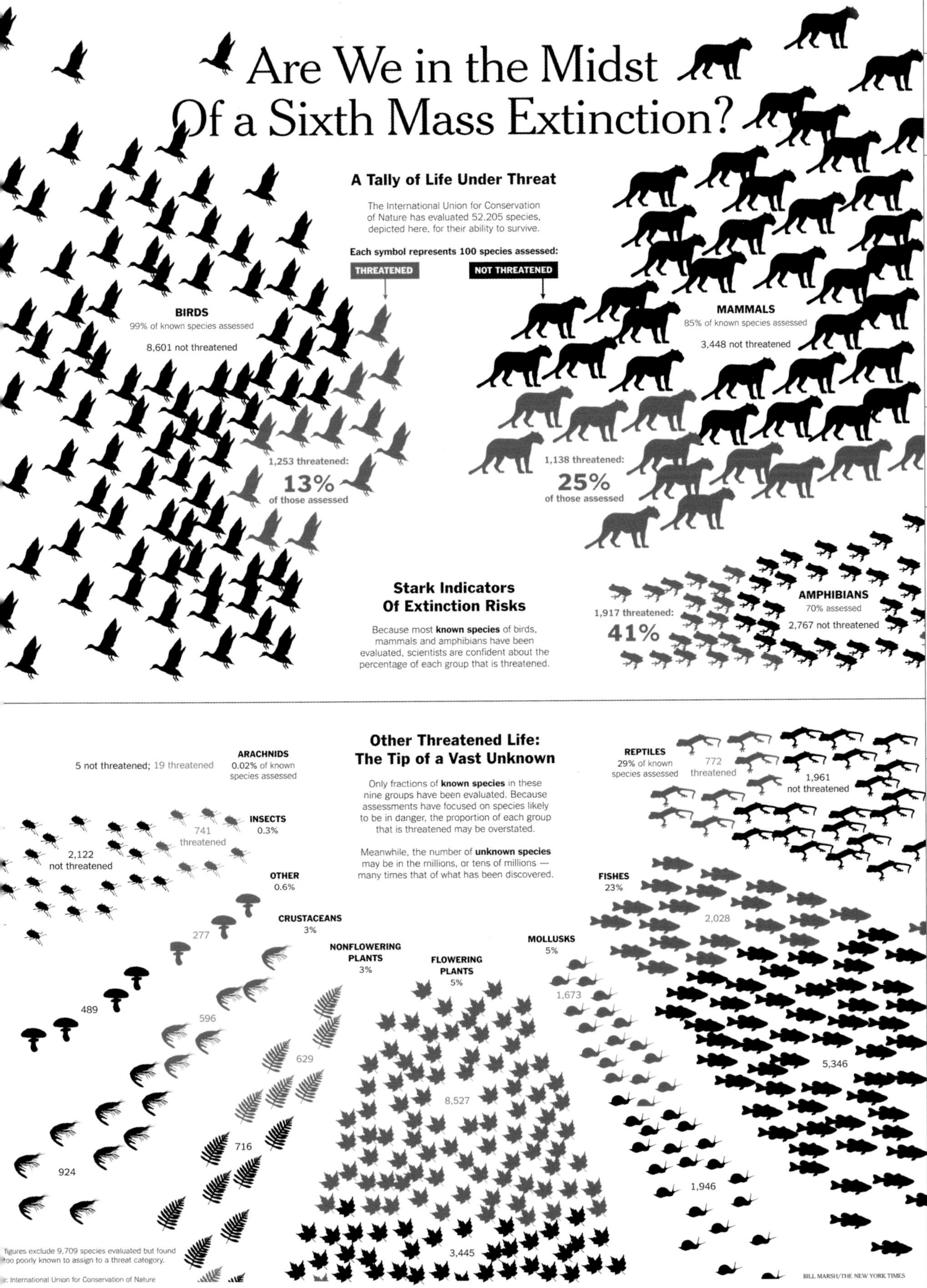

A Tally of Life Under Threat

The International Union for Conservation of Nature has evaluated 52,205 species, depicted here, for their ability to survive.

Each symbol represents 100 species assessed:

THREATENED — NOT THREATENED

BIRDS
99% of known species assessed
8,601 not threatened
1,253 threatened:
13%
of those assessed

MAMMALS
85% of known species assessed
3,448 not threatened
1,138 threatened:
25%
of those assessed

AMPHIBIANS
70% assessed
2,767 not threatened
1,917 threatened:
41%

Stark Indicators Of Extinction Risks

Because most **known species** of birds, mammals and amphibians have been evaluated, scientists are confident about the percentage of each group that is threatened.

Other Threatened Life: The Tip of a Vast Unknown

Only fractions of **known species** in these nine groups have been evaluated. Because assessments have focused on species likely to be in danger, the proportion of each group that is threatened may be overstated.

Meanwhile, the number of **unknown species** may be in the millions, or tens of millions — many times that of what has been discovered.

ARACHNIDS
0.02% of known species assessed
5 not threatened; 19 threatened

INSECTS
0.3%
741 threatened
2,122 not threatened

OTHER
0.6%
277
489

CRUSTACEANS
3%
596
924

NONFLOWERING PLANTS
3%
629
716

FLOWERING PLANTS
5%
8,527
3,445

MOLLUSKS
5%
1,673
1,946

FISHES
23%
2,028
5,346

REPTILES
29% of known species assessed
772 threatened
1,961 not threatened

figures exclude 9,709 species evaluated but found too poorly known to assign to a threat category.

:: International Union for Conservation of Nature

BILL MARSH/THE NEW YORK TIMES

The Shuttle's Moving Day

How the Endeavour was driven through downtown Los Angeles.

ARTISTS Tom Reinken, Raoul Rañoa, and Les Dunseith, the *Los Angeles Times*.

STATEMENT We had meetings and interviews with a wide-ranging cast of sources including engineers, movers, and city officials, plus NASA and museum personnel. The shuttles were a presence in Americans' lives for thirty years, providing both magic and tragic moments. The end of the program was a big story in itself. But bringing one to Los Angeles made it a once-in-a-lifetime local event.

Although we had worked with NASA on other projects, this was a unique occurrence, so there was a lot to learn. The transport device, for example, is strong enough to carry seven shuttles. And the transport vehicles were controlled via a remote control that looks very similar to a video game controller.

PUBLICATION *Los Angeles Times* (October 11, 2012)

A complex Endeavour

The shuttle's 12-mile, two-day journey from LAX to the California Science Center will require four computer-controlled transporters to work together through a series of complex turns and back-and-forth slides to avoid streetside obstacles.

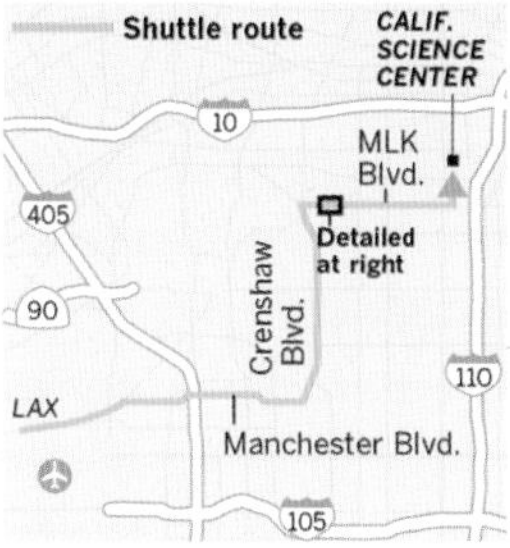

Shuttle route
CALIF. SCIENCE CENTER
MLK Blvd.
Detailed at right
Crenshaw Blvd.
Manchester Blvd.
LAX
10
405
90
110
105

Avoiding obstacles Movements ● Trees kept ● Light post removed

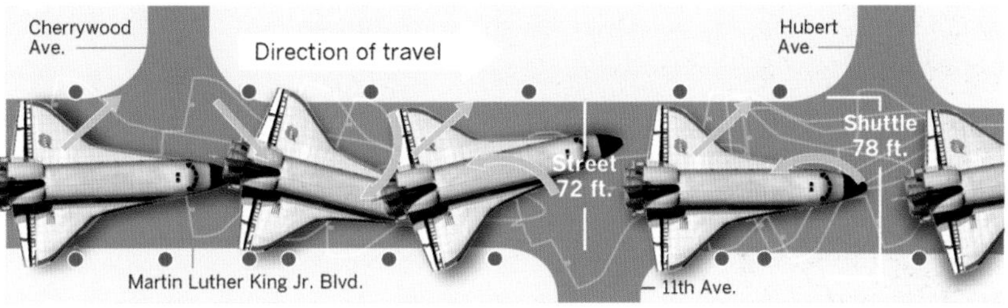

Cherrywood Ave.
Direction of travel
Hubert Ave.
Street 72 ft.
Shuttle 78 ft.
Martin Luther King Jr. Blvd.
11th Ave.

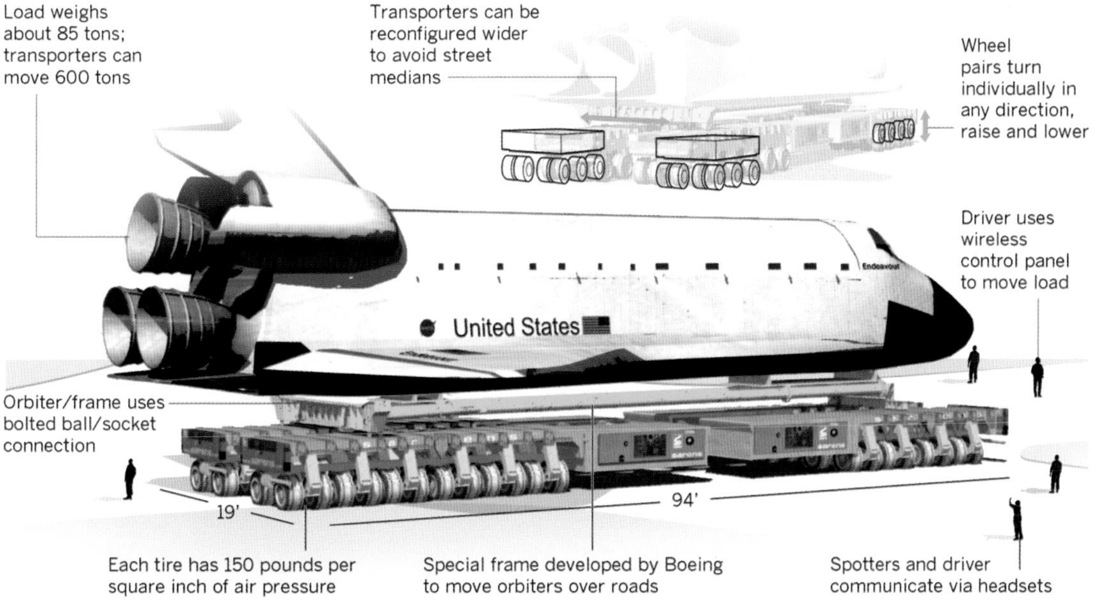

Load weighs about 85 tons; transporters can move 600 tons

Transporters can be reconfigured wider to avoid street medians

Wheel pairs turn individually in any direction, raise and lower

Driver uses wireless control panel to move load

United States

Endeavour

Orbiter/frame uses bolted ball/socket connection

19'

94'

Each tire has 150 pounds per square inch of air pressure

Special frame developed by Boeing to move orbiters over roads

Spotters and driver communicate via headsets

Maneuvering the shuttle

Three primary types of movement will allow Endeavor to successfully navigate city streets.

Carousel

❶ Orbiter is moved into position for a sharp right turn.

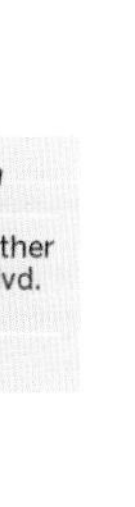
Crenshaw Blvd.
Wheel direction
Martin Luther King Jr.Blvd.

❷ Wheels realign, spin shuttle 90 degrees to point east.

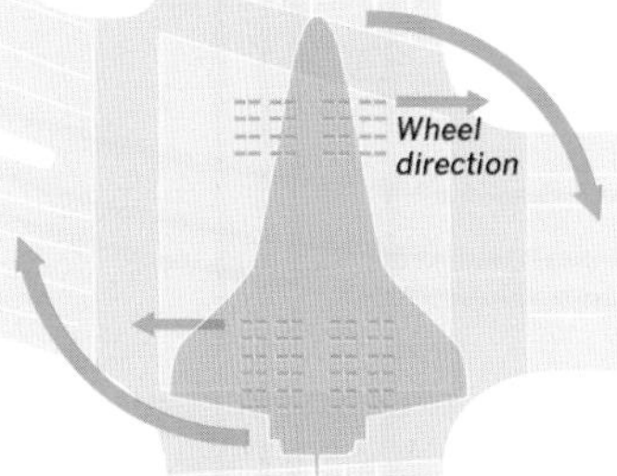
Wheel direction

❸ Wheels resume former position, all turning in same direction.

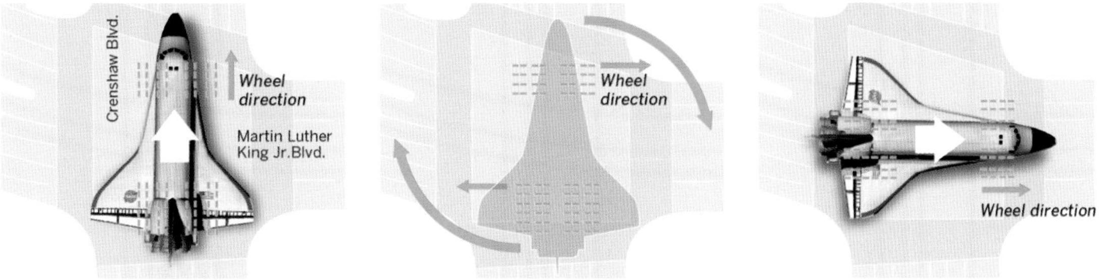

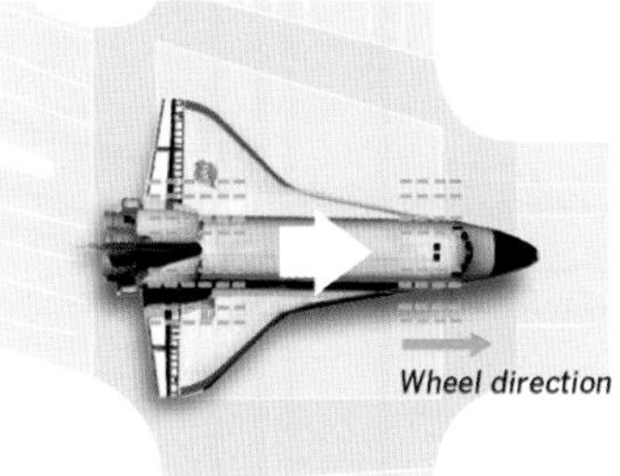
Wheel direction

Crabbing

With all wheels turned in the same direction, a diagonal or side-to-side movement is made.

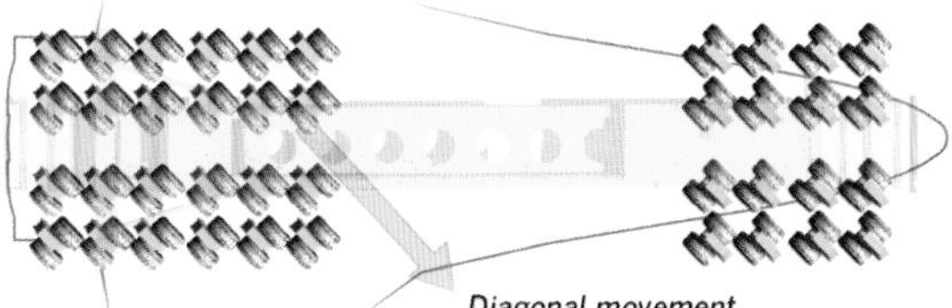
Diagonal movement

Standard turn

Wheels gradually turn in different directions at incremental angles to make more conventional turns.

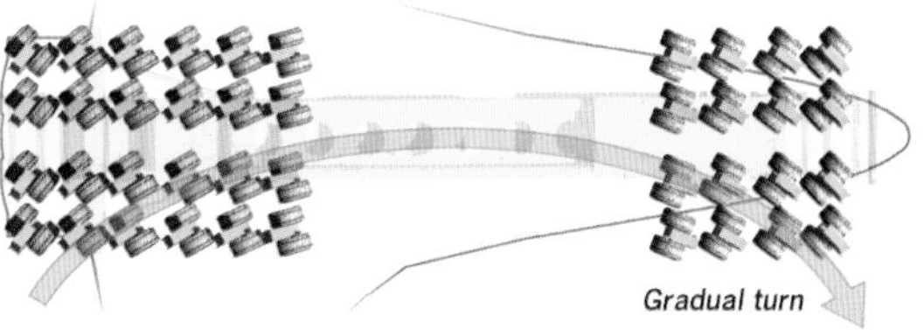
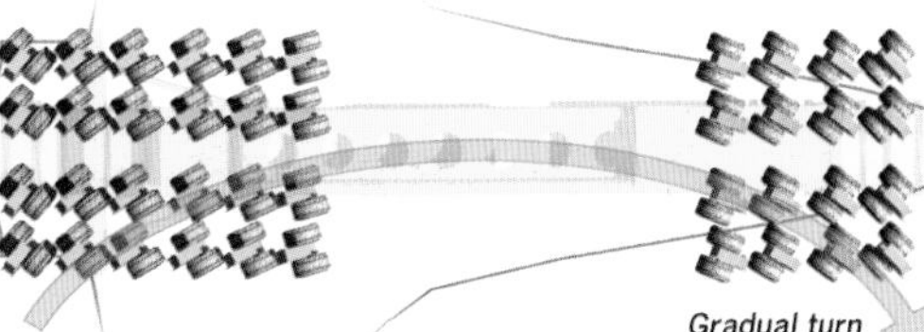
Gradual turn

An Army for the Afterlife

The first complete reconstruction, in color, of the main pit at the Terra-cotta Army site in Xi'an, China.

ARTISTS Pure Rendering GmbH in Berlin; Juan Velasco and Ann Williams, *National Geographic.*

STATEMENT Emperor Qin Shi Huang Di buried himself with a fabulous army of more than 6,000 terra-cotta figures. For the first time we had enough clues from pigment fragments to have a very accurate idea of the colors in the army.

I (Juan Velasco) traveled to the site in China to research this project and to spend time with the scientists working on the preservation of the color pigments. Until now, any tiny fragments of paint would disappear in a few minutes after new figures were unearthed. Story photographer Lou Mazzatenta showed me some panoramic photos of the pit, and we thought it would be amazing to show a full view of the army in all of its splendor. Once in China, the photographers at the site's museum showed me a beautiful panoramic photo. When you come to the page, you see the photo before you open a double gatefold from the same point of view, revealing the whole full-color army.

All of the illustrations for this piece were created by Pure Rendering GmbH, a German CGI company that does architectural and product renderings, animation, and matte painting.

PUBLICATION *National Geographic* (June 2012)

Pigments
Various materials provided color, including precious stones ground into powder.
Color unknown
General, Pit 1
RED: Cinnabar
BLACK: Charcoal
PURPLE: Cinnabar and barium copper silicate
BLUE: Azurite
DARK RED: Iron oxide
WHITE: Bones burned at a high temperature
GREEN: Malachite
BROWN, BLACK, AND GROUND LAYER: Lacquer made from the sap of a local tree

Fragile Paint

The army's rich coloring is reproduced on this figure (left), one of the few found with enough traces of paint so that experts could determine almost all of its original colors. On each warrior, egg-based paint was applied over two layers of lacquer. When archaeologists began to uncover the army, the lacquer dried and flaked off, taking the paint with it. Today new techniques are saving the ancient hues.

PHOTOS: ROBERT CLARK (PIGMENTS)

CONTINUED

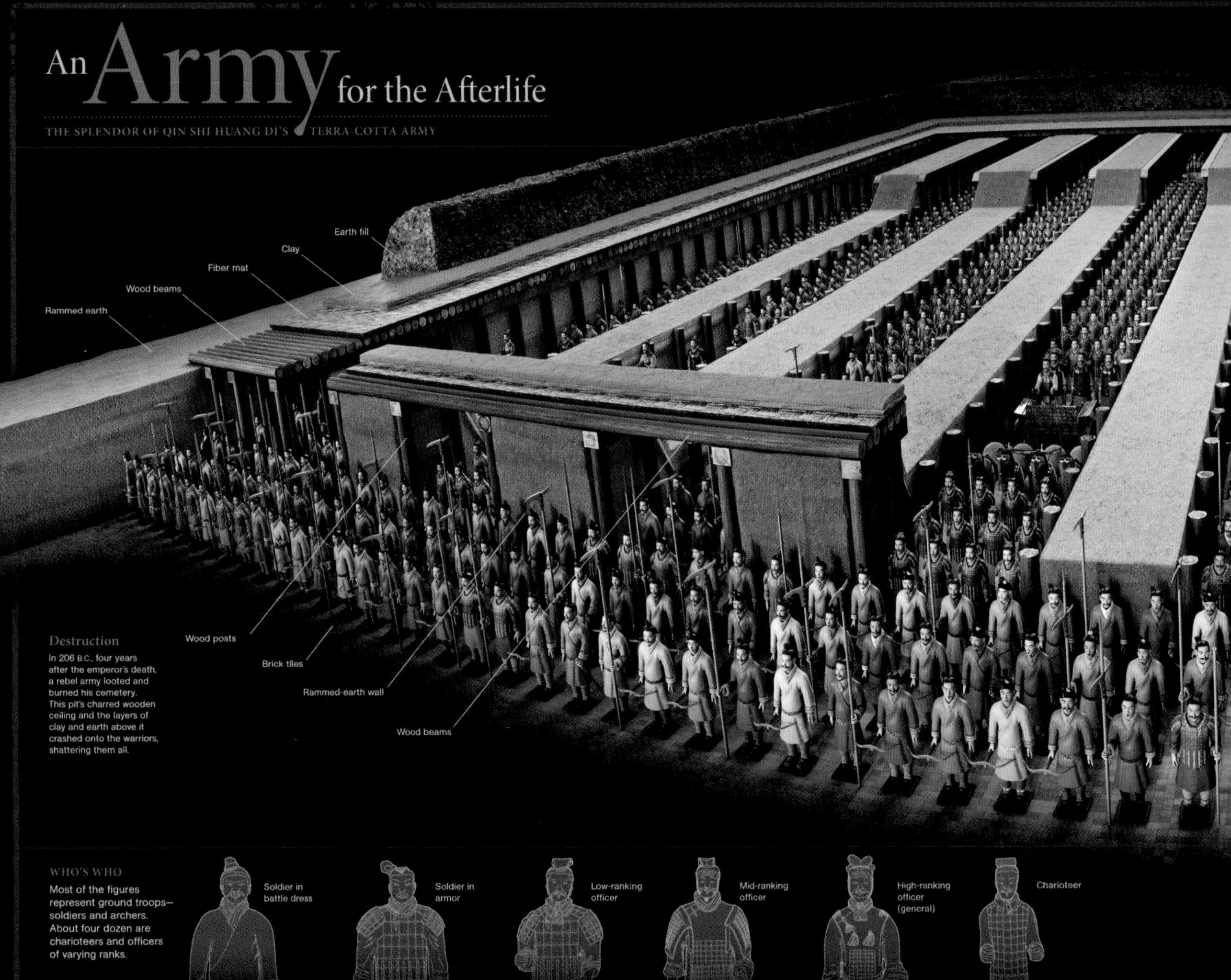
An Army for the Afterlife
THE SPLENDOR OF QIN SHI HUANG DI'S TERRA-COTTA ARMY
Earth fill
Clay
Fiber mat
Wood beams
Rammed earth
Destruction
In 206 B.C., four years after the emperor's death, a rebel army looted and burned his cemetery. This pit's charred wooden ceiling and the layers of clay and earth above it crashed onto the warriors, shattering them all.
Wood posts
Brick tiles
Rammed-earth wall
Wood beams
WHO'S WHO
Most of the figures represent ground troops—soldiers and archers. About four dozen are charioteers and officers of varying ranks.
Soldier in battle dress
Soldier in armor
Low-ranking officer
Mid-ranking officer
High-ranking officer (general)
Charioteer

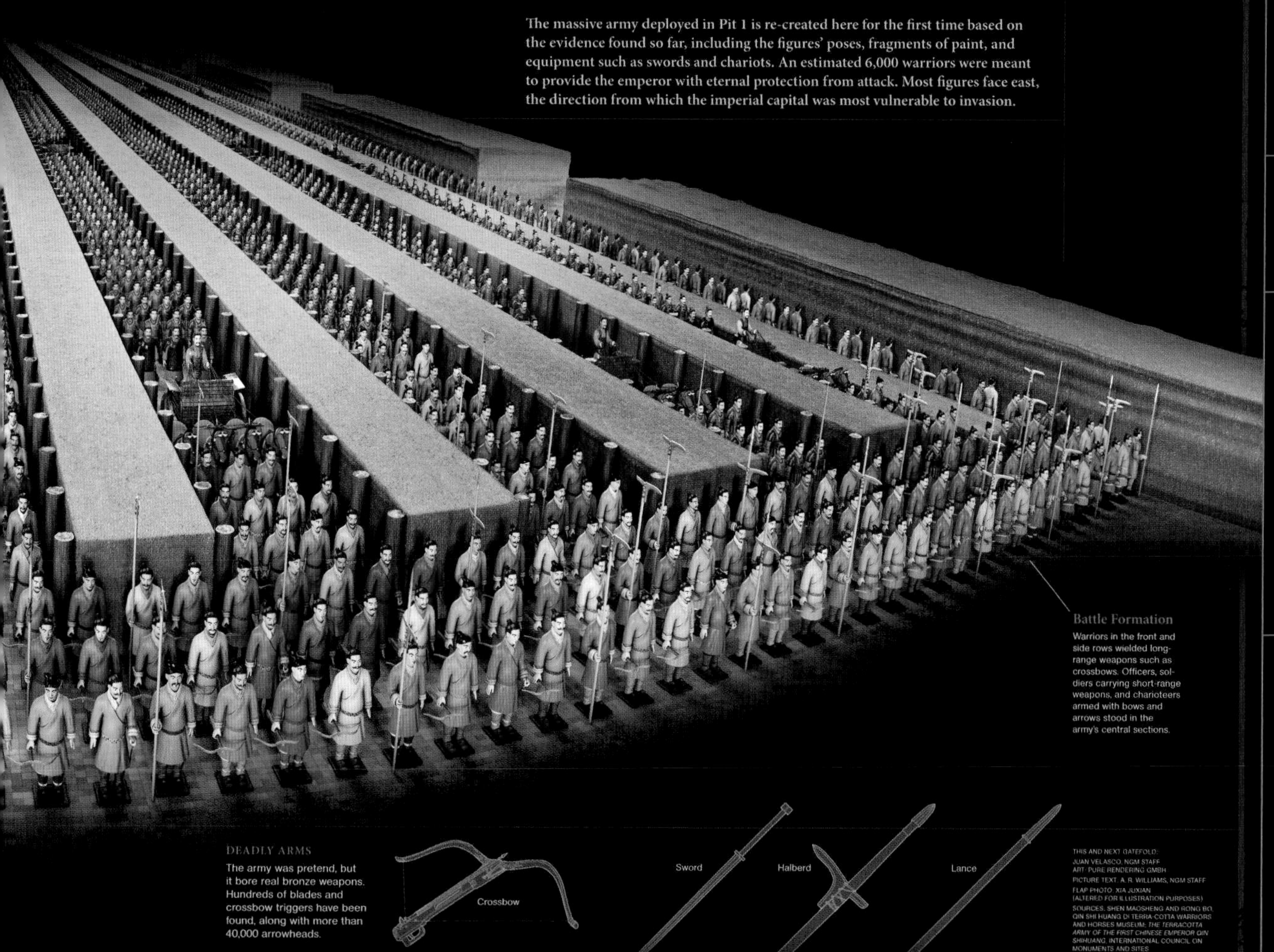
Crossbow
Sword
Halberd
Lance

The massive army deployed in Pit 1 is re-created here for the first time based on the evidence found so far, including the figures' poses, fragments of paint, and equipment such as swords and chariots. An estimated 6,000 warriors were meant to provide the emperor with eternal protection from attack. Most figures face east, the direction from which the imperial capital was most vulnerable to invasion.

Battle Formation

Warriors in the front and side rows wielded long-range weapons such as crossbows. Officers, soldiers carrying short-range weapons, and charioteers armed with bows and arrows stood in the army's central sections.

DEADLY ARMS

The army was pretend, but it bore real bronze weapons. Hundreds of blades and crossbow triggers have been found, along with more than 40,000 arrowheads.

THIS AND NEXT GATEFOLD:
JUAN VELASCO, NGM STAFF
ART: PURE RENDERING GMBH
PICTURE TEXT: A. R. WILLIAMS, NGM STAFF
FLAP PHOTO: XIA JUXIAN
(ALTERED FOR ILLUSTRATION PURPOSES)
SOURCES: SHEN MAOSHENG AND RONG BO, QIN SHI HUANG DI TERRA-COTTA WARRIORS AND HORSES MUSEUM; *THE TERRACOTTA ARMY OF THE FIRST CHINESE EMPEROR QIN SHIHUANG*, INTERNATIONAL COUNCIL ON MONUMENTS AND SITES

The Disappearing Desktop

Working habits or tools that are destined for extinction.

ARTIST Nicolas Rapp, graphics director, *Fortune.*

STATEMENT LinkedIn recently asked more than seven thousand members of its professional network in eighteen countries about which office supplies they see going the way of the dodo in the next five years. Topping the list was the tape recorder. The effort to find more hard data behind the disappearance of these items was fruitless. Since the graphic became qualitative than quantitative, I wanted to have some fun with the rendering style. It was done in a 3-D application and details were added in Adobe Illustrator.

PUBLICATION *Fortune* (November 12, 2012)

1 **TAPE RECORDERS** are expected to be gone by 2017, according to 79% of respondents.

2 **ZIP DRIVES** will decline as the global market for cloud computing grows from $40.7 billion in 2011 to more than $241 billion in 2020.

3 **PALM PILOTS,** along with sales of other PDAs, went down 94% between 2002 and 2012.

4 **CUBICLES** are getting replaced by collaborative and shared space—19% of LinkedIn respondents expect the cubicle to disappear in the next five years.

7
4
8
5
6
3
2
1

5 **DESKTOP COMPUTERS** will be replaced by tablets. By 2016 consumers are expected to buy 375 million tablets worldwide, with almost a third sold directly to businesses, according to the research firm Forrester.

6 **ROLODEXES** are increasingly irrelevant, thanks to social networks and smartphones.

7 **FIXED SCHEDULES** are disappearing. In 2008, according to the Alfred P. Sloan Foundation, 79% of employers allowed some workers to periodically change their arrival and departure time, up from 68% in 1998.

8 **BUSINESS ATTIRE** is no longer *de rigueur*. Casual Friday increasingly extends to the rest of the week.

Between Five Bells

2011 WHITE WINE

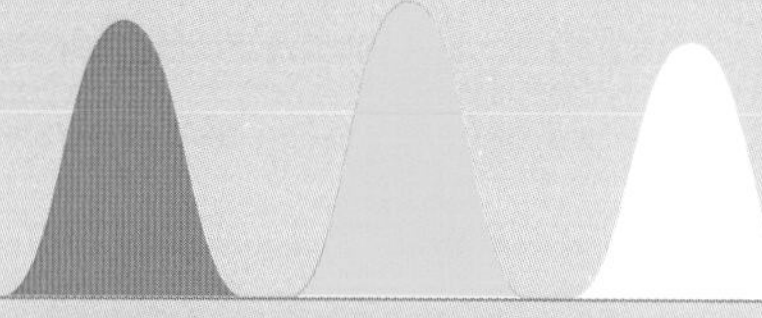

Chardonnay Pinot Gris Riesling Pinot Meunier

For no other reason than to be delicious. This is our first White, and we hope it makes sense. When it should be drunk is up to you, probably not long after it comes into your possession. *Made at Lethbridge Winery, Geelong, by the Between Five Bells team.*

WINE OF AUSTRALIA

Realised by Between Five Bells

149 Francis St, Lilyfield 2040 NSW

BAUME
12.3
CHARDONNAY
12
11.6
RIESLIN
14.5°
LOWEST TEMPERATURE

Precision Wine

Labels for the Between Five Bells Vineyard that visualize various dimensions of the component grapes.

ARTIST Nicholas Felton, cofounder of Daytum.com and a member of the product design team at Facebook.

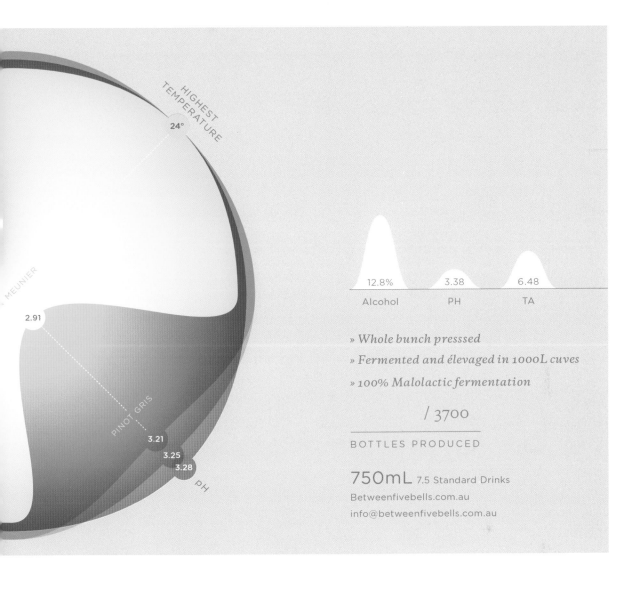

HIGHEST TEMPERATURE
24°
MEUNIER
2.91
PINOT GRIS
3.21
3.25
3.28
pH

12.8% Alcohol

3.38 PH

6.48 TA

» *Whole bunch presssed*

» *Fermented and élevaged in 1000L cuves*

» *100% Malolactic fermentation*

/ 3700

BOTTLES PRODUCED

750mL 7.5 Standard Drinks

Betweenfivebells.com.au

info@betweenfivebells.com.au

Between
Five Bells

STATEMENT The label series for this wine is the direct result of the winemaker's philosophy: "In the very early days, long before I had a feeling for the aesthetics of the labels, I had some convictions about what should, and should not, be on them. I like the idea of transparency from winemakers, and the primary tool of communication is a wine's label. Now I know that very few people care about such things, but I still felt it important to let people know they can access that information if they want it. And, even if it's a side effect, to let people know that there's nothing about the wines we are trying to hide. The labels on these wines should tell you something about the wine inside, be honest about it, and maybe even inspire a bit of research."

PUBLICATION Australian wine labels (2012)

Your Microbiome

An annotated chart of microbes that live in and on the human body. A circular family tree of bacteria is surrounded by colored bars that show where on the body each species is found and how common it is.

ARTIST Jonathan Corum, the *New York Times*.

STATEMENT The Human Microbiome Project sent me an elaborate family tree that looked interesting but seemed much too complicated. I focused on quieting and simplifying the design by removing vibrant colors, unnecessary symbols, brightly colored text, and scattered photographs of bacteria. Once I had a spare, stripped-down version of the family tree, I built it back up by adding new labels and annotations to help readers better understand the complex chart. I also changed the orientation and introduced a set of muted colors that work well together.

The end result is still a vibrant and complex image, but the graphic is hopefully easier to read and navigate. Although most readers (including myself) will not understand all of the details of the different bacteria, the graphic hints at the complex population of microbes living on and inside our bodies.

PUBLICATION *New York Times* (June 18, 2012)

idents

ome Project has spent two years surveying bacteria and other microbes at different sites on 242 healthy people. The chart below hints inations of microbes living in and on the human body.

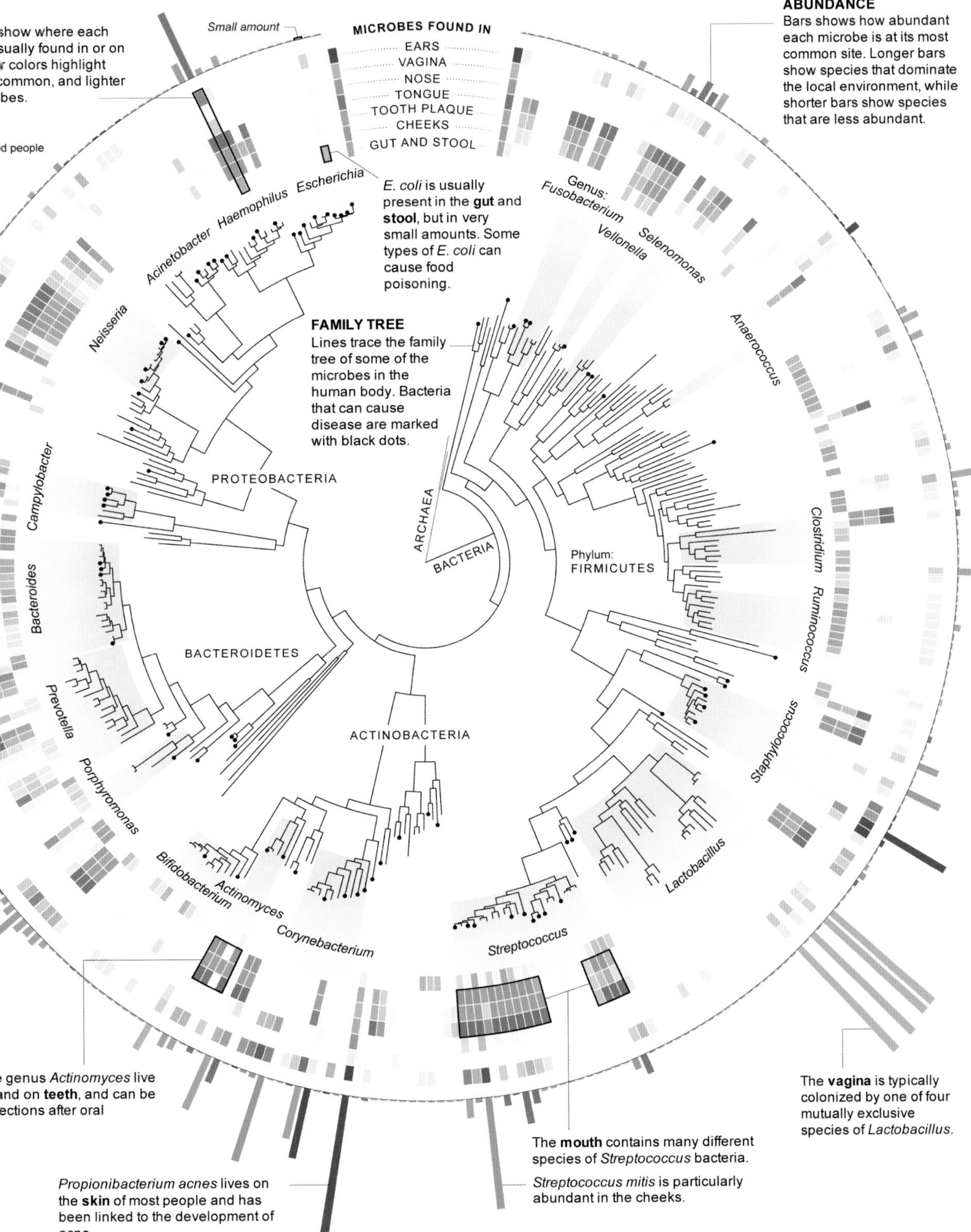

show where each
sually found in or on
r colors highlight
common, and lighter
bes.
d people
Small amount
MICROBES FOUND IN
EARS
VAGINA
NOSE
TONGUE
TOOTH PLAQUE
CHEEKS
GUT AND STOOL
ABUNDANCE
Bars shows how abundant each microbe is at its most common site. Longer bars show species that dominate the local environment, while shorter bars show species that are less abundant.
E. coli is usually present in the gut and stool, but in very small amounts. Some types of E. coli can cause food poisoning.
FAMILY TREE
Lines trace the family tree of some of the microbes in the human body. Bacteria that can cause disease are marked with black dots.
Escherichia
Haemophilus
Acinetobacter
Neisseria
Campylobacter
Bacteroides
Prevotella
Porphyromonas
Bifidobacterium
Actinomyces
Corynebacterium
Streptococcus
Lactobacillus
Staphylococcus
Ruminococcus
Clostridium
Anaerococcus
Selenomonas
Vellonella
Genus:
Fusobacterium
PROTEOBACTERIA
BACTEROIDETES
ACTINOBACTERIA
ARCHAEA
BACTERIA
Phylum:
FIRMICUTES
genus Actinomyces live
nd on teeth, and can be
ections after oral
Propionibacterium acnes lives on the skin of most people and has been linked to the development of acne.
The mouth contains many different species of Streptococcus bacteria.
Streptococcus mitis is particularly abundant in the cheeks.
The vagina is typically colonized by one of four mutually exclusive species of Lactobacillus.

Sources: Curtis Huttenhower and Nicola Segata, Harvard School of Public Health; National Institutes of Health Human Microbiome Project

The Illusion of Joey

BY BONNIE BERKOWITZ AND ALBERTO CUADRA

Hanging motionless backstage, the puppet star of "War Horse" looks only vaguely equine, like framework on which someone plans to build an animal. But the preening, snorting, galloping Joey that bursts onstage is, without question, a *horse*. The difference, say its creators, is the movement and the audience. "I think part of what's special about puppets is that you're working with a thing that is dead, and you have to struggle every second on the stage to make it live," said Basil Jones, executive producer of Handspring Puppet Co. in South Africa, which created all the show's puppets. "Once there is enough puppet pulling you in, you start filling in the rest," said Adrian Kohler, Handspring's artistic director and Jones's partner of 41 years. "But you've got to be convinced in the beginning, and that's the hard part." Here is a look at Joey and the puppeteers who bring him to life.

Eyes are the most natural-looking element in the puppet, Kohler said, even though Joey's don't move. Clear resin is affixed over the painted iris and highly polished, so there is a wet look to it. "The way it catches light keeps it alive," he said. Puppet eyes are so important that Handspring has an entire eye department.

A horse's evolution

Joey is the culmination of years of Kohler's experimentation in designing and refining puppets that move like animals.

1992

Joey's **leg mechanism** can be traced to the play "Woyzeck on the Highveld," in which a miniature rhinoceros needed to tap its front leg to pretend to count. The jointed leg was controlled from behind with a lever and pulleys.

1994

Two years later, a cynical, anthropomorphic hyena in "Faustus in Africa" had to be able to play checkers, so a **more articulated paw** was created in which two movements were controlled by a single cable. It was this puppet that future "War Horse" co-director Tom Morris saw and kept in mind.

2000

The lead character in "The Chimp Project" required extremely **flexible limbs and hands**, because in the story, a domesticated chimp teaches sign language to wild chimps. It also needed to be able to bare its teeth, so the **head control system** became more complex.

2004

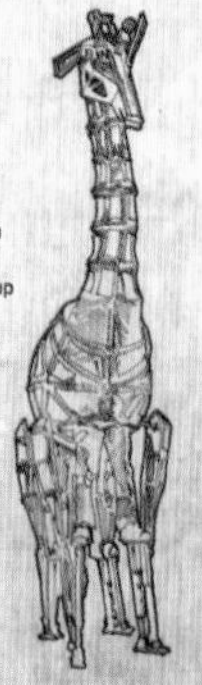

The production of "Tall Horse" required a massive but lightweight giraffe with human puppeteers inside, so the Handspring craftsmen came up with the **cane frame and transparent mesh skin** that they would use for Joey and rival horse Topthorn in 2007.

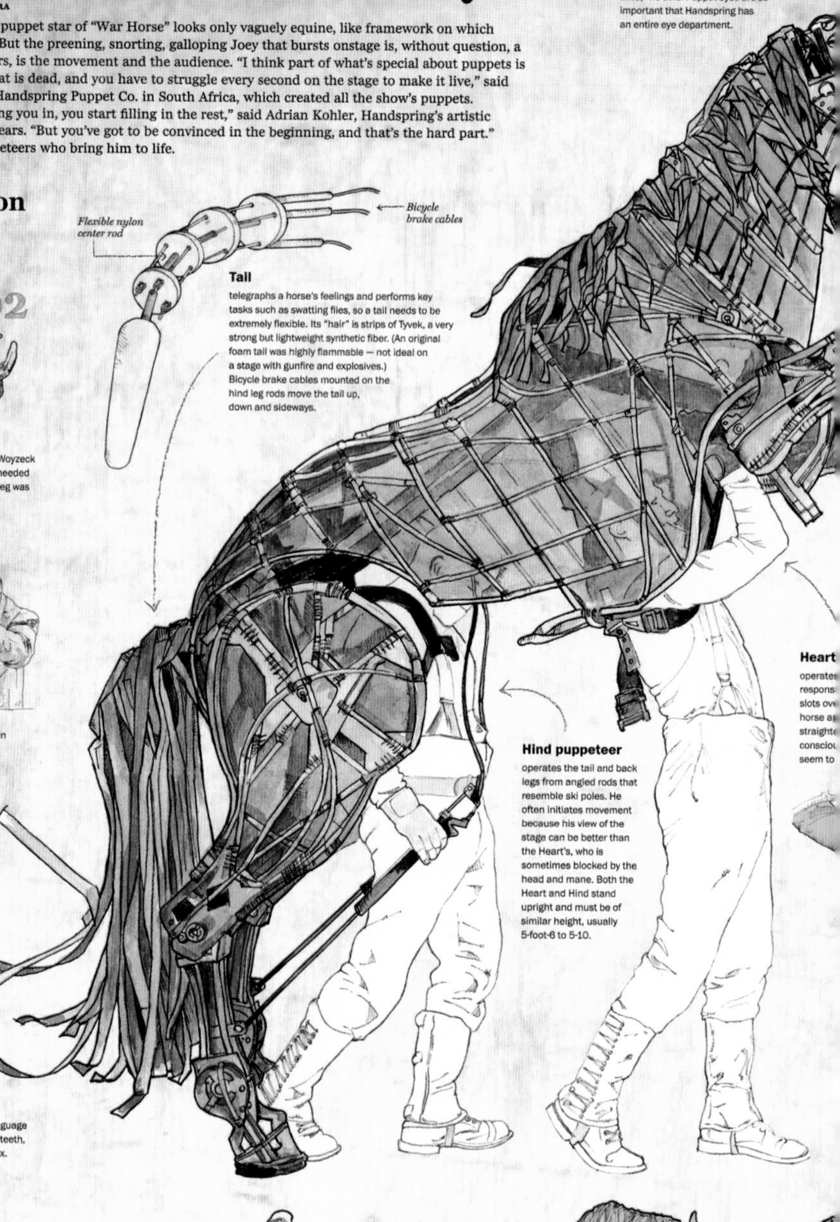

Sources: Adrian Kohler and Basil Jones of Handspring Puppet Co., The Lincoln Theater, The Kennedy Center, puppeteers Christopher Mai, Derek Stratton and Rob Laqui

Flexible nylon center rod

Bicycle brake cables

Tail telegraphs a horse's feelings and performs key tasks such as swatting flies, so a tail needs to be extremely flexible. Its "hair" is strips of Tyvek, a very strong but lightweight synthetic fiber. (An original foam tail was highly flammable — not ideal on a stage with gunfire and explosives.) Bicycle brake cables mounted on the hind leg rods move the tail up, down and sideways.

Hind puppeteer operates the tail and back legs from angled rods that resemble ski poles. He often initiates movement because his view of the stage can be better than the Heart's, who is sometimes blocked by the head and mane. Both the Heart and Hind stand upright and must be of similar height, usually 5-foot-6 to 5-10.

Heart
operates
respons
slots ov
horse a
straight
consciou
seem to

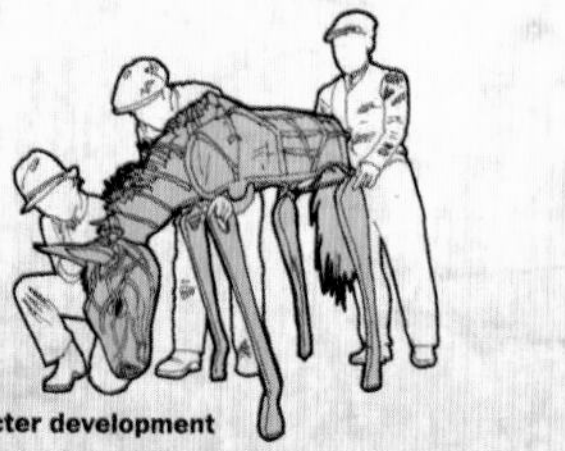

Character development

Joey begins as a foal, a cross between a thoroughbred and a draft horse. This puppet is less flexible than the adult version but still requires three puppeteers. No puppets in the show contain electronics or robotics (with the exception of a tank made by another company). Kohler prefers simple mechanisms operated by people, so that each performance is unique.

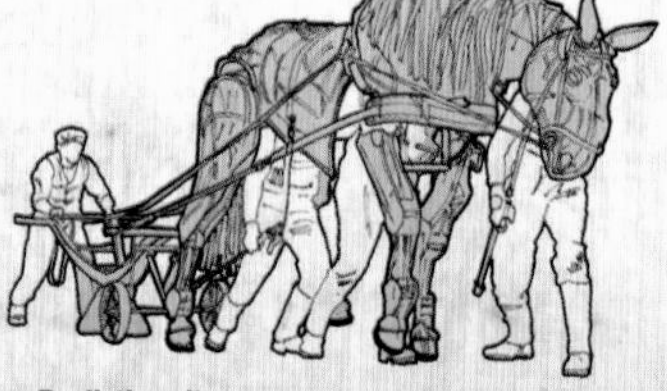

Realistic gait

From early in training, puppeteers concentrate on walking, trotting, galloping, and even pulling a plow and limping as a horse would. Walking is a specific four-count pattern: Front right, back left; front left, back right. Trotting is two counts as hooves move in pairs. Galloping is six counts: One-two, three-four, with five-six being air time. Within weeks, the gait becomes automatic.

Lightwe

The puppet'
wet, but is
together fi
flexibility. T
lighting. Joe

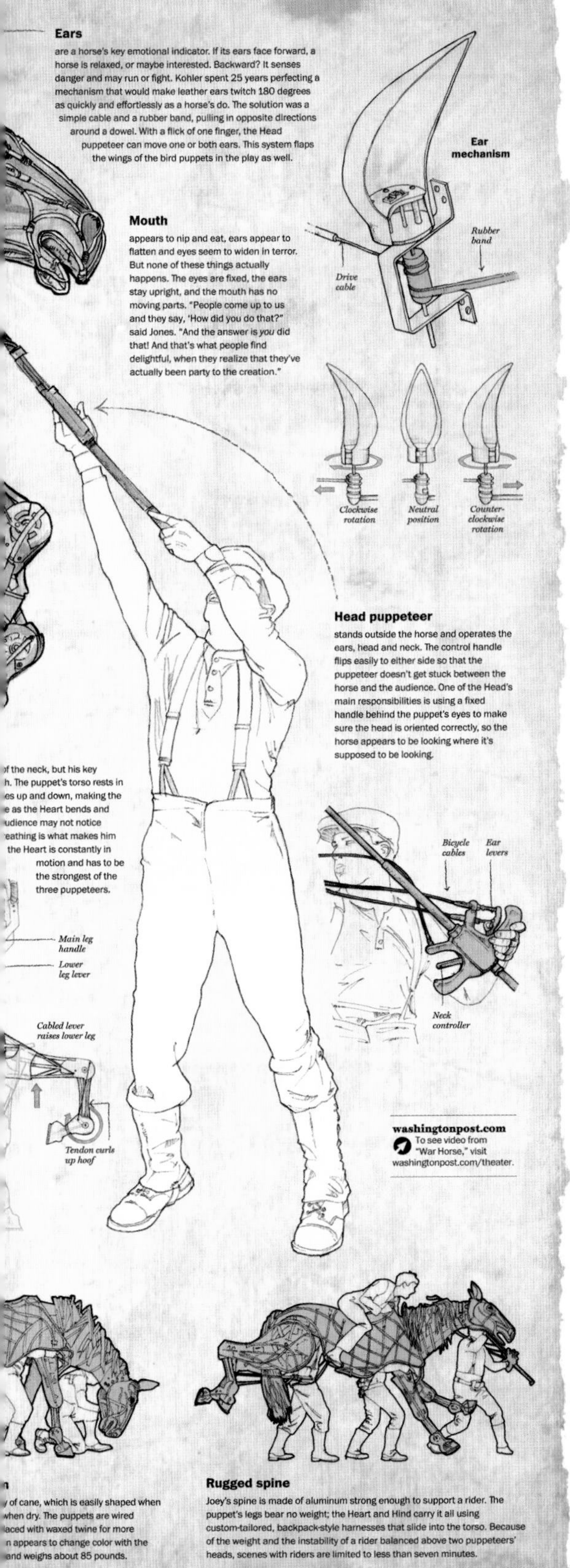

Ears
are a horse's key emotional indicator. If its ears face forward, a horse is relaxed, or maybe interested. Backward? It senses danger and may run or fight. Kohler spent 25 years perfecting a mechanism that would make leather ears twitch 180 degrees as quickly and effortlessly as a horse's do. The solution was a simple cable and a rubber band, pulling in opposite directions around a dowel. With a flick of one finger, the Head puppeteer can move one or both ears. This system flaps the wings of the bird puppets in the play as well.
Ear mechanism
Rubber band
Drive cable
Mouth
appears to nip and eat, ears appear to flatten and eyes seem to widen in terror. But none of these things actually happens. The eyes are fixed, the ears stay upright, and the mouth has no moving parts. "People come up to us and they say, 'How did you do that?'" said Jones. "And the answer is *you* did that! And that's what people find delightful, when they realize that they've actually been party to the creation."
Clockwise rotation
Neutral position
Counter-clockwise rotation
Head puppeteer
stands outside the horse and operates the ears, head and neck. The control handle flips easily to either side so that the puppeteer doesn't get stuck between the horse and the audience. One of the Head's main responsibilities is using a fixed handle behind the puppet's eyes to make sure the head is oriented correctly, so the horse appears to be looking where it's supposed to be looking.
of the neck, but his key
h. The puppet's torso rests in
es up and down, making the
e as the Heart bends and
udience may not notice
eathing is what makes him
the Heart is constantly in
motion and has to be
the strongest of the
three puppeteers.
Bicycle cables
Ear levers
Neck controller
Main leg handle
Lower leg lever
Cabled lever raises lower leg
Tendon curls up hoof
washingtonpost.com
To see video from "War Horse," visit washingtonpost.com/theater.
Rugged spine
Joey's spine is made of aluminum strong enough to support a rider. The puppet's legs bear no weight; the Heart and Hind carry it all using custom-tailored, backpack-style harnesses that slide into the torso. Because of the weight and the instability of a rider balanced above two puppeteers' heads, scenes with riders are limited to less than seven minutes.
of cane, which is easily shaped when
when dry. The puppets are wired
laced with waxed twine for more
n appears to change color with the
and weighs about 85 pounds.

A Magnificent Horse Is Brought to Life

Inside the magic of *War Horse*, a play set during World War I.

ARTISTS Alberto Cuadra is a graphic artist and Bonnie Berkowitz is a graphics reporter for the *Washington Post* in Washington, D.C.

STATEMENT The show *War Horse* was coming to the Kennedy Center, and our original assignment was to tell readers how the mechanical puppet worked. This could've been a simple and bare-bones explanation, showing only joints and strings and harnesses. But as soon as we saw it on Broadway, we knew we had to try to convey not just how the puppet worked but how its creators and puppeteers managed to make an audience emotionally involved with a collection of sticks and cables. The extraordinary puppetmakers Adrian Kohler and Basil Jones shared both the nuts and bolts of the puppet design and the philosophies behind them. We titled our piece "The Illusion of Joey" because even we were fooled by the expert puppeteering into thinking that the puppet was doing things that it wasn't.

Bonnie wrote the text for the graphic and the accompanying story; Alberto drew, by hand, all the artwork and even the numbers and arrows, then painted each piece using watercolors.

PUBLICATION *Washington Post* (October 21, 2012)

A Deep History of the Brōcelet

A timeline of masculine bracelets through the ages.

ARTISTS Raul Aguila, Thomas Alberty, Mark Nerys, and Clint Rainey, *New York.*

STATEMENT Observing a trend—eclectic high-fashion bracelets worn by men—the editors wanted a historical timeline. And what better linear representation of the millennia than a very, very, very long arm? The subject of the infographic is somewhat frivolous, so the treatment needed to be sort of goofy. A long, squiggly arm certainly qualifies, and the scraggly bits of arm hair add to that quality, while also reinforcing the fact that this is a man's arm rather than a woman's. The bracelets themselves add sparks of color on the neutral background of the beige skin, and thus pop off the arm and catch the eye (as jewelry does in real life).

PUBLICATION *New York*
(March 12 to March 19, 2012)

Intelligencer

BRŌCELETS THROUGH THE AGES

Bracelets are back in for dudes, fueling a surge in men's accessories that has forecasters predicting twenty-year sales highs. As the rich history of male wrist adornment shows, Allen Iverson, James Dean, and Gork the Caveman would approve. CLINT RAINEY

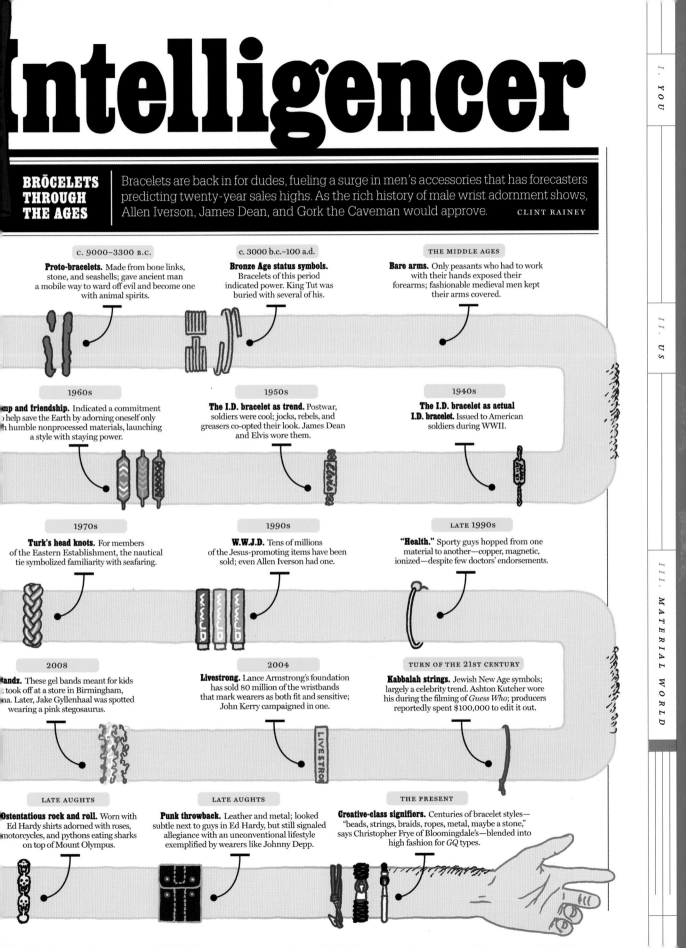

c. 9000–3300 B.C.

Proto-bracelets. Made from bone links, stone, and seashells; gave ancient man a mobile way to ward off evil and become one with animal spirits.

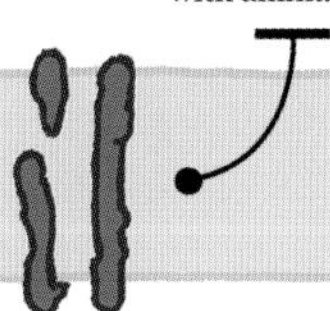

c. 3000 b.c.–100 a.d.

Bronze Age status symbols. Bracelets of this period indicated power. King Tut was buried with several of his.

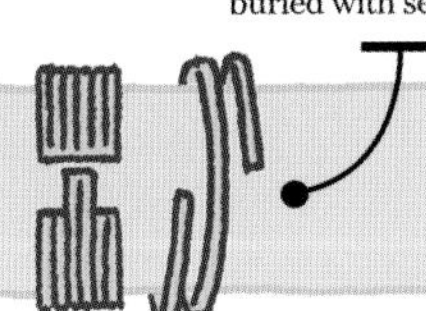

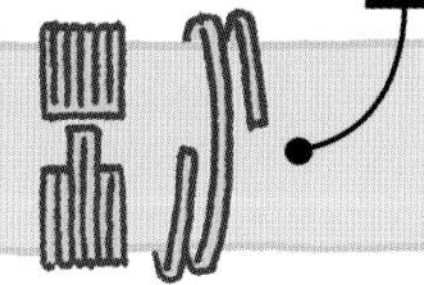

THE MIDDLE AGES

Bare arms. Only peasants who had to work with their hands exposed their forearms; fashionable medieval men kept their arms covered.

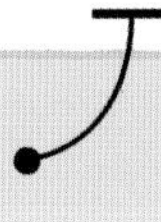

1940s

The I.D. bracelet as actual I.D. bracelet. Issued to American soldiers during WWII.

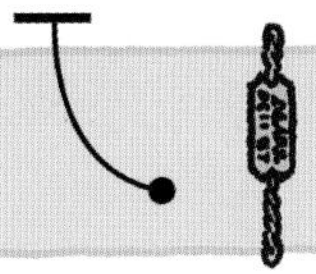

1950s

The I.D. bracelet as trend. Postwar, soldiers were cool; jocks, rebels, and greasers co-opted their look. James Dean and Elvis wore them.

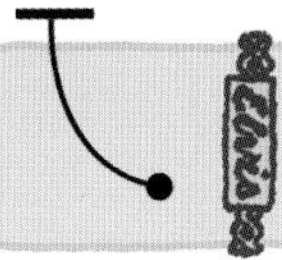

1960s

mp and friendship. Indicated a commitment) help save the Earth by adorning oneself only h humble nonprocessed materials, launching a style with staying power.

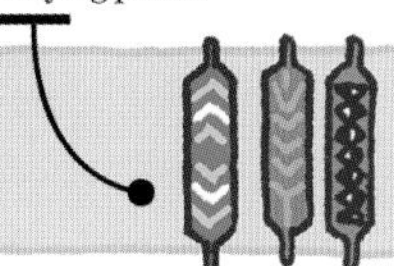

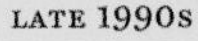

1970s

Turk's head knots. For members of the Eastern Establishment, the nautical tie symbolized familiarity with seafaring.

1990s

W.W.J.D. Tens of millions of the Jesus-promoting items have been sold; even Allen Iverson had one.

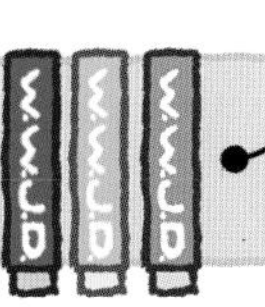
W.W.J.D
W.W.J.D
W.W.J.D

LATE 1990s

"Health." Sporty guys hopped from one material to another—copper, magnetic, ionized—despite few doctors' endorsements.

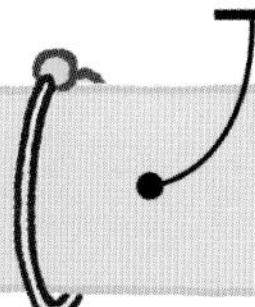

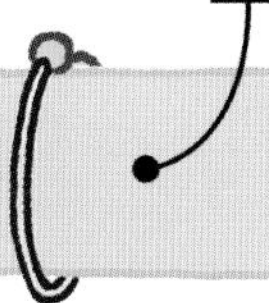

TURN OF THE 21ST CENTURY

Kabbalah strings. Jewish New Age symbols; largely a celebrity trend. Ashton Kutcher wore his during the filming of *Guess Who*; producers reportedly spent $100,000 to edit it out.

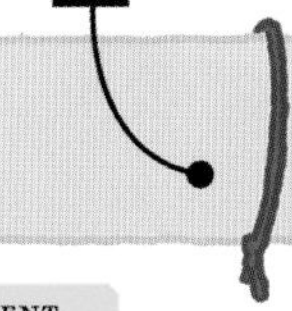

2004

Livestrong. Lance Armstrong's foundation has sold 80 million of the wristbands that mark wearers as both fit and sensitive; John Kerry campaigned in one.

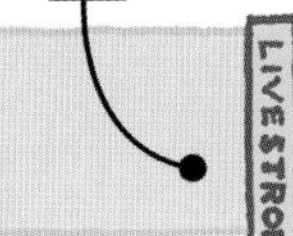

LIVESTRO

2008

andz. These gel bands meant for kids : took off at a store in Birmingham, na. Later, Jake Gyllenhaal was spotted wearing a pink stegosaurus.

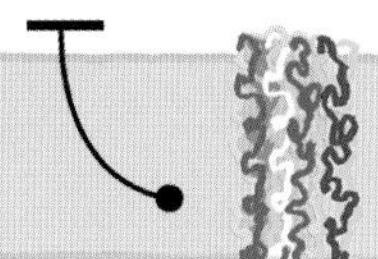

LATE AUGHTS

Ostentatious rock and roll. Worn with Ed Hardy shirts adorned with roses, motorcycles, and pythons eating sharks on top of Mount Olympus.

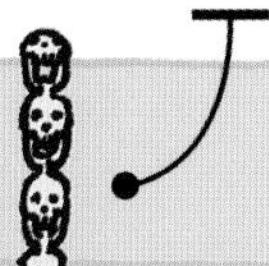

LATE AUGHTS

Punk throwback. Leather and metal; looked subtle next to guys in Ed Hardy, but still signaled allegiance with an unconventional lifestyle exemplified by wearers like Johnny Depp.

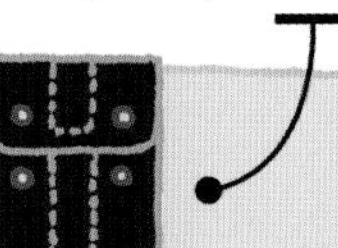

THE PRESENT

Creative-class signifiers. Centuries of bracelet styles—"beads, strings, braids, ropes, metal, maybe a stone," says Christopher Frye of Bloomingdale's—blended into high fashion for *GQ* types.

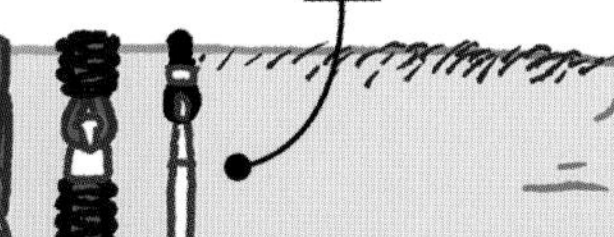

Under the Border

NOGALES **AZ** **MEXICO**

January 1999
Agents discover two tunnels, in a home and adjoining apartment across from a Catholic school. While the longer of the two appeared to stretch 400 feet, it was never fully explored because of safety concerns.

October 1999
Investigators trace 1,089 pounds of marijuana and 1,254 pounds of cocaine to a tunnel on Loma Street. While interviewing neighbors, agents find a second tunnel under construction next door.

LOMA STREET

August 1995
The first known tunnel was found in the basement of an abandoned Methodist church (now an empty lot). The tunnel went down 40 feet to the Grand Avenue storm conduit. No drugs were seized.

August 2010
A tunnel beneath the DeConcini port of entry is discovered when the road collapses beneath a bus crossing into Mexico.

OAK ST

SACRED HEART CATHOLIC SCHOOL

November 2011
Authorities find a tunnel under a deck at one home and, fifteen days later, a second under the bedroom of a house down the block.

December 2009
A sinkhole at the border crossing leads to the discovery of a smuggling tunnel.

N. GRAND AVE

September 2003
A 330-yard-long tunnel equipped with rails for moving cocaine is discovered. Authorities arrest "Don Rigo" Gaxiola, the only senior cartel figure yet prosecuted for tunnel-building in Nogales.

DUNBAR DR

NELSON AVE

DECONCINI PORT OF ENTRY

U.S. MEXICO BORDER

W INTERNATIONAL ST.

E INTERNATIONAL ST.

A

The "parkin
to the San

PHOTOS: AP PHOTOS(1); REUTERS(2); ZUMA(1)
GRAPHIC BY BLOOMBERG BUSINESSWEEK; SATELLITE IMAGE: USGS

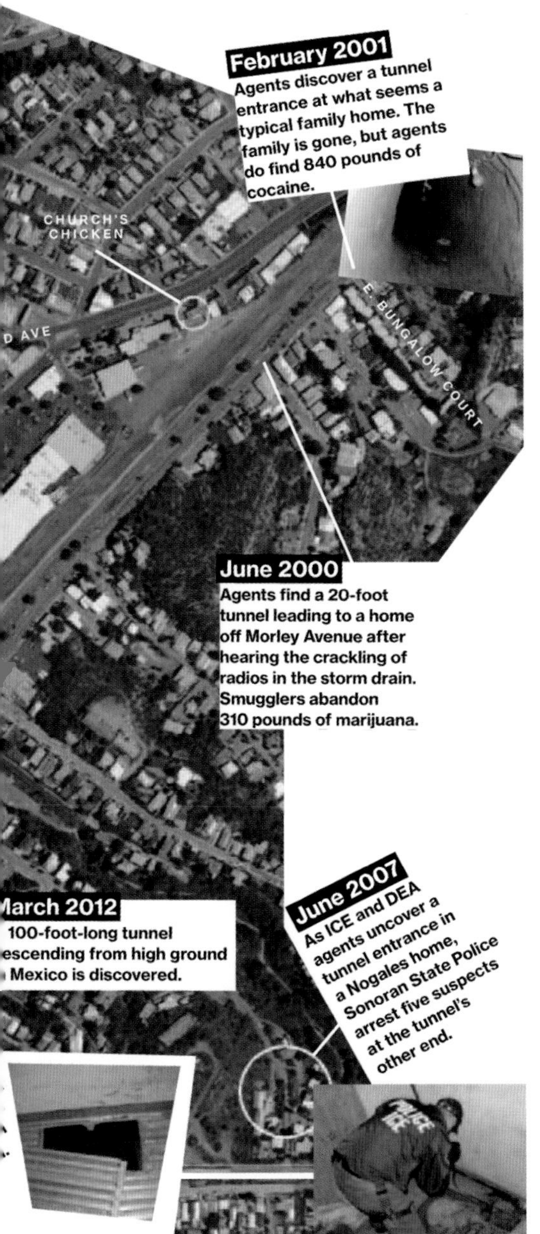
February 2001
Agents discover a tunnel entrance at what seems a typical family home. The family is gone, but agents do find 840 pounds of cocaine.
CHURCH'S CHICKEN
D AVE
E. BUNGALOW COURT
June 2000
Agents find a 20-foot tunnel leading to a home off Morley Avenue after hearing the crackling of radios in the storm drain. Smugglers abandon 310 pounds of marijuana.
arch 2012
100-foot-long tunnel
escending from high ground
Mexico is discovered.
June 2007
As ICE and DEA agents uncover a tunnel entrance in a Nogales home, Sonoran State Police arrest five suspects at the tunnel's other end.

Digging for Drugs

Smuggling tunnels discovered by the FBI in Nogales, Arizona.

ARTISTS Jennifer Daniel and Emily Keegin, *Bloomberg Businessweek.*

STATEMENT The first known drug-smuggling tunnel in Nogales, Arizona, was found in August 1995 beneath an abandoned church 150 yards from the border. Since then, more than ninety illicit underground passageways have been discovered in various states of completion. Using police reports from U.S. Immigration and Customs Enforcement and local news witness reports ("across the street from Burger King," "on the corner by Nogales Car Wash," etc.), we were able to pinpoint twelve tunnels. Execution was a combination of GIS satellite imagery, Google maps, and InDesign.

PUBLICATION *Bloomberg Businessweek* (August 9, 2012)

The Clatter Beneath the Waves

Average noise levels in the North Atlantic from cargo ships and other manmade sources.

ARTIST Jonathan Corum, the *New York Times.*

STATEMENT This map of noise levels led to some loud discussions at the *Times.* I was skeptical that the maps would work at a large size, because the data was so low resolution, but the Science desk thought the idea of mapping ocean noise was interesting enough to merit a large graphic.

My challenge was to build a graphic to fill the cover of the Science section, but without high-resolution data. My early sketches were all failures because I was trying to find ways to minimize pixelation by using a large number of maps at small size. Finally I gave up and decided to embrace the chunkiness of the data set. I overlaid the noise data with high-resolution map borders, which emphasized the pixelation, and added as few labels as possible, to keep the reader focused on the water. Normally I would have used a much more muted color scale, but for a map about ocean noise this loud and colorful scale seemed to work.

PUBLICATION *New York Times* (December 11, 2012)

Mapping Ocean Noise

A project to document and map man-made noise
a range of frequencies. Sources of noise include s

NORTH ATLANTIC *Noise levels from tankers, cargo an*

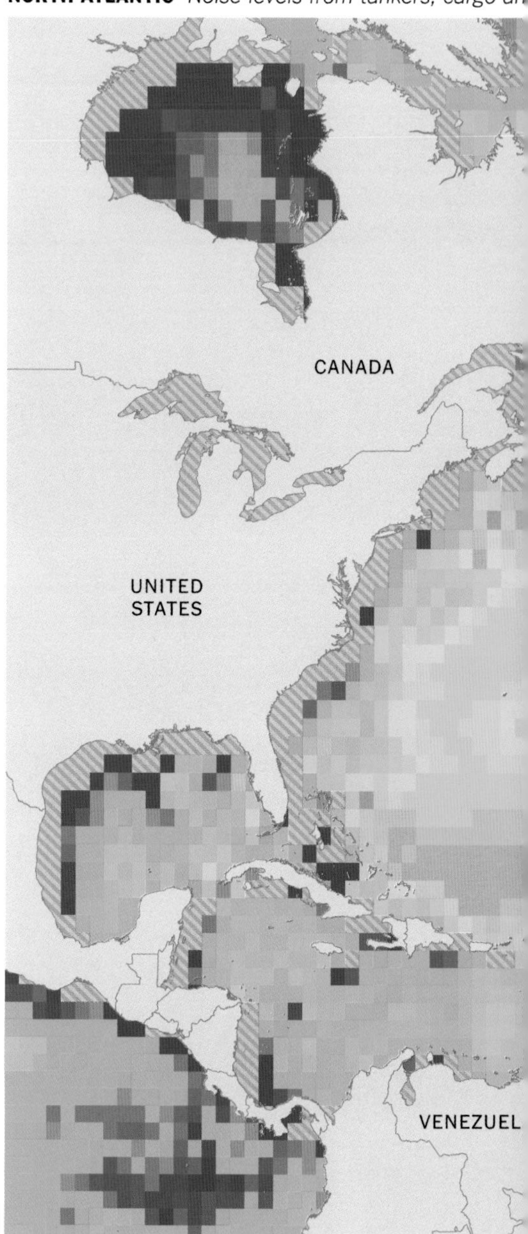
CANADA
UNITED STATES
VENEZUEL

Sources: NOAA Underwater Sound Field Mapping Working Group; H

an estimated average annual underwater noise across
veys, commercial shipping and passenger ships.

r ships. Sound frequencies are in a ⅓-octave band centered on 400 Hz.

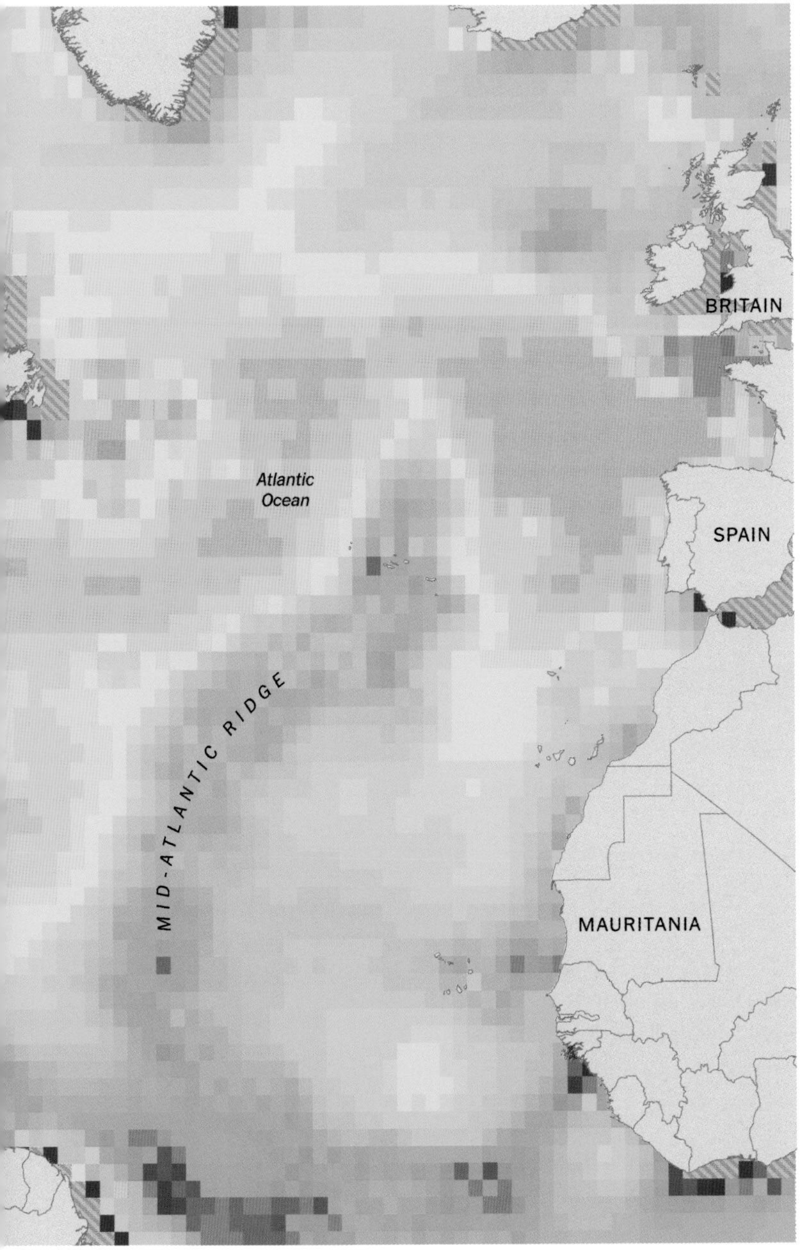

BRITAIN

Atlantic
Ocean

SPAIN

MID-ATLANTIC RIDGE

MAURITANIA

ESTIMATED NOISE LEVELS
40 decibels
115
N.A.
NORTH ATLANTIC 50 Hz
U.S.
NORTH ATLANTIC SHIPPING
A map of commercial shipping traffic, used to estimate sound levels.
U.S.
NEAR LONG ISLAND 400 Hz and 50 Hz
N.Y.
Conn.
N.J.
Atlantic
Ocean

NCEAS Note: Maps show noise at a depth of 50 feet and a standard reference sound pressure of 1 micropascal. JONATHAN CORUM/THE NEW YORK TIMES

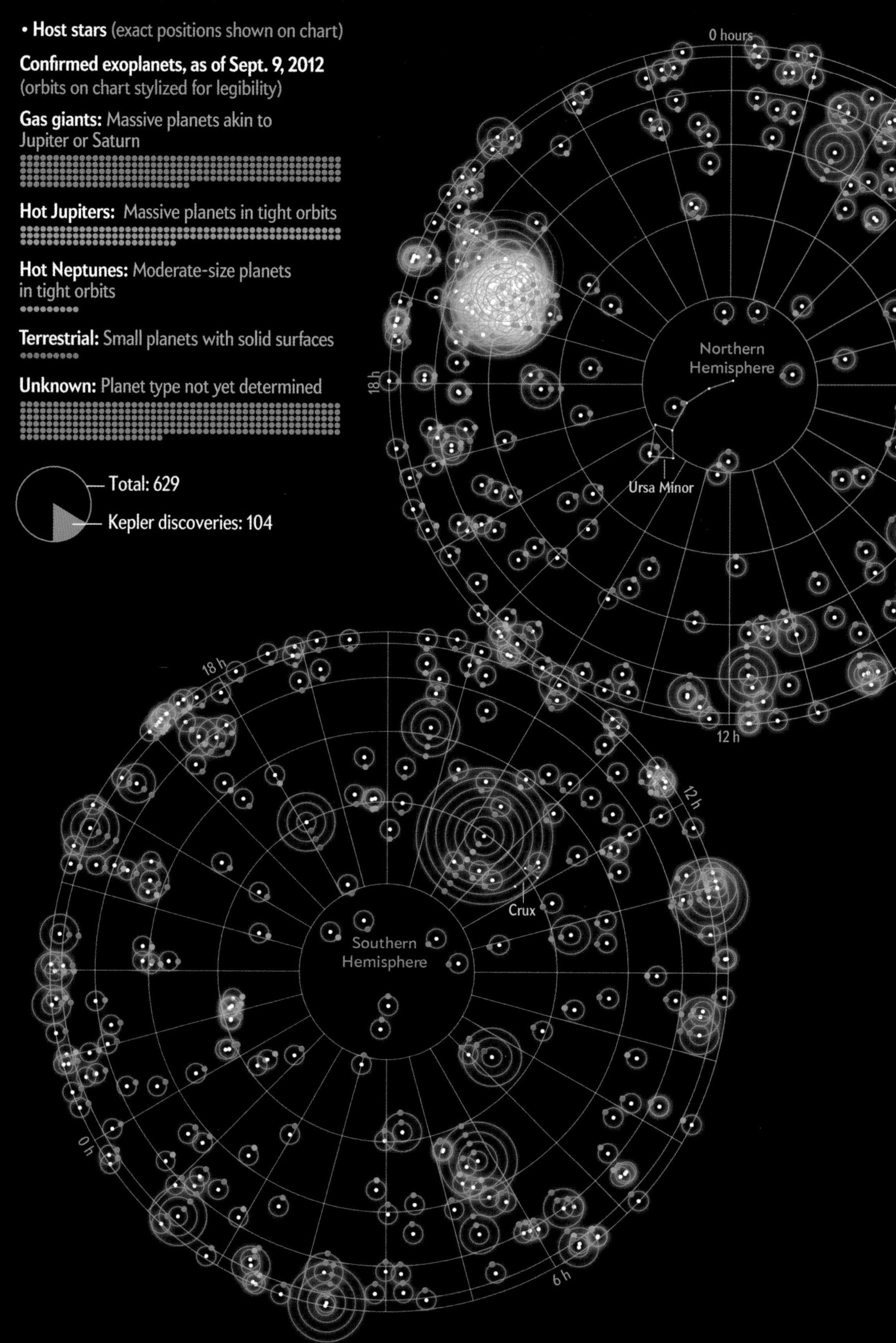

• Host stars (exact positions shown on chart)
Confirmed exoplanets, as of Sept. 9, 2012
(orbits on chart stylized for legibility)
Gas giants: Massive planets akin to Jupiter or Saturn
Hot Jupiters: Massive planets in tight orbits
Hot Neptunes: Moderate-size planets in tight orbits
Terrestrial: Small planets with solid surfaces
Unknown: Planet type not yet determined
Total: 629
Kepler discoveries: 104
0 hours
18 h
12 h
Northern Hemisphere
Ursa Minor
18 h
12 h
0 h
6 h
Southern Hemisphere
Crux

Planets Everywhere

All of the planets discovered outside the Solar System.

ARTIST Jan Willem Tulp, a freelance information visualizer based in The Hague, Netherlands.

STATEMENT The graphic shows the northern and the southern hemisphere, and each white dot represents a host star. Each host star contains one or more exoplanets. Each exoplanet is represented with a colored dot and a circle representing its orbit around its host star. The color represents the type of the exoplanet, such as Gas Giant or Hot Jupiter. To aid in the orientation of the graphic, the two most well-known constellations have been added: Ursa Minor (Little Dipper) on the northern hemisphere and Crux (Southern Cross) on the southern hemisphere.

As with most data visualizations, it was very exciting to see the first visual representation of the data set. I could immediately see the potential for an interesting graphic.

PUBLICATION *Scientific American* (December 2012)

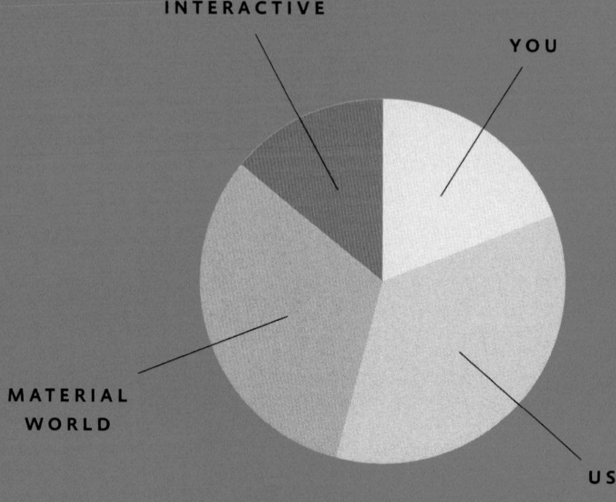
INTERACTIVE
YOU
MATERIAL WORLD
US

THE TOP TEN BEST AMERICAN INTERACTIVE INFOGRAPHICS OF 2013

by ERIC RODENBECK

LOOKING BACK AT 2012, it's safe to say that the world faced immense change during its 366 days. While change may be a constant for any era, one thing marks our little blip on the timeline more than all previous: absolutely huge amounts of information, processed by humans and machines at greater quantities and rates than ever before. These days we are even able to pan and zoom, from macro to micro, to see both forest and trees—and if we want to, the amount of water near a particular maple tree, many miles distant. Nowness and visibility are at the heart of what makes all of this—the state of our world and the ways we express its quantified loveliness—so compelling.

It's with these thoughts in mind that I selected the ten best interactive infographics of the year. For example, "Bear 71," which I also think of (somewhat sadly) as "the last great Flash piece," is the true story of a female grizzly bear—Bear 71—monitored by wildlife conservation officers from 2001 to 2009. In addition to illustrating the hidden life of the forest through a gorgeous, enticing interface, the work—itself a curation of thousands of photos and video—sheds an eerie light on what it means to be surveilled and turned into data. In the winner from Carbon Visuals, "New York's Carbon Emissions—in Real Time," the carbon dioxide released into New York's atmosphere each day is made concrete using an accumulation of black spheres, rendered at scale. The *pop-pop-pop* of the giant balls lifting up out of city streets made me draw a sharp breath: We're doing *what* to the atmosphere?! And "Wind Map" is an elegant illustration of the direction and speed of wind at this very moment, using the barest of graphics—the black silhouette of the United States, the wind represented as moving white hairs.

Each of these works captures something we couldn't see before (carbon in the atmosphere, life from a bear's perspective) and turns it into something tangible and beautiful. It's through seeing our world in this way, and perhaps comparing it to the past, that we can get a sense for where we are going—and, if we choose, change paths.

Eric Rodenbeck is the CEO and creative director of Stamen Design, a San Francisco design and technology studio he founded in 2001. Stamen is a leader in the emerging genres of interactive online mapping and live data visualization.

TO SEE THE INTERACTIVE WINNERS, GO TO WWW.HMHBOOKS.COM/INFOGRAPHICS2013

Wind Map

The wind map shows the delicate tracery of wind flowing over the United States, in near real time.

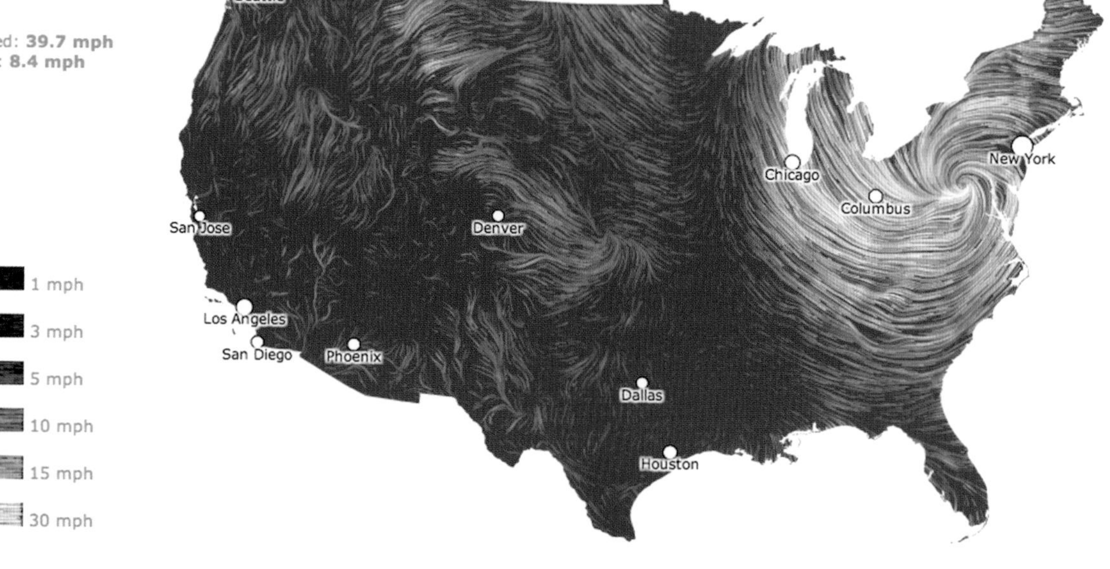
October 30, 2012
6:59 am EST
(time of forecast download)
top speed: 39.7 mph
average: 8.4 mph
1 mph
3 mph
5 mph
10 mph
15 mph
30 mph
Seattle
San Jose
Los Angeles
San Diego
Phoenix
Denver
Dallas
Houston
Chicago
Columbus
New York

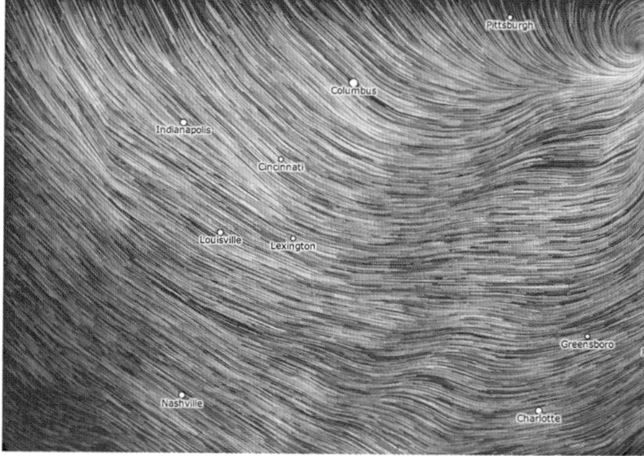
Pittsburgh
Columbus
Indianapolis
Cincinnati
Louisville
Lexington
Greensboro
Nashville
Charlotte

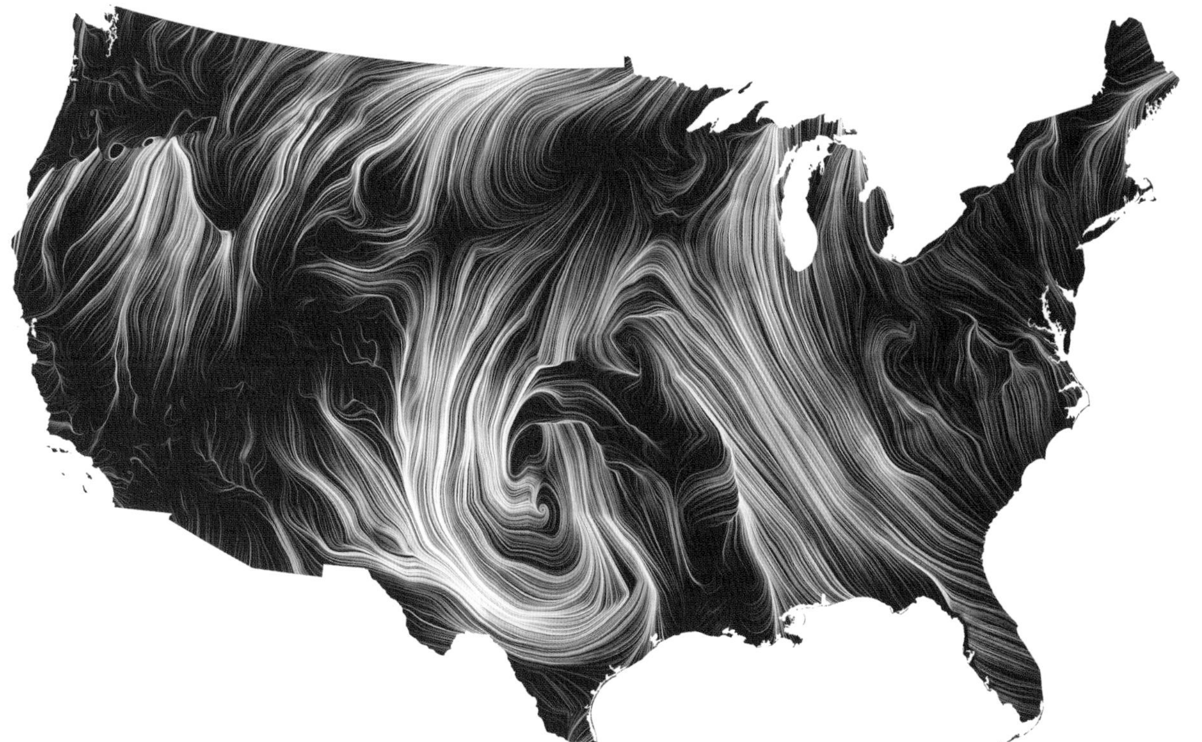

ARTISTS Fernanda Viégas and Martin Wattenberg, leaders of Google's data visualization research group in Boston. The wind map was a personal art project.

STATEMENT We had a couple of surprising experiences with the map. We didn't realize how many people obsess over the weather. Surfers, firefighters, even scientists who track butterfly migration—we got fan mail from communities we never expected. The second surprise to us was the map's emotional power during storms. We were both transfixed watching Hurricane Sandy make landfall, and we heard from many other people that they were too. The wind map was the first of our visualizations that scared us.

The design of the map reflects a careful balance. Most of the visualization is in constant motion, which could be overwhelming, so we took a restrained approach to everything else. We stuck to a monochrome palette and avoided overlaying more information. Another important consideration was that everyone would have a different perspective on the map, focusing on particular places they might have lived in, visited, or read about. That's part of why we added zooming. We also added a tiny trace of our own history: Every U.S. city that either of us has lived in is marked on the map.

PUBLICATION hint.fm/wind (March 28, 2012)

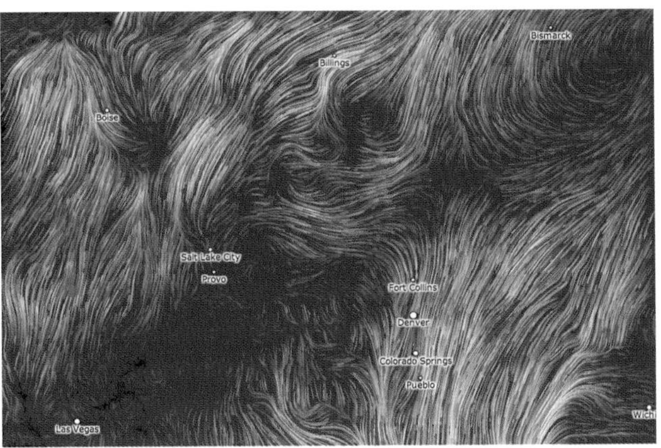
Bismarck
Billings
Boise
Salt Lake City
Provo
Fort Collins
Denver
Colorado Springs
Pueblo
Las Vegas

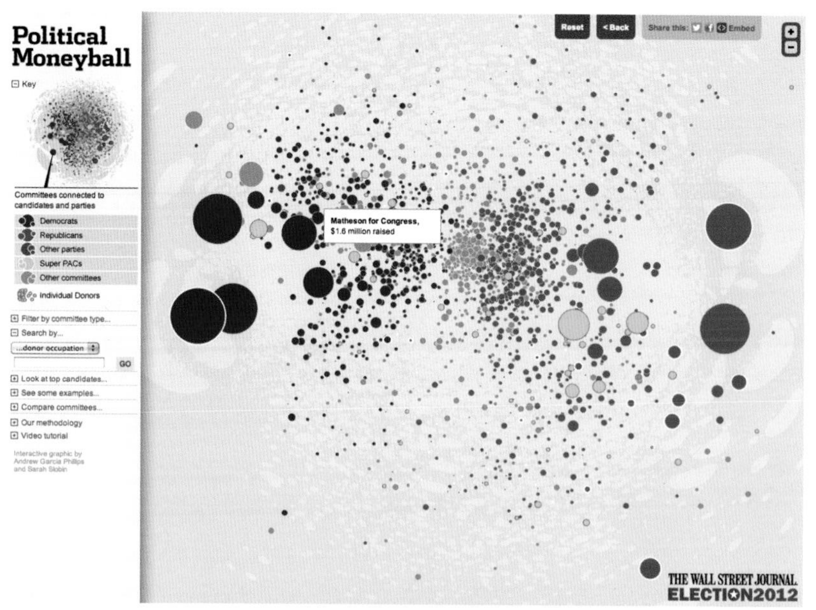
Political Moneyball
Key
Committees connected to candidates and parties
Democrats
Republicans
Other parties
Super PACs
Other committees
Individual Donors
Filter by committee type...
Search by...
...donor occupation
GO
Look at top candidates...
See some examples...
Compare committees...
Our methodology
Video tutorial
Interactive graphic by Andrew Garcia Phillips and Sarah Slobin
Reset
<Back
Share this:
Embed
Matheson for Congress,
$1.6 million raised
THE WALL STREET JOURNAL.
ELECTION2012

Money given by
Switch direction »
Ideological/Single-Issue committees | $50
To other committees
64.2% to Democrats
33.6% to Republicans
List view »

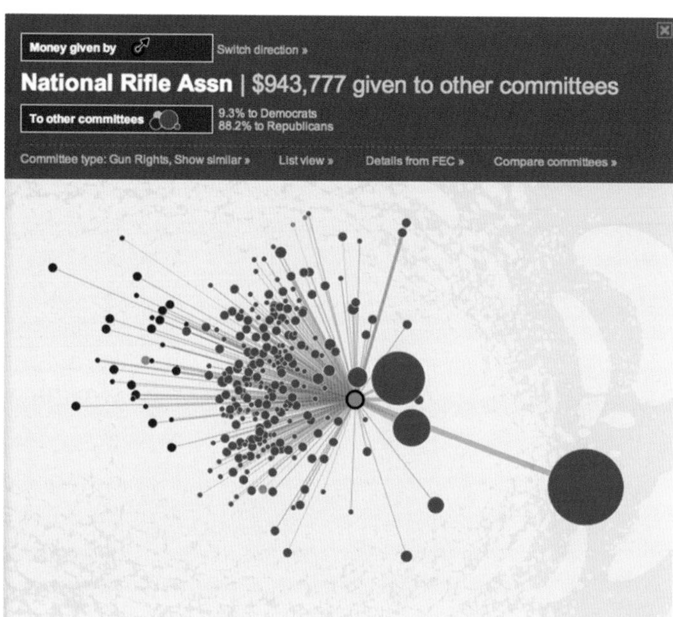
Money given by
Switch direction »
National Rifle Assn | $943,777 given to other committees
To other committees
9.3% to Democrats
88.2% to Republicans
Committee type: Gun Rights, Show similar »
List view »
Details from FEC »
Compare committees »

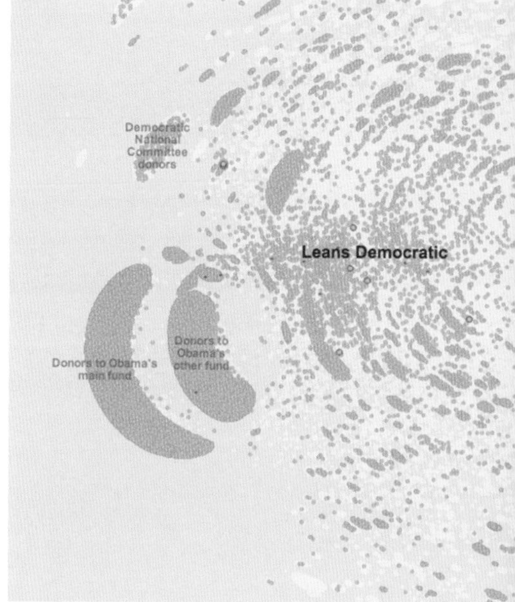
Democratic National Committee donors
Leans Democratic
Donors to Obama's main fund
Donors to Obama's other fund

The Money in Politics Navigator

A map of the universe of money in U.S. federal politics.

ARTIST Andrew Garcia Phillips, senior graphics editor, the *Wall Street Journal.*

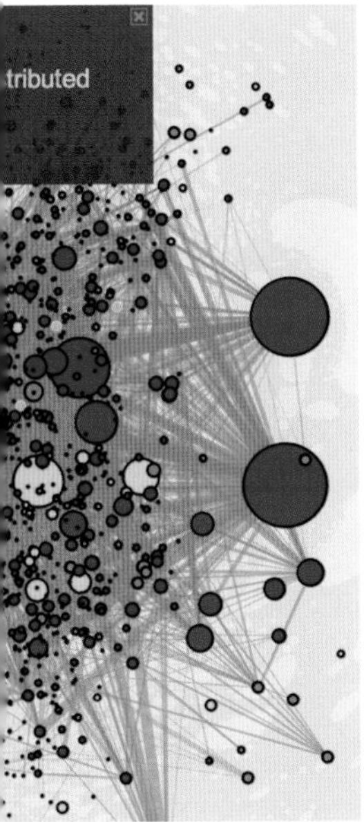
tributed

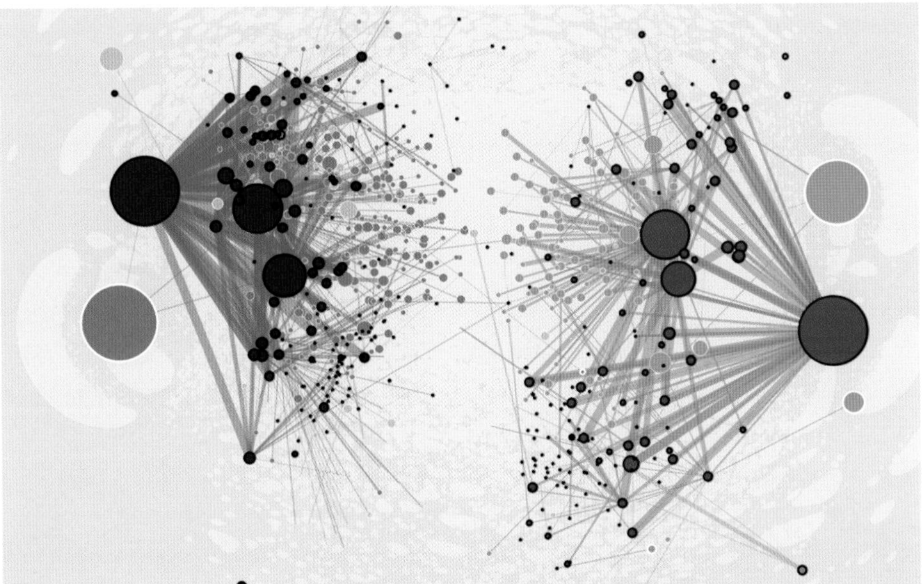

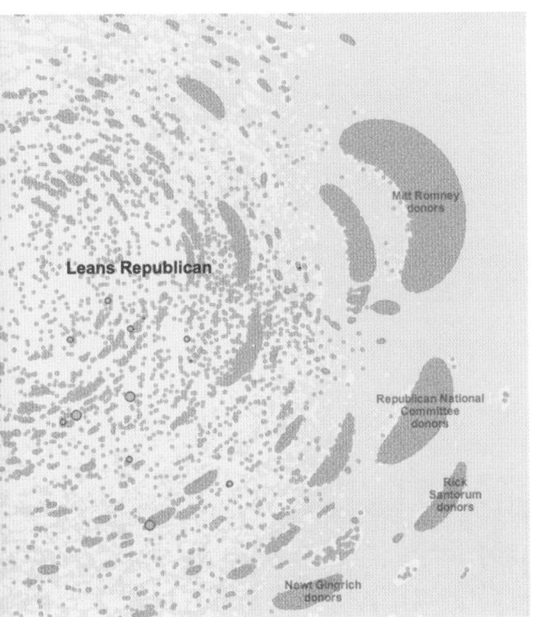
Leans Republican
Mitt Romney donors
Republican National Committee donors
Rick Santorum donors
Newt Gingrich donors

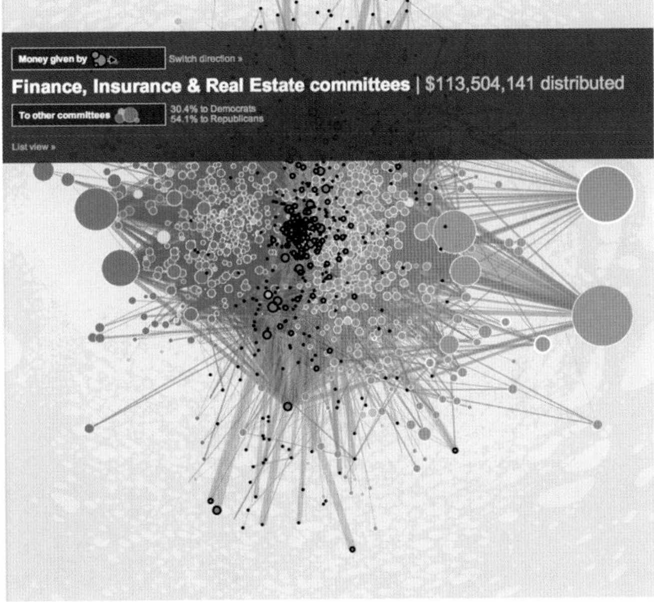
Money given by
Switch direction »
Finance, Insurance & Real Estate committees | $113,504,141 distributed
To other committees
30.4% to Democrats
54.1% to Republicans
List view »

STATEMENT Vast amounts of data are made available by the Federal Election Commission, but accessing it and understanding it is difficult for a typical reader or citizen—or even for professionals. By mapping the players based on their relationships to one another, we provided an interface for that data, allowing users to sort by connections, industry groups, donor identification, and so on. Outliers in the patterns that this creates help point us to stories that deserve extra attention.

The graphic uses some terrific technology, like Tulip (which helped us find the correct arrangement of nodes) and CartoDB (which we used for creating tiles to display the graphic on a blank map interface). The data set grew to about two million nodes, creating more complexity (which we would handle differently if we had to start from scratch).

PUBLICATION *Wall Street Journal* (www.wsj.com) (July 25, 2012)

Women as Academic Authors, 1665–2010

The gender of authors in nearly 1,800 fields and subfields, across four centuries.

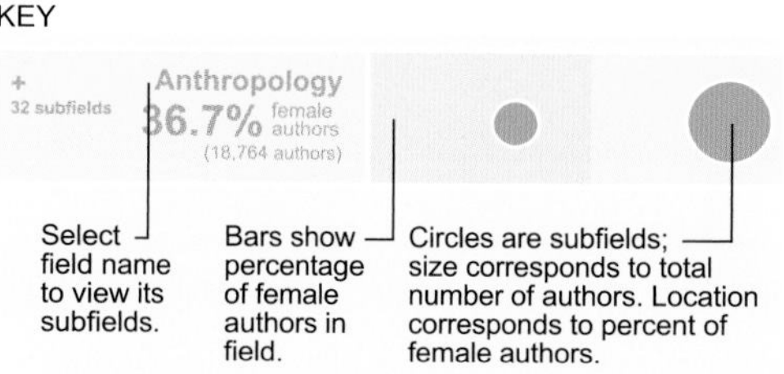
KEY
+
32 subfields
Anthropology
36.7% female authors
(18,764 authors)
Select field name to view its subfields.
Bars show percentage of female authors in field.
Circles are subfields; size corresponds to total number of authors. Location corresponds to percent of female authors.

ARTISTS Brian O'Leary and Josh Keller, the *Chronicle of Higher Education;* Jevin West and Jennifer Jacquet, the University of Washington's Eigenfactor Project.

STATEMENT Women's presence in higher education has increased, but as authors of scholarly papers—keys to career success—their publishing patterns differ from those of men. We set out to build a news application that enabled our audience to find their own stories in the data by comparing fields and disciplines with which they are familiar. Those who take the time to explore will discover a great disparity between fields and disciplines with regard to female authorship.

We are now on the lookout for new partnerships to bring together research and analysis by scholars with data visualization and presentation by the *Chronicle*. We believe this has potential to be an excellent model, interesting our audience, and benefiting the scholars by providing them with visualizations that can aid them in their research.

PUBLICATION chronicle.com (October 22, 2012)

CHOOSE A TIME PERIOD
1665-1970
321,368 authors
1971-1990
609,635 authors
1991-2010
1.1 million authors
All years
2.0 million authors
SORT Percentage of female authors
Percentage of female authors
AUTHOR POSITION
What is this?
All authors
10
20
30
40
50
60
70+
Ecology and evolution
24 subfields
8.4% female authors
(56,152 authors)
Molecular & Cell biology
39 subfields
15.7% female authors
(16,889 authors)
Economics
16 subfields
4.0% female authors
(15,968 authors)
Sociology
22 subfields
13.4% female authors
(15,522 authors)
Probability and statistics
20 subfields
8.9% female authors
(6,547 authors)
Organizational and marketing

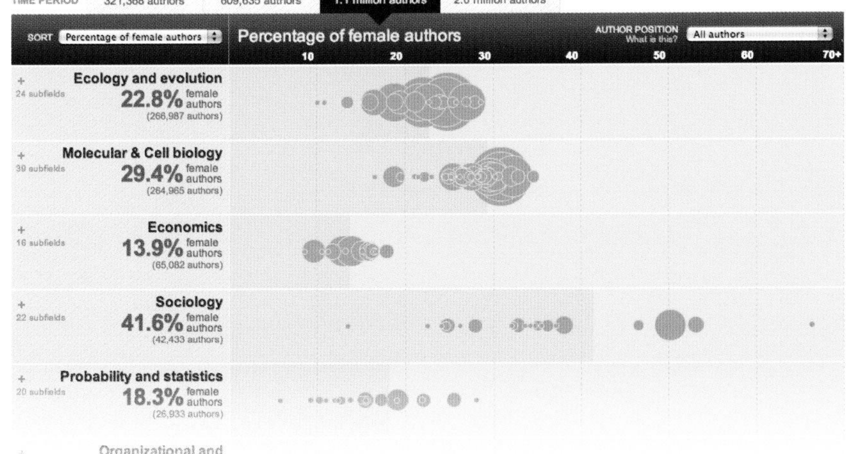
CHOOSE A TIME PERIOD
1665-1970
321,368 authors
1971-1990
609,635 authors
1991-2010
1.1 million authors
All years
2.0 million authors
SORT Percentage of female authors
Percentage of female authors
AUTHOR POSITION
What is this?
All authors
10
20
30
40
50
60
70+
Ecology and evolution
24 subfields
22.8% female authors
(266,987 authors)
Molecular & Cell biology
39 subfields
29.4% female authors
(264,965 authors)
Economics
16 subfields
13.9% female authors
(65,082 authors)
Sociology
22 subfields
41.6% female authors
(42,433 authors)
Probability and statistics
20 subfields
18.3% female authors
(26,933 authors)
Organizational and marketing

CHOOSE A TIME PERIOD
1665-1970
321,368 authors
1971-1990
609,635 authors
1991-2010
1.1 million authors
All years
2.0 million authors

SORT Percentage of female authors
Percentage of female authors
AUTHOR POSITION
What is this?
All authors

10 20 30 40 50 60 70+

Ecology and evolution
24 subfields
18.5% female authors
(427,476 authors)

Molecular & Cell biology
39 subfields
26.7% female authors
(392,159 authors)

Economics
16 subfields
9.7% female authors
(129,059 authors)

Sociology
22 subfields
31.4% female authors
(90,506 authors)

Probability and statistics
20 subfields
14.1% female authors
(51,026 authors)

Organizational and marketing

FRONTLINE
A PERFECT TERRORIST
WATCH THE FILM »
A PERFECT TERRORIST
David Coleman Headley's Web of Betrayal
How did David Coleman Headley veer from a life of privilege to drugs, crime and, finally, terrorism? His dedication to one thing beyond all else: Himself.
We recommend using the Chrome browser to view this interactive experience.
An interactive analysis by Tom Jennings
BEGIN

U.S. Law
Enforcement
& Intelligence

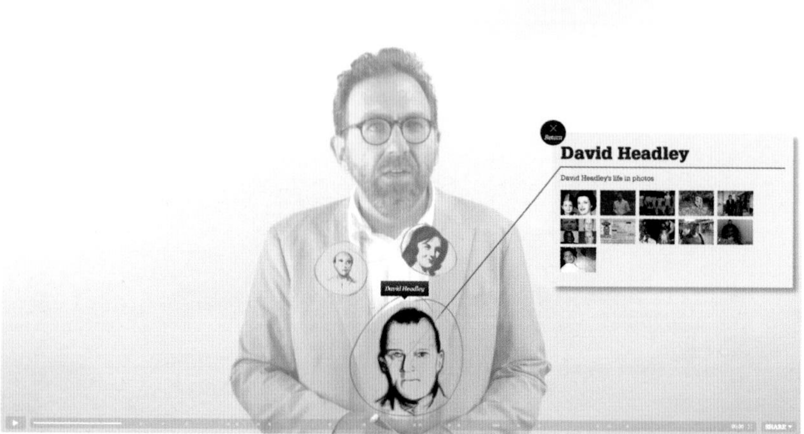
David Headley
David Headley's life in photos

Return
Sajid Mir
Sajid Mir is the Lashkar e Taiba official who is credited as one of the primary architects of the Mumbai terror attack. Years before that, French prosecutor Jean-Louis BruguiÃ/Ã"re successfuly prosecuted Mir in absentia for training a sleeper agent and placing him in France. Mir, he believes, was the force behind LET's plan to emulate Al Qaeda by launching terror attacks around the world. Using David Coleman Headely to plot the Mumbai attacks was part of this broader goal.

A Network of Violence

An interactive documentary telling the story of an American-born terrorist who plotted the November 2008 attack in Mumbai that killed 166 people.

Terrorism
Affiliates
SHARE

CLICK ON A CIRCLE TO LEARN MORE
SHARE

New York Wife
New York Wife
David Headley married a woman from Canada in 2002 in part to give her US citizenship. In the 1990s, when Headley was incarcerated and was working with the DEA to get out of jail, she worked to get him out. Their relationship changed after Headley became involved with Lashkar e Taiba on visits to Pakistan. She stayed in New York and helped run a video store he owned. It was here she says he assaulted her in 2005. In turn, she called the Joint Terrorism Task Force hotline, reporting him to the FBI.
DOCUMENTS

SHARE

ARTISTS Tom Jennings and Sabrina Shankman, the independent film company 2over10; Andrew Golis, *PBS Frontline;* James Milward, Pietro Gagliano, and Ashlee Lougheed, the digital design group Secret Location, in Toronto.

STATEMENT Taking the whiteboard concept to a new level, the narrator speaks while drawing clickable circles that appear before him and represent the people, places, and events that made up David Coleman Headley's life. By the end of the six-minute narrative, there are twenty-four subject areas the viewer can explore in depth. This project was the result of a collaboration between *PBS Frontline* and Secret Location that started with a weekend hackathon in April 2012. The brainchild of *Frontline*'s Andrew Golis, the creative session occurred at Harvard and brought together documentary producers and web designers in a two-day, free-for-all experimental collaboration.

One of *Frontline*'s recent films, "A Perfect Terrorist" (directed by Tom Jennings), was used as a test bed to explore a new form of digital documentary storytelling. Pietro Gagliano of Secret Location spearheaded a design concept in consultation with Jennings. From this session came a skeletal structure of what would become the full interactive in the following months. After conference calls and late-night planning sessions, a key concept of doing a whiteboardlike presentation was hit upon, with the twist of dimensionalizing the elements by having the narrator seemingly draw them in air before the camera. The 1950 film of Pablo Picasso painting on glass, by Belgian filmmaker Paul Haesaerts, provided inspiration.

PUBLICATION pbs.org (November 29, 2012)

The Red State, Blue State Shuffle

How the states stacked up in the 2012 election and how they have shifted over past elections.

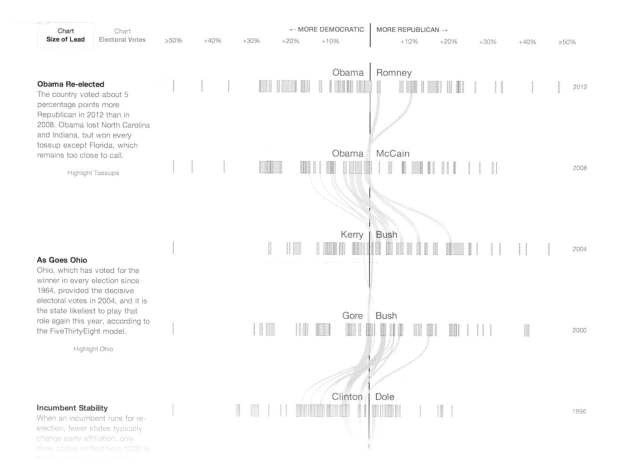

Chart Size of Lead | Chart Electoral Votes

← MORE DEMOCRATIC | MORE REPUBLICAN →

≥50% +40% +30% +20% +10% | +10% +20% +30% +40% ≥50%

Obama | Romney 2012

Obama | McCain 2008

Kerry | Bush 2004

Gore | Bush 2000

Clinton | Dole 1996

Obama Re-elected
The country voted about 5 percentage points more Republican in 2012 than in 2008. Obama lost North Carolina and Indiana, but won every tossup except Florida, which remains too close to call.

Highlight Tossups

As Goes Ohio
Ohio, which has voted for the winner in every election since 1964, provided the decisive electoral votes in 2004, and it is the state likeliest to play that role again this year, according to the FiveThirtyEight model.

Highlight Ohio

Incumbent Stability
When an incumbent runs for re-election, fewer states typically change party affiliation; only three states shifted from 2000 to

ARTISTS Mike Bostock, Shan Carter, and Amanda Cox, the *New York Times*.

STATEMENT Recent elections have placed a heavy emphasis on "swing states"—Ohio, Florida, and the other competitive states. Yet in the past, many more states shifted between the Democratic and Republican parties.

Our department has long been frustrated with election choropleth maps, such as the familiar red state/blue state maps. Given the Electoral College, a state's importance is not proportional to its geographic area; a blowout by one party can falsely appear a win by the other. We've solved this problem previously by varying chart forms, such as bubble maps, but those solutions gave a good view of only current results. With increasingly close elections and fewer states shifting allegiance, we wanted to put current electoral predictions in historical context.

PUBLICATION *New York Times* online (www.nytimes.com) (October 15, 2012)

Over the Decades, How States Have Shifted

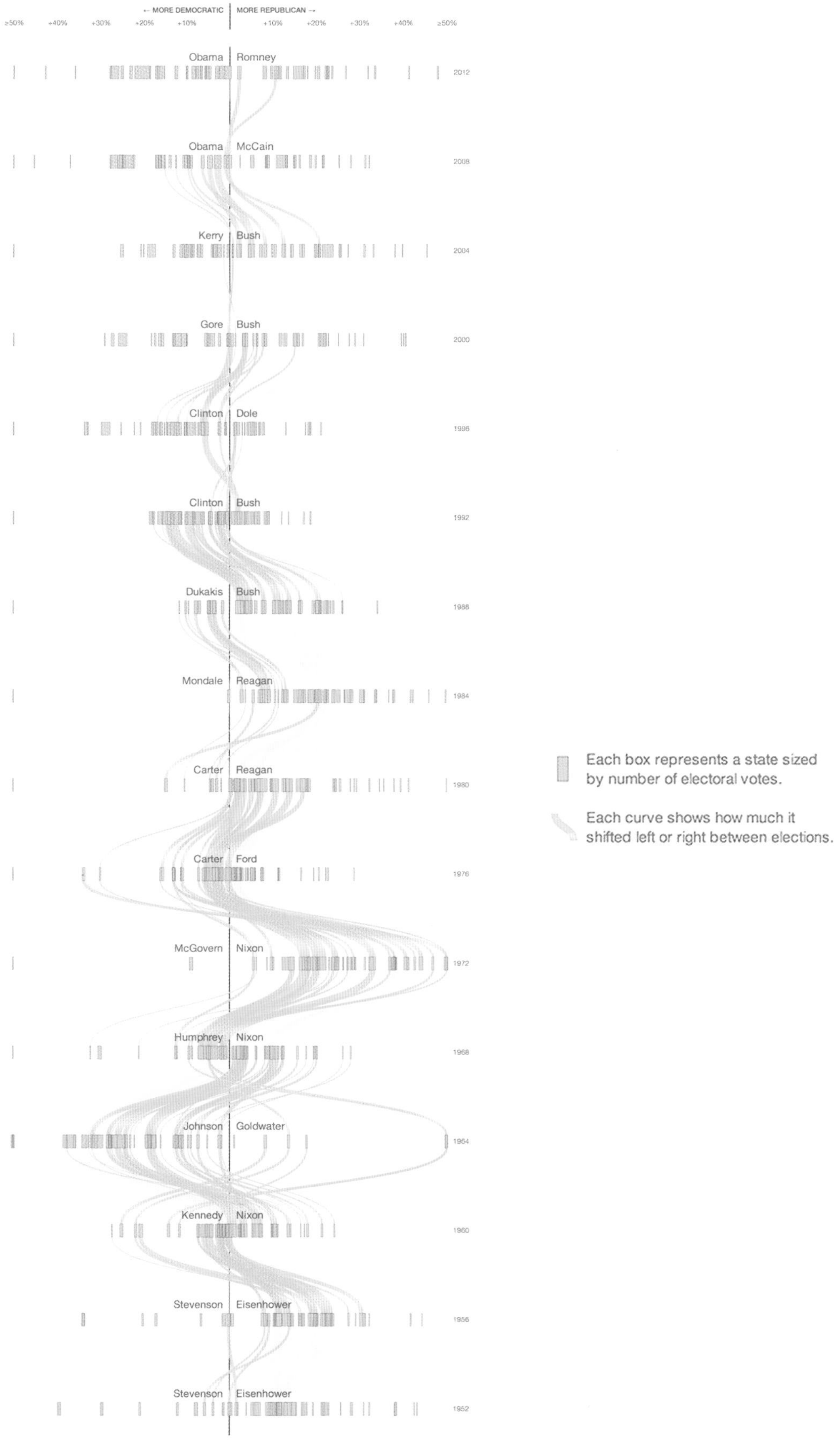

← MORE DEMOCRATIC
MORE REPUBLICAN →
≥50%
+40%
+30%
+20%
+10%
+10%
+20%
+30%
+40%
≥50%
Obama | Romney 2012
Obama | McCain 2008
Kerry | Bush 2004
Gore | Bush 2000
Clinton | Dole 1996
Clinton | Bush 1992
Dukakis | Bush 1988
Mondale | Reagan 1984
Carter | Reagan 1980
Carter | Ford 1976
McGovern | Nixon 1972
Humphrey | Nixon 1968
Johnson | Goldwater 1964
Kennedy | Nixon 1960
Stevenson | Eisenhower 1956
Stevenson | Eisenhower 1952
Each box represents a state sized by number of electoral votes.
Each curve shows how much it shifted left or right between elections.

In 1960, 1968 and 1972, some electoral votes were unpledged or allocated to a third-party candidate; for these years, the displayed electoral vote totals are less than 538.

Source: Dave Leip's Atlas of U.S. Presidential Elections

TIMES INVESTIGATION

Life on the line: 911 bre

BY ROBERT J. LOPEZ, KATE LINTHICUM AND BEN WELSH

Controversy over the Los Angeles Fire Department's response times erupted in March after The Times reported that fire officials admitted publishing incorrect statistics that overstated how fast rescuers arrive at emergencies.

The Times has followed up with a series of investigative stories and a data analysis that uncovered deep-rooted problems in a safety net millions of Angelenos rely on when they dial 911.

Top stories

HOW IT STARTED

Politics lights a fire under LAFD

COMMUNICATION BREAKDOW

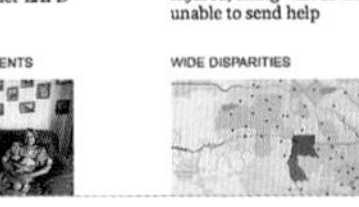

Injured, ailing wait as dis unable to send help

DISCONNECTED DEPARTMENTS

WIDE DISPARITIES

The LA Fire Department: Too Slow

Rescuers are expected to respond to nearly all 911 calls within six minutes, a national standard that the Los Angeles Fire Department routinely fails to meet.

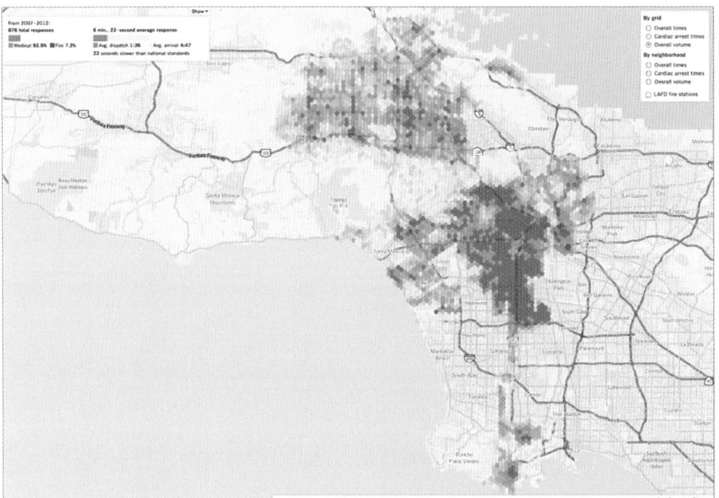

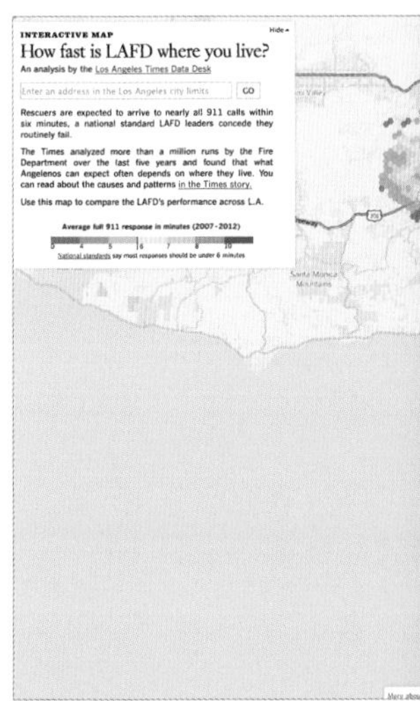
INTERACTIVE MAP
How fast is LAFD where you live?
An analysis by the Los Angeles Times Data Desk

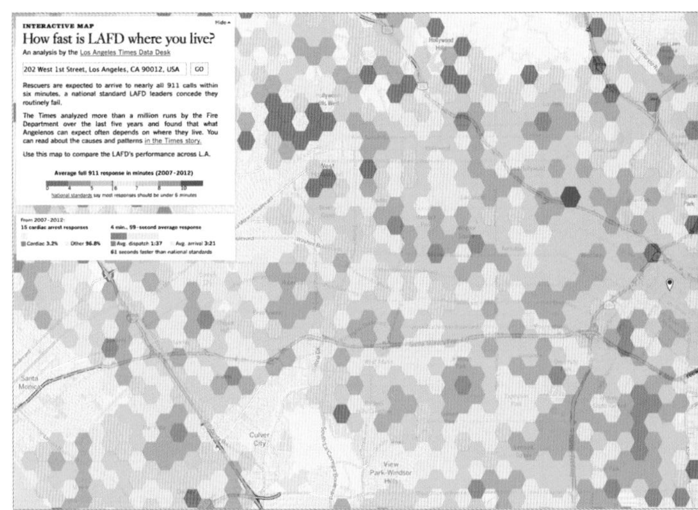
INTERACTIVE MAP
How fast is LAFD where you live?
An analysis by the Los Angeles Times Data Desk
202 West 1st Street, Los Angeles, CA 90012, USA
GO
Rescuers are expected to arrive to nearly all 911 calls within six minutes, a national standard LAFD leaders concede they routinely fail.
The Times analyzed more than a million runs by the Fire Department over the last five years and found that what Angelenos can expect often depends on where they live. You can read about the causes and patterns in the Times story.
Use this map to compare the LAFD's performance across L.A.
Average full 911 response in minutes (2007-2012)

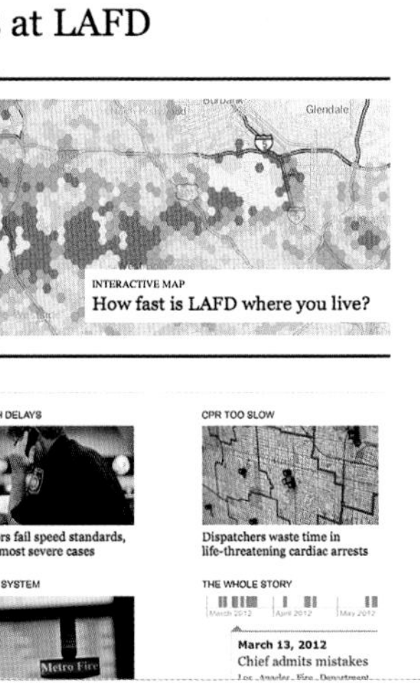
at LAFD
INTERACTIVE MAP
How fast is LAFD where you live?
CPR TOO SLOW
Dispatchers waste time in life-threatening cardiac arrests
THE WHOLE STORY
March 13, 2012
Chief admits mistakes

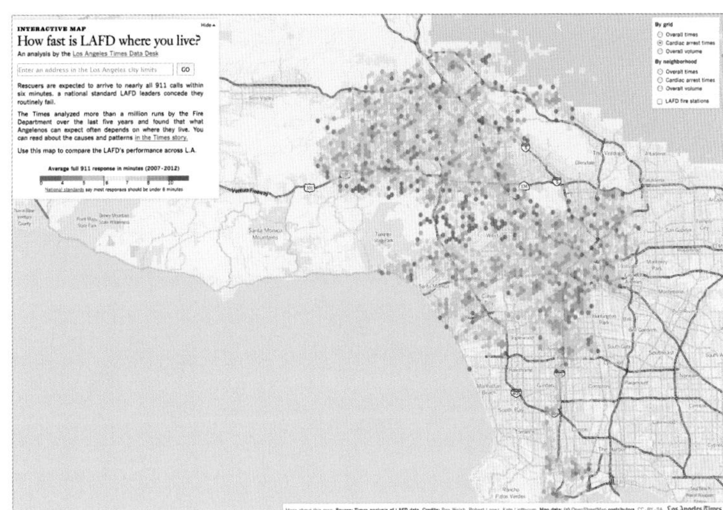
INTERACTIVE MAP
How fast is LAFD where you live?
An analysis by the Los Angeles Times Data Desk
GO
Use this map to compare the LAFD's performance across L.A.
By grid
Overall times
Cardiac arrest times
Overall volume
By neighborhood
Overall times
Cardiac arrest times
Overall volume
LAFD fire stations

By grid
Overall times
Cardiac arrest times
Overall volume
By neighborhood
Overall times
Cardiac arrest times
Overall volume
LAFD fire stations

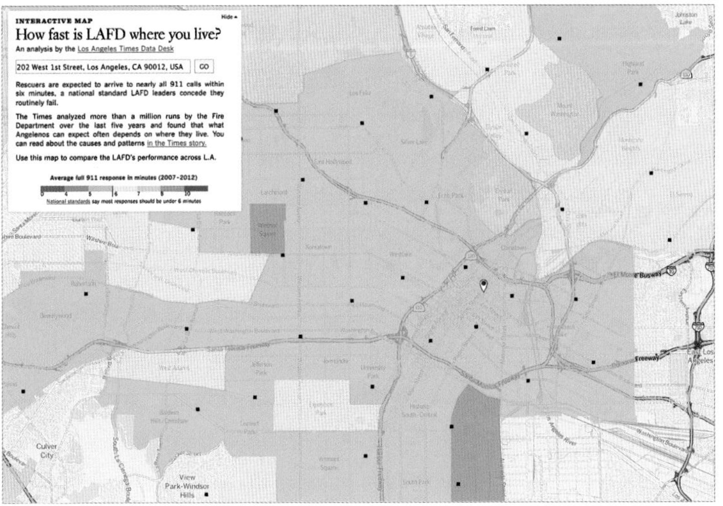
INTERACTIVE MAP
How fast is LAFD where you live?
An analysis by the Los Angeles Times Data Desk
202 West 1st Street, Los Angeles, CA 90012, USA
GO
Rescuers are expected to arrive to nearly all 911 calls within six minutes, a national standard LAFD leaders concede they routinely fail.
The Times analyzed more than a million runs by the Fire Department over the last five years and found that what Angelenos can expect often depends on where they live. You can read about the causes and patterns in the Times story.
Use this map to compare the LAFD's performance across L.A.
Average full 911 response in minutes (2007-2012)
National standards say most responses should be under 6 minutes
Culver City
View Park-Windsor Hills

ARTISTS Ben Welsh, Robert J. Lopez, and Kate Linthicum, the *Los Angeles Times.*

STATEMENT Controversy over the Los Angeles Fire Department's response times erupted in March 2012 after the *Times* reported that fire officials admitted publishing statistics that overstated how fast rescuers arrive at emergencies. The *Times* has followed up with a series of investigative stories and a data analysis that uncovered deep-rooted problems in a safety net that millions of Angelenos rely on when they dial 911.

The *Times* analyzed more than a million 911 responses by the Fire Department over the last five years and found that what Angelenos can expect often depends on where they live. The map was the first independent, block-by-block analysis of how long it takes LAFD units to reach victims after the agency picks up a 911 call. The findings reinforce the obvious risks of living in L.A.'s scenic and desirable canyon enclaves, where wildfires and mudslides are a perennial concern and narrow and winding roads can slow rescue vehicles. Readers can search their address and find out how long they can expect to wait if they dial 911.

PUBLICATION Los Angeles Times online (www.latimes.com) (November 15, 2012)

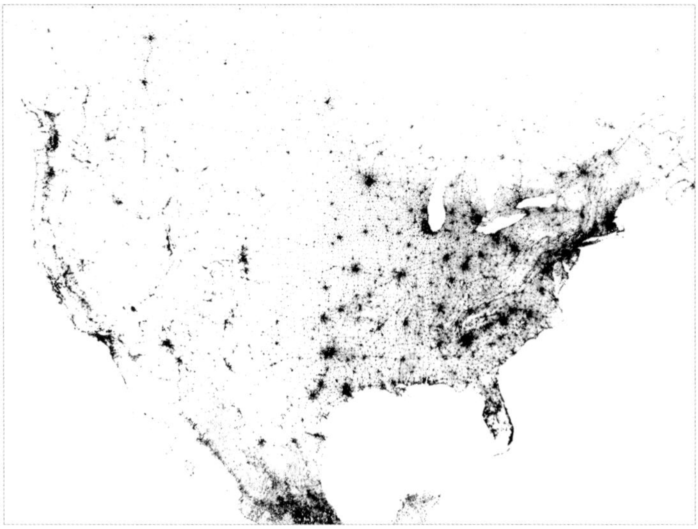

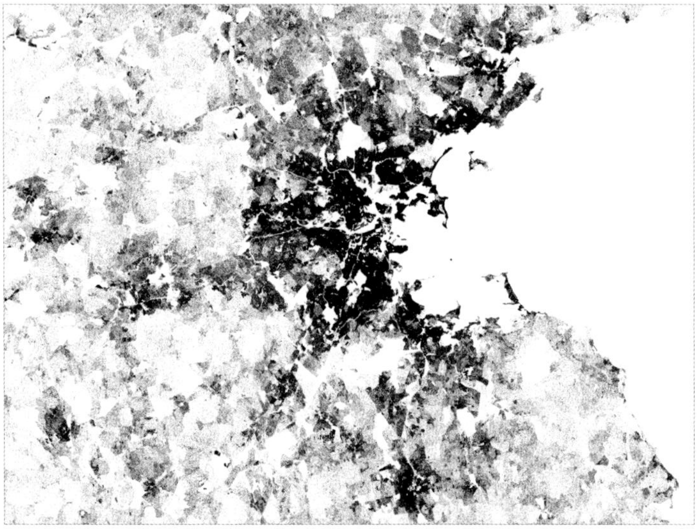

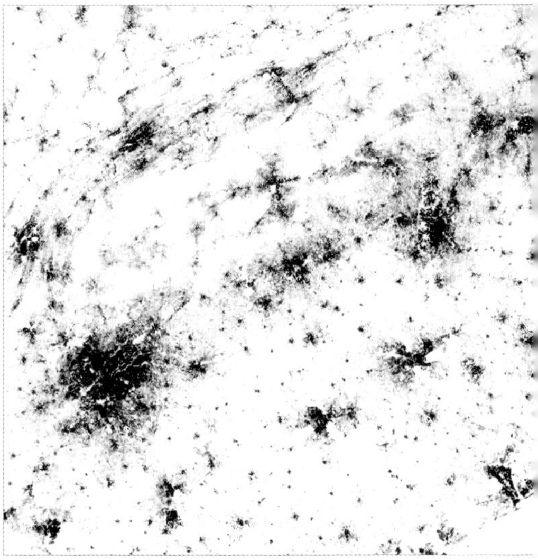

Census Dotmap

454,064,098 dots, a dot for every person in the United States, Canada, and Mexico, with no other features—no roads, borders, or coastlines.

ARTIST Brandon Martin-Anderson, a researcher at the MIT Media Lab.

STATEMENT Infographics tend to reduce and simplify, to project the data in such a way that supports the creator's thesis. I wanted to do the opposite, to show the data without reducing and without telling viewers what they're supposed to see. I believe that information designers often underestimate the capacity of the human eye to take in and synthesize data when presented in a very dense way. The image is made from about 250 million data points—the number of rods and cones in a pair of normal human eyes—and yet you can synthesize it all into a coherent whole.

People are surprisingly comfortable with zooming. I thought I'd have to explain to everyone in slow and patient terms that they can zoom in and out of the image, but people do it on their own. Google and Apple have spent a lot of time and effort getting people comfortable with the idea of diving through different scales as a way of understanding a very large data set, and their efforts have paid off.

PUBLICATION
bmander.com (December 25, 2012)

Explore Playlists Channels Blog Interactive Search

+ Story

2005-06-11 13:06:19 M 4/4 20°C

HIGHWAY

WOLVER

GRIZZLY BEAR 114

Trail Cam 01 - North Bend

ROAD

The First Rule of Survival | Music: Bloom - Radiohead

ABOUT READ THE STORY CREDITS

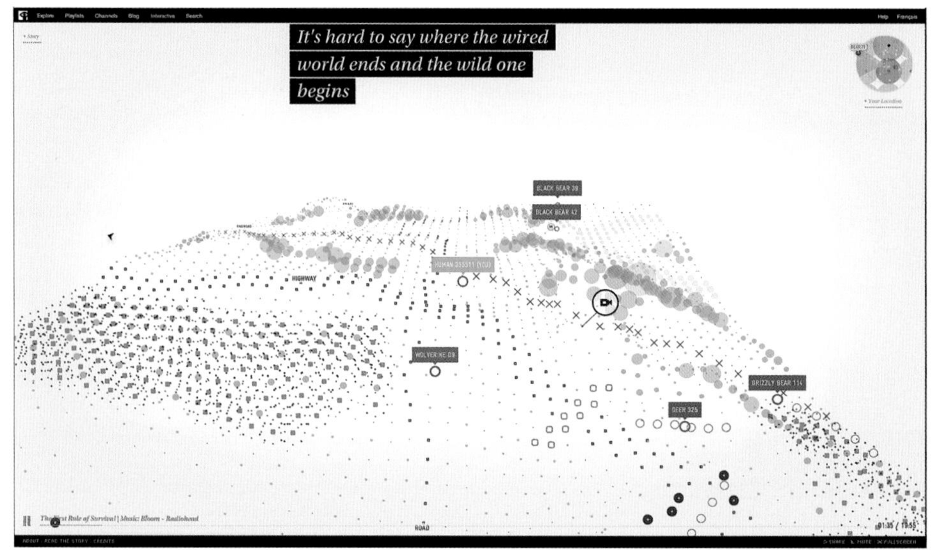
It's hard to say where the wired world ends and the wild one begins
BLACK BEAR 38
BLACK BEAR 42
HIGHWAY
WOLVERINE 09
GRIZZLY BEAR 114
DEER 325
ROAD

Help Français
BEAR 71
+ Your Location
01:58 / 19:55
SHARE | MUTE | FULLSCREEN

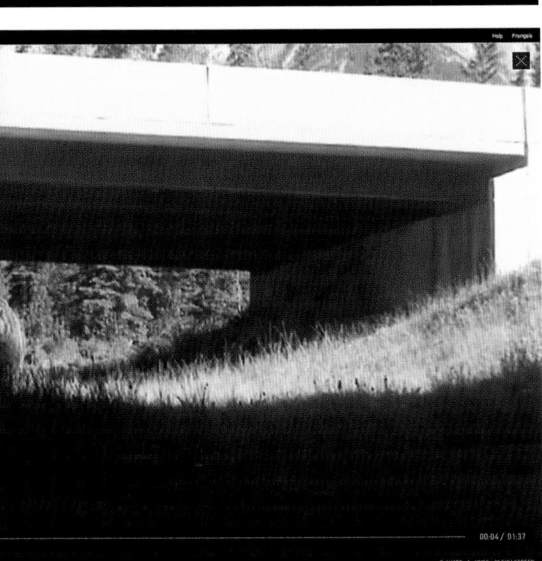

Bear 71

An interactive multiuser experience told from the point of view of an omniscient female grizzly bear, dubbed "Bear 71" by the park rangers in Alberta's Banff National Park.

ARTISTS Jeremy Mendes, Leanne Allison, and the digital studio of the National Film Board of Canada.

STATEMENT Bear 71's story speaks to how we coexist with wildlife in the age of networks, surveillance, and digital information en masse. The bear's world is revealed through a script written by JB McKinnon, and brought to life by actress Mia Kirshner against a rich musical and natural soundscape. The bear's story is played out on a landscape dubbed "the grid," a technological reimagining of nature. Exploring this environment, visitors to the site can open up hundreds of "trail cam" images of wildlife in the Rocky Mountains captured over the last ten years. These images, displayed as interactive infographics, relay key facts about the animals in the bear's environment. Visitors can become part of the bear's world by turning on their webcams and appearing as another creature in the bear's landscape. Ultimately, Bear 71 carries a potent reminder that what we think of as "wilderness" is changing, as the wired world and the wild one intersect.

PUBLICATION nfb.ca/bear71, launched at Sundance, New Frontier (January 19, 2012)

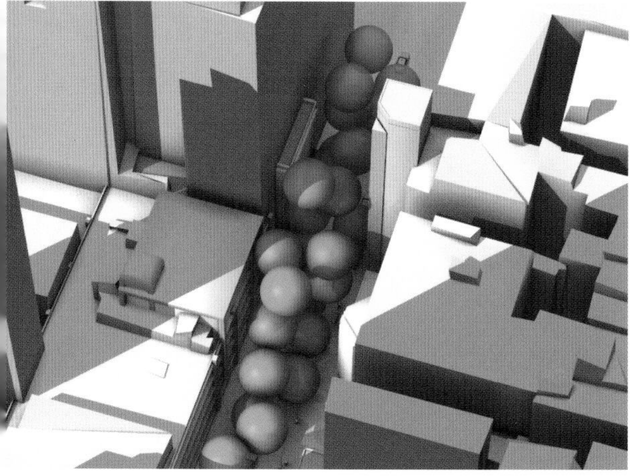

New York's Carbon Emissions—in Real Time

In 2010 New York City added the equivalent of 54 million metric tons of carbon dioxide to the atmosphere. Carbon Visuals and the Environmental Defense Fund wanted to make it feel a little more real.

ARTISTS Adam Nieman of Carbon Visuals, a British data visualization company that specializes in reaching "nonengaged" audiences; Chris Rabét, a freelance British director and digital visual effects artist.

STATEMENT Most visualization involves a process of abstraction, but sometimes it is useful to illustrate actual quantities of stuff so viewers can relate to the data physically. New Yorkers know what it's like to walk across Manhattan; and they know in their bodies, not just their minds, how tall the Empire State Building is. We can use that to make an important number feel a little more real.

Using the real world as a canvas for visualization brings with it a new set of challenges. The film must be "true" to the data. We wanted to give carbon dioxide substance but didn't want to make it seem too substantial. It is a delicate balance. Rather than one continuous volume of gas, we chose individual spheres because the human mind is better at counting things than it is at judging volume.

PUBLICATION YouTube and carbonvisuals.com (October 19, 2012)

512 Paths to the White House

Select a winner in the most competitive states below to see all the paths to victory available for either can

Fla.	Ohio	N.C.	Va.	Wis.	Colo.	Iowa	Nev.
Dem Rep	Dem Rep	Dem Rep	Dem Rep	Dem Rep	Dem Rep	Dem Rep	Dem Rep

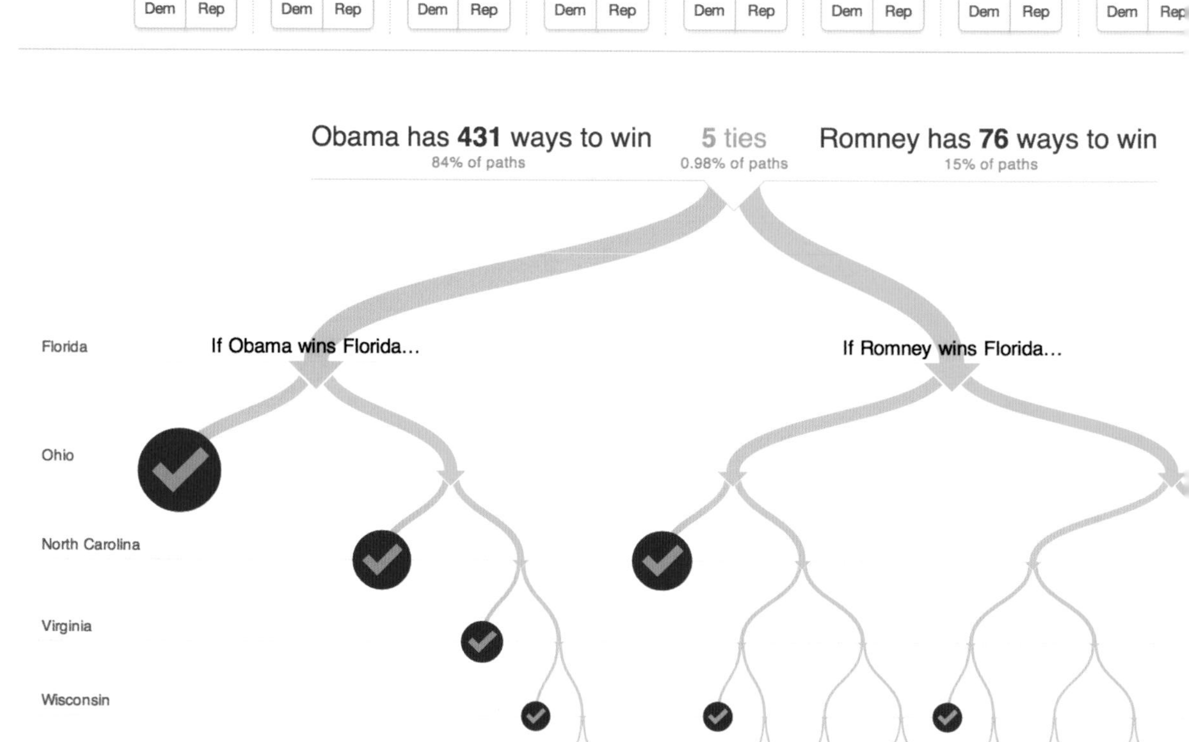
Obama has **431** ways to win
84% of paths
5 ties
0.98% of paths
Romney has **76** ways to win
15% of paths
Florida
If Obama wins Florida...
If Romney wins Florida...
Ohio
North Carolina
Virginia
Wisconsin

Colorado

Iowa

Nevada

New Hampshire

Florida is a Must Win for Romney
If Mr. Romney loses Florida, he has only one way to victory: through all the other battleground states. He has led most polls there, however, and is the favorite. If Mr. Romney wins Florida, he has 75 paths open to him.

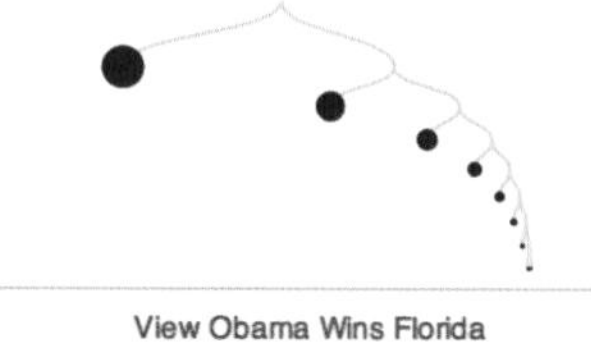

View Obama Wins Florida

Ohio: Obama's Firewall
Of the three largest battleground states, Mr. Obama has the largest lead in Ohio – partly because of a strong local economy and the auto industry bailout. If he loses here, it's likely he will trail in Florida and North Carolina too. Losing all three leaves him with only 14 ways to win.

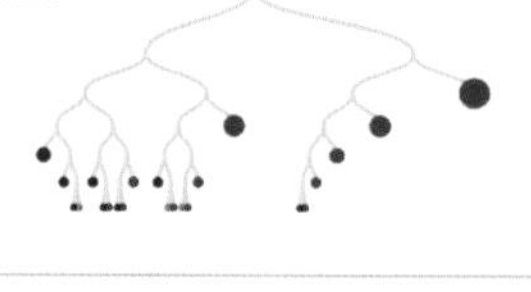

View Romney Wins Ohio, Fla. & N.C.

Times's Battlegrounds
Nine states are shown above, but The Times rates only seven of them as battlegrounds. If Nevada goes to Mr. Obama and North Carolina goes to Mr. Romney, as The Times's ratings suggest, the president will have four times as many paths to victory as his opponent.

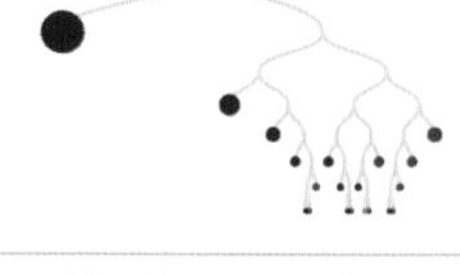

View Battleground States

Edge of
There are
the newly
Represen
president
Senate w
(possibly

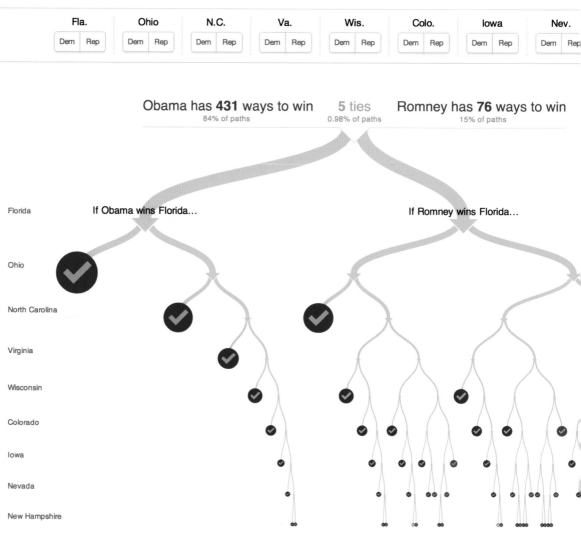

Road to Victory

A tool to explore all the likely outcomes of the 2012 presidential election. It was available before the election and was updated on election night as results flowed in, removing paths that had been eliminated.

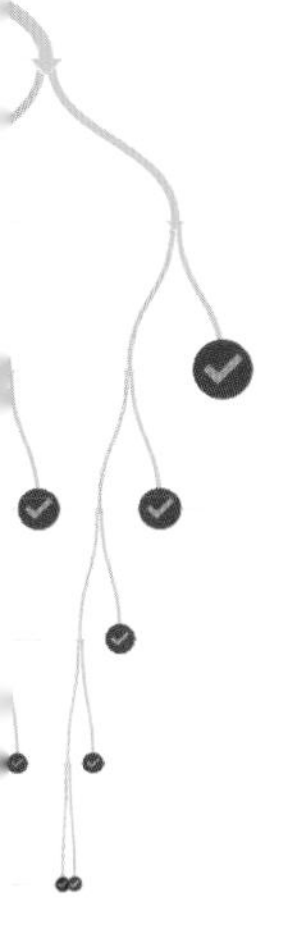

ARTISTS Mike Bostock and Shan Carter, the *New York Times*.

STATEMENT After building electoral calculators for two presidential election cycles, I had developed an intense frustration with how tedious the traditional electoral calculators were to use—they allowed one to explore a universe of possible outcomes, but only one at a time. If instead of forcing people to explore this forest by taking a single path at a time, Mike and I thought, "Couldn't we just show the map of the area?" From that idea, we developed this interactive bird's-eye view of all 512 paths available to Barack Obama and Mitt Romney.

PUBLICATION *New York Times* online (www.nytimes.com) (November 2, 2012)

BEST AMERICAN INFOGRAPHICS BRAIN TRUST

THOMAS ALBERTY was brought on as the design director of *New York* magazine in 2012. Prior to that, he worked at *GQ* for eight years. His work has been recognized by the Society of Publication Designers and the Type Directors Club. He lives in Brooklyn, New York.

SAMUEL ARBESMAN is an applied mathematician and network scientist. He is a senior scholar at the Ewing Marion Kauffman Foundation and a fellow at the Institute for Quantitative Social Science at Harvard University. He is the author of *The Half-Life of Facts*.

ALBERTO CAIRO teaches infographics and visualization at the University of Miami. He has been a professor at the University of North Carolina at Chapel Hill and the infographics and multimedia director at various media organizations in Spain and Brazil. He is the author of *The Functional Art: An Introduction to Information Graphics and Visualization*.

JEN CHRISTIANSEN is the art director of information graphics at *Scientific American*. Previously she was an assistant art director and then a designer at *National Geographic*. She completed her undergraduate studies in geology and art at Smith College and her graduate studies in science illustration at the University of California, Santa Cruz.

AMANDA COX joined the *New York Times* graphics desk in 2005. She holds a master's degree in statistics from the University of Washington.

CARL DETORRES is a multidisciplinary graphic designer operating at the intersection of design, illustration, and information graphics. He is a longtime contributor to publications such as *Nature*, *Wired*, *Fortune*, *Time*, and the *New York Times* and regularly partners with corporations and institutions like IBM, Facebook, IEEE, and the George Lucas Educational Foundation. His studio is located in Oakland, California.

MARIETTE DICHRISTINA is the editor-in-chief and senior vice president of *Scientific American* and oversees the magazine as well as ScientificAmerican.com, *Scientific American Mind*, and all newsstand special editions. Under her leadership, the magazine received a 2011 National Magazine Award for General Excellence.

JOHN GRIMWADE is the graphics director of *Condé Nast Traveler* and has his own information graphics business. He has produced infographics for over thirty magazines. Before moving to the United States, he worked for fourteen years at newspapers in London, spending six years as head of graphics at *The Times*. He cohosts the annual Malofiej Show, Don't Tell infographics workshop in Pamplona, Spain, and teaches information graphics at the School of Visual Arts in Manhattan.

NIGEL HOLMES is the founder of Explanation Graphics, a design company that helps people understand complex processes and statistics. He was the graphics director for *Time* from 1978 to 1994. The Society for News Design gave him a Lifetime Achievement Award in 2009, and a retrospective exhibition of his work was shown at Stevenson University in Baltimore in 2011. His most recent book, *The Book of Everything*, was published by Lonely Planet in 2012. With his son, Rowland, he makes short animated films.

GEOFF MCGHEE develops interactive media at the Bill Lane Center for the American West at Stanford University. Previously, he spent a decade doing infographics, multimedia, and video at the *New York Times*, ABC News, and *Le Monde*. In 2009–2010, he was a John S. Knight Journalism

Fellow at Stanford University and studied data visualization, which resulted in the web documentary *Journalism in the Age of Data*.

JOHN NELSON is an interaction designer and cartographer at IDV Solutions, a software company specializing in risk visualization and management. He runs the data visualization and research site uxblog.idvsolutions.com.

MARIA POPOVA is the founder and editor of *Brain Pickings* (brainpickings.org), an inventory of cross-disciplinary interestingness. She has written for *Wired UK, The Atlantic, Nieman Journalism Lab*, the *New York Times*, *Smithsonian*, and *Design Observer*, among others, and is an MIT Futures of Entertainment Fellow. She is on Twitter as @brainpicker.

KIM REES is a cofounder of Periscopic, a socially conscious data visualization firm.

SIMON ROGERS is the editor of the *Guardian*'s *Datablog* and *Datastore*, blogs that publish and analyze the data behind the news. In 2012 he won a Royal Statistical Society award for statistical excellence in journalism.

DREW SKAU is the visualization architect at Visually, a community for infographic and data visualization creators to showcase their work and connect with clients. He is pursuing a PhD in computer science at the University of North Carolina at Charlotte with a focus on supporting creativity in visualization design.

JUAN VELASCO has been the art director of *National Geographic* since 2008. Previously he worked as a graphics artist for *El Mundo* and as the graphics art director for the *New York Times*. In 2001 he founded his own consulting company, 5W Infographics, which is based in New York City and Madrid. He is an instructor for the Show, Don't Tell infographics workshop, part of the SND-e Malofiej conference at the University of Pamplona in Spain, and a visiting teacher of information graphics for the University of Hong Kong.

FERNANDA B. VIÉGAS is a computational designer whose work focuses on the social, collaborative, and artistic aspects of information visualization. She is a coleader, with Martin Wattenberg, of Google's Big Picture data visualization research group in Cambridge, Massachusetts.

MARTIN WATTENBERG is a computer scientist and artist whose work focuses on visual explorations of culturally significant data. With Fernanda Viégas, he leads Google's Big Picture visualization research group. A particular interest is using visual tools to foster collaboration and collective discovery.

BANG WONG is the creative director of the Broad Institute of MIT and Harvard and an adjunct assistant professor in the Department of Art as Applied to Medicine at the Johns Hopkins University School of Medicine. His work focuses on developing visual strategies to meet the analytical challenges posed by the unprecedented scale, resolution, and variety of data in biomedical research.

NATHAN YAU has a PhD in statistics from the University of California, Los Angeles, and is the author of *Visualize This* and *Data Points*. He writes about visualization and statistics at FlowingData.com.

DAN ZEDEK is the assistant managing editor/design at the *Boston Globe,* where he leads the print and online design and infographics teams. In 2012 BostonGlobe.com was named the world's best-designed website by the Society for News Design.

CREDITS "Can I Make Stuff Up? A Visual Guide" by L. V. Anderson, David Haglund, Natalie Matthews-Ramo, and Jim Pagels. First published in *Slate,* March 21, 2012. Copyright © 2012 by *Slate.* Reprinted by permission of *Slate.* "Short Guys Can Dunk" by Bonnie Berkowitz and Alberto Cuadra. First published in the *Washington Post,* March 6, 2012. "Warhorse" by Bonnie Berkowitz and Alberto Cuadra. First published in the *Washington Post,* October 21, 2012. Copyright © 2013 by the *Washington Post.* Reprinted by permission of Bonnie Berkowitz and Alberto Cuadra. "A Survey of Destruction by Hurricane Sandy in New York City" by Matthew Block, Ford Fessenden, Alan McLean, Archie Tse, and Derek Watkins. First published in the *New York Times,* November 20, 2012. Copyright © 2012 by the *New York Times.* Reprinted by permission of New York Times Graphics. "512 Paths to the White House" by Mike Bostock and Shan Carter. First published in the *New York Times,* November 2, 2012. Copyright © 2012 by the *New York Times.* Reprinted by permission of New York Times Graphics. "Ten Artists, Ten Years" by Arthur Buxton. First published on his blog arthurbuxton.com, June 3, 2012. Copyright © 2013 by Arthur Buxton. Reprinted by permission of Arthur Buxton. "Gay Rights in the U.S., State by State" by Feilding Cage and Gabriel Dance. First published in the *Guardian US* interactive, May 8, 2012. Copyright Guardian News & Media Ltd © 2012. Reprinted by permission. "Death of the Titanic" Courtesy of James Cameron. Art Direction: Kaitlin M. Yarnall; Design and Production: Matthew Twombly; NGM Staff Artist: Nick Kaloterakis; Sources: James Cameron, Ken Marschall, Casey Schatz, Lt. Cmdr. Parks Stephenson, USN (Ret), Cmdr. Jeffrey Stettler, USN, PhD. "The Anatomy of Speed" by Bryan Christie Design, from "Cheetahs on the Edge" by Roff Smith. First published in *National Geographic,* 2012. Copyright © 2012 by Bryan Christie Design. Reprinted by permission of Bryan Christie Design. "Women as Academic Authors, 1665–2010" from the *Chronicle of Higher Education* http://chronicle.com/article/Women-as-Academic-Authors/135192/. Copyright © 2013 by the *Chronicle of Higher Education.* Reprinted by permission of the *Chronicle of Higher Education.* "A Campaign Map, Morphed by Money" by Adam Cole. First published in "It's All Politics," NPR, November 1, 2012. Copyright © 2012 by National Public Radio, Inc. Reprinted by permission of NPR. "What Happens After the I.P.O.?" by Amanda Cox and Seth W. Feaster. First published in the *New York Times,* 2012. Copyright © 2012 by the *New York Times.* Reprinted by permission of New York Times Graphics. "Obama Was Not as Strong as in 2008, but Strong Enough" by Amanda Cox, Alicia DeSantis, and Ford Fessenden. First published in the *New York Times,* November 7, 2012. Copyright © 2012 by the *New York Times.* Reprinted by permission of New York Times Graphics. "Under the Border" by Jennifer Daniel. First published in *Bloomberg Businessweek,* August 2, 2012. Copyright © 2012 by Jennifer Daniel/*Bloomberg Businessweek.* Reprinted by permission of *Bloomberg Businessweek.* "Bear 71" by Loc Dao. Copyright © 2012 National Film Board of Canada. All rights reserved. "The 1% Next Door" by Alicia DeSantis, Ford Fessenden, and Rob Gebeloff. First published in the *New York Times,* January 15, 2012. Copyright © 2012 by the *New York Times.* Reprinted by permission of New York Times Graphics. "Is Life Good?" by Gustavo Vieira Dias. First published on islifegood.tumbler.com, February 2012. Copyright © 2013 by Gustavo Vieira Dias. Reprinted by permission of Gustavo Vieira Dias. "Going, Going, Gone?" First published in *ESPN The Magazine,* April 2, 2012. Page layout copyright © ESPN *Magazine,* LLC 2012. Graphic copyright © 2012 by Carl DeTorres. Reprinted by permission of *ESPN The Magazine.* "Springfield Is a Maddening Mess. Cold, Hard Metrics Clean It Up." First published in *ESPN The Magazine,* December 24, 2012. Page layout copyright © ESPN *Magazine,* LLC 2012. Graphic copyright © 2012 by Pop Chart Lab. Reprinted by permission of *ESPN The Magazine.* "The 2010/2011 Feltron Biennial Report" by Nick Felton. First published in Feltron.com. Copyright © 2012 by Nicholas Felton. Reprinted by permission of Nicholas Felton. "Between Five Bells 2011 White Wine Label" by Nick Felton. First published in BetweenFiveBells.com. Copyright © 2013 by David Fesq. Reprinted by permission of David Fesq. "Is This the Structure of New York City" by Eric Fischer. Base map data © OpenStreetMap contributors, CC-BY-SA. Copyright © 2012 by Eric Fischer. Reprinted by permission of Eric Fisher. "Number of Guns per 100 People" by Max Fisher. First published in Washington*Post*.com, December 15, 2012, http://www.washingtonpost.com/blogs/worldviews/. Copyright © 2013 by Maxwell Fisher. Reprinted by permission of Maxwell Fisher. "The United States Redrawn as Fifty States with Equal Population" by Neil Freeman. First published in fakeisthenewreal.com, December 5, 2012. Copyright © 2012 by Neil Freeman. Reprinted by permission of Neil Freeman. "Fifty States of Grey" from http://www.goodreads.com/blog/show/365-fifty-states-of-grey-infographic. Copyright © 2012 by Goodreads. Reprinted by permission of Goodreads. "7 Minutes of Terror" by Eric Hand. First published in *Nature,* August 1, 2012. Copyright © 2012 by *Nature* Publishing Group. Reprinted by permission of *Nature*/NPG. "Tornado Tracks" by IDV Solutions, LLC and John Nelson. First published in http://www.flickr.com/photos/idvsolutions/7394756396/in/photostream/lightbox/. Copyright © 2012 IDV Solutions, LLC. Reprinted by permission of John Dougherty, VP of Operations, IDV Solutions, LLC. "The Gaffe-O-Meter" by Heather Jones. First published in *Time,* November 7, 2012. "Influence: A Brief History" by Heather Jones. First published in *Time,* April 18, 2012. Copyright © 2012 by *Time.* Reprinted by permission of Heather Jones. "The N.F.L. Players Mentioned Most on 'Sports Center'" by Ritchie S. King, Kevin Quealy, and Graham Roberts. First published in the *New York Times,* February 4, 2012. Copyright © 2012 by the *New York Times.* Reprinted by permission of New York Times Graphics. "A National Report Card" Graphics by Kiss Me I'm Polish. First published in *The Atlantic,* October 2012, and "How We Spend" Graphics by Kiss Me I'm Polish. First published in *The Atlantic,* March 2012. Graphics copyright © 2013 by Kiss Me I'm Polish. Reprinted by permission of Kiss Me I›m Polish. "The Death Toll in Breaking Bad" by John D. LaRue. First published on his blog TDYLF. Copyright © 2012 by John D. LaRue. Reprinted by permission of John D. LaRue. Breaking Bad © 2013 Sony Pictures Television Inc. "The Common Cook's How-Many Guide to Kitchen Conversions" by Shannon Lattin. First published on sblattindesign.wordpress.com. Copyright © 2012 by Shannon Lattin. Reprinted by permission of Shannon Lattin."Untranslatable Emotions in Languages other than English v.s. Parrott's Emotion Classification" by Pei-Ying Lin. First published on her blog http://uniquelang.peiyinglin.net/01untranslatable.html. Copyright © 2013 by Pei-Ying Lin. Reprinted by permission of Pei-Ying Lin. "The Last 45 Seconds" by Todd Lindemann. First published in the *Washington Post,* May 19, 2012. Copyright © 2012 by the *Washington Post.* Reprinted by permission. "The Gender Divide" by Brian McGill. First published in *National Journal*'s The Next Economy Supplement, Spring 2012. Copyright © 2012 by *National Journal.* Reprinted by permission. "Should I Check E-mail?" by Wendy MacNaughton. First published by Dell, Inc., in FORBES.com, 2012. Copyright © 2012 by Wendy MacNaughton. Reprinted by permission of the author. "Census Dotmap" by Brandon Martin-Anderson. Public domain. "Lakes and Oceans" by Randall Munroe. First published in XKCD webcomic, April 9, 2012. Copyright © 2012 by Randall Munroe. Reprinted by permission of Randall Munroe. "Family Ties" from "How to Build a Dog." First published in *National Geographic,* February 2012. Copyright © 2012 by National Geographic Society. Reprinted by permission. "Are We in the Midst of a Sixth Mass Extinction?" First published in the *New York Times Sunday Review,* June 1, 2012. Copyright © 2012 by the *New York Times.* Reprinted by permission of New York Times Graphics. "Invisible Residents." First published in the *New York Times,* June 18, 2012. Copyright © 2012 by the *New York Times.* Reprinted by permission of New York Times Graphics. "Mapping Ocean Noise." First published in the *New York Times,* December 10, 2012. Copyright © 2012 by the *New York Times.* Reprinted by permission of New York Times Graphics. "Over the Decades, How States Have Shifted." First published in the *New York Times,* November 7, 2012. Copyright © 2012 by the *New York Times.* Reprinted by permission of New York Times Graphics. "Pampered Like Royalty, or Canned Like Sardines." First published in the *New York Times,* June 9, 2012. Copyright © 2012 by the *New York Times.* Reprinted by permission of New York Times Graphics. "Usain Bolt Against the Olympic Medalist Field Since 1896." First published in the *New York Times,* August 6, 2012. Copyright © 2012 by the *New York Times.* Reprinted by permission of New York Times Graphics. "New York's Carbon Emissions—in Real *Time*" by Adam Nieman, Antony Turner, and Chris Rabet. First published in Carbon Visuals Ltd. Copyright © 2013 by Carbon Visuals Ltd. Reprinted by permission of the authors. "Prevalence of U.S. Influenza Infections (Est.)" by Katie Peek and Ryan Bradley, illustration by Pitch Interactive. First published in *Popular Science.* "The Warmup" by Katie Peek. First published in *Popular Science,* December 18, 2012. Used with permission of *Popular Science.* Copyright © 2013. All rights reserved. "Political Moneyball" by Andrew Garcia Phillips and Sarah Slobin. First published in the *Wall Street Journal,* July 26, 2012. Reprinted with permission of the *Wall Street Journal.* Copyright © 2012 Dow Jones & Company, Inc. All Rights Reserved Worldwide. "Constitutions of Classic Cocktails" by Pop Chart Lab. First published in http://popchartlab.com/collections/prints/products/constitutions-of-classic-cocktails. Copyright © 2012 by Pop Chart Lab, Inc. Reprinted by permission of Pop Chart Lab, Inc. "The Popification of the Top 40" by Gavin Potenza. First published in *Billboard,* September 29, 2012. Copyright © 2012 by Gavin Potenza. Reprinted by permission of Gavin Potenza. "Brocelets Through the Ages" by Clint Rainey; Illustration by Mark Nerys; Design Director: Thomas Alberty. First published in *New York Magazine,* March 12–19, 2012. Copyright © 2012 by New York Media, LLC. Reprinted by permission of New York Media. "The Disappearing Desktop" by Nicolas Rapp. First published in *Fortune,* November 14, 2012. Copyright © 2012 by Nicolas Rapp/*Fortune Magazine.* Reprinted by permission of Nicolas Rapp. "A Complex Endeavor" by Tom Reinken and Raoul Rañoa. First published in the *Los Angeles Times,* October 11, 2012. Copyright © 2012 by the *Los Angeles Times.* Reprinted with permission. "Mapping Best Picture." First published in *New York Magazine,* February 6, 2012. Designer: Stevie Remsberg; Art Director: Randy Minor. Copyright © 2012 by New York Media. Reprinted by permission of New York Media. "Multi-Touch Finger Paintings" by Evan Roth. First published in *Manifesto.* Copyright © 2012 by Evan Roth. Reprinted by permission of Evan Roth. "What Were the Gayest (And Straightest) Super Bowl Halftime Shows?" by Tom Scocca. First published on http://deadspin.com/5880648/ on January 30, 2012. Copyright © 2012 by Gawker Media, LLC. Reprinted by permission of Gawker Media, LLC. "Lifting a Coffee Cup, with Thoughts" by Damien Scogin. First published in *The Atavist,* April 16, 2012. Copyright © 2012 by Damien Scogin. Reprinted by permission of Damien Scogin. "Social Media Explained" by Corey Smith. First published on February 12, 2012, at http://www.coreysmith.ws/blog/social-media-explained-bacon. Copyright © 2012 by Corey Smith. Reprinted by permission of Corey Smith. "How Common Is Your Birthday?" by Matt Stiles. First published in http://thedailyviz.com/2012/05/12/how-common-is-your-birthday/. Copyright © 2012 by Matt Stiles. Reprinted by permission of Matt Stiles. "Planets Everywhere" by Jan Willem Tulp. First published in *Scientific American,* December 2012. Copyright © 2012 by Jan Willem Tulp —TULP Interactive. Reprinted by permission of TULP Interactive. "Seasonal Produce" by Russell van Kraayenberg. First published in http://chasingdelicious.com/produce-calendars. Copyright © 2012 by Russell van Kraayenberg. Reprinted by permission of Russell van Kraayenberg. "An Army for the Afterlife" from "Terra Cotta Warriors" by Juan Velasco. First published in *National Geographic,* June 2012. Copyright © 2012 by National Geographic Society. Reprinted by permission. "Wind Map" by Fernanda Viégas and Martin Wattenberg. First published in http://hint.fm/wind. Copyright © 2013 by Fernanda Viégas and Martin Wattenberg. Reprinted by permission of the authors. "How Fast Is LAFD Where You Live?" by Ben Welsh, Robert Lopez, Kate Linthicum, the *Los Angeles Times,* 2012. Copyright © 2012 *Los Angeles Times.* Reprinted with permission. "Proposed Nutrition Label" by Werner Design Werks for the *New York Times.* First published in the *New York Times,* October 13, 2012. Copyright © 2012 by the *New York Times.* Reprinted by permission of Werner Design Works, Inc. —Sharon Werner. "A Perfect Terrorist" produced by Yellow Truck Productions and WGBH Educational Foundation. First published on *Frontline,* 2012. Copyright © 2012 by WGBH Educational Foundation. Reprinted by permission of WGBH Educational Foundation.